Programming Models for Parallel Computing

T0265315

Scientific and Engineering Computation
William Gropp and Ewing Lusk, editors; Janusz Kowalik, founding editor

A list of books published in the Scientific and Engineering Computation series appears at the back of this book.

Programming Models for Parallel Computing

Edited by Pavan Balaji

The MIT Press
Cambridge, Massachusetts
London, England

This book was set in LaTeX by the authors.

Library of Congress Cataloging-in-Publication Data is available.

ISBN: 978-0-262-52881-8

To my daughter, Mimi, without whom this book would have been completed two years earlier, and my wife Rinku, without whom it never would have been completed at all.

Contents

Series Foreword

The Scientific and Engineering Series from MIT Press presents accessible accounts of computing research areas normally presented in research papers and specialized conferences. Elements of modern computing that have appeared thus far in the series include parallelism, language design and implementation, system software, and numerical libraries. The scope of the series continues to expand with the spread of ideas from computing into new aspects of science.

Programming models and the software systems that implement them are a crucial aspect of all computing, since they provide the concrete mechanisms by which a programmer prepares algorithms for execution on a computer and communicates these ideas to the machine. In the case of parallel systems, the complexity of the task has spurred innovative research. This book collects in one place definitive expositions of a wide variety of programming systems by highly regarded authors, including both language-based systems and library-based systems. Some are heavily used and defined by standards bodies; others are research projects with smaller user bases. All are currently being used in scientific and engineering applications for parallel computers.

William Gropp and Ewing Lusk, Editors

Preface

A *programming model* can be thought of as the abstract machine for which a programmer is writing instructions. Programming models typically are instantiated in languages and libraries. Such models form a rich topic for computer science research because programmers prefer them to be *productive* (capable of expressing any abstract algorithm with ease), *portable* (capable of being used on any computer architecture), *performant* (capable of delivering performance commensurate with that of the underlying hardware), and *expressive* (capable of expressing a broad range of algorithms)—the four pillars of programming. Achieving one or perhaps even two of these features simultaneously is relatively easy, but achieving all of them is nearly impossible. This situation accounts for the great multiplicity of programming models, each choosing a different set of compromises.

With the coming of the parallel computing era, computer science researchers have shifted focus to designing programming models that are well suited for high-performance parallel computing and supercomputing systems. Parallel programming models typically include an execution model (what path the code execution takes) and a memory model (how data moves in the system between computing nodes and in the memory hierarchy of each computing node). Programming parallel systems is complicated by the fact that multiple processing units are simultaneously computing and moving data, thus often increasing the nondeterminism in the execution in terms of both correctness and performance.

Also important is the distinction between *programming models* and *programming systems*. Technically speaking, the former refers to a style of programming—such as bulk synchronous or implicit compiler-assisted parallelization—while the latter refers to actual abstract interfaces that the user would program to. Over the years, however, the parallel computing community has blurred this distinction; and in practice today a programming model refers to both the style of programming and the abstract interfaces exposed by the instantiation of the model.

Contrary to common belief, most parallel systems do not expose a single parallel programming model to users. Different users prefer different levels of abstraction and different sets of tradeoffs among the four pillars of programming. Broadly speaking, domain scientists and those developing end applications often prefer a high-level programming model that is biased toward higher productivity, even if it is specialized to a small class of algorithms and lacks the expressivity required by other algorithms. On the other hand, developers of domain-specific languages and libraries might prefer a low-level programming model that is biased toward performance, even if it is not as easy to use. Of course, these are general statements, and exceptions exist on both sides.

About this book

This book provides an overview of some of the most prominent parallel programming models used on high-performance computing and supercomputing systems today. The book aims at covering a wide range of parallel programming models at various levels of the productivity, portability, performance, and expressability spectrum, allowing the reader to learn about and understand what tradeoffs each of these models has to offer.

We begin in Chapter 1 with a discussion of the Message Passing Interface (MPI), which is the most prominent parallel programming model for distributed-memory computing today. This chapter provides an overview of the most commonly used capabilities of MPI, leading up to the third major version of the standard—MPI-3.

In Chapters 2 to 5, we cover one-sided communication models, ranging from low-level runtime libraries to high-level programming models. Chapter 2 covers GASNet (global address space networking), a low-level programming model designed to serve as a common portable runtime system for a number of partitioned global address space (PGAS) models. Chapter 3 discusses OpenSHMEM, a one-sided communication library designed to directly expose native hardware communication capabilities to end users. OpenSHMEM mimics many of the capabilities of PGAS models, but in library form as opposed to relying on language extensions and compiler support for processing those extensions. Chapter 4 provides an overview of the Unified Parallel C (UPC) programming model. UPC is a C language–based PGAS model that provides both language extensions and library interfaces for creating and managing global address space memory. Chapter 5 covers Global Arrays (GA), another library-based one-sided communication model like OpenSHMEM but providing a higher-level abstraction—based on multidimensional arrays—for users to program with.

Chapter 6 discusses Chapel, a high-productivity programming model that allows applications to be expressed with both task and data parallelism. Chapel also has first-class language concepts for expressing and reasoning about locality that are orthogonal to its features for parallelism.

In Chapters 7 to 11, we present task-oriented programming models that allow users to describe their computation and data units as tasks, allowing the runtime system to manage the computation and data movement as necessary. Of these models, we first discuss the Charm++ programming model in Chapter 7. Charm++ provides an abstract model that relies on overdecomposition of work in order to dynamically manage the work across the available computational units. Next we delve into the Asynchronous Dynamic Load Balancing (ADLB) library in Chapter 8, which provides another task-oriented approach for sharing work based on an MPI-based low-level communication model. In Chapter 9 we discuss the Scalable Collection of Task Objects (Scioto) programming model, which relies on PGAS-like one-sided communication frameworks to achieve load balancing through work stealing. Chapter 10 describes Swift, a high-level scripting language that allows users to describe their computation in high-level semantics and internally translates it to other task-oriented models such as ADLB. Chapter 11 describes Concurrent Collections (CnC), a high-level declarative model that allows users to describe their applications as a graph of kernels communicating with one another.

In the final collection of chapters, Chapter 12 to 16, we present parallel programming models intended for on-node parallelism in the context of multicore architectures, attached accelerators, or both. In this collection, we first discuss OpenMP in Chapter 12. OpenMP is the most prominent on-node parallel programming model for scientific computing today. The chapter describes the evolution of OpenMP and its core set of features, leading up to OpenMP 4.0. In Chapter 13 we discuss the Cilk Plus programming model, a parallel extension of C and C++ languages for exploiting regular and irregular parallelism on modern shared-memory multicore machines. In Chapter 14 we discuss Intel Threading Building Blocks (TBB), which, like Cilk Plus, aims at providing parallelism on shared-memory multicore architectures but using a library based on C++ template classes. The Compute Unified Device Architecture (CUDA) programming model from NVIDIA is discussed in Chapter 15. CUDA provides parallelism based on single instruction, multiple thread blocks suitable for NVIDIA graphics processing units. Although CUDA is a proprietary programming model restricted to NVIDIA devices, the broad interest in the community and the wide range of applications using it make it a worthy programming model for inclusion in this book. In Chapter 16, we describe the Open Computing Language (OpenCL) model, which provides a low-level, vendor-independent programming model to program various heterogeneous architectures, including graphics processing units.

This book describes the various programming models at a level that is difficult to find elsewhere. Specifically, the chapters present material in a tutorial fashion, rather than the more formal approach found in research publications. Nor is this book a reference manual aimed at comprehensively describing all of the syntax and semantics defined by each programming model. Rather, the goal of this book is to describe the general approaches to parallel programming taken by each of the presented models and what they aim to achieve. Nevertheless, the chapters provide some syntactic and semantic definitions of a core set of interfaces they offer. These definitions are meant to be examples of the abstractions offered by the programming model. They are provided in order to improve the readability of the chapter. They are not meant to be taken as the most important or even the most commonly used interfaces, but just as examples of how one would use that programming model.

Acknowledgments

I first thank all the authors who contributed the various chapters to this book:

William D. Gropp, University of Illinois, Urbana-Champaign

Rajeev Thakur, Argonne National Laboratory

Paul Hargrove, Lawrence Berkeley National Laboratory

Jeffery A. Kuehn, Oak Ridge National Laboratory

Stephen W. Poole, Oak Ridge National Laboratory

Kathy Yelick, University of California, Berkeley, and Lawrence Berkeley National Laboratory

Yili Zheng, Lawrence Berkeley National Laboratory

Sriram Krishnamoorthy, Pacific Northwest National Laboratory

Jeff Daily, Pacific Northwest National Laboratory

Abhinav Vishnu, Pacific Northwest National Laboratory

Bruce Palmer, Pacific Northwest National Laboratory

Bradford L. Chamberlain, Cray Inc.

Laxmikant Kale, University of Illinois, Urbana-Champaign

Nikhil Jain, University of Illinois, Urbana-Champaign

Jonathan Lifflander, University of Illinois, Urbana-Champaign

Ewing Lusk, Argonne National Laboratory

Ralph Butler, Middle Tennessee State University

Steven C. Pieper, Argonne National Laboratory

James Dinan, Intel

Timothy Armstrong, The University of Chicago

Justin M. Wozniak, Argonne National Laboratory and the University of Chicago

Michael Wilde, Argonne National Laboratory and the University of Chicago

Ian T. Foster, Argonne National Laboratory and the University of Chicago

Kath Knobe, Rice University

Michael G. Burke, Rice University

Frank Schlimbach, Intel

Barbara Chapman, University of Houston

Deepak Eachempati, University of Houston

Sunita Chandrasekaran, University of Houston

Arch D. Robison, Intel

Charles E. Leiserson, MIT

Alexey Kukanov, Intel

Wen-mei Hwu, University of Illinois, Urbana-Champaign

David Kirk, NVIDIA

Tim Mattson, Intel

Special thanks to Ewing Lusk and William Gropp for their contributions to the book as a whole and for improving the prose substantially.

I also thank Gail Pieper, technical writer in the Mathematics and Computer Science Division at Argonne National Laboratory, for her indispensable guidance in matters of style and usage, which vastly improved the readability of the prose.

Programming Models for Parallel Computing

1 Message Passing Interface

William D. Gropp, University of Illinois, Urbana-Champaign
Rajeev Thakur, Argonne National Laboratory

1.1 Introduction

MPI is a standard, portable interface for communication in parallel programs that use a distributed-memory programming model. It provides a rich set of features for expressing the communication commonly needed in parallel programs and also includes additional features such as support for parallel file I/O. It supports the MPMD (multiple program, multiple data) programming model. It is a library-based system, not a compiler or language specification. MPI functions can be called from multiple languages—it has official bindings for C and Fortran. MPI itself refers to the definition of the interface specification (the function names, arguments, and semantics), not any particular implementation of those functions. MPI was defined by an organization known as the MPI Forum, a broadly based group of experts and users from industry, academia, and research laboratories. Many high-performance implementations of the MPI specification are available (both free and commercial) for all platforms (laptops, desktops, servers, clusters and supercomputers of all sizes) and all architectures and operating systems. As a result, it is possible to write parallel applications that can be run portably on any platform, while at the same time achieving good performance. This feature has contributed to MPI becoming the most widely used programming system for parallel scientific applications.

MPI Background

The effort to define a single, standard interface for message passing began in 1992. It was motivated by the presence of too many different, nonportable APIs—both vendor supported (e.g., Intel NX [232], IBM EUI [119], Thinking Machines CMMD [272], nCUBE [207]) and research libraries (e.g., PVM [121], p4 [51], Chameleon [130], Zipcode [254]). Applications written to any one of these APIs either could not be run on different machines or would not run efficiently. If any HPC vendor went out of business, applications written to that vendor's API could not be run elsewhere. It was recognized that this multiplicity of APIs was hampering progress in application development, and the need for a single, standard interface defined with broad input from everyone was evident.

The first version of the MPI specification (MPI-1) was released in 1994, and it covered basic message-passing features, such as point-to-point communication, collective communication, datatypes, and nonblocking communication. In 1997, the MPI Forum released the second major version of MPI (MPI-2), which extended the basic message-passing model to include features such as one-sided communication, parallel I/O, and dynamic processes. The third major release of MPI (MPI-3) was in 2012, and it included new features such as nonblocking collectives, neighborhood collectives, a tools information interface, and significant extensions to the one-sided communication interface. We discuss many of these features in this chapter.

1.2   MPI Basics

The core of MPI is communication between processes, following the communicating sequential processes (CSP) model. Each process executes in its own address space. Declared variables (e.g., `int b[10];`) are private to each process; the `b` in one process is distinct from the `b` in another process. In MPI, there are two major types of communication: communication between two processes, called point-to-point communication, and communication among a group of processes, called collective communication.

Each MPI process is a member of a group of processes and is identified by its *rank* in that group. Ranks start from zero, so in a group of four processes, the processes are numbered 0, 1, 2, 3. All communication in MPI is made with respect to a *communicator*. This object contains the group of processes and a (hidden) communication context. The communication context ensures that library software written using MPI can guarantee that messages remain within the library, which is a critical feature that enables MPI applications to use third-party libraries. The communicator object is a *handle*, which is just a way to say "opaque type." In C, the communicator handle is of type `MPI_Comm`; in Fortran, it is of type `TYPE(MPI_Comm)` (for the Fortran 2008 interface) or `INTEGER` (for earlier versions of Fortran). When an MPI program begins, there are two predefined communicators: `MPI_COMM_WORLD` and `MPI_COMM_SELF`. The former contains all the processes in the MPI execution; the latter just the process running that instance of the program. MPI provides routines to discover the rank of a process in a communicator (`MPI_Comm_rank`), to discover the number of processes in a communicator (`MPI_Comm_size`), and to create new communicators from old ones.

A complete, but very basic, MPI program is shown in Figure 1.1. This program shows the use of `MPI_Init` to initialize MPI and `MPI_Finalize` to finalize MPI. With a few exceptions, all other MPI routines must be called after `MPI_Init` (or `MPI_Init_thread`) and before `MPI_Finalize`. The odd arguments to `MPI_Init` were intended to support systems where the command-line arguments in a parallel program were not available from `main` but had to be provided to the processes by MPI.

Figure 1.1 illustrates another feature of MPI: anything that is *not* an MPI call executes independently. In this case, the `printf`s will execute in an arbitrary order; it is not even required that the output appear one line at a time.

The examples presented are in C, but it is important to note that MPI is defined by a language-neutral specification and a set of language bindings to that specification. MPI

```
#include "mpi.h"
#include <stdio.h>

int main(int argc, char *argv[])
{
    int wrank, srank, wsize;
    MPI_Init(&argc, &argv);
    MPI_Comm_rank(MPI_COMM_WORLD, &wrank);
    MPI_Comm_size(MPI_COMM_WORLD, &wsize);
    MPI_Comm_rank(MPI_COMM_SELF,  &srank);
    printf("World rank %d, world size %d, self rank %d\n",
            wrank, wsize, srank);
    MPI_Finalize();
    return 0;
}
```

Figure 1.1: A complete MPI program that illustrates communicator rank and size.

currently supports language bindings in C and Fortran. (C++ programs can use the C bindings.)

1.3 Point-to-Point Communication

The most basic communication in MPI is between pairs of processes. One process sends data, and the other receives it. The sending process must specify the data to send, the process to which that data is to be sent, and a communicator. In addition, following a feature from some of the earliest message-passing systems, each message also has a message *tag*, which is a single nonnegative integer. The receiving process must specify where the data is to be received, the process that is the source of the data, the communicator, and the message tag. In addition, it may provide a parameter in which MPI will return information about the received message; this is called the message status.

Early message-passing systems, and most I/O libraries, specify data buffers as a tuple containing the address and the number of bytes. MPI generalizes this as a triple: address, datatype, and count (the number of datatype elements). In the simplest case, the datatype corresponds to the basic language types. For example, to specify a buffer of 10 ints in C, MPI uses (address, 10, MPI_INT). This approach allows easier handling of data for the programmer, who does not need to know or discover the number of bytes in each basic type. It also allows the MPI library to perform data conversions if the MPI program is running on a mix of hardware that has different data representations (this was more important when MPI was created than it is today). In addition, as described in Section 1.4, it allows the specification of data buffers that are not contiguous in memory.

```
int msg[MAX_MSG_SIZE];
...
MPI_Comm_rank(MPI_COMM_WORLD, &rank);
MPI_Comm_size(MPI_COMM_WORLD, &size);
if (rank == 0) {
   for (i=1; i<size; i++)
      MPI_Send(msg, msgsize, MPI_INT, i, 0, MPI_COMM_WORLD);
} else {
   MPI_Recv(msg, MAX_MSG_SIZE, MPI_INT, 0, 0, MPI_COMM_WORLD,
            MPI_STATUS_IGNORE);
   doWork(msg);
}
```

Figure 1.2: Example of the use of MPI to send data (in the integer array msg of length msgsize from the process with rank zero to all other processes).

The process to which data is sent is specified by a rank in a communicator; that communicator also provides the communication context. The message tag is a nonnegative integer; the maximum allowed value depends on the MPI implementation but must be at least 32767. These are the arguments to MPI_Send.

The arguments for receiving a message are similar. One difference is that the receive function is allowed to specify a size larger than the data actually being sent. The tag and source rank may be used to either specify an exact value (e.g., tag of 15 and source of 3) or any value by using what are called *wild card* values (MPI_ANY_TAG and MPI_ANY_SOURCE, respectively). The use of MPI_ANY_TAG allows the user to send one additional integer item of data (as the tag value); the use of MPI_ANY_SOURCE allows the implementation of nondeterministic algorithms. A status argument provides access to the tag value provided by the sender and the source rank of the sender. When this information is not needed, the value MPI_STATUS_IGNORE may be used. Figure 1.2 shows a program that sends the same data from the process with rank zero in MPI_COMM_WORLD to all other processes.

MPI provides a number of different send modes; what has been described here is the basic or *standard* send mode. Other modes include a synchronous send, ready send, and buffered send. Nonblocking communication is described in Section 1.5.

1.4   Datatypes

As explained earlier, one of the special features of MPI is that all communication functions take a "datatype" argument. The datatype is used to describe the type of data being sent or received, instead of just bytes. For example, if communicating an array of integers, the datatype argument would be set to MPI_INT in C or MPI_INTEGER in Fortran. One purpose for such a datatype argument is to enable communication in a heterogeneous environment, e.g., communication between machines with different endianness or different lengths of basic datatypes. When the datatype is specified as part of the communication, the MPI implementation can internally perform the necessary byte transformations so that the data makes sense at the destination. MPI supports all the language types specified in C99 and Fortran 2008.

Another purpose of datatypes is to enable the user to describe noncontiguous layouts of data in memory and communicate the data with a single MPI function call. MPI provides several datatype constructor functions to describe noncontiguous data layouts. A high-quality implementation can optimize the noncontiguous data transfer such that it performs better than manual packing/unpacking and contiguous communication by the user.

MPI datatypes can describe any layout in memory. The predefined types corresponding to basic language types, such as MPI_FLOAT (C float) or MPI_COMPLEX (Fortran COMPLEX), provide the starting points. New datatypes can be constructed from old ones using a variety of layouts. For example,

---

MPI_Type_vector(count, blocklength, stride, oldtype, newtype)

---

creates a new datatype where there are count blocks, each consisting of blocklength contiguous copies of oldtype, with each block separated by a distance of stride, where stride is in units of the size of the oldtype. This provides a convenient (and, with a good MPI implementation, more efficient [139]) way to describe data that is separated by a regular stride.

Other MPI routines can be used to describe more general data layouts. MPI_Type_indexed is a generalization of MPI_Type_vector where each block can have a different number of copies of the oldtype and a different displacement. MPI_Type_create_struct is the most general datatype constructor, which further generalizes MPI_Type_indexed allowing each block to consist of replications of different datatypes. Convenience functions for describing layouts for subarrays and distributed arrays are also provided; these functions are particularly useful when using the parallel file I/O interface in MPI. All these functions can be called recursively to build datatypes describing any arbitrary layout.

Figure 1.3 shows an example of sending a column of a two-dimensional array in C. The column is noncontiguous because C stores arrays in row-major order. By using a vector datatype to define the memory layout, one can send the entire column with a single MPI send function. Note that it is necessary to call MPI_Type_commit before a derived

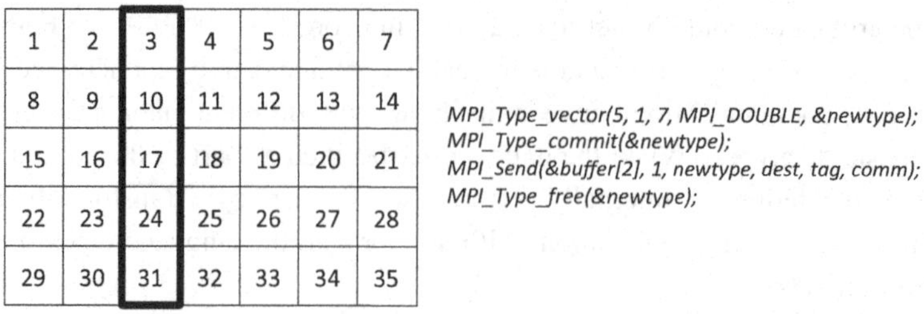

Figure 1.3: Using an MPI derived datatype to send a column of a 2D array in C

datatype can be used in a communication function. This function provides the implementation an opportunity to analyze the datatype and store a compact representation in order to optimize the communication of noncontiguous data during the subsequent communication function.

1.5 Nonblocking Communication

An important feature of MPI is the availability of *nonblocking* communication routines. These routines are used to initiate a communication but not wait for it to complete. This feature provides two benefits. First, it enables (but does not require) the MPI implementation to perform the communication asynchronously with other activities, such as computations. Second, it permits the description of complex communication patterns without requiring careful management of communication order and memory space. To understand the second requirement, consider this communication between two processes, where partner is the rank of the other process and both processes execute this code:

```
MPI_Send(buf,  100000000, MPI_INT, partner, 0, MPI_COMM_WORLD);
MPI_Recv(rbuf, 100000000, MPI_INT, partner, 0, MPI_COMM_WORLD,
         MPI_STATUS_IGNORE);
```

For the MPI_Send to complete, the data in buf, all one hundred million words of it, will need to be copied into some buffer somewhere (most likely either at the source or destination process). If this memory is not available, then the program will wait within the MPI_Send call for that memory to become available, e.g., the receive buffer that would be available when the destination process calls a receive routine such as MPI_Recv. That will not happen in the example above because both processes call MPI_Send first, and so the program might hang forever. Such programs are called *unsafe* because their correct

```
if (rank & 0x1) {
    /* Odd rank, do send first */
    MPI_Send(...);
    MPI_Recv(...);
}
else {
    /* Even rank, do receive first */
    MPI_Recv(...);
    MPI_Send(...);
}
```

Figure 1.4: Fixing deadlock by having some processes receive while others send. This method requires knowledge of the communication pattern at compile time.

execution depends on how much memory is available and used for buffering messages for which there is no matching receive at the time of the send.

The classic fix for this is to order the sends and receives so that no process has to wait, and is shown in Figure 1.4. However, this approach only works if the communication pattern is simple and known at compile time. More complex patterns can be handled at run time, but such code rapidly becomes too complex to maintain. The alternative is to allow the MPI operations to return before the communication is complete. In MPI, such routines are called *nonblocking* and are often (but not always) named with an "I" before the operation. For example, the nonblocking version of MPI_Send is MPI_Isend. The parameters for these routines are very similar to those for the blocking versions. The one change is an additional output parameter of type MPI_Request. This is a handle (in the MPI sense) that can be used to query about the status of the operation and to wait for its completion. Figure 1.5 shows the use of nonblocking send and receive routines. Note that the user is required to call a test or wait function to complete the nonblocking operation. MPI_Wait will block until the operation completes. A nonblocking alternative is to use the function MPI_Test, which returns immediately and indicates whether the operation has completed or not. Variants of test and wait operations are available for checking completion of multiple requests at a time, such as MPI_Waitall in Figure 1.5.

In many applications, the same communication pattern is executed repeatedly. For this case, MPI provides a version of nonblocking operation that uses *persistent* requests; that is, requests that persist and may be used repeatedly to initiate communication. These are created with routines such as MPI_Send_init (the persistent counterpart to MPI_Isend) and MPI_Recv_init (the persistent counterpart to MPI_Irecv). In the persistent case, the request is first created but the communication is not yet started. Starting the communication is accomplished with MPI_Start (and MPI_Startall for a collection of

```
int msg[MAX_MSG_SIZE];
MPI_Request *r;
...
MPI_Comm_rank(MPI_COMM_WORLD, &rank);
MPI_Comm_size(MPI_COMM_WORLD, &size);
if (rank == 0) {
    r = (MPI_Request *) malloc((size-1) * sizeof(MPI_Request));
    if (!r) ... error
    for (i=1; i<size; i++)
        MPI_Isend(msg, msgsize, MPI_INT, i, 0, MPI_COMM_WORLD,
                  &r[i-1]);
    ... Could perform some work
    MPI_Waitall(size-1, r, MPI_STATUSES_IGNORE);
    free(r);
} else {
    MPI_Request rr;
    MPI_Irecv(msg, msgsize, MPI_INT, 0, 0, MPI_COMM_WORLD, &rr);
    ... perform other work
    MPI_Wait(&rr, MPI_STATUS_IGNORE);
    doWork(msg);
}
```

Figure 1.5: An alternative to the code in Figure 1.2 that permits the overlapping of communication and computation

requests). Once that communication has completed, for example, after MPI_Wait returns on that request, it may be started again by calling MPI_Start. When the request is no longer needed, it is freed by calling MPI_Request_free.

1.6   Collective Communication

In addition to the point-to-point communication functions that exchange data between pairs of processes, MPI provides a large set of functions that perform communication among a group of processes. This type of communication is called *collective* communication. All processes in the communicator passed to a collective communication function must call the function, and the function is said to be "collective over the communicator." Collective communication functions are widely used in parallel programming because they represent commonly needed communication patterns and a vast amount of research in efficient collective communication algorithms has resulted in high-performance implementations [73, 270, 284].

Collective communication functions are of three types:

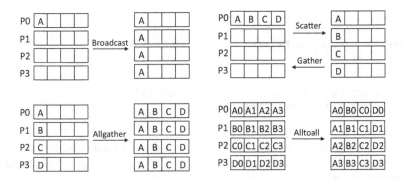

Figure 1.6: Some of the collective operations in MPI

1. *Synchronization.* MPI_Barrier is a collective function that synchronizes all processes in the communicator passed to the function. No process can return from the barrier until all processes have reached the barrier.

2. *Data Movement.* MPI has a large set of functions to perform commonly needed collective data movement operations. For example, MPI_Bcast sends data from one process (the root) to all other processes in the communicator. MPI_Scatter sends different parts of a buffer from a root process to other processes. MPI_Gather does the reverse of scatter: it collects data from other processes to a buffer at the root. MPI_Allgather is similar to gather except that all processes get the result, not just the root. MPI_Alltoall does the most general form of collective communication in which each process sends a different data item to every other process. Figure 1.6 illustrates these collective communication operations. Variants of these basic operations also exist that allow users to communicate unequal amounts of data.

3. *Collective Computation.* MPI also provides reduction and scan operations that perform arithmetic operations on data, such as minimum, maximum, sum, product, and logical OR, and also user-defined operations. MPI_Reduce performs a reduction operation and returns the result at the root process; MPI_Allreduce returns the result to all processes. MPI_Scan performs a scan (or parallel prefix) operation in which the reduction result at a process is the result of the operations performed on data items contributed by the process itself and all processes ranked less than it. MPI_Exscan does an exclusive scan in which the result does not include the contribution from the calling process. MPI_Reduce_scatter combines reduce and scatter.

```
int result[MAX_MSG_SIZE];
...
MPI_Bcast(msg, msgsize, MPI_INT, 0, MPI_COMM_WORLD);
if (rank != 0) {
   doWork(msg, result);
}
MPI_Reduce(MPI_IN_PLACE, result, msgsize, MPI_INT,
           MPI_SUM, 0, MPI_COMM_WORLD);
```

Figure 1.7: An alternative (and more efficient) way than in Figure 1.2 for sending data from one process to all others. It also includes an MPI_Reduce call to accumulate the results on one process (the process with rank zero in MPI_COMM_WORLD).

Both blocking and nonblocking versions of all collective communication functions are available. The functions mentioned above are blocking functions, i.e., they return only after the operation has locally completed at the calling process. Their nonblocking versions have an "I" in their name, e.g., MPI_Ibcast or MPI_Ireduce. These functions initiate the collective operation and return an MPI_Request object, similar to point-to-point functions. The operations must be completed by calling a test or wait function. Nonblocking collectives provide much needed support for overlapping collective communication with computation. MPI even provides a nonblocking version of barrier, called MPI_Ibarrier.

Figure 1.7 shows the use of MPI_Bcast to send the same data from one process (the "root" process) to all other processes in the same communicator. It also shows the use of MPI_Reduce with the sum operation (given by the MPI predefined operation, MPI_SUM) to add all the results from each process and store them on the specified root process, which in this case is the process with rank zero.

1.7   One-Sided Communication

In point-to-point or collective operations, communication between processes requires participation by both the sender and the receiver. An alternative approach is to have one process specify both the source and destination of the data. This approach is called *one-sided communication* and is the major method used for communication in programming systems such as ARMCI/GA (see Chapter 5), UPC (see Chapter 4), and OpenSHMEM (see Chapter 3). This approach is also called *remote memory access* or RMA.

The one-sided model in MPI has three major components. First is the creation of an MPI_Win object, also called a *window object*. This describes the region of memory, or memory *window* on each process, that other processes can access. Second are routines for moving data between processes; these include routines to *put*, *get*, and *update* data in a memory window on a remote process. Third are routines to ensure completion of the one-sided operations. Each of these components has a unique MPI flavor.

MPI provides four routines for creating memory windows, each addressing a specific application need. Three of the routines, MPI_Win_create, MPI_Win_allocate, and MPI_Win_allocate_shared, specify the memory that can be read or changed by another process. These routines, unlike the ones in many other one-sided programming models, are collective. The fourth routine, MPI_Win_create_dynamic, allows memory to be attached (and detached) by individual processes independently by calling additional routines.

The communication routines are simple (at least in concept) and are in the three categories of put, get, and update. The simplest routines (and the only ones in the original MPI-2 RMA) are one to put data to a remote process (MPI_Put), one to get data from a remote process (MPI_Get), and one to update data in a remote process by using one of the predefined MPI reduction operations (MPI_Accumulate). MPI-3 added additional communication routines in each of these categories. Each of these routines is nonblocking in the MPI sense, which permits the MPI implementation great flexibility in implementing these operations.

The fact that these operations are nonblocking emphasizes that a third set of functions are needed. These functions define when the one-sided communications complete. Any one-sided model must address this issue. In MPI, there are three ways to complete one-sided operations. The simplest is a collective MPI_Win_fence. This function completes all operations that originated at the calling process as well as those that targeted the calling process. When the "fence" exits, the calling process knows that all the operations started on this process have completed (thus, the data buffers provided can now be reused or changed) and that all operations targeting this process have also completed (thus, any access to the local memory that was defined for the MPI_Win has completed, and the local process may freely access or update that memory). This description simplifies the actual situation somewhat; the reader is encouraged to consult the MPI standard for the precise details. In particular, MPI_Win_fence really *separates* groups of RMA operations; thus a fence both precedes and follows the use of the MPI RMA communication calls.

Figure 1.8 shows the use of one-sided communication to implement an alternative to the use of MPI_Reduce in Figure 1.7. Note that this is not an exact replacement. By using one-sided operations, we can update the result asynchronously; in fact, a single process could update the result multiple times. Conversely, there are potential scalability issues with this approach, and it is used as an example only.

MPI provides two additional methods for completing one-sided operations. One can be thought of as a generalization of MPI_Win_fence. This is called the *scalable syn-*

```
MPI_Win_allocate((rank==0)?result:NULL,
                 (rank==0)?msgsize:0, sizeof(int),
                 MPI_INFO_NULL, MPI_COMM_WORLD, &result, &win);
MPI_Win_fence(0, win);
...
   doWork(msg, myresult);
   MPI_Accumulate(myresult, msgsize, MPI_INT, 0,
                  0, msgsize, MPI_INT, MPI_SUM, win);
...
MPI_Win_fence(0, win);
... process 0 has data in result
MPI_Win_free(&win);
```

Figure 1.8: Using MPI one-sided operations to accumulate (reduce) a result at a single process.

chronization method and uses four routines—MPI_Win_post, MPI_Win_start, MPI_-Win_complete, and MPI_Win_wait. As input, these routines take the MPI window and a group of processes that specify either the processes that are the targets or the origins of a one-sided communication operation. This method is considered scalable because it does not require barrier synchronization across all processes in the communicator used to create the window. Because both this scalable synchronization approach and the fence approach require that synchronization routines be called by both origin and target processes, these synchronization methods are called *active target synchronization*.

A third form of one-sided synchronization requires only calls at the origin process. This form is called *passive target synchronization*. The use of this form is illustrated in Figure 1.9. Note that the process with rank zero does not need to call any MPI routines within the while loop to cause RMA operations that target process zero to complete. The MPI_Win_lock and MPI_Win_unlock routines ensure that the MPI RMA operations (MPI_Accumulate in this example) complete at the origin (calling) process and that the data is deposited at the target process. The routines MPI_Win_lockall and MPI_Win_-unlockall permit one process to perform RMA communication to all other processes in the window object. In addition, MPI_Win_flush may be used within the *passive target synchronization* to complete the RMA operations issued so far to a particular target; there are additional routines to complete only locally and to complete RMA operations to all targets. There are also versions of put, get, and accumulate operations that return an MPI_Request object; the user can use any of the MPI_Test or MPI_Wait functions to check for local completion, without having to wait until the next RMA synchronization call.

Also note that process zero *does* need to call MPI_Win_lock before accessing the

```
MPI_Win_allocate((rank==0)?result:NULL,
                 (rank==0)?msgsize:0, sizeof(int),
                 MPI_INFO_NULL, MPI_COMM_WORLD, &result, &win);

while (not done) {
    ...
    doWork(msg, myresult);
    MPI_Win_lock(MPI_LOCK_SHARED, 0, 0, win);
    MPI_Accumulate(myresult, msgsize, MPI_INT, 0,
                   0, msgsize, MPI_INT, MPI_SUM, win);
    MPI_Win_unlock(0, win);
    ...
}
MPI_Barrier(MPI_COMM_WORLD);    // Ensure all processes done
if (rank == 0) {
    MPI_Win_lock(MPI_LOCK_EXCLUSIVE, 0, 0, win);
    printf("Result is %d\n", result[0]);
    ...
    MPI_Win_unlock(0, win);
}
MPI_Win_free(&win);
```

Figure 1.9: Using MPI one-sided operations to accumulate (reduce) a result at a single process, using passive target synchronization.

result buffer that it used to create the MPI window. This ensures that any pending memory operations have completed at the target process. This is a subtle aspect of shared and remote memory programming models that is often misunderstood by programmers (see [45] for some examples of common errors in using shared memory). MPI defines a *memory model* for the one-sided operations that ensures that users will obtain consistent and correct results, even on systems without fully cache-coherent memory (at the time of MPI-2's definition, the fastest machines in the world had this feature, and systems in the future again may not be fully cache coherent). While the standard is careful to describe the minimum requirements for correctly using one-sided operations, it also provides slightly more restrictive yet simpler rules that are sufficient for programmers on most systems. MPI-3 introduced a new "unified memory model" in addition to the existing memory model, which is now called "separate memory model." The user can query (via MPI_Win_get_attr) whether the implementation supports a unified memory model (e.g., on a cache-coherent system), and if so, the memory consistency semantics that the user must follow are greatly simplified.

MPI-3 significantly extended the one-sided communication interface defined in MPI-2 in order to fix some of the limitations of the MPI-2 interface and to enable MPI RMA be more broadly usable in libraries and applications, while also supporting portability and high performance. For example, new functions have been added to support atomic read-modify-write operations, such as fetch-and-add (`MPI_Fetch_and_op`) and compare-and-swap (`MPI_Compare_and_swap`), which are essential in many parallel algorithms. Another new feature is the ability to create a window of shared memory (where shared memory is available, such as within a single node) that can be used for direct load/store accesses in addition to RMA operations. If you considered the MPI-2 RMA programming features and found them wanting, you should look at the new features in MPI-3.

1.8   Parallel I/O

Many parallel scientific applications need to read or write large amounts of data from or to files for a number of reasons such as reading input meshes, checkpoint/restart, data analysis, and visualization. If file I/O is not performed efficiently, it is often the bottleneck in such applications. MPI provides an interface for parallel file I/O that enables application and library writers to express the "big picture" of the I/O access pattern concisely and thereby enable MPI implementations to optimize file access.

The MPI interface for I/O retains the look and feel of MPI and also supports the common operations in POSIX file I/O such as open, close, seek, read, and write. In addition, it supports many advanced features such as the ability to express noncontiguous accesses in memory and in the file using MPI derived datatypes, collective I/O functions, and passing performance-related hints to the MPI implementation.

Let us consider a simple example where each process needs to read data from a different location in a shared file in parallel as shown in Figure 1.10. There are many ways of doing this using MPI. The simplest way is by using independent file I/O functions and individual file pointers, as shown in Figure 1.11. Each process opens the file by using `MPI_File_open`, which is collective over the communicator passed as the first argument to the function, in this case `MPI_COMM_WORLD`. The second parameter is the name of the file being opened, which could include a directory path. The third parameter is the mode in which the file is being opened. The fourth parameter can be used to pass hints to the implementation by attaching key-value pairs to an `MPI_Info` object. Example hints include parameters for file striping, sizes of internal buffers used by MPI for I/O optimizations, etc. In the simple example in Figure 1.11, we pass `MPI_INFO_NULL` so that default values are used. The last parameter is the file handle returned by MPI (of type `MPI_File`), which is used in future operations on the file.

Each process then calls `MPI_File_seek` to move the file pointer to the offset corresponding to the first byte it needs to read. This is called the individual file pointer since it is local to each process. (MPI also has another file pointer, called the shared file pointer,

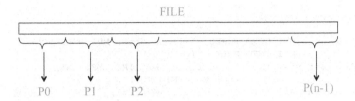

Figure 1.10: Each process needs to read a chunk of data from a common file

```
MPI_File fh;
...
rc = MPI_File_open(MPI_COMM_WORLD, "myfile.dat", MPI_MODE_RDONLY,
                   MPI_INFO_NULL, &fh);
rc = MPI_File_seek(fh, rank*bufsize*sizeof(int), MPI_SEEK_SET);
rc = MPI_File_read(fh, msg, msgsize, MPI_INT, MPI_STATUS_IGNORE);
MPI_File_close(&fh);
```

Figure 1.11: Reading data with independent I/O functions and individual file pointers

that is shared among processes and requires a separate set of functions to access and use.) Data is read by each process using MPI_File_read, which reads msgsize integers into the memory buffer from the current location of the file pointer. MPI_File_close closes the file. Note that this method of doing file I/O is very similar to the way one would do it with POSIX I/O functions.

A second way of reading the same data is to avoid using file pointers and instead specify the starting offset in the file directly to the read function. This can be done by using the function MPI_File_read_at, which takes an additional "offset" parameter. MPI_File_seek does not need to be called in this case. This function also provides a thread-safe way to access the file, since it does not require a notion of "current" position in the file.

MPI_File_read and MPI_File_read_at are called *independent* I/O functions because they have no collective semantics. Each process calls them independently; there is no requirement that if one process calls them, then all processes must call them. In other words, an MPI implementation does not know how many processes may call these functions and hence cannot perform any optimizations across processes.

MPI also provides *collective* versions of all read and write functions. These functions have an _all in their name, e.g., MPI_File_read_all and MPI_File_read_at_all. They have the same syntax as their independent counterparts, but they have collective semantics; i.e., they must be called on all processes in the communicator with which the file

```
MPI_File fh;
...
rc = MPI_File_open(MPI_COMM_WORLD, "myfile.dat", MPI_MODE_RDONLY,
                   MPI_INFO_NULL, &fh);
rc = MPI_File_set_view(fh, rank*bufsize, MPI_INT, MPI_INT,
                       "native", MPI_INFO_NULL);
rc = MPI_File_read_all(fh, msg, msgsize, MPI_INT,
                       MPI_STATUS_IGNORE);
MPI_File_close(&fh);
```

Figure 1.12: Reading data in parallel, with each process receiving a different part of the input file

was opened. With this guarantee, an MPI implementation has the opportunity to optimize the accesses based on the combined request of all processes, an optimization known as collective I/O [268, 269]. In general, it is recommended to use collective I/O over independent I/O whenever possible.

A third way of reading the data in Figure 1.10 is to use the notion of "file views" defined in MPI, as shown in Figure 1.12. MPI_File_set_view is used to set the file view, whereby a process can specify its view of the file, i.e., which parts of the file it intends to read/write and which parts it wants to skip. The file view is specified as a triplet of *displacement*, *etype*, and *filetype*: displacement is the offset to be skipped from the start of the file (such as a header), etype is the elementary type describing the basic unit of data access, and filetype is an MPI type constructed out of etypes. The file view consists of the layout described by a repeated tiling of filetypes starting at an offset of "displacement" from the start of the file.

In Figure 1.12, each process specifies the displacement as its rank $\times$ msgsize, etype as MPI_INT, and filetype also as MPI_INT. The next parameter specifies the data representation in the file; "native" means the data representation is the same as in memory. The last parameter can be used to pass hints. We could use either independent or collective read functions to read the data; we choose to use the collective function MPI_File_read_all. Each process reads msgsize integers into the memory buffer from the file view defined for that process. Since each process has a different displacement in the file view, offset by its rank, it reads a different portion of the file.

MPI's I/O functionality is quite sophisticated, particularly for cases where I/O accesses from individual processes are not contiguous in the file, such as when accessing subarrays and distributed arrays. In such cases, MPI-I/O can provide very large performance benefits over using POSIX I/O directly; in some cases, it is over 1,000 times as fast. We refer the reader to [127] for a more detailed discussion of MPI's I/O capabilities.

```
#include "mpi.h"
#include <stdio.h>

static double syncTime = 0.0;

int MPI_Bcast(void *buf, int len, MPI_Datatype dtype, int root,
              MPI_Comm comm)
{
  double t1;
  t1 = MPI_Wtime();
  PMPI_Barrier(comm);
  syncTime += MPI_Wtime() - t1;
  return PMPI_Bcast(buf, len, dtype, root, comm);
}

int MPI_Finalize(void)
{
  printf("Synchronization time in MPI_Bcast was %.2e seconds\n",
         syncTime); fflush(stdout);
  return PMPI_Finalize();
}
```

Figure 1.13: Example use of the profiling interface to record an estimate of the amount of time that an MPI_Bcast is waiting for all processes to enter the MPI_Bcast call.

1.9   Other Features

MPI includes a rich set of features intended to support developing and using large-scale software. One innovative feature (now available in some other tools) is a set of alternate entry points for each routine that makes it easy to interpose special code between any MPI routine. For each MPI routine, there is another entry point that uses PMPI as the prefix. This is known as the MPI profiling interface. For example, PMPI_Bcast is the profiling entry point for MPI_Bcast. The PMPI version of the routine performs exactly the same operations as the MPI version. The one difference is that the user may define their own version of any MPI routine but not of the PMPI routines. An example is shown in Figure 1.13. Linking the object file created from this file with a program that includes calls to MPI_Bcast will create a program that will print out the amount of time spent waiting for all the processes to call MPI_Bcast.

To enable users to write hybrid MPI and threaded programs, MPI also precisely specifies the interaction between MPI calls and threads. MPI supports four "levels" of thread-safety that a user must explicitly select:

MPI_THREAD_SINGLE: A process has only one thread of execution.

`MPI_THREAD_FUNNELED`: A process may be multithreaded, but only the thread that
initialized MPI can make MPI calls.

`MPI_THREAD_SERIALIZED`: A process may be multithreaded, but only one thread can
make MPI calls at a time.

`MPI_THREAD_MULTIPLE`: A process may be multithreaded and multiple threads can
call MPI functions simultaneously.

The user must call the function `MPI_Init_thread` to indicate the level of thread-safety
desired, and the MPI implementation will return the level it supports. It is the user's responsibility to meet the restrictions of the level supported. An implementation is not required
to support a level higher than `MPI_THREAD_SINGLE`, but a fully thread-safe implementation will support `MPI_THREAD_MULTIPLE`. MPI specifies thread safety in this manner
so that the implementation does not need to support more than what the user needs and
unnecessarily incur the potential performance penalties.

MPI also enables an application to spawn additional processes (by using `MPI_Comm_-`
`spawn` or `MPI_Comm_spawn_multiple`) and separately started MPI applications to
connect with each other and communicate (by using `MPI_Comm_connect` and `MPI_-`
`Comm_accept` or `MPI_Join`).

MPI provides neighborhood collective operations (`MPI_Neighbor_allgather` and
`MPI_Neighbor_alltoall` and their variants) that define collective operations among
a process and its neighbors as defined by a cartesian or graph virtual process topology in
MPI. These functions are useful, for example, in stencil computations that require nearest-
neighbor exchanges. They also represent sparse all-to-many communication concisely,
which is essential when running on many thousands of processes.

MPI also has functionality to expose some internal aspects of an MPI implementation that may be useful for libraries. These features include functions to decode derived datatypes and functions to associate arbitrary nonblocking operations with an `MPI_-`
`Request` (known as generalized requests). New in MPI-3 is a facility, known as the
`MPI_T` interface, that provides access to internal variables that either control the operation
of the MPI implementation or expose performance information.

1.10 Best Practices

Like any programming approach, making effective use of MPI requires using it as it was
intended, taking into account the strengths and weaknesses of the approach. Perhaps the
most important consideration is that MPI is a library. This means that any MPI operation
requires one or more function calls and might not be the most efficient for very short data

transfers where even function-call overheads matter. Therefore, wherever possible, communication should be aggregated so as to move as much data in one MPI call as possible.

MPI contains features to support the construction of software libraries. These features should be used. For example, rather than adding MPI calls throughout your application, it is often better to define important abstractions and implement them in MPI. Most of the application code then makes use of these abstractions, which permits the code to be cleaner as well as simplifies the process of tuning the use of MPI. This is the approach used in several important computational libraries and frameworks, such as PETSc [229, 26] and Trilinos [137]. In these libraries, MPI calls rarely, if ever, appear in the user's code.

Locality at all levels is important for performance, and MPI, because it is based on processes, helps users maintain locality. In fact, this feature is sometimes considered both a strength and weakness of MPI: a strength because requiring users to plan for and respect locality helps develop efficient programs; a weakness because users *must* take locality into account. We note that locality at other levels of the memory hierarchy, particularly between cache and main memory, is also necessary (possibly more so) for achieving high performance.

Programs often do not behave as expected, and having tools to investigate the behavior, both in terms of correctness and performance, is essential. The MPI profiling interface has provided an excellent interface for tool development, and a number of tools are available that can help in the visualization of MPI program behavior [72, 145, 253, 300]. The profiling interface can also be used by end users [285], and good program design will take advantage of this feature.

There are many good practices to follow when using MPI. Some of the most important are the following.

1. Avoid assumptions about buffering (see the discussion above on safe programs)

2. Avoid unnecessary synchronization in programs. This means avoiding forcing an order on the communication of data when it is not necessary. Implementing this often means using nonblocking communication and multiple-completion routines (e.g., MPI_Waitall).

3. Use persistent communication where possible and when communicating small to medium amounts of data (the definition of medium depends on the speed of your network, MPI implementation, and processor). This can reduce the overhead of MPI.

4. Use MPI derived datatypes when possible and when your MPI implementation provides a high-quality implementation of this feature. This can reduce unnecessary memory motion for noncontiguous data.

5. For I/O, use collective I/O where possible. Pay attention to any performance limitations of your file system (some have extreme penalties for accesses that are not aligned on disk block boundaries).

6. `MPI_Barrier` is rarely required and usually reduces performance. See [252] for an automated way to detect "functionally irrelevant barriers." Though there are a few exceptions, most uses of `MPI_Barrier` are, at best, sloppy programming and, at worst, incorrect because they assume that `MPI_Barrier` has some side effects. A correct MPI program will rarely need `MPI_Barrier`. (We mention this because the analysis of many programs reveals that `MPI_Barrier` is one of the most common MPI collective routines even though it is not necessary.)

1.11 Summary

MPI has been an outstanding success. At this writing, the MPI specification is over 21 years old and continues to be the dominant programming system for highly parallel applications in computational science.

Why has MPI has been so successful? In brief, it is because MPI provides a robust solution for parallel programming that allows users to achieve their goals. A thorough examination of the reasons for MPI's success may be found in [129]. The open process by which MPI was defined also contributed to its success; MPI avoided errors committed in some other, less open, programming system designs. Another contributor to the success of MPI is its deliberate support for "programming in the large"—for the creation of software modules that operate in parallel. A number of libraries have been built on top of MPI, permitting application developers to write programs at a high level and still achieve performance. Several of these have won the Gordon Bell prize for outstanding achievements in high-performance computing and/or R&D 100 awards [4, 9, 12, 24, 137].

As the number of cores continues to grow in the most powerful systems, one frequent question is "Can MPI scale to millions of processes?" The answer is yes, though it will require careful implementation of the MPI library [23]. It is also likely that for such systems, MPI will be combined with another approach, exploiting MPI's thread-safe design. Users are already combining MPI with OpenMP. Using OpenMP or another node programming language, combined with MPI, would allow the use of MPI with millions of MPI processes, with each process using thousands of cores (e.g., via threads).

There is a rich research literature on the use and implementation of MPI, including the annual EuroMPI meeting. A tutorial introduction to MPI is available in [127, 128]. The official version of the MPI standard [202] is freely available at www.mpi-forum.org.

This chapter provided an introduction to MPI but could not cover the richness of MPI. The references above, as well as your favorite search engine, can help you discover the full power of the MPI programming model.

2 Global Address Space Networking

Paul Hargrove, Lawrence Berkeley National Laboratory

2.1 Background and Motivation

In 2002 a team of researchers at the University of California Berkeley and Lawrence Berkeley National Laboratory began work on a compiler for the Unified Parallel C (UPC) language (see Chapter 4). A portion of that team had also worked on the compiler and runtime library for Titanium [277], a parallel dialect of Java. This motivated the design of a language-independent library to support the network communication needs of both UPC and Titanium, with the intent to be applicable to an even wider range of global address space language and library implementations. The result of those efforts is the **G**lobal **A**ddress **S**pace **Net**working library, known more commonly as simply "GASNet" (pronounced just as written: "gas net"). GASNet has language bindings only for C, but is "safe" to use from C++ as well.

At the time of this writing, the current revision of the GASNet specification is v1.8. The most current revision can always be found on the GASNet project webpage [174].

Since its inception, GASNet has become the networking layer for numerous global address space language implementations. In addition to the Berkeley UPC compiler [173], the Open Source UPC compilers from Intrepid Technology [146] (GUPC) and the University of Houston [278] (OpenUH) use GASNet. Rice University chose GASNet for both their original Co-Array Fortran (CAF) and CAF-2.0 compilers [239]. Cray's UPC and CAF compilers [96] use GASNet for the Cray XT series, and Cray Chapel (see Chapter 6) uses GASNet on multiple platforms. The OpenSHMEM (see Chapter 3) reference implementation from the University of Houston and Oak Ridge National Laboratory is also implemented over GASNet. In addition to these languages and libraries, some of which are described in later chapters of this book, GASNet has been used in numerous other research projects.

2.2 Overview of GASNet

GASNet was originally designed to support languages compiled by source-to-source translation techniques in which the compiler converts a program written in a parallel language into serial code (almost always in C) with library calls to implement the parallel communication and other distinguishing aspects of the language, such as global memory allocation and locks in UPC. Since GASNet is language-independent by design, translated code typically calls a language-specific runtime library. Calls to GASNet to implement the communication might be made either directly by the translated code or indirectly by the language-specific runtime library. Since source-to-source translation was the original motivating usage case, GASNet has been designed for use in automatically generated code and for use by expert programmers who are authoring parallel runtime libraries. Where performance and ease-of-use conflict, the design favors choices that will achieve high performance. One consequence of this is GASNet's API specifies the "interfaces" or "calls" which GASNet implements, but does not require that any of these be implemented as a function. Therefore, in many cases a GASNet call may be implemented as a C preprocessor macro (especially when there is a simple mapping from a GASNet interface to a call in the vendor-provided network API).

GASNet is also designed with wide portability in mind and one consequence is that the capabilities expressed directly in GASNet's interfaces are those one should be able to implement efficiently on nearly any platform. At the time of this writing, GASNet has "native" implementations—in terms of the network APIs—of all of the common cluster interconnects, and those of the currently available supercomputers from IBM and Cray. Also at the time of this writing, porting of GASNet to the largest systems in Japan and China is known to be in progress by researchers affiliated with those systems.

The remainder of this section will introduce the terminology used in the GASNet specification and in this chapter, and provide an overview of the functionality found in GASNet. Later sections expand in more detail upon this overview, provide usage examples and describe some of the plans for GASNet's future.

2.2.1 Terminology

Below are several terms that are used extensively in the GASNet specification and in this chapter. Before reading further, familiarize yourself with these terms or bookmark this page for easy reference.

Client	The software using GASNet, most often a parallel language runtime rather than an "end-user" code.
Conduit	The implementation of GASNet for a specific network API. Example: "mpi-conduit" and "udp-conduit" are maximally portable implementations to allow use on platforms without "native" support.
Node	GASNet uses the term "node" to mean an O/S process rather than a network endpoint.
Supernode	A collection of nodes running under the same OS instance. On supported platforms, GASNet will use shared-memory communication among such groups of nodes.
Segment	The range of virtual addresses that are permitted as the remote address (part of the Extended API described in Section 2.4).
Local Completion	When memory associated with input(s) on the initiating node is safe for reuse.
Remote Completion	When memory associated with output(s) has been written.

2.2.2   Threading

GASNet is intended to be "thread neutral" and allow the client to use threads as it sees fit. By default GASNet will build three variants of the library for each supported network to support different client threading models. These are known as the "seq", "parsync" and "par" builds, where the names correspond both to the library file name and to the preprocessor tokens GASNET_SEQ, GASNET_PARSYNC and GASNET_PAR. Exactly one of these three must be defined by the client when it includes gasnet.h and the library to which it is linked must correspond to the correct preprocessor token.[1] The three models are:

- GASNET_SEQ
  In this mode the client is permitted to make GASNet calls from only a single thread in each process. There is no restriction on how many threads the client may use, but exactly one of them must be used to make all GASNet calls.

- GASNET_PARSYNC
  In this mode at most one thread may make GASNet calls *concurrently*. Multiple

---

1. There is some name-shifting under the covers to catch mismatches.

threads may make GASNet calls with appropriate mutual exclusion. GASNet does *not* provide the mechanism for such mutual exclusion, which is the client's responsibility.

- GASNET_PAR

  This is the most general mode, allowing multiple client threads to enter GASNet concurrently.

When using SEQ or PARSYNC modes, the restriction on the client's calls to GASNet is *only* a restriction on the client. It is legal, even in a SEQ build, for GASNet to use threads internally, and these internal threads may be used to execute the client's AM handlers. For this reason the client code must make proper use of GASNet's mechanisms for concurrency control (described in Section 2.3.4) regardless of the threading mode.

2.2.3   API Organization

GASNet divides its interfaces into two groups—the "Core API" and the "Extended API." The latter of these contains interfaces for remote memory access, while everything else in contained in the former. The core includes the most basic needs in any parallel runtime with interfaces to initialize and finalize the runtime, query the number of parallel entities (GASNet "nodes", in this case), and the identity of the calling entity (the node number in GASNet).

In addition to the Core and Extended API as documented in the GASNet specification, there are several additional features in GASNet to assist in the writing and debugging of portable GASNet clients.

2.3   Core API

GASNet's flexibility in implementing parallel language runtimes comes from the inclusion of a remote procedure call mechanism based on Berkeley Active Messages [183]. While GASNet's Active Message (just "AM" from here on) interfaces are significantly reduced relative to the Berkeley AM design, they provide the caller with significant flexibility subject to constraints that allow an implementation to guarantee deadlock freedom while using bounded resources. Briefly, the idea is that a client may send an AM Request to a node (including itself) which results in running code (a "handler") that was registered by the call to gasnet_attach. The handler receives a small number of integer arguments provided by the AMRequest call, plus an optional payload which may either be buffered by the implementation or delivered to a location given by the client. The handler is permitted calls to only a subset of the GASNet Core API (and none of the Extended); the only communication permitted is at most one AMReply to the requesting node. A significant portion of this chapter will be devoted to showing how to use GASNet's AMs.

The GASNet Core API contains everything one needs to write an AM-based code.[2] This section picks up from the brief introduction given in Section 2.2.3 to provide some detail on the Core API. This information will be put into practice in several examples in Section 2.6.

2.3.1 Beginnings and Endings

There seems to be an almost universal imperative to provide a "Hello, World!" example for every programming language. With parallel languages there is an expectation that one can print some information about the job size and the caller's rank. Such an example is provided in Section 2.6.2, but we introduce here the corresponding portions of the Core API:

```
int gasnet_init(int *argcp, char ***argvp);
int gasnet_attach(gasnet_handlerentry_t *table, int numentries,
                  uintptr_t segsize, uintptr_t minheapoffset);
void gasnet_exit(int exitcode);
gasnet_node_t gasnet_nodes(void);
gasnet_node_t gasnet_mynode(void);
char * gasnet_getenv(const char *name);
uintptr_t gasnet_getMaxLocalSegmentSize(void);
uintptr_t gasnet_getMaxGlobalSegmentSize(void);
```

Any GASNet client will begin with a call to gasnet_init which takes pointers to the standard argc and argv parameters to main(). The job environment prior to calling gasnet_init is very vague (see the specification for details), and the user is strongly encouraged not to do much, if anything, before this call. However, after the call to gasnet_init, the command-line will have been cleansed of any arguments used internally by GASNet, and environment variables will be accessible using gasnet_getenv. Additionally, the jobs's stdout and stderr will be setup by this init call. GASNet does *not* make any guarantees about stdin.

Only after gasnet_init returns do the other calls in the list above become legal. The next step in initialization of a GASNet job is a call to gasnet_attach to allocate the GASNet segment and reserve any network resources required for the job. The arguments to gasnet_attach give the client's table of AM handlers, and the client's segment requirements:

---

2. It is also the minimum one must port to a new platform, because there is a reference implementation of everything in the Extended API in terms of the Core.

- `gasnet_handlerentry_t *table`
  This is a pointer to an array of C structs:

```
typedef struct {
    gasnet_handler_t index;
    void (*fnptr)();
} gasnet_handlerentry_t;
```

The `fnptr` is the function to be invoked as the AM handler at the respective integer `index`. The signature of AM handlers will be covered in Section 2.3.5. Values for `index` of 128–255 are available to the client, while the special value of 0 indicates "don't care" and will be overwritten by a unique value by `gasnet_attach`.

- `int numentries`
  The number of entries in the handler entry table.

- `uintptr_t segsize`
  The requested size of the GASNet segment.
  Must be a multiple of `GASNET_PAGESIZE`, and no larger than the value returned by `gasnet_getMaxLocalSegmentSize` (see below).
  Ignored for `GASNET_SEGMENT_EVERYTHING`.

- `uintptr_t minheapoffset`
  The requested minimum distance between GASNet's segment and the current top of the heap.[3] On systems where the layout in virtual memory forces GASNet's segment and the heap to compete for space, this ensures that at least this amount of space will be left for heap allocation after allocation of the segment. While not recommended, it is legal to pass zero. The value passed by all nodes must be equal.
  Ignored for `GASNET_SEGMENT_EVERYTHING`.

There are two calls to determine what segment size one may request in the attach call. The function `gasnet_getMaxLocalSegmentSize` returns the maximum amount of memory that GASNet has determined is available for the segment on the calling node, while `gasnet_getMaxGlobalSegmentSize` returns the minimum of all the "local" values. Keep in mind that on many platforms, the GASNet segment and the malloc heap must compete for the same space, meaning that these `SegmentSize` queries should be treated as the maximum of the *sum* of `segsize` and `minheapoffset`. A client that

---

3. The range of memory used to satisfy calls to the `malloc` family of functions.

finds the available segment size too small for its requirements may call `gasnet_exit` to terminate the job rather than calling `gasnet_attach`.

In addition to the two segment size query calls and access to environment variables using `gasnet_getenv`, clients may call `gasnet_nodes` to query the number of GASNet nodes in the job, and `gasnet_mynode` to determine the caller's rank within the job (ranks start from zero). The calls listed above are the only ones permitted between `gasnet_init` and `gasnet_attach`. The two segment size query calls are unique in that they are *only* legal between `gasnet_init` and `gasnet_attach`.

After `gasnet_attach` comes the client's "real" code using the interfaces described in the sections that follow. When all the real work is done, `gasnet_exit` is the mechanism for reliable job termination. The call to `gasnet_exit` takes an exit code as its only argument and *does not* return to the caller. GASNet makes a strong effort to ensure that if any node provides a nonzero exit code that the job as a whole (spawned by some platform-specific mechanism) will also return a nonzero code. It also tries to preserve the actual value when possible.

A call to `gasnet_exit` by a single node is sufficient to cause the entire parallel job to terminate. Any node which does not call `gasnet_exit` at the same time as one or more others, will receive a `SIGQUIT` signal if possible.[4] This is the only signal for which a client may portably register a signal handler, because GASNet reserves all others for internal use. To avoid unintentionally triggering their mechanism, a client performing a "normal" exit should perform a barrier (see Section 2.3.3) immediately before the call to `gasnet_exit`.

2.3.2   Segment Info

The `segsize` argument to `gasnet_attach` is the client's *requested* size. GASNet may allocate a smaller segment. At any time following the call to `gasnet_attach` a client may determine information about the segments allocated to all nodes by calling `gasnet_getSegmentInfo`:

```
typedef struct {
   void *addr;
   uintptr_t size;
} gasnet_seginfo_t;
int gasnet_getSegmentInfo(gasnet_seginfo_t *seginfo_table,
                    int numentries);
```

4. Except on platforms without POSIX signals.

This call populates the lesser of `numentries` or `gasnet_nodes()` entries of type `gasnet_seginfo_t` in the client-owned memory at `seginfo_table`, and returns an error code on failure (see Section 2.3.8). The ith entry in the array gives the address and size of the segment on node i. When conditions permit, GASNet *favors* assigning segments with the same base address on all nodes. If an implementation can guarantee that this property is always satisfied, then the preprocessor token `GASNET_ALIGNED_SEGMENTS` is defined to 1.

In the `GASNET_SEGMENT_EVERYTHING` configuration, the segment is all of virtual memory. In this configuration, the `addr` fields will always be zero and the `size` will always be `(uintptr_t)(-1)`.

2.3.3 Barriers

The next set of Core API calls to describe are those for performing a barrier:

```
#define GASNET_BARRIERFLAG_ANONYMOUS ...
#define GASNET_BARRIERFLAG_MISMATCH ...
void gasnet_barrier_notify(int id, int flags);
int gasnet_barrier_wait(int id, int flags);
int gasnet_barrier_try(int id, int flags);
```

Unlike many barrier implementation, the one in GASNet is "split-phase" and supports optional id matching.

The "split-phase" nature of GASNet's barrier is evident in the specification's description of `gasnet_barrier_wait` which states "This is a blocking operation that returns only after all remote nodes have called `gasnet_barrier_notify()`." In simple terms imagine that "notify" increments an arrival counter and that "wait" blocks until that counter equals the job size.[5] The call `gasnet_barrier_try` checks the same condition, but returns immediately with the value `GASNET_ERROR_NOT_READY` if the condition is not yet satisfied. Regardless of whether one uses "wait" or "try" to complete the barrier, it *is* legal to perform most GASNet operations between the initiation and completion.

The `id` and `flags` arguments to the barrier functions implement optional matching at the barriers. This feature is best understood by a careful reading of the specification, but two common use cases are easy to understand:

- Anonymous barrier
  The simplest case is when one does not wish to use the id matching support. In this case, the constant `GASNET_BARRIERFLAG_ANONYMOUS` is passed for the `flags`

---

5. Rest assured that more scalable algorithms are used in practice.

argument to the barrier functions. Any value can be passed as the `id` (though `0` is most common), since it will be ignored.

- Named barrier
  The simplest case that makes use of the id matching logic is a blocking (as opposed to split-phase) barrier with an integer argument that is expected to be equal across all callers:

```c
int named_barrier(int name) {
  gasnet_barrier_notify(name, 0);
  int err = gasnet_barrier_wait(name, 0);
  if (err == GASNET_OK) {
    return 0; // Success — all nodes specified same name
  } else if (err == GASNET_ERR_BARRIER_MISMATCH) {
    return 1; // Failure — names did not all match
  }
  return -1; // Something unexpected happened!
}
```

GASNet's split-phase barrier comes with some usage restrictions which might not initially be obvious. Here we will consider a successful "try" equivalent to a "wait" to keep the descriptions brief. The first restriction is the most intuitive: one must alternate between "notify" and "wait" to ensure that barrier operations do not overlap one another. The second is that in a GASNET_PARSYNC or GASNET_PAR build, the "notify" and "wait" should only be performed once per node (the client is free to choose which thread does the work, and need not pick the same thread for the two phases). The third is a potentially nonobvious consequence of the first two: in a GASNET_PAR build the client has the burden of ensuring that at most one client thread is in *any* barrier call at any given instant.

2.3.4   Locks and Interrupts

In Section 2.2.2 we learned that GASNet might run AM handlers concurrent with client code even when the client is single threaded. We also learned above that multi-threaded clients must prevent concurrent calls to GASNet's barrier functions. So now we take a look at GASNet's mechanisms for controlling concurrency.

GASNet has interfaces specifically for dealing with thread-safety, which are of importance even in single-threaded clients due to the possibility of multi-threaded implementations of GASNet. The main mechanism is a simple mutex, known as a "handler-safe lock", or "HSL", based on the mutex type, `gasnet_hsl_t`. The implementation of this mutex type is ensured to be appropriate for the given implementation (which includes being a no-op when both the GASNet client and implementation are single-threaded).

```
#define GASNET_HSL_INITIALIZER ...
void gasnetc_hsl_init(gasnet_hsl_t *hsl);
void gasnetc_hsl_destroy(gasnet_hsl_t *hsl);
void gasnetc_hsl_lock(gasnet_hsl_t *hsl);
void gasnetc_hsl_unlock(gasnet_hsl_t *hsl);
int gasnetc_hsl_trylock(gasnet_hsl_t *hsl);
```

Other than minor details given in the GASNet specification, these are equivalent to the analogous constants and functions on pthread_mutex_t. Like the POSIX threads analogues, these can be used to prevent concurrent access to data structures or regions of code. A general tutorial on the use of a mutex are outside the scope of this chapter. Note that these are node-local mutexes, and GASNet does not provide mechanisms for cross-node mutual exclusion. However, the example in Section 2.6.5 shows how one can use AMs to implement a well-known shared memory algorithm for mutual exclusion.

In addition to the previously introduced idea of internal threads for executing the client's AM handlers, the GASNet specification allows for the possibility of interrupt-driven implementations. Though at the time of this writing there are no such implementations, we will introduce this concept briefly:

```
void gasnet_hold_interrupts();
void gasnet_resume_interrupts();
```

These two calls, used in pairs, delimit sections of code which may not be interrupted by execution of AM handlers *on the calling thread*. This is different from use of an HSL to prevent multiple threads from concurrently accessing given code or data. The intended use of no-interrupt sections is to protect client code which is nonreentrant and can potentially be reached from both handler and nonhandler code in the client. No-interrupt sections are seldom necessary for two key reasons: 1) holding an HSL implicitly enters a no-interrupt section; 2) AM handlers run in implicit no-interrupt sections. Note that these calls do *not* nest and the client is therefore responsible for managing no-interrupt sections when nesting might occur dynamically.

It is worth noting that in a GASNET_SEQ build the mutex calls may compile away to "nothing" if and only if the GASNet implementation is using neither threads nor interrupts internally to execute the client's AM handlers.

2.3.5 Active Messages

The real meat of the GASNet Core API is the AM interfaces. The principle of an AM is that a call on the initiating node transfers to the target node some small number of arguments, and an optional payload, all of which are passed to a function run on the target node. Functions to be run are known as AM "handlers" and are named by an index of type `gasnet_handler_t`, where the mapping between these indices and actual functions was established by the handler table passed to (and possibly modified by) the call to `gasnet_attach`.

Arguments to AM handlers are 32-bit integers.[6] There are implementation-dependent limits on the argument count, which can be queried at runtime:

```
size_t gasnet_AMMaxArgs(void);
```

The value *must* be at least 8 on 32-bit platforms and at least 16 on 64-bit platforms. This ensures a client can always pass at least 8 pointer-sized values to a handler.

In addition to the arguments, there is an optional payload. There are three "categories" of AMs depending on the treatment of the payload:

- **Short** AMs have no payload. The signature of a Short AM handler looks like:

```
void ShortExample(gasnet_token_t token ...);
```

- **Medium** AMs carry a payload which is held in an implementation-provided temporary buffer on the target. The AM handler is given the address and length of this buffer, which will be destroyed/recycled when the handler completes. The handler *is* permitted to modify the payload in-place if desired. The signature of a Medium AM handler looks like:

```
void MediumExample(gasnet_token_t token, void *buf,
                   size_t nbytes ...);
```

- **Long** AMs carry a payload that is placed at an address on the target node that is provided by the initiating node. This address must lie in the GASNet segment. The signature of a Long AM handler looks like:

```
void LongExample(gasnet_token_t token, void *buf,
                 size_t nbytes ...);
```

---

6. GASNet's `gasnet_handlerarg_t` type is always equivalent to `uint32_t`, but GASNet supports C89 compilers which may not have `uint32_t`.

In all three handler signatures above, the "..." denotes up to `gasnet_AMMaxArgs()` additional arguments. Since the Medium and Long AM handler signatures are identical, it is permissible to use the same handler for either category of AM.

Payload size is subject to implementation-dependent limit, which can be queried at runtime:

```
size_t gasnet_AMMaxMedium(void);
size_t gasnet_AMMaxLongRequest(void);
size_t gasnet_AMMaxLongReply(void);
```

The GASNet specification requires that all implementations support payloads of at least 512 bytes, and typical values are much higher for platforms with RMA support in hardware. It is important to notice the distinction between the Request and Reply limits for Long AMs.[7]

To invoke an AM handler on a target node one issues an AM request using one of the following:

```
int gasnet_AMRequestShort[N](gasnet_node_t dest,
                        gasnet_handler_t handler ...);
int gasnet_AMRequestMedium[N](gasnet_node_t dest,
                        gasnet_handler_t handler,
                        void *src_addr, size_t nbytes ...);
int gasnet_AMRequestLong[N](gasnet_node_t dest,
                        gasnet_handler_t handler,
                        void *src_addr, size_t nbytes,
                        void * dest_addr ...);
int gasnet_AMRequestLongAsync[N](gasnet_node_t dest,
                        gasnet_handler_t handler,
                        void *src_addr, size_t nbytes,
                        void * dest_addr ...);
```

Each of the above prototypes represents an entire family of calls, where the "[N]" above is replaced with the values from 0 through `gasnet_AMMaxArgs()`. As before, the "..." denotes the placement of the 32-bit arguments to pass to the handler. For the Medium and Long requests, the calls return as soon as the payload memory is safe to reuse (also known as "local completion"). The implementation is *not* required to make a copy of the payload, and thus these calls may block temporarily until the network can send the payload. While blocked, AMs sent to the calling node by others may be executed. The LongAsync request

---

7. This difference arises from the fact that a Reply can only be initiated within a request handler, and it may not be possible in this context to allocate resources for a large Reply. Therefore, when the limits for LongRequest and LongReply differ, the Request value will be the larger of the two.

differs from the Long case in that it returns *without* waiting for local completion (though it may still block waiting for resources). The client must *not* modify the payload until the corresponding AM reply handler begins running—that is the only indication of local completion. This is a difficult semantic to apply correctly, but can be powerful.

When an AM handler runs, code is executed in an environment known as "handler context" in which several restrictions apply. These restrictions will be enumerated later, but at this point we focus on the one that for many is the defining feature of Berkeley AM, and thus of GASNet. This is the "at most one reply" rule which states that 1) the only communication permitted in the handler for an AM Request is one optional Reply to the node initiating the Request; and 2) no communication is permitted in the handler for an AM Reply. An AM Reply is sent with one of the following:[8]

```
int gasnet_AMReplyShort[N](gasnet_token_t token,
                 gasnet_handler_t handler ...);
int gasnet_AMReplyMedium[N](gasnet_token_t token,
                 gasnet_handler_t handler,
                 void *src_addr, size_t nbytes ...);
int gasnet_AMReplyLong[N](gasnet_token_t token,
                 gasnet_handler_t handler,
                 void *src_addr, size_t nbytes,
                 void * dest_addr ...);
```

The use of "...", again, denotes the 32-bit hander arguments, and [N] indicates that these three prototypes are templates for instances from 0 to `gasnet_AMMaxArgs()` arguments.

Other than the names, the key difference between the calls to send an AM Reply versus those for a Request is the type of the first argument: `gasnet_token_t`. This type was first seen, without any explanation, when the prototypes for the three categories of AM handlers were given. It is an opaque type that contains (at least) the source node of an AM. Since there is no way to construct an object of this type the only way to invoke an AMReply function is using the token received as an argument to the Request handler. For situations where one does need to known the source node for an AM (either Request or Reply), one can query:

```
int gasnet_AMGetMsgSource(gasnet_token_t token,
                 gasnet_node_t *srcindex);
```

This call can be made only from the handler context and the only valid value for the `token` argument is the one received as an argument to the handler function.

---

8. Note that the lack of an AMReplyLongAsync is a consequence of the fact that the "at most one reply" rule prevents the AM Reply handler from issuing any communication that would serve to indicate the local completion.

2.3.6   Active Message Progress

It has been mentioned that GASNet may run AM handlers using internal threads or with interrupts. While important for writing correct client code, those should not be considered the
common case as many implementations lack both of those mechanisms for asynchronous
progress. Instead, the progress of a typical AM-driven GASNet application is dependent
on the client making entries to GASNet. A client can be assured that AM initiating calls
will also poll for incoming AMs, but that is not always sufficient. So, there are two ways
to explicitly poll for incoming AMs:

```
int gasnet_AMPoll(void);
#define GASNET_BLOCKUNTIL(condition) ...
```

The call gasnet_AMPoll checks for incoming AMs (both Requests and Replies) and
will execute some implementation-dependent maximum number of them before returning. Thus, there is no guarantee that at the time this call returns that are no additional
AMs waiting. This call is typically used in the clients' own progress loop, or before and
after client operations that are known not to poll for long periods of time. The macro
GASNET_BLOCKUNTIL is used to block until a condition becomes true. It takes as an
argument a C expression to evaluate, and GASNet executes code functionally equivalent
to:

```
#define GASNET_BLOCKUNTIL(cond) while (!(cond)) gasnet_AMPoll()
```

It is possible, however, for GASNET_BLOCKUNTIL to use implementation-specific mechanisms instead of this naive mechanism. It is important to note that it is only valid to use
GASNET_BLOCKUNTIL to block waiting for a condition which will change due to the action of an AM—code which uses GASNET_BLOCKUNTIL to block for an Extended API
call to change memory could block indefinitely.[9]

2.3.7   Active Message Rules and Restrictions

The GASNet specification is the most complete reference for the details, but the following
are the primary rules which must be followed to write correct/portable AM codes with
GASNet. Keep in mind that not all implementations enforce all of these rules, but clients
must follow them all or risk incorrect operation on some implementation.

---

9. If it helps to understand this rule, try visualize an implementation using a condition variable which is broadcast
by GASNet each time a handler execution completes.

- A handler running as the result of an AM Request is permitted communication only via a single optional call to an AMReply function.

- A handler running as the result of an AM Reply is not permitted any communication.

- No handler may call the GASNet barrier functions, initiate AM Requests or call any portion of the Extended API (these involve prohibited communication).

- A handler *may* block temporarily in a call to obtain an HSL, but must release any held HSL before returning.

- A handler may *not* call GASNET_BLOCKUNTIL.

- The GASNet implementation is *not* required to ensure AMs are executed in order and client code must be constructed to be deadlock-free in the presence of reordered messages.[10]

- Client code must be written in a thread-safe manner (through the proper use of HSL) in recognition that even with single-threaded clients, GASNet may run AM handlers asynchronously.

- The expression passed to GASNET_BLOCKUNTIL does *not* have an exception to the previous rule and must consider the possibility that the expression could be evaluated concurrently with execution of AM handlers.

2.3.8   Error Codes

While only a few were mentioned in prior discussions, most of the Core API has integer return values taken from the following:

- GASNET_OK
  Guaranteed to be zero, this value indicates success.

- GASNET_ERR_RESOURCE
  A fairly generic error indicating that a call failed because some finite resource was unavailable.

- GASNET_ERR_BAD_ARG
  Similar to errno == EINVAL, this indicates that the client passed an invalid argument.

---

10. GASNet will *not* drop or replay AMs. So the client *may* assume "exactly once" delivery.

- GASNET_ERR_NOT_INIT
  Client has not yet called `gasnet_init`

- GASNET_ERR_BARRIER_MISMATCH
  Either the id-matching logic of GASNet's barrier has *detected* a mismatch (see the specification for the matching rules), or a caller has *indicated* one by passing GASNET_BARRIERFLAG_MISMATCH.

- GASNET_ERR_NOT_READY
  A (temporary) indication that a split-phase operation is incomplete. In the Core API this occurs when calling `gasnet_barrier_try` before all nodes have called `gasnet_barrier_notify`.

Additionally, one can convert the numerical error code into a string (GASNET_ERR-prefixed) name, or an English language description of the error value using the following:

```
char * gasnet_ErrorName(int errval);
char * gasnet_ErrorDesc(int errval);
```

2.4   Extended API

The Extended API provides a rich set of interfaces for remote memory access (Puts and Gets) with a variety of semantics intended to ease automatic code generation, especially from source-to-source translation of partitioned global address space (PGAS) Languages. At this time GASNet provides standardized RMA interfaces only for Put and Get of contiguous regions, but see Section 2.7 for information on proposed "Vector-Index-Strided" interfaces).

2.4.1   The GASNet Segment

As previously mentioned, the Extended API can only access remote addresses that lie in a portion of memory known as the GASNet segment and established at `gasnet_attach` time. The two original GASNet clients, implementations of UPC and Titanium, differ in terms of what portion of memory should be remotely accessible. In UPC, only memory allocated by the language-specific shared allocation functions can be the remote operand to an RMA operation, while in Titanium there is no such specialization of memory allocation and consequently all objects can potentially be accessed remotely with GASNet Extended API calls. GASNet recognizes this distinction, plus one additional gradation in the form of the "segment configuration" which must be selected when the GASNet library is built

from source. The default configuration is known as GASNET_SEGMENT_FAST, or just
SEGMENT_FAST for short. In this configuration the implementation provides the fastest
(lowest latency and/or highest bandwidth) implementation possible, even if this results in
making trade-offs which significantly reduce the size of the segment. The second option,
SEGMENT_LARGE, supports the largest contiguous segment possible (within reason) even
when this support may require "bounce buffers" or other mechanisms that reduce the speed
of remote accesses. The final option is GASNET_SEGMENT_EVERYTHING in which the
entire virtual address space is considered "in-segment."

2.4.2   Ordering and Memory Model

As a general design principle, GASNet attempts to define as few semantics as possible
to allow both efficient implementation and freedom for the client to determine its own
semantics. In this vein, GASNet's Extended API operations are unordered and the state
of destination memory is undefined between the initiation of an operation and its remote
completion. Clients which require ordering "A precedes B" must complete operation "A"
before initiating operation "B." Local completion semantics for Puts depends on the client's
choice of "bulk" or "nonbulk" operations as described below. GASNet makes no guarantees about the results of concurrent operations where an operation's destination overlaps
the source or destination of another (including undefined result for a loopback operation
with overlapping source and destination).

2.4.3   Blocking and Nonblocking

Blocking operations are both locally and remotely complete when they return. Therefore, a
sequence of blocking operations is trivially ordered, but only with respect to other blocking
operations. Nonblocking operations come in two flavors: "explicit handle" and "implicit
handle." Explicit-handle operations have an "_nb" suffix and return an opaque handle,
gasnet_handle_t, with which one can poll on or block for completion of individual
operations or on arrays of handles (known as "syncing" a handle). Implicit-handle nonblocking operations have an "_nbi" suffix and treat a sequence of RMA operations as a
group. A client can sync all outstanding implicit-handle Puts, Gets, or both. One cannot
sync individual implicit-handle operations, but can manage a sequence of such operations
without needing to track a collection of explicit handles. It is also possible to create an
"nbi access region" which collects all implicit-handle operations occurring dynamically
between the begin and end calls together under a single handle which can then be used
with the explicit-handle sync operations.

2.4.4 Bulk and Nonbulk

GASNet combines the concepts of data alignment and local completion together into the concept of "bulk" transfers. A "bulk" operation has an extra "_bulk" suffix and imposes no alignment restrictions for either source or destination addresses. A "nonbulk" operation imposes a "natural alignment constraint" on both the source and destination addresses. GASNet uses "natural alignment" to mean that for power-of-two transfer sizes not larger than the machine word size (4 or 8 bytes) the source and destination addresses must both be multiples of the transfer size. For sizes larger than the word size or not a power-of-two, there is no restriction.

In addition to the alignment restriction, the nonblocking nonbulk Put operations delay their return until local completion (possibly making an internal copy[11]). The nonblocking bulk Put operations, on the other hand, return as soon as possible without delaying for local completion. In this case there is no mechanism by which one can determine local completion independent of syncing the operation for remote completion. Get operations also have bulk and nonbulk flavors with the corresponding alignment restriction on the nonbulk version. However, the local completion distinction is absent, since the initiator's buffer is the destination, rather than source, of the operation.

2.4.5 Register-Memory and Remote `memset` Operations

GASNet's Extended API does have a few odd-ball interfaces that can be very useful in some cases. In addition to the bulk and nonbulk operations for data, GASNet offers value-based operations for moving data that fits in a register (up to 4 or 8 bytes, depending on platform) to or from remote memory. For Puts, blocking and nonblocking variants (with explicit and implicit handles) are supported. For Gets, there is a blocking variant and an explicit-handle variant with its own distinct handle type, `gasnet_valget_handle_t`. The GASNet API also provides a corresponding call to sync the operation and return the value: `gasnet_wait_syncnb_valget`.

GASNet supports blocking and nonblocking (with explicit and implicit handles) remote `memset` calls with the same completion semantics as Put. These calls do not have the time or space overheads of constructing a source buffer initialized to the desired constant value.

2.4.6 Extended API Summary

The following summarizes the various operations in the GASNet Extended API:

---

11. The README for each conduit includes documentation on protocol switch points that control such behaviors, and most offer environment variables to adjust them.

```
// Blocking Get and Put operations :
void gasnet_get(void *dest, gasnet_node_t node, void *src,
          size_t nbytes);
void gasnet_get_bulk(void *dest, gasnet_node_t node, void *src,
            size_t nbytes);
void gasnet_put(gasnet_node_t node, void *dest, void *src,
          size_t nbytes);
void gasnet_put_bulk(gasnet_node_t node, void *dest, void *src,
            size_t nbytes);

// Explicit —handle nonblocking Get and Put operations :
gasnet_handle_t gasnet_get_nb(void *dest, gasnet_node_t node,
                  void *src, size_t nbytes);
gasnet_handle_t gasnet_get_nb_bulk(void *dest, gasnet_node_t node,
                    void *src, size_t nbytes);
gasnet_handle_t gasnet_put_nb(gasnet_node_t node, void *dest,
                  void *src, size_t nbytes);
gasnet_handle_t gasnet_put_nb_bulk(gasnet_node_t node, void *dest,
                    void *src, size_t nbytes);

// Explicit —handle synchronization functions :
void gasnet_wait_syncnb(gasnet_handle_t handle);
void gasnet_wait_syncnb_all(gasnet_handle_t *handles,
              size_t count);
void gasnet_wait_syncnb_some(gasnet_handle_t *handles,
               size_t count);
int gasnet_try_syncnb(gasnet_handle_t handle);
int gasnet_try_syncnb_all(gasnet_handle_t *handles, size_t count);
int gasnet_try_syncnb_some(gasnet_handle_t *handles,
             size_t count);

// Implicit —handle nonblocking Get and Put operations :
void gasnet_get_nbi(void *dest, gasnet_node_t node, void *src,
          size_t nbytes);
void gasnet_get_nbi_bulk(void *dest, gasnet_node_t node,
            void *src, size_t nbytes);
void gasnet_put_nbi(gasnet_node_t node, void *dest, void *src,
          size_t nbytes);
void gasnet_put_nbi_bulk(gasnet_node_t node, void *dest,
            void *src, size_t nbytes);

// Implicit —handle synchronization functions :
void gasnet_wait_syncnbi_gets(void);
void gasnet_wait_syncnbi_puts(void);
void gasnet_wait_syncnbi_all(void);
int gasnet_try_syncnbi_gets(void);
int gasnet_try_syncnbi_puts(void);
int gasnet_try_syncnbi_all(void);

// Implicit —handle access regions :
void gasnet_begin_nbi_accessregion(void);
```

```
gasnet_handle_t gasnet_end_nbi_accessregion(void);

// Remote memset functions:
void gasnet_memset(gasnet_node_t node, void *dest, int val,
                size_t nbytes);
gasnet_handle_t gasnet_memset_nb(gasnet_node_t node, void *dest,
                        int val, size_t nbytes);
void gasnet_memset_nbi(gasnet_node_t node, void *dest, int val,
                size_t nbytes);

// Register −memory Put functions:
void gasnet_put_val(gasnet_node_t node, void *dest,
                gasnet_register_value_t value, size_t nbytes);
gasnet_handle_t gasnet_put_nb_val(gasnet_node_t node, void *dest,
                        gasnet_register_value_t value,
                        size_t nbytes);
void gasnet_put_nbi_val(gasnet_node_t node, void *dest,
                gasnet_register_value_t value,
                size_t nbytes);

// Register −memory Get functions:
gasnet_register_value_t gasnet_get_val(gasnet_node_t node,
                        void *src, size_t nbytes);
gasnet_valget_handle_t gasnet_get_nb_val(gasnet_node_t node,
                        void *src,
                        size_t nbytes);
gasnet_register_value_t gasnet_wait_syncnb_valget(
                        asnet_valget_handle_t handle);
```

2.5   Extras

In addition to the GASNet Core and Extended APIs as defined in the specification, there are some additional capabilities in GASNet, documented in its README file. There are also two other software components that ship with GASNet called "GASNet Tools." One can download just these "GASNet Tools" from the same locations as the full GASNet package.

When GASNet has been configured with --enable-debug, many usage restrictions, constraints on arguments, and other rules given in the specification will be checked at runtime. This debugging code was developed in part to detect errors in the GASNet implementation itself, but a lot of the debug code is devoted to checking the client's arguments and detecting violations of usage restrictions (such as calls which are not legal in certain contexts). It is a good idea to perform initial development work using a debugging build of GASNet to help catch these sorts of errors quickly.

GASNet also provides an optional mechanism for detailed event tracing and statistical collection, again designed for the developers of GASNet and its clients. These features are described in GASNet's `README` file, and are enabled by passing `--enable-tracing` and/or `--enable-stats` to configure, though both are enabled automatically when one passes `--enable-debug`.

2.5.1 GASNet Tools

In the course of implementing GASNet for a wide range of systems, the development team found a variety of abstractions that needed to be supported uniformly. As the same team was also responsible for the UPC and Titanium language runtimes, it quickly became obvious that the same abstractions would need to be replicated three times (together with their convoluted autoconf logic and C preprocessor macros), unless GASNet provided a common implementation for use by its clients. Thus the "GASNet Tools" interfaces were born, independent of the GASNet specification. While included with GASnet, one can also obtain a stand-alone GASNet Tools distribution without the rest of GASNet (no Core or Extended API). Regardless of whether one obtains the tools as part of GASNet or from a stand-alone distribution, the interfaces are fully documented in the file `README-tools`. Below is a brief summary of some of the features in the tools API:

- Memory barriers—e.g., for writing spin lock constructs, especially for architectures with memory models weaker than the x86.

- Atomics—e.g., for writing lock-free data structures.

- Compiler annotations—to allow portable use of GNU C `__attribute__` and equivalent pragmas in other compilers.

- Branch prediction—to portably apply branch prediction hints.

- Backtrace—to obtain stack traces from a variety of C library implementations and external debuggers.

2.5.2 Portable Platform Header

Even with resources such as the GASNet tools, there is often a need to write platform-specific code. This may include, for instance, optimizations that are specific to one operating system, or work-arounds for bugs specific to certain versions of a given compiler. The header `portable_platform.h` is intended to simplify the C preprocessor logic required to manage platform-specific code. This improves maintainability and avoids mistakes that may arise when *ad hoc* solutions are used. This header contains the C preprocessor logic to recognize the operating system, compiler, CPU and several other platform characteristics, and exports this information in a uniform name space. The categories of information detected include:

- `PLATFORM_OS_*` for operating system.

- `PLATFORM_COMPILER_*` for compiler family and language (C vs. C++).

- `PLATFORM_COMPILER_VERSION*` for compiler version in numerical and string representations, and macros for comparing numerical versions.

- `PLATFORM_ARCH_{32,64}` for word size (pointer width).

- `PLATFORM_ARCH_{BIG,LITTLE}_ENDIAN` for byte order.

- `PLATFORM_ARCH_*` for processor family. .

Representative examples include `PLATFORM_OS_LINUX`, `PLATFORM_COMPILER_GNU`, and `PLATFORM_ARCH_X86_64`.

2.6   Examples

This section contains a series of examples intended to put into practice the lessons of the preceding sections. The examples illustrate how you can use GASNet to accomplish various tasks that one might find useful in a language runtime. Examples are devoted to the Core API only. This is not intended to diminish the importance or value of the Extended API for implementation of PGAS language runtimes. Rather, the concentration on the Core API is intended to highlight one of GASNet's distinguishing features. Several other chapters in this volume provide examples of RMA and PGAS programming which can easily be translated into GASNet Extended API calls by the reader.[12] The reader is also encouraged to look at the codes in the `tests/` directory of the GASNet distribution. While many are performance or correctness tests, they also serve to demonstrate uses of nearly every aspect of the GASNet APIs.

2.6.1   Building and Running Examples

GASNet handles the tricky issue of getting the correct compiler and linker for each platform by creating `Makefile` fragments for each conduit and threading mode that can

---

12. Alternatively, since runtimes for several of the languages or libraries in this book have been implemented over GASNet, one can instead look at how those source-to-source compilers and/or libraries map their respective API or language onto GASNet's.

be used to compile and link. GASNet's README file provides the following sample Makefile, which assumes a version of make that supports the include directive:

```
include /install/path/include/mpi-conduit/mpi-seq.mak

.c.o:
    $(GASNET_CC) $(GASNET_CPPFLAGS) $(GASNET_CFLAGS) -c -o $@ $<

myprog: myprog.o
    $(GASNET_LD) $(GASNET_LDFLAGS) -o $@ $< $(GASNET_LIBS)
```

The remainder of this section will assume you are either using this sort of a Makefile, or have inspected an appropriate .mak file to get all the necessary compiler flags. We will also assume that you have read the conduit-specific documentation on how to run GASNet applications on your platform.

2.6.2 Hello World Example

The first example is a GASNet version of the classic "Hello, World!" C program, and can be found as Listing 2.1, appearing on page 45. Beginning on line 5 is a macro we will be using to wrap most calls to GASNet, which demonstrates the use of GASNet's facilities for getting string versions of error codes. Lines 19 and 20 are the AM handler table—which for this example is effectively empty—and a macro giving its length.

```c
1  #include <gasnet.h>
2  #include <stdio.h>
3
4  // Macro to check return code and terminate with a useful message
5  #define SAFE_CALL(fncall) do {                              \
6    int _retval = fncall;                                     \
7    if (_retval != GASNET_OK) {                               \
8      fprintf(stderr,                                         \
9         "ERROR calling: %s\n at: %s:%i\n error: %s (%s)\n", \
10        #fncall, __FILE__, __LINE__,                         \
11        gasnet_ErrorName(_retval), gasnet_ErrorDesc(_retval)); \
12      fflush(stderr);                                         \
13      gasnet_exit(_retval);                                   \
14    }                                                         \
15  } while(0)
16
17  gasnet_node_t rank, size; // globals
18
19  gasnet_handlerentry_t htable[] = { { 0, NULL } };
20  #define HTABLE_LEN (sizeof(htable) / sizeof(htable[0]))
21
```

```
22  int main(int argc, char **argv)
23  {
24    SAFE_CALL(gasnet_init(&argc, &argv));
25    SAFE_CALL(gasnet_attach(htable, HTABLE_LEN,
26                      GASNET_PAGESIZE, GASNET_PAGESIZE));
27    rank = gasnet_mynode();
28    size = gasnet_nodes();
29
30    // Only first and last print here — reduces screen clutter
31    if (!rank || (rank == size-1))
32      printf("Hello_from_node_%d_of_%d\n", (int)rank, (int)size);
33
34    // Spec says client should include barrier before gasnet_exit()
35    gasnet_barrier_notify(0,GASNET_BARRIERFLAG_ANONYMOUS);
36    gasnet_barrier_wait(0,GASNET_BARRIERFLAG_ANONYMOUS);
37
38    gasnet_exit(0);
39
40    // Not reached, but keeps some compilers from warning
41    return 0;
42  }
```

Listing 2.1: GASNet Hello World

In main(), we see the skeleton of any GASNet application: calls to gasnet_init, gasnet_attach and gasnet_exit. For the initialization steps, this example does not query the segment size limits and simply requests a 1-page segment (and at least 1 page of heap space). There are also calls to gasnet_nodes and gasnet_mynode to personalize the greeting. As was mentioned previously, GASNet recommends a barrier prior to exit to avoid triggering the logic that performs cleanup if less than all nodes exit. So, there is an anonymous barrier on lines 35 and 36.

That is pretty much all there is to this example, but in the remainder of the examples we will reuse "Hello, World!" as a template, providing just the portions which need replacement.

2.6.3   AM Ping-Pong Example

While the "Hello, World!" example demonstrates the basics needed to begin and end every GASNet application, it performs no communication other than that which is implicit in the barrier. So, in the second example we will demonstrate a very simple use of GASNet's AMs to perform a "ping-pong" communication between pairs of nodes.[13]

---

13. If run with an odd number of nodes, the last one communicates with itself, demonstrating that loopback use of AMs is fully supported.

```
1   // Handlers for PingPong Example
2
3   gasnett_atomic_t pong_count = gasnett_atomic_init(0);
4
5   #define PingHandlerIdx 128
6   #define PongHandlerIdx 129
7
8   void PingHandler(gasnet_token_t token, gasnet_handlerarg_t arg0) {
9     gasnet_node_t peer;
10    SAFE_CALL(getMsgSource(token, &peer));
11    printf("Node_%d_receive_Ping_#%d_from_%d\n",
12          (int)gasnet_mynode, (int)arg0, (int)peer);
13    SAFE_CALL(gasnet_AMReplyShort1(token, PongHandlerIdx, arg0));
14  }
15
16  void PongHandler(gasnet_token_t token, gasnet_handlerarg_t arg0) {
17    gasnet_node_t peer;
18    SAFE_CALL(getMsgSource(token, &peer));
19    printf("Node_%d_receive_Pong_#%d_from_%d\n",
20          (int)mynode, (int)arg0, (int)src);
21    gasnett_atomic_increment(&pong_count, 0);
22  }
23
24  gasnet_handlerentry_t htable[] = {
25    { PingHandlerIdx, &PingHandler },
26    { PongHandlerIdx, &PongHandler }
27  };
```

Listing 2.2: PingPong Handlers

```
1   // Fragment of main() for Ping—Pong Example
2
3   int count = (argc == 1) ? 2 : atoi(argv[1]); // default is 2
4
5   // Pair up the nodes.  If nodes odd, last one sends to self.
6   gasnet_node_t peer = mynode ^ 1;
7   if (peer == nodes) peer = mynode;
8
9   // First node in each pair sends Ping messages
10  if (mynode <= peer) { // equals case catches loopback
11    for (int i = 0; i < count; ++i) {
12      // Send a single "ping" to our peer
13      SAFE_CALL(gasnet_AMRequestShort1(peer, PingHandlerIdx, i));
14      // Wait for the next "pong" to arrive before continuing
15      GASNET_BLOCKUNTIL(gasnett_atomic_read(&pong_count,0) == i+1);
16    }
17  }
```

```
18
19   // Spec says client should include barrier before gasnet_exit()
20   gasnet_barrier_notify(0,GASNET_BARRIERFLAG_ANONYMOUS);
21   gasnet_barrier_wait(0,GASNET_BARRIERFLAG_ANONYMOUS);
```

Listing 2.3: PingPong Main

The first portion of this example is the necessary AM handlers, shown in Listing 2.2, appearing on page 47. This code can be dropped in to the framework of the "Hello, World!" example to replace line 19. In this example there are two AM handlers, each of which is expecting an AM Short with a single argument. The "Ping" handler will run in response to an AM Request and performs just two actions: print a message containing the value of the argument and issue an AM Reply to invoke the "Pong" handler with the same argument. The "Pong" handler prints a slightly different message and increments a counter. It is worth noting that the counter has been implemented using an atomic increment from GASNet Tools to ensure thread-safety (the counter will also be read from `main()`). Alternatively, `pong_counter++` could have been used, but would require the protection of an HSL.

The second portion of this example is the `main()` logic, shown in Listing 2.3. This code can be dropped into the framework of the "Hello, World!" example to replace lines 32–34. The code on line 3 defaults to 2 iterations, but will obtain an alternate value from the command line if one were provided. The code on lines 6 and 7 pair up the nodes (0 and 1, 2 and 3, etc.), taking care to pair the last node with itself if running on an odd number of nodes. On line 10 the interesting work finally begins. The lower-numbered node in each pair loops for `count` iterations, sending an AM Request to its partner and then blocking until the peer's AM Reply has incremented the `pong_count` atomic variable. Meanwhile, the higher-numbered node in each pair has no corresponding work to perform in `main()`, and proceeds to the barrier call that appears on lines 20 and 21. Both nodes in each pair must make progress running AMs for this example to work. It is therefore important that the even nodes wait for "Pongs" by using GASNET_BLOCKUNTIL. GASNet implementations without asynchronous progress threads would deadlock if the code had instead read:

```
    do {} while (gasnett_atomic_read(&pong_count,0) != i+1);  // NO
```

If one compiles this example and runs on 3 nodes with no command line arguments, the output should look like the following, except that output lines from the 3 nodes may interleave differently depending on timing:

```
Node 2 receive Ping #0 from 2
Node 2 receive Pong #0 from 2
Node 2 receive Ping #1 from 2
Node 2 receive Pong #1 from 2
Node 1 receive Ping #0 from 0
Node 0 receive Pong #0 from 1
Node 1 receive Ping #1 from 0
Node 0 receive Pong #1 from 1
```

2.6.4 AM Ring Example

In the "Ping-Pong" example the communication was limited to a Request and a Reply to the sender. This is the only sort of communication permitted using the simple logic of that example. However, more realistic applications require at least "A-to-B-to-C" communications patterns, and the "Ring" example (Listings 2.4 and 2.5) demonstrates how that is typically accomplished. As with the "Ping-Pong" example, these two listings should be used to replace lines 19–21 and 32–34 of the "Hello, World!" example.

```
1   // Handlers for Ring Example
2
3   // Two functions  left "as an exercise  for  the  reader"
4   //    Enqueue adds (dest,arg) pair  to  a FIFO queue
5   //    Dequeue returns 0 when the queue is empty, or else
6   //           removes one such pair and returns non−zero
7   extern void Enqueue(gasnet_node_t dest, int arg);
8   extern int Dequeue(gasnet_node_t *dest_p, int *arg_p);
9
10  #define RingHandlerIdx 128
11
12  void RingHandler(gasnet_token_t token, void *msg, size_t len,
13              gasnet_handerarg_t arg0) {
14    gasnet_node_t peer;
15    SAFE_CALL(getMsgSource(token, &peer));
16    printf("Node %d receive message %d '%s' from %d\n",
17        (int)mynode, (int)arg0, msg, (int)peer);
18    if (0 == mynode) ++arg0; // Advance as we pass the origin
19    Enqueue((mynode+1) % nodes, arg0);
20  }
21
22  gasnet_handlerentry_t htable[] = {
23    { RingHandlerIdx, &RingHandler },
24  };
```

Listing 2.4: Ring Handler

```
1    // Fragment of main() for Ring Example
2
3    int count = (argc == 1) ? 2 : atoi(argv[1]);  // default is 2
4
5    // Compose a message to send
6    char msg[32];
7    size_t len = 1 + snprintf(msg, sizeof(msg), "sent_by_%d", mynode);
8
9    // Node zero starts the message travelling around the ring:
10   if (0 == mynode) {
11     gasnet_node_t peer = (nodes > 1) ? 1 : 0;
12     SAFE_CALL(gasnet_AMRequestMedium1(peer, msg, len, 1));
13   }
14
15   // All nodes work to pass the message 'count' times
16   gasnet_node_t dest;
17   int arg = 0;
18   do {
19     gasnet_AMPoll();  // Make progress
20     if (!Dequeue(&dest, &arg)) continue;
21     if (arg <= count)  // See the text for an explanation
22       SAFE_CALL(gasnet_AMRequestMedium1(dest, msg, len, arg));
23   } while (arg <= count);
```

Listing 2.5: Ring Main

The idea of this example is to pass an imaginary token multiple times around a ring which begins on node 0 and passes through the nodes in ascending order, wrapping back to node 0 after the highest-numbered node. Since each node must receive from its predecessor and send to its successor, the Request+Reply logic of the "Ping-Pong" example is only sufficient/correct for 1 or 2 nodes. For larger node counts a different approach is needed. Specifically, when a node receives the AM, it must defer sending of the next message until control returns back to nonhandler code. This is a very important concept to master, as "deferred work" is the solution to many "how can I do X with Active Messages?" questions. So, we have made this "Ring" example slightly more general than strictly necessary.

This example has a single handler, this time expecting a Medium AM, that prints a message containing the AM payload before enqueuing[14] information to be retrieved by code running in main(). Note that when run on node 0, the received argument is incremented before it is enqueued to ensure that the ring traversal will eventually end. In this example the intent is to traverse the ring in order, which accounts for the expression

---

14. For brevity, we have omitted code for Enqueue() and Dequeue() functions to implement a FIFO work queue. However, the reader should find very little challenge in implementing these, taking care to use GASNet's handler-safe locks to serialize manipulation of the queue data structure.

((mynode+1)%nodes) passed as the first argument to Enqueue().[15] However, in a real application the destination of the next message could easily be a function of some combination of the handler arguments and payload, which would describe a more complex task.

Turning our attention now to Listing 2.5 for the logic in main(), we see the same logic as the previous example for determining the trip count, followed by construction of a very simple node-specific message. The actual communication begins with node 0 sending the first AM Request to the "next" node in the ring, which could be itself if running a single node, with the payload "sent by 0" and a single argument with value 1. All nodes then enter a polling loop in which they alternate calls to gasnet_AMPoll and Dequeue. Since gasnet_AMPoll processes AMs *without* blocking if none have arrived, the common return from the Dequeue call is most likely to be 0, indicating no queued work. However, when there is work queued by the AM handler a new AM Request is sent to the queued destination, carrying the senders personalized msg and the queued argument. Each node terminates the loop after receiving the message with the argument equal to the desired total trip count. A bit of nonobvious logic is also in place to prevent node 0 from sending an "extra" message when finished.

Keeping in mind that output from distinct nodes can be reordered, the expected output for a 3-node run with no command line arguments is approximately:

```
Node 1 receive message 1 'sent_by_0' from 0
Node 2 receive message 1 'sent_by_1' from 1
Node 0 receive message 1 'sent_by_2' from 2
Node 1 receive message 2 'sent_by_0' from 0
Node 2 receive message 2 'sent_by_1' from 1
Node 0 receive message 2 'sent_by_2' from 2
```

2.6.5   MCS Locks Example

This final example demonstrates transformation of a portion of a well-known shared-memory algorithm to an AM based implementation for distributed memory. The algorithm to be addressed is the lock-acquire function for MCS Locks [189]. Only the lock acquisition is presented, and the reader is encouraged to pursue initialization and lock release on their own. The reader is strongly encouraged to take some time now to look at the MCS Locks paper, especially Algorithm 5 in Section 2.4. An understanding of the shared-memory implementation is crucial to understanding this example.

---

15. The curious and adventurous reader is encouraged to try replacing this with (rand()%nodes) and devise a corresponding termination condition for the loop in main().

A translation into C of the MCS Lock data types and lock acquisition for shared-memory are given below in Listing 2.6.

```
 1   // C version of MCS list—based queue lock
 2
 3   typedef struct qnode {
 4     struct qnode *next;
 5     bool locked;
 6   } qnode;
 7
 8   typedef struct qnode *lock; // initialized to NULL
 9
10   void acquire_lock(lock *L, qnode *I) {
11     I->next = NULL;
12     qnode *predecessor = fetch_and_store(L, I);
13     if (predecessor != NULL) { // queue was non—empty
14       I->locked = true;
15       wmb();
16       predecessor->next = I;
17       while (I->locked) sched_yield(); // spin
18     }
19   }
```

Listing 2.6: MCS List-Based Queue Lock in C

The key observations to make are:

1. The lock data type is the head of a linked list in shared-memory.

2. The qnode data type forms the elements of the linked list.

3. The qnode data type contains a locked field to allow polling in local memory by a thread blocked on lock acquisition.

The goal of this example is to reproduce these properties in a distributed-memory implementation. To do this, we begin with a transformation of the data types as shown in Listing 2.7.

```
 1   #include <stdint.h>
 2   #include <stdio.h>
 3   #include <stdbool.h>
 4   #include "gasnet.h"
 5   #include "gasnet_tools.h"
 6
 7   // Forward type declarations :
 8   struct qnode_s; struct lock_s;
 9
```

```
10   // "wide pointer" types:
11   typedef struct { gasnet_node_t node;
12                    struct qnode_s *addr; } qnode_ptr_t;
13   typedef struct { gasnet_node_t node;
14                    struct lock_s *addr; } lock_ptr_t;
15
16   typedef struct qnode_s { // The qnode type:
17     qnode_ptr_t next;
18     bool locked;
19     qnode_ptr_t predecessor; // NEW: fetch_and_store return value
20   } qnode_t;
21
22   typedef struct lock_s { // The lock type:
23     qnode_ptr_t qnode;
24     gasnet_hsl_t hsl; // NEW: serializes access to qnode field
25   } lock_t;
```

Listing 2.7: AM MCS Lock, Part 1/4

Lines 11 to 14 define two "wide pointer" types, each containing a node and an address. In the definitions of the types `lock_t` and `qnode_t`, the pointers to linked list nodes have been replaced with the "wide" equivalent. This is a common idiom in the transformation from shared- to distributed-memory. The definitions of these two types also includes fields identified as "NEW", the use of which will be described in what follows.

Before continuing with the transformation of the MCS lock acquisition, we must take the reader on a short digression. This is the first example in which one must pass pointers as AM arguments. As was noted previously, the arguments to GASNet AM's are always unsigned 32-bit integers. This necessitates passing any 64-bit pointers as 2 arguments. If one is only concerned with writing for 64-bit platforms then some simple C preprocessor macros could accomplish this. However, writing legible code for both 32- and 64-bit platforms requires some nontrivial use of the C preprocessor. Each client using GASNet has some version of this idiom, and Listing 2.8 provides just the logic necessary to construct the three AM handlers that will be required for this example. The one nonobvious aspect of these macros is that `Request2P` and `Reply2P1I` take a doubly parenthesized list of arguments, which will ensure that the C preprocessor will performs its expansions in the proper order.

```
26   // Some tricks for word-size independence of AM code:
27   #if PLATFORM_ARCH_32
28   # define SEND_PTR(ptr) ((gasnet_handlerarg_t) ptr)
29   # define RECV_PTR(a0) ((void *) a0)
30   # define Request2P(args) gasnet_AMRequestShort2 args
31   # define Reply2P1I(args) gasnet_AMReplyShort3 args
32   # define PtrArg1   gasnet_handlerarg_t arg0
33   # define PtrArg2   gasnet_handlerarg_t arg1
```

```
34  # define Ptr1        RECV_PTR(arg0)
35  # define Ptr2        RECV_PTR(arg1)
36  #elif PLATFORM_ARCH_64
37  # define SEND_PTR(ptr) \
38               ((gasnet_handlerarg_t)((uintptr_t)(ptr)>>32)), \
39               ((gasnet_handlerarg_t) (uintptr_t)(ptr))
40  # define RECV_PTR(a0,a1) \
41               ((void *) ((uint64_t)(a0) << 32 (uint64_t)(a1)))
42  # define Request2P(args) gasnet_AMRequestShort4 args
43  # define Reply2P1I(args) gasnet_AMReplyShort5 args
44  # define PtrArg1 \
45           gasnet_handlerarg_t arg0, gasnet_handlerarg_t arg1
46  # define PtrArg2 \
47           gasnet_handlerarg_t arg2, gasnet_handlerarg_t arg3
48  # define Ptr1 RECV_PTR(arg0,arg1)
49  # define Ptr2 RECV_PTR(arg2,arg3)
50  #else
51  # error
52  #endif
```

Listing 2.8: AM MCS Lock, Part 2/4

Returning from our digression, we direct the reader's attention back to the shared-memory C code in Listing 2.6, and especially to Lines 12 and 16. These two lines contain the only references to nonlocal memory in the original algorithm and therefore their implementation in terms of AMs, shown in Listing 2.9, forms the "meat" of this example.

```
53  void
54  FetchAndStoreRequest(gasnet_token_t token, PtrArg1, PtrArg2) {
55    lock_t *lock = Ptr1;
56
57    gasnet_hsl_lock(&lock->hsl);
58      qnode_ptr_t prev = lock->qnode;
59      gasnet_AMGetMsgSource(token, &lock->qnode.node);
60      lock->qnode.addr = Ptr2;
61    gasnet_hsl_unlock(&lock->hsl);
62
63    Reply2P1I((token, FetchAndStoreReplyIdx,
64          SEND_PTR(Ptr2),
65          SEND_PTR(prev.addr), prev.node));
66  }
67
68  void
69  FetchAndStoreReply(gasnet_token_t token,
70                  PtrArg1, PtrArg2, gasnet_handlerarg_t node) {
71    qnode_t *I = Ptr1;
72
73    I->predecessor.addr = Ptr2;
74    gasnett_local_wmb(); // for ordering
```

```
75    I->predecessor.node = node;
76  }
77
78  void StoreNextRequest(gasnet_token_t token, PtrArg1, PtrArg2) {
79    qnode_t *I = Ptr1;
80
81    I->next.addr = Ptr2;
82    gasnett_local_wmb(); // for ordering
83    gasnet_AMGetMsgSource(token, &I->next.node);
84  }
```

Listing 2.9: AM MCS Lock, Part 3/4

The `fetch_and_store()` of the shared-memory code replaces the linked list head with the caller's `I` while returning the prior value, and doing so atomically with respect to other threads performing the same update. This operation in distributed-memory is implemented by the AM request handler `FetchAndStoreRequest` and its corresponding reply handler `FetchAndStoreReply`. The atomicity requirement is met through the use of a GASNet handler-safe lock. Within the lock-protected critical section, the existing value of the wide pointer is saved in `prev` and the new value is written. The handler arguments pass only the address portion of the new value since the node portion is (at least for this algorithm) always that of the request's sender and thus available via `gasnet_GetMsgSource`. Finally, `FetchAndStoreRequest` send a reply containing the value of `prev` (with the node portion explicit since it could be any node).

The AM reply handler `FetchAndStoreReply` receives the value sent back by the `FetchAndStoreRequest` request handler. The arguments also contain the `Ptr2` value passed in the original request. This allows the reply handler to identify the corresponding request, and thus store the "Fetched" value in the `predecessor` field of the correct `qnode_t` variable. This round-trip passing of an address on the requester is a common idiom in construction of AM-based algorithms, as is the reservation of space for receiving a "return value" (as in the `predecessor` field we added to the `qnode_t` type). The call to `gasnett_local_wmb()` will be explained later when we examine the code for `AcquireLock`.

The third AM handler in Listing 2.9 is `StoreNextRequest` and serves to implement "`predecessor->next = I`" from the shared-memory version of the algorithm. It is similar to `FetchAndStoreReply`, differing only in which field is written and the fact that the node number is passed implicitly rather than as an argument. There is no reply required.

Finally, we direct the reader to Listing 2.10 for the implementation of `AcquireLock`.

```
85  void AcquireLock(lock_ptr_t *L, qnode_t *I) {
86    I->next.node = nodes; // "nil"
87    I->predecessor.node = nodes; // "nil"
88    Request2P((L->node, FetchAndStoreRequestIdx,
89            SEND_PTR(L->addr), SEND_PTR(I)));
90    GASNET_BLOCKUNTIL(I->predecessor.node != nodes);
91    if (I->predecessor.addr != NULL) {
92      I->locked = true;
93      Request2P((I->predecessor.node, StoreNextRequestIdx,
94              SEND_PTR(I->predecessor.addr), SEND_PTR(I)));
95      GASNET_BLOCKUNTIL(! I->locked); // spin
96    }
97  }
```

Listing 2.10: AM MCS Lock, Part 4/4

The code follows the same sequence of steps as the shared-memory algorithm with some small additions. The caller's I is first initialized to have no successor in the linked list,[16] and additionally marks the predecessor as "nil." Then the AM version of fetch-and-store is invoked and a call to GASNET_BLOCKUNTIL waits until predecessor is no longer a "nil" value. The next step is to branch on the value of predecessor->addr and this is where the GASNet Tools call, gasnett_local_wmb(), becomes important. This call is a memory fence to ensure that the write to the addr field is globally visible prior to the write to the node field. Combined with the presence of a corresponding read fence inside of GASNET_BLOCKUNTIL, this fencing ensures we can read only a consistent value for the (node,addr) pair without the need for a mutex.

Branching on the value of predecessor->addr, the distributed-memory algorithm continues to follow the logic of the shared-memory version by marking I as "locked", by writing the address of I to the predecessor's next field, and spinning for I->lock to be cleared. The clearing of this flag is accomplished in the LockRelease code which we have not supplied. The reader is encouraged to practice what they have learned by constructing LockRelease.

2.7   Future Directions

At the time of this writing GASNet includes implementations of two major API areas that are not yet documented in the official specification. However, the Berkeley UPC Runtime already makes use of both and addition to the specification should just be a matter of time.

---

16. Our implementation of wide pointers considers a value of the node field equal to the node count as signifying a "nil" pointer without regard to the addr field. This is an otherwise impossible value, while a NULL value of addr can legally occur. This distinction simplifies the implementation.

The first area is interfaces for RMA operations on noncontiguous data, and is known as "Vector, Indexed, Strided", or "VIS" for short. Description for the GASNet VIS interfaces is available as a portion of a document [47] proposing analogous interfaces for the UPC language, and function prototypes also appear in the file `gasnet_vis.h` in the GASNet distribution.

The second area is GASNet Collectives, which are described in some detail in the file `docs/collective_notes.txt` and prototypes appear in `gasnet_coll.h`.

There are also directions that are more forward-looking, including the following ideas being pursued for extensions to the Core and Extended APIs:

1. Nonblocking AMs with a "sync" for local completion. This would eliminate the need for excessive (re)copying of Medium payloads (which are often constructed in temporary buffers by the client) and would be more usable than LongAsync for payloads delivered to the remote segment.

2. "Immediate" nonblocking RMA operations that return failure if the network is not ready to accept additional traffic. This would allow clients the opportunity to perform useful work prior to trying the RMA operation, rather than allow GASNet to spin waiting for the network to become ready as is current practice.

3. Ability to sync local completion of nonblocking bulk Put operations as a distinct event. There is currently no means to determine local completion of a nonblocking bulk Put independent of its remote completion. Adding such a mechanism would allow better control of temporary buffers and of memory, in general.

3 OpenSHMEM

Jeffery A. Kuehn, Oak Ridge National Laboratory
Stephen W. Poole, Oak Ridge National Laboratory

3.1 Introduction

OpenSHMEM [74, 138, 223][1] is a modern derivative of the SHMEM API [88, 87] originally developed in 1993 by Cray Research, Inc. for efficient programming of the Cray T3D computer system [85]. The SHMEM API was transferred to SGI [251] when it purchased Cray Research in 1996. The rights to use SHMEM were then transferred with the Cray business unit when it was sold to Tera, Inc., which subsequently renamed itself to Cray, Inc. in 2000. At each product generation within these three companies, the SHMEM API proved itself to be both robust and flexible on systems of the largest scales. The SHMEM API developed a strong following among users tasked with developing software on systems of the very largest scales at each generation, leading many vendors, including IBM, Quadrics (Vega UK, Ltd.) [235], Hewlett Packard, QLogic, and Mellanox to develop their own implementations of the SHMEM API. While these implementations were mostly consistent, there were several small issues which inhibited application portability between implementations, and thus in 2009 the Extreme Scale Systems Center at Oak Ridge National Laboratory engaged in an effort to standardize the API.[2] The standardized API is OpenSHMEM. As such, it is the modern state-of-the-art incarnation of two decades of use, research, and development at the largest available scales of computing capability. At the time of this writing, version 1.0 of the OpenSHMEM specification [138, 223] and reference implementation are publicly available, and community work on version 1.1 is proceeding.

OpenSHMEM describes an API through which the user explicitly programs data transfers (as one would with a message passing model [200, 201, 120, 170]) and synchronizations (as one would with a shared memory model). However, its data structures and pointers permit global access to memory partitioned across nodes as via a partitioned global address space (PGAS) model [48]. Finally, OpenSHMEM is designed to expose low-level hardware capabilities with minimal overhead, so that it may be used as a foundation for implementing other programming models described in this book. This efficiency, though, is not without compromise. While most message passing and PGAS models provide some implicit synchronization guarantees, OpenSHMEM decouples data transfer and synchronization, placing upon the user the burden of designing appropriate synchronization into the algorithm. While this may seem to be a significant drawback, by virtue of decoupled data transfer and synchronization, OpenSHMEM, and its SHMEM-derived predecessors, are exceptionally well suited to designing extremely asynchronous scalable software systems.

---

1. SHMEM and OpenSHMEM are trademarks of SGI
2. This work and its authors were supported by the Department of Defense. The Extreme Scale Systems Center is supported by the Department of Defense.

3.2   Design Philosophy and Considerations

SHMEM and OpenSHMEM were conceived and have evolved with the assumption of an integral relationship with the underlying hardware system architecture. The Cray T3D and Cray T3E computer systems developed and marketed by Cray Research Inc., included several advanced hardware acceleration features in their network architectures, which were codesigned with SHMEM to maximize the available bandwidth and minimize the latency across the systems' 3D Torus network [85]. Cray, Inc., the modern namesake of the original Cray Research, Inc., carries this same philosophy forward in its most recent "Gemini" network infrastructure [86, 90]. When SGI acquired Cray Research in 1996, it also acquired the SHMEM intellectual property. SGI designed its NUMAlink architecture [250] and its shared memory capabilities to maximize performance and SHMEM was once again the best API to exploit those capabilities. Both companies continue to focus on ensuring very high performance implementations of the hardware and software which enable the capabilities of SHMEM/OpenSHMEM API.

IBM, under the DARPA HPCS program, developed a proprietary networking device called Torrent [266]. One of the primary goals of the design of Torrent was to enable hardware acceleration of the capabilities of PGAS programming paradigms like OpenSHMEM. Torrent has a number of advanced network acceleration features, including remote memory access capability (RMA), a Collective Acceleration Unit (CAU), and support for a rich set of atomic memory operations (AMOs). AMO features included both fixed point (NOP, SUM, MIN, MAX, OR, AND, XOR (signed and unsigned)), and floating point (MIN, MAX, SUM, PROD (single and double precision)) capabilities. With these features, Torrent enables both MPI and OpenSHMEM to exploit the full performance capability of the hardware and provide a foundation for PGAS languages. Figure 3.1 depicts the IBM Torrent networking chip, an exemplar of the level of integration possible between the compute/memory elements of the system and the networking portion of the environment. For extreme scale systems (exascale) it is imperative that this level of integration exist in order to bring networking in a peer position with the memory and processing capabilities. This will allow an increase in capability, decrease in latency and increase in bandwidth. This will have a positive effect on *all* PGAS style programming models.

Until recently, these capabilities and levels of integration have only existed in high-end systems with a large proprietary network investment, like those from Cray, SGI and IBM. But in 2011 both Mellanox [188] and HP, under guidance from the Extreme Scale Systems Center at Oak Ridge National Laboratory, announced support for the OpenSHMEM API and many of the underlying hardware features key to fully enabling this model. Though the codesign effort was focused on providing accelerated OpenSHMEM support, these capabilities will also help enable other PGAS programming models. This will be the first

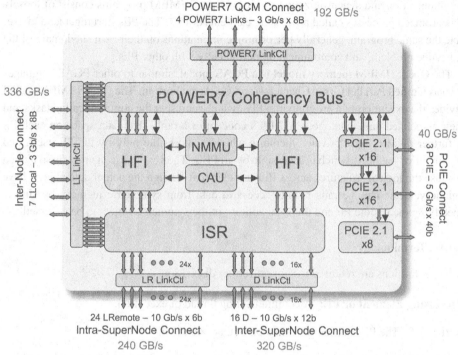

Figure 3.1: Torrent Block Diagram

time that commodity networks have been engineered to include hardware, firmware, and system software that support the foundational elements of OpenSHMEM. In addition to the improvements in proprietary networks and those proposed in commodity networks, we have seen projects that embed the capabilities of the OpenSHMEM API in FPGAs [267]. These lightweight implementations will open up the performance capabilities of the hardware that will be deployed in future extreme scale systems. With the load being placed on current peta-OP systems and future exa-OP systems, moving networking into a "first class citizen" position is essential.

3.3   The OpenSHMEM Memory Model

OpenSHMEM is a single program, multiple data (SPMD) programming model, characteristically emphasizing one-sided messaging and a decoupling of data motion and synchronization. It is implemented as a library that provides high-performance, high scalability communication and synchronization routines. OpenSHMEM programs consist of loosely synchronized processes called processing elements or PEs. The PEs start together and execute the same program, generally performing computations on their own subdomain of the collective problem, and communicating periodically with other PEs.

The OpenSHMEM memory model is a PGAS model, similar to other PGAS languages such as Unified Parallel C (see Chapter 4) and Co-Array Fortran. The OpenSHMEM model divides the execution of a program into PEs, which represent the communicating tasks and their associated data, analogous to MPI's concept of a rank. The data space on each PE is further divided into "private" memory, which is accessible only by the PE itself, and "symmetric" memory, which is accessible by all PE's. The symmetric memory is so named because the logical structures across PEs are identical, though the actual data objects have unique values. This permits remote access to data from symmetric memory by simply specifying the remote PE and the local address of the symmetric object to be accessed.

3.3.1   Terminology

A few definitions are required to support further discussion.

Processing Element or PE: A communicating thread of execution.

Active Set: The PEs participating in a particular operation.

Symmetric Memory: The collection of memory which is visible to all PEs. This will include statically allocated memory and memory allocated dynamically with the symmetric allocation function: `shmalloc()`.

Asymmetric Memory: The memory which is private to an individual PE, including stack space and memory dynamically allocated by other means (e.g., `malloc()`).

Active Side: In one-sided communication, the side which makes an API call to initiate data motion.

Passive Side: In one-sided communication, the side which does not make an API call related to the communication.

Source: The memory location(s) to be read.

Target: The memory location(s) to be updated.

Put: A remote write operation, in which the source data from the (local) active side is copied into the target address on the (remote) passive side.

Get: A remote read operation, in which the source data on the (remote) passive side is copied into the target address on the (local) active side.

Synchronization: A guarantee on the ordering of operations or consistency of memory between two or more PEs.

Atomic Memory Operation: An operation or block of operations which complete as a unit without interference from other operations.

Reduction: An operation across primitive data types on multiple PEs, such as finding a minimum or maximum.

Collective Communication: A one-to-N, N-to-one, or N-to-N communication (e.g., a one-to-all broadcast).

3.4   Managing the Symmetric Heap and the Basics

The OpenSHMEM API provides functions for initializing and querying the status of the symmetric memory, and allocating and deallocating symmetric memory. While the initialization and query functions are straightforward, attention must be paid to maintaining consistency in the symmetric heap when using the allocation and deallocation routines.

3.4.1   Initialization and Query

Initialization is accomplished with `start_pes(0)`. Basic queries regarding the size of the active set and the identity of a PE in the active set are accomplished with calls to `shmem_n_pes()` and `shmem_my_pe()`. Listing 3.1 illustrates a simple "hello world" example including these calls. As Version 1.0 of the OpenSHMEM specification did not include a "finalize" call, it is considered good practice to enforce a barrier (using `shmem_barrier_all()`) before the program exits, to prevent attempts to reference PEs after they have exited.

```
/* include file for OpenSHMEM macros, declarations, and prototypes */
#include <shmem.h>

main() {
        int i, mype, numpes;

        /* Initialize OpenSHMEM */
        start_pes(0);

        /* How many PEs are in the active set? */
```

```
        numpes = shmem_n_pes();

        /* What is my identity within the active set?  */
        mype   = shmem_my_pe();

        printf("Hello World from PE %d of %d\n", mype, numpes);

        /* sync before exit  */
        shmem_barrier_all();
        return 0;
}
```

Listing 3.1: OpenSHMEM Hello World.

3.4.2 Allocation and Deallocation

The symmetric heap allocation and deallocation routines work much like the standard allocation and deallocation functions in the C language. The only complicating factor is that the user must ensure that each PE performs exactly the same series of allocations, both in size and order. Doing so guarantees consistency in the symmetric heap, thus allowing each PE to locate symmetric objects using the address of its own object.

> *Symmetry Principle: The allocation and deallocation operations should be performed in the same order, with the same arguments, on every PE. Failing to maintain the required symmetry will, at best, cause the program to hang since allocation is a global synchronization event.*

Listing 3.2 illustrates this principle by creating three symmetric objects. The arrays a and b are symmetric by virtue of the `static` keyword and the pointer c points to another block of symmetric memory (an array of ten integers) allocated by `shmalloc()` and then freed by `shfree()`. Since an identical series of declarations and dynamic allocations occur in every PE instance, the heap is symmetric.

```
#include <shmem.h>

static int a[10];

main() {
        static int b[10];
        int *c;
        int i, mype, numpes;

        start_pes(0);
        numpes = shmem_n_pes();
```

```
mype    = shmem_my_pe();

/* dynamically allocate and free memory */
c = (int*)shmalloc(10*sizeof(int));
shfree(c);

shmem_barrier_all();
return 0;
}
```

Listing 3.2: Correct Allocation.

Listing 3.3 illustrates several violations of the symmetry principle. Note that the common thread of error among the problems in this program is that the execution, order, or size of the allocations is in some way dependent on data which differs from one PE to the next.

```
#include <shmem.h>

static int a[10];

main() {
        static int b[10];
        int *c, *d, *e, *f, *g;
        int i, mype, numpes;

        start_pes(0);
        numpes = shmem_n_pes();
        mype    = shmem_my_pe();

        /* NO: order must be the same on each PE */
        if (mype%2 == 0) {
                c = (int*)shmalloc(10*sizeof(int));
                d = (int*)shmalloc(20*sizeof(int));
        } else {
                d = (int*)shmalloc(20*sizeof(int));
                c = (int*)shmalloc(10*sizeof(int));
        }

        /* NO: shmalloc() size must match across all PEs */
        e = (int*)shmalloc(10*sizeof(int)+mype);

        /* NO: shmalloc() must occur on every PE */
        if (mype == 0) f = (int*)shmalloc(10*sizeof(int));

        shmem_barrier_all();
        return 0;
}
```

Listing 3.3: Incorrect Allocation.

3.4.3   A Final Note on Allocation and the Symmetric Heap

While the OpenSHMEM API uses local addresses of objects to find the same objects on remote PEs, it must be noted that for version 1.0 of OpenSHMEM, this does not imply that each PE has placed their instance of the object at the same virtual address. Future version of the API may provide such a guarantee.

3.5   Remote Memory Access: Put and Get

OpenSHMEM's functions for remote memory access (RMA) provide the basic building blocks of a highly scalable parallel communication paradigm for reading and writing remote data. These functions, generically referred to as `put` or `get` functions, allow one PE to write (`put`) or read (`get`) memory locations within the symmetric data space of any other PE with no required synchronization.

3.5.1   RMA Function Semantics

OpenSHMEM's programming model decouples data transfer and synchronization to improve scalability. The semantics of the decoupling are relatively straightforward to understand. The PE that calls the RMA function (`put` or `get`) is referred to as the "active side" of the transfer. The other PE (which is likely unaware of the transfer) is referred to as the "passive side". OpenSHMEM's only implicit consistency guarantees for `put` and `get` operations occur on the active side. Consistency, however, can still be enforced on the passive side, when desired, by adding synchronization to the program.

> ***Active Side Completion Principle:*** *When a single RMA call (`put` or `get`) returns on the active side, the program may assume that the memory state on the active side is consistent with the completion of that operation.*

> ***Passive Side Completion Principle:*** *When a single RMA call (`put` or `get`) returns on the active side, the program should not assume that the operations have completed on the passive side or that they will complete in any particular order, without explicit synchronization.*

Warning: Note that in situations in which a `put` immediately follows a `get` for the same data, both principles must be considered. Because the passive side of the `put` cannot be assumed to have reached completion before the `get`, correctness requires a synchronization to enforce ordering between the `put` and the `get`. Without that synchronization, the `get` may retrieve the remote data *before* the `put` completes. We will discuss synchronization in more detail in a later section, and for now we will simply use a barrier.

3.5.2 RMA Function Usage

The OpenSHMEM API has three different categories of `put` and `get` functions: generic, typed, and strided. The generic `put` and `get` functions for RMA are type-agnostic and simply serve to transfer a block of bytes. These two generic functions are sufficient for most transfers, but lack the convenience of the typed and strided interfaces. The typed `put` and `get` functions provided by OpenSHMEM operate on contiguous blocks of primitive types with either the bit-width or the type of the object being specified in the function name (thus there are 20 `put` functions and 20 `get` functions that specify the data type or size of the objects being referenced). Strided access routines are also provided by OpenSHMEM and allow both the source and target memory to be accessed with a particular stride (e.g., every n^{th} element of an array). Listings 3.4, 3.5, and 3.6 describe the API for the generic, typed and strided `put` and `get` functions, respectively.

```
#include <shmem.h>

void
shmem_putmem
shmem_getmem(              void *target,
                          const void *source,
                          size_t len,
                          int pe);
```

Listing 3.4: OpenSHMEM Generic Put/Get Functions.

```
#include <shmem.h>

/* by native type */
void
shmem_double_get
shmem_double_put
shmem_float_get
shmem_float_put
shmem_int_get
shmem_int_put
shmem_long_get
shmem_long_put
shmem_longdouble_get
shmem_longdouble_put
shmem_longlong_get
shmem_longlong_put
shmem_short_get
shmem_short_put(          <TYPE> *target,
                          const <TYPE> *source,
                          size_t len,
```

```
                                    int pe);
/* by type width */
void
shmem_get32
shmem_put32
shmem_get64
shmem_put64
shmem_get128
shmem_put128(              void *target,
                          const void *source,
                          size_t len,
                          int pe);
```

Listing 3.5: OpenSHMEM Typed Put/Get Functions.

```
#include <shmem.h>

/* by native type */
void
shmem_double_iget
shmem_double_iput
shmem_float_iget
shmem_float_iput
shmem_int_iget
shmem_int_iput
shmem_long_iget
shmem_long_iput
shmem_longdouble_iget
shmem_longdouble_iput
shmem_longlong_iget
shmem_longlong_iput
shmem_short_iget
shmem_short_iput(         <TYPE> *target,
                          const <TYPE> *source,
                          ptrdiff_t tst,
                          ptrdiff_t sst,
                          size_t len,
                          int pe);
/* by width in bits */
void
shmem_iget32
shmem_iput32
shmem_iget64
shmem_iput64
shmem_iget128
shmem_iput128(            void *target,
                          const void *source,
```

```
                    ptrdiff_t tst,
                    ptrdiff_t sst,
                    size_t len,
                    int pe);
```

Listing 3.6: OpenSHMEM Strided Put/Get Functions.

The first two arguments for each function identify the (target) location to be updated and the (source) location from which the data will be copied. For put functions, the target is remote (on the passive-side PE) and identified by the last argument (pe). The source is local on the active-side PE. For get functions, the target location to be updated is on the local, active-side PE, and the source is on the remote, passive-side PE. It is worth noting that while the location specified on the passive-side PE must lie within its symmetric memory, the location on the active-side is permitted to lie in either symmetric memory or asymmetric memory. The second to last parameter, len, specifies the amount of data to be transferred, as number of bytes for the generic routines, or as number of the specified primitive types in the case of the typed and strided routines. The stride parameters tst and sst specify the strides through the target and source arrays, respectively, in units of the type specified by the function name. Setting the stride to 1 would result in a contiguous transfer, as with the typed versions of these functions. Listing 3.7 shows a simple example of ring communication using get and put. Note that in this example, the only synchronization required is the barrier between when self is set and when it could be read by another PE.

```
/* circular shift clockwise and counter-clockwise */
#include <shmem.h>

int main() {
        /* symmetric by virtue of static */
        static int c_up, cc_up, self, c_down, cc_down;

        /* asymmetric */
        int npes, successor, predecessor;

        start_pes(0);

        self = shmem_my_pe();
        /* don't start moving data until everyone s set 'self' */
        shmem_barrier_all();

        npes = shmem_n_pes();
        successor = (self+1)%npes;
        predecessor = (self-1+npes)%npes;

        /* clockwise */
```

```
    /* overwrite successor's 'down' with local 'up' */
    shmem_int_put(&c_down, &self, 1, successor);

    /* overwrite local 'up' with successor's 'self' */
    shmem_int_get(&c_up, &self, 1, successor);

    /* counter-clockwise */

    /* overwrite predecessor's 'down' with local 'up' */
    shmem_int_put(&cc_down, &self, 1, predecessor);

    /* overwrite local 'up' with predecessor's 'self' */
    shmem_int_get(&cc_up, &self, 1, predecessor);

    /* wait for all to finish */
    shmem_barrier_all();

    return 0;
}
```

Listing 3.7: OpenSHMEM Put/Get Example.

3.6 Ordering and Synchronization

The ability to explicitly enforce ordering and synchronization is a critical capability in an OpenSHMEM paradigm dominated by asynchronous communications. The availability of a spectrum of such capabilities from lightweight and/or local to heavyweight and/or global provides the programmer with crucial flexibility in minimizing the impact of synchronization overhead and leveraging OpenSHMEM's extreme scalability. In addition to the global barrier outlined in the previous examples, OpenSHMEM also provides a nonglobal barrier, mutual exclusion locks, mechanisms for ordering RMA operations from a single active partner or globally (fence and quiet, respectively), and mechanisms for fine-grained data synchronization (wait and wait_until). These tools provide a rich set of synchronization primitives, giving the developer great flexibility to direct ordering of RMA operations and synchronization between PEs. While this may seem to be a large set, these tools permit the programmer to design the minimum of synchronization required for program correctness.

3.6.1 Global Barrier Synchronization

Global barrier is a synchronization mechanism common to most parallel programming models. The concept is clear and provides for easy reasoning, though the impact on scalability can leave something to be desired. Essentially, all PEs call the barrier function, which guarantees that none of the calls will return before all the participating PEs have arrived. For this reason, barrier is often added as an aid to debugging when race conditions are suspected. In addition to the global barrier, `shmem_barrier_all()`, OpenSHMEM also provides a collective barrier, `shmem_barrier()`, which can operate on subsets of PEs. This will be discussed under the section on Collective Operations since the subset selection mechanism is common across this group.

```
#include <shmem.h>

void shmem_barrier_all();
```

Listing 3.8: OpenSHMEM Barrier Functions.

3.6.2 Fence and Quiet: Ordering of RMA Operations

In cases where barrier creates a heavyweight synchronization, `fence` and `quiet` are much more lightweight (and thus scale better), but the guarantee they provide is weaker. A `fence` only enforces a "before and after" ordering on operations from a single active PE as seen by an individual passive PE. In the example in Listing 3.10, a `fence` is used between the `put` and `get` to ensure that the result of the `put` is visible before the `get` occurs. The `fence` is sufficient in this case because the RMAs involve only this PE and its successor. In essence, when the `fence` function is called between two groups of RMA operations, the guarantee provided is thus:

> **Fence Semantics:** *For a series of transfers from a particular active PE to a particular passive PE, if the active PE calls the `fence` function, a guarantee occurs on the passive side that all of the operations initiated by the active PE before the `fence` will be visible on the passive side before any of the transfers initiated after the `fence` become visible.*

In cases where all of the PEs are actively initiating transfers, passively participating in transfers, and calling the `fence` function, pairwise ordering guarantee can be insufficient for ensuring proper ordering of memory updates. If global before/after ordering is desired, the `quiet` function should be used instead. Listing 3.11 demonstrates an example where each PE updates a value on its successor with a `put`, and then reads its predecessor's updated value with a `get`. In this case a pairwise ordering is not sufficient and `quiet` is used to enforce global ordering.

Where `fence` only imposes a pairwise ordering of those operations before and after the `fence`, a `quiet` imposes a stronger (but more expensive) condition of globally ordering the RMA operations before and after the `quiet`. However, this is still much better than a barrier, since it only demands ordering of the inbound operations on each PE without dictating synchronization between PEs.

> ***Quiet Semantics:*** *For a series of transfers between active PEs and passive PEs, a call to the* `quiet` *function will cause all of the RMA operations initiated before the* `quiet` *call to be globally visible before any RMA operation initiated after the* `quiet` *becomes visible.*

```
#include <shmem.h>

void shmem_quiet(void);
void shmem_fence(void);
```

Listing 3.9: OpenSHMEM Fence and Quiet Functions.

```
/* circular shift clockwise and counter-clockwise */
#include <shmem.h>

int main() {
        static int a, b, c;        /* symmetric */

        int npes, successor;       /* asymmetric */

        start_pes(0);
        a = shmem_my_pe();
        shmem_barrier_all();

        npes = shmem_n_pes();
        successor = (self+1)%npes;

        shmem_int_put(&b, &a, 1, successor);
        shmem_fence();             /* put visible before get */
        shmem_int_get(&c, &b, 1, successor);

        shmem_barrier_all();

        return 0;
}
```

Listing 3.10: OpenSHMEM Fence Example.

```
/* circular shift clockwise and counter-clockwise */
#include <shmem.h>

int main() {
        static int a, b, c;                    /* symmetric */
        int npes, successor, predecessor;      /* asymmetric */
```

```
start_pes(0);
a = shmem_my_pe();
shmem_barrier_all();

npes = shmem_n_pes();
successor = (self+1)%npes;
predecessor = (self-1+npes)%npes;

shmem_int_put(&b, &a, 1, successor);
shmem_quiet();              /* all puts visible */
shmem_int_get(&c, &b, 1, predecessor);

shmem_barrier_all();

return 0;
}
```

Listing 3.11: OpenSHMEM Quiet Example.

3.6.3 Locks

The OpenSHMEM lock functions implement mutual exclusion locks in symmetric memory. The prototypes for the functions are shown below in Listing 3.12. The lock argument must exist in the symmetric memory space and be initialized to zero before any attempted use. It is common to either declare these at global scope as static variables initialized to zero, or for the programmer to perform a global barrier call after the lock is initialized but before it is used. The shmem_set_lock() function will return after it obtains the lock, waiting until the lock is cleared, if necessary. The shmem_clear_lock() function will release the lock and should only be called by the PE which obtained the lock with the set function. The shmem_test_lock() function will attempt to obtain the lock and return 0 if it was successful or 1 if the lock is already set. As with locks in other paradigms, it is incumbent upon the programmer to ensure that the program does not create deadlocks.


```
#include <shmem.h>

void shmem_set_lock(long *lock);
void shmem_clear_lock(long *lock);
int  shmem_test_lock(long *lock);
```

Listing 3.12: OpenSHMEM Lock Functions.

3.6.4 Wait and Wait_Until

Frequently, the only synchronization a PE requires is to ensure that it does not proceed before data it requires has arrived. While this synchronization is predicated on an update of symmetric data, the operation itself is local. As the name implies, the wait routines simply wait until their condition is met. Specifically, `shmem_wait()` will return when its trigger variable, `ivar`, is changed to a value different from its comparison value `value`, and `shmem_wait_until()` will return when the condition expressed by `ivar cmp value` is true.

```
include <shmem.h>

void shmem_wait(long *ivar, long value);
void shmem_wait_until(long *ivar, int cmp, long value);

where cmp is one of:
        SHMEM_CMP_NE
        SHMEM_CMP_GE
        SHMEM_CMP_GT
        SHMEM_CMP_EQ
        SHMEM_CMP_LT
        SHMEM_CMP_LE
```

Listing 3.13: OpenSHMEM Wait Functions.

3.7 Collective Operations

OpenSHMEM provides several functions that are typically considered "collective" operations falling into four categories: broadcast, collect, reduce (which all operate on symmetric memory), and a nonglobal barrier (which is sometimes grouped with synchronizations but included here because it depends on the same synchronization array (sync array) structure as the other collectives). Each of these implies synchronization and requires the use of a symmetric sync array. These operations are designed to operate either on all PEs or on subsets thereof. *If a collective is being executed on only a subset of the PEs, only those PEs participating in the collective should call the collective routine—if nonparticipating PEs attempt to call the collective operation, the results are undefined.* It should also be noted that while a collective implies synchronization, for OpenSHMEM collectives, it is best to consider this in a more relaxed "before and after" sense. For example, in a broadcast, it can be reasoned that the receivers cannot complete the operation before the sender transmits its data, but this does not imply any ordering on the start times or finish times of the participating PEs beyond that which the sender must have started before any receiver could complete.

3.7.1 Selecting the Participants for a Collective

To participate in a collective operation, each member of the collective must call the same collective function with the same source and target arguments, and they must each specify the same set of PEs to participate in the collective. Each collective operation requires three arguments to describe which PEs will participate in the operation: a start PE, a $log_2(PE\_stride)$, and the number of PEs to participate. Thus, setting these to (0,2,6) respectively, would mean that the collective operation would include PE0, PE4, PE8, PE12, PE16, and PE20, whereas setting these values instead to (1,0,6) would include PE1, PE2, PE3, PE4, PE5, and PE6 (when $log_2(PE\_stride) = 0$, the stride is 1).

> *Recognizing Heavyweight Synchronizations: The presence of a sync array in the calling sequence of an OpenSHMEM function can be taken as an indicator of the presence of a heavyweight synchronization. This can negatively impact scalability on some platforms. Additionally, while the number of PEs participating is not required to be a power of 2, non-power-of-2 values can have further performance implications for some implementations of collective operations. Finally, synchronizations are implied by other functions that do not require a sync array, including the global barrier and the symmetric allocation functions. Careful attention to when these functions are required (or can be avoided) is a key to leveraging the scalability advantages offered by OpenSHMEM.*

3.7.2 Sync Arrays and Work Arrays

Collective routines require symmetric sync arrays (and symmetric work arrays for reduce operations) to be appropriately sized and initialized for the specific operation and the subset of PEs used. These arrays represent a global state, and the symmetric components of each array should be treated as a whole. For the purposes of this description, when reference is made to a sync array or work array, this should be understood to refer to the full collection of symmetric images of the named array across all PEs. These arrays are subject to several important points to note about sync/work arrays.

- **Initialization:** The program must ensure that the allocation and initialization of the sync array and allocation of the work array is complete on all PEs before a collective operation begins using them. This can be enforced by using arrays that are statically allocated or with a global barrier after a dynamic allocation. Typically, all such arrays are allocated near program startup, so at most one global barrier is required.

- **Exclusivity:** Once a collective operation is started, the program must protect the operation's sync/work array from modification by any other activity (e.g., memory operation, RMA, other collective) until all PEs have completed the operation. This implies that these arrays cannot be immediately reused for consecutive collective operations.

- **Value on Completion:** On completion across all PEs, the sync/work arrays are returned to a state suitable for reuse.

- **Protecting Reuse:** To protect the sync/work arrays for reuse in a series of collective operations, the program may either include a global barrier before reusing the sync/work arrays (bad) or alternate between two sync/work arrays (better).

- **Same PE Set Required for Reuse:** The sync arrays can be reused without reinitialization by subsequent operations of the same type (barrier, broadcast, collect, reduce) if and only if the subset of PEs participating in the operation remains the same, i.e., the starting PE, the number of PEs participating, and the $log_2(PEstride)$ are the same. Work arrays may be reused if they are appropriately sized (number and type of elements) for the operation.

3.7.3 Nonglobal Barrier

Like the global barrier, the nonglobal barrier provides the guarantee that none of the barrier calls on the participating PEs will return before all of the participating PEs have arrived. The nonglobal barrier allows the programmer to select a subset of PEs (including a global subset) to participate by specifying a start PE, a stride through the PEs (specified as the $log_2(PEstride)$ rather than the actual stride), the number of participating PEs, and a symmetric sync array of length _SHMEM_BARRIER_SYNC_SIZE. This array must be initialized to zero on all PEs before being used, thus requiring some synchronization between initialization and use, for instance, a global barrier. The sync array can be reused on a subsequent barrier if and only if the active set of PEs remains unchanged.

```
#include <shmem.h>

void
shmem_barrier(       int PE_start,
                     int logPE_stride,
                     int PE_size,
                     long *pSync);
```

Listing 3.14: OpenSHMEM Nonglobal Barrier Function.

3.7.4 Broadcast

The broadcast functions copy a contiguous block of 32 bit or 64 bit elements from one PE (the root) to the other PEs. As with the other collective functions, the broadcast functions allow the programmer to select a subset of PEs to participate in the synchronization by specifying a start PE, a $log_2(PEstride)$ through the PEs, the number of PEs to participate in the broadcast, and a symmetric sync array of long integers of length _SHMEM_BCAST_SYNC_SIZE. The user must initialize this array to the predefined value _SHMEM_SYNC_VALUE on all PEs before it is used, thus requiring some synchronization between initialization and use, such as a global barrier. However, as mentioned earlier, two sync arrays can be used, and once the post-initialization global synchronization is performed, the program can simply alternate between sync arrays instead of imposing a barrier in advance of each broadcast. The sync arrays can be reused (without reinitializing) on subsequent alternating broadcasts if the active set of PEs is identical each time the sync array is used.

```
#include <shmem.h>

void
shmem_broadcast32
shmem_broadcast64(        void *target,
                          const void *source,
                          size_t nelems,
                          int PE_root,
                          int PE_start,
                          int logPE_stride,
                          int PE_size,
                          long *pSync);
```

Listing 3.15: OpenSHMEM Broadcast Functions.

```
for (i=0; i < _SHMEM_BCAST_SYNC_SIZE; i++) {
        pSync[i] = _SHMEM_SYNC_VALUE;
        qSync[i] = _SHMEM_SYNC_VALUE;
}
shmem_barrier_all(); /* Wait for all PEs to initialize sync-arrays */

/* broadcast on alternating syncs without barriers */
shmem_broadcast64(target1, source1, nelems, 0, 4, 0, 4, pSync);
shmem_broadcast64(target2, source2, nelems, 0, 4, 0, 4, qSync);
shmem_broadcast64(target3, source3, nelems, 0, 4, 0, 4, pSync);
shmem_broadcast64(target4, source4, nelems, 0, 4, 0, 4, qSync);
```

Listing 3.16: OpenSHMEM Broadcast Example.

78   Chapter 3

3.7.5 Collect

The collect functions perform an aggregating gather, copying a block of elements from the symmetric source object of each participating PE and replicating them consecutively into (larger) symmetric target arrays on every PE participating in the collective. It is incumbent upon the programmer to ensure that the symmetric target arrays are large enough to receive the aggregated data. Collect functions exist for both 32 bit and 64 bit data types and for each, there are two variants of the collect functions: a general *collect* which allows each PE to contribute a different number of elements, and a fixed-size *fcollect* which requires that each PE contribute the same number of elements. As with the other collective functions, the collect functions allow the programmer to select a subset of PEs to participate in the aggregation by specifying a start PE, $log_2(PEstride)$ stride through the PEs, the number of participating PEs, and a symmetric sync array of length _SHMEM_COLLECT_SYNC_SIZE. This array must be initialized to the defined value _SHMEM_SYNC_VALUE on all PEs before being used, which requires a synchronization between initialization and use, such as, a global barrier. However, as mentioned earlier, two sync arrays can be used, and once the post-initialization global synchronization is performed, the program can simply alternate between sync arrays instead of imposing a barrier in advance of each collect. The sync arrays can be reused (without reinitializing) on subsequent alternating collects if the active set of PEs is identical each time the sync array is used. Listing 3.18 demonstrates the general collect function. Two sync arrays allow the collect functions to be called back-to-back by alternating which sync array is used to control the collective operation. On the completion of each collective, each PE's target array contains the series of data blocks provided by each participant in the collective.

```
#include <shmem.h>

void
shmem_collect32
shmem_collect64
shmem_fcollect32
shmem_fcollect64(          void *target,
                           const void *source,
                           size_t nelems,
                           int PE_start,
                           int logPE_stride,
                           int PE_size,
                           long *pSync);
```

Listing 3.17: OpenSHMEM Collect Functions.

```
for (i=0; i < _SHMEM_COLLECT_SYNC_SIZE; i++) {
  rSync[i] = _SHMEM_SYNC_VALUE;
  sSync[i] = _SHMEM_SYNC_VALUE;
}
shmem_barrier_all(); /* Wait for all PEs to initialize sync arrays */

/* collects, alternate sync arrays, number of elements vary per PE */
nelem = myPE+1;
shmem_collect32(targ4, src4, nelem, startPE, logPEstr, PEsz, rSync);
shmem_collect32(targ5, src5, nelem, startPE, logPEstr, PEsz, sSync);
shmem_collect32(targ6, src6, nelem, startPE, logPEstr, PEsz, rSync);
shmem_collect32(targ7, src7, nelem, startPE, logPEstr, PEsz, sSync);

/* targets now hold 1 element from PE0, 2 from PE1, 3 from PE3, etc */
```

Listing 3.18: OpenSHMEM Collect Example.

3.7.6 Reduce

The reduce functions perform a primitive operation on corresponding elements of the symmetric sources of the participating PEs, and place the results of these operations into the corresponding elements of each participating PE's symmetric target (e.g., finding the maximum of the first element of the source arrays across the participating PEs and placing this maximum into the first element of each participating PE's target array, and so on for the remaining elements of the source arrays). Reduce operation variants exist for most noncharacter types, including: short, int, long, long long, float, and double. These variants implement several primitive operators: bitwise AND, bitwise OR, bitwise XOR, native type SUM, and native type PRODUCT. The various reduce functions are named for the type on which they operate and the operator which they implement. As with the other collective functions, the reduce functions allow the programmer to select a subset of PEs to participate in the reduction by specifying a start PE, a $log_2(PEstride)$ through the PEs, and the number of PEs to participate in the reduction. A symmetric sync array of length _SHMEM_REDUCE_SYNC_SIZE is required and must be initialized to _SHMEM_SYNC_VALUE on all PEs before being used (again, generally requiring a global barrier). Reduction operations also require a work array large enough to hold $max(nreduce/2+1,$_SHMEM_REDUCE_MIN_WRKDATA_SIZE$)$ elements of the type being reduced.

However, as mentioned above, two sync/work array pairs can be used, and once the post-initialization global synchronization is performed, the program can simply alternate between sync/work array pairs instead of imposing a barrier in advance of each reduction. The sync arrays can be reused (without reinitializing) on subsequent alternating reductions

if the active set of PEs is identical each time the sync arrays are used. The work arrays can
be reused under the same conditions as long as the number of elements does not exceed the
original allocation. Listing 3.20 demonstrates the use of a sum reduction function. Two
sync/work array pairs allow the reduce functions to be called back-to-back by alternating
which pair is used to control the operation. On the completion of each collective, each
PE's target array contains the sum of the corresponding elements of the source arrays on
each PE.

```
#include <shmem.h>

void
shmem_int_and_to_all
shmem_long_and_to_all
shmem_longlong_and_to_all
shmem_short_and_to_all
shmem_double_max_to_all
shmem_float_max_to_all
shmem_int_max_to_all
shmem_long_max_to_all
shmem_longlong_max_to_all
shmem_short_max_to_all
shmem_double_min_to_all
shmem_float_min_to_all
shmem_int_min_to_all
shmem_long_min_to_all
shmem_longlong_min_to_all
shmem_short_min_to_all
shmem_double_sum_to_all
shmem_float_sum_to_all
shmem_int_sum_to_all
shmem_long_sum_to_all
shmem_longlong_sum_to_all
shmem_short_sum_to_all
shmem_double_prod_to_all
shmem_float_prod_to_all
shmem_int_prod_to_all
shmem_long_prod_to_all
shmem_longlong_prod_to_all
shmem_short_prod_to_all
shmem_int_or_to_all
shmem_long_or_to_all
shmem_longlong_or_to_all
shmem_short_or_to_all
shmem_int_xor_to_all
shmem_long_xor_to_all
shmem_longlong_xor_to_all
shmem_short_xor_to_all(          <TYPE> *target,
                                 <TYPE> *source,
```

```
int nreduce,
int PE_start,
int logPE_stride,
int PE_size,
<TYPE> *pWrk,
long *pSync);
```

Listing 3.19: OpenSHMEM Reduce Functions.

```
/* allocate and initialize the sync arrays */
psync = (long*)shmalloc(_SHMEM_REDUCE_SYNC_SIZE*sizeof(long));
qsync = (long*)shmalloc(_SHMEM_REDUCE_SYNC_SIZE*sizeof(long));
for (i=0; i < _SHMEM_REDUCE_SYNC_SIZE; i++) {
  psync[i] = _SHMEM_SYNC_VALUE;
  qsync[i] = _SHMEM_SYNC_VALUE;
}

/* allocate the work arrays */
worksize = nreduce/2 + 1;
if (worksize < _SHMEM_REDUCE_MIN_WRKDATA_SIZE)
      worksize =_SHMEM_REDUCE_MIN_WRKDATA_SIZE;
pwork = (long*)shmalloc(worksize*sizeof(int));
qwork = (long*)shmalloc(worksize*sizeof(int));

/* Wait for all PEs to initialize sync arrays */
shmem_barrier_all();

/* perform reductions, alternating sync/work arrays */
/* note: work array only re-usable for same nreduce or smaller */
shmem_int_sum_to_all(tg1, sr1, nreduce, 0, 0, npes, pwork, psync );
shmem_int_sum_to_all(tg2, sr2, nreduce, 0, 0, npes, qwork, qsync );
shmem_int_sum_to_all(tg3, sr3, nreduce, 0, 0, npes, pwork, psync );
shmem_int_sum_to_all(tg4, sr4, nreduce, 0, 0, npes, qwork, qsync );
/* target[i] now contains sum( source[i]@PE0 ... source[i]@PEn) */
```

Listing 3.20: OpenSHMEM Reduce Example.

3.8 Atomic Memory Operations

Atomic memory operations (AMOs) are an extension of OpenSHMEM's RMA capability, which provide for performing simple operations on the passive side of an RMA operation. Because AMOs are very low-level operations which leverage RMA capability, they are amenable to hardware acceleration on systems which provide hardware support for RMA. When coupled with a `wait` or `wait_until` operation on the passive side, very flexible synchronization structures can be created, which with very modest hardware support can scale to extremely large systems. The current set of AMOs will allow the active side of the operation to update a memory location in the passive side's symmetric memory and optionally retrieve the value that was in that location prior to the operation. The operations available are: increment, add, swap, and cswap (conditional swap). All of the operators are compatible with integer operands (int, long, and long long) for their target on the remote (passive) side. The swap operator additionally accepts floating point operands (float and double).

3.8.1   Atomic Add and Increment

The add AMO adds its value argument to the target in the passive PE's symmetric memory. The increment AMO (inc) behaves likewise, except that the value argument is implied to be unity. These AMOs make no strong guarantees on ordering, though fence and quiet can be used to create appropriate guarantees. Additionally, these AMOs can be used with the wait functions to trigger more complex locking and event mechanisms on the passive side.

```
#include <shmem.h>

void
shmem_longlong_add
shmem_long_add
shmem_int_add(          <TYPE> *target,
                        <TYPE> value,
                        int pe);
void
shmem_longlong_inc
shmem_long_inc
shmem_int_inc(          <TYPE> *target,
                        int pe);
```

Listing 3.21: OpenSHMEM Add and Increment AMO Functions.

3.8.2   Atomic Fetch-Add and Fetch-Increment

The fetch-add AMO (fadd) and the fetch-increment AMO (finc) are very similar to their add and inc counterparts, except that they also return the value that was in the target location before the operation. This has two side effects. First, it returns state information from the passive side of the AMO, and more importantly, it creates a slightly strong ordering principle since the active side has received data from the passive side. This is analogous to the difference between a put and a get. Like the add and inc AMOs, they are sometimes paired with wait functions on the passive side of the AMO.

```
#include <mpp/shmem.h>

<TYPE>
shmem_longlong_fadd
shmem_long_fadd
shmem_int_fadd(          <TYPE> *target,
                        <TYPE> value,
                        int pe);

<TYPE>
shmem_longlong_finc
shmem_long_finc
shmem_int_finc(          <TYPE>  *target,
                        int pe);
```

Listing 3.22: OpenSHMEM Fetch-Add AMO Functions.

3.8.3 Atomic Swap and Conditional Swap

The swap AMO will exchange the target operand on the remote PE with the value operand
from its argument list and it will return the value of the target prior to the AMO to the active
PE. The conditional swap AMO (cswap) will test the target operand, and if it is equal to
the condition argument, the value operand from the argument list will replace the value
in the target; in either case, the value of the target prior to the AMO will be returned to
the active PE. As with the fetch-add and fetch-increment operators, the return of a swap
operator implies a slightly stronger ordering than the add and inc AMOs. Like the other
AMOs, the swap AMOs are sometime used to trigger progress in a passive side wait
function. Listing 3.24 demonstrates the use of the swap AMO in which the odd numbered
PEs perform a swap on the symmetric memory of their successor, and print the retrieved
value. Note that the swap provides all the necessary synchronization.

```
#include <shmem.h>

<TYPE>
shmem_double_swap
shmem_float_swap
shmem_longlong_swap
shmem_long_swap
shmem_int_swap (         <TYPE> *target,
                        <TYPE> value,
                        int pe);

long shmem_swap(        long *target,
                        long value,
```

```
                             int pe);

<TYPE>
shmem_longlong_cswap
shmem_long_cswap
shmem_int_cswap(            <TYPE> *target,
                           <TYPE> cond,
                           <TYPE> value,
                           int pe);
```

Listing 3.23: OpenSHMEM Swap AMO Functions.

```
/*
 * swap values between odd numbered PEs and their
 * right (module) neighbor.  Show result of swap.
 */

#include <stdio.h>
#include <shmem.h>

int main() {
  long *target;
  int me, npes;
  long swapped_val, new_val;

  start_pes(0);
  me      = shmem_my_pe();
  npes    = shmem_n_pes();
  target  = (long *) shmalloc( sizeof(*target) );
  *target = me;

  shmem_barrier_all(); /* complete all symmetric alloc/init */

  new_val = me;

  if (me & 1) {
    swapped_val = shmem_long_swap(target, new_val, (me+1)%npes);
     printf("%d: target = %d, swapped = %d\n", me, *target, swapped_val);
  }

  shfree(target);

  return 0;
}
```

Listing 3.24: OpenSHMEM Swap AMO Example.

3.9   Future Directions

At the time of this writing, there are a number of developments in progress relevant to the state of OpenSHMEM, largely driven by procurement requirements for OpenSHMEM which began appearing in 2010. As mentioned in Section 3.2, several vendors have announced accelerated hardware and firmware support for network primitives which will significantly simplify the implementation of OpenSHMEM and dramatically improve performance and robustness on not only extreme scale systems, but also commodity based systems. This would include hardware support for OpenSHMEM collectives and atomic memory operations, performance improvements for small messages, as well as adaptive routing and congestion management for large system interconnects. Participants on the OpenSHMEM forum and mailing lists have suggested adopting extensions from the Quadrics implementation which included a very useful set of nonblocking primitives along with other API improvements. Along with this, an extended atomic operator set which includes bitwise operators (i.e., SHIFT, AND, OR, XOR), logical operators, and MIN/MAX operators has been suggested. These enhancements will most certainly be utilized in the proposed exascale systems currently under design by the U.S. Department of Energy (DOE) and the U.S. Department of Defense.

An additional byproduct of the co-design of OpenSHMEM hardware/software capabilities, described in Section 3.2, is that the energy required to move the data around an extreme scale system using OpenSHMEM (or other PGAS programming models) can be significantly less than the energy required by normal message passing methods which do not decouple data motion and synchronization. As energy will be one of the major constraints for future systems, this will have a major impact on the viability of future interconnect designs and will be a forcing function on most, if not all, designs for extreme-scale systems.

Of the future technologies required to enable exascale computing, memory and networking are currently the major focal points for hardware improvements, placing a codesign emphasis on enabling support for active messages via OpenSHMEM expanding the programming model to allow moving either computation to data or data to computation, based on the cost (time or energy) required for the move. While research in this area is still in the early stages, we expect to see additional Hardware and Firmware capabilities soon which will enable this to happen. The foundations for such a *Data Motion Machine* are certainly in OpenSHMEM's future—particularly since hardware improvements alone are most unlikely to meet the 20MW power constraint proposed in the DOE exascale roadmap at the time of this writing. OpenSHMEM's deep history of codesign should continue to facilitate the path forward.

4 Unified Parallel C

Kathy Yelick, University of California, Berkeley and Lawrence Berkeley National Laboratory

Yili Zheng, Lawrence Berkeley National Laboratory

Unified Parallel C (UPC) is a C language extension with global address space support for parallel programming. UPC provides mechanisms for both bulk-synchronous and fine-grain parallel programming styles and thus users have the freedom to choose one or combine two programming styles with the same language. In this chapter, we will survey a brief history about UPC, discuss the high-level programming model of UPC, have a quick tour of practical UPC programming, and walk through a few examples of UPC programs. Finally, we will summarize the roadmap ahead in the last section.

4.1 Brief History of UPC

UPC was influenced by the experience gained from its predecessors such as Split-C [165], AC [60] and PCP [53]. The first UPC Specification (version 0.9) was introduced in a technical report by Carlson et al. [59]. Subsequently, the UPC consortium was formed by a group of UPC implementers and users from government, industry and academia. The current UPC Specification V1.3 based on C99 was released in November 2013. The main new features in UPC 1.3 include nonblocking data transfer, atomic memory operations and shared-to-private pointer castability functions. Nonblocking data transfer functions enable users to hide communication latency by overlapping it with other activities. Atomic memory operations are aimed to avoid using locks and leverage hardware support to deliver better performance for operations that need atomicity. The challenge here is to design an API that allows high performance implementations when hardware support is available, while maintaining general portability when such support is absent. Shared-to-private pointer castability enables UPC programs to directly access the shared data in other threads' partitions through a regular C pointer (a virtual memory address) if the underlying hardware supports such accesses. For instance, this can be achieved by cross-mapping the virtual memory address space of different processes (e.g., through `mmap()`), if the UPC threads are implemented as OS processes.

Back in the early days of UPC, though many people agreed that PGAS languages could improve the programming productivity of applications with dynamic data access patterns, few in the HPC community believed PGAS languages could deliver high performance. UPC was the first PGAS language that demonstrated excellent scalable performance on hundreds of thousands of cores in the HPC Challenge Class 2 (productivity) competition at the Supercomputing (SC) conference in 2005 [141]. Since then, other PGAS languages including Co-Array Fortran, X10 and Chapel have also won productivity awards in HPCC competitions for a balance of productivity and performance.

As hardware RDMA support becomes pervasive, the PGAS programming model thrives as well. Today there are a diverse portfolio of production-quality UPC implementations available to interested users. Open-source implementations include Berkeley UPC,[1] GCC UPC,[2] and Clang UPC.[3] Commercial UPC compilers are offered by Cray, IBM, HP and SGI. The increasing importance of data locality encourages more programmers to try out UPC not only for distributed-memory systems but for shared-memory systems with NUMA architectures as well. The whole UPC ecosystem is growing—more and more supercomputing centers procure systems with vendor UPC compilers.

4.2   UPC Programming Model

4.2.1   Terminology

To help better understand the UPC programming model, we first explain some of the common terms in UPC. Readers who are interested in the formal definition of UPC concepts can refer to the UPC specification document [279].

- **UPC thread** is a logical execution unit that has an independent instruction stream, its own execution state, a private data space, and a partition of the global address space.

- **Shared data** are data stored in the global address space, which can be accessed by any thread. Please note that a thread usually has faster access time to the shared data stored in its local partition than to those stored in the remote partitions of other threads.

- **Private data** are data stored in the private address space, which can only be accessed by the thread that owns that private space. A UPC thread's stack and local heap are in its private address space.

- **Pointer-to-shared** is a pointer data type that is used to reference shared data. It is also called a global address space pointer.

- **Pointer-to-local** is a pointer date type that is used to reference private data. It is also called a private or local address, which is the same as a regular pointer in C.

- **Affinity** is the logical association between a shared object and a thread. A shared object is said to have affinity to a thread if it is located within the thread's partition

---

1. Berkeley UPC: http://upc.lbl.gov/
2. GCC UPC: http://www.gccupc.org/
3. Clang UPC: https://github.com/Intrepid/clang-upc

of global address space. A thread can access a shared object that it has affinity to through a regular C pointer obtained by casting the pointer-to-shared for that object to a pointer-to-local.

4.2.2 Global Address Space

The defining feature of the UPC programming model is its partitioned global address space (PGAS) as depicted in Figure 4.1. Unlike conventional shared memory programming models that provide a uniformly-shared global address space abstraction, UPC divides the global address space into partitions and thus allows the compiler to explicitly generate communication operations when data accesses are across different partitions. This design not only greatly simplifies the implementation complexity of the UPC runtime on distributed memory systems, it also helps the programmer to be more aware of data locality and manage it carefully.

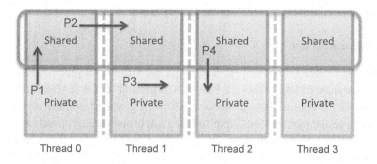

Figure 4.1: Partitioned Global Address Space in UPC: vertical boundaries distinguish local and remote partitions while horizontal boundaries separate private and shared segments. P1 is a private variable of pointer-to-shared type; P2 is a shared variable of pointer-to-shared type; P3 is a private variable of pointer-to-local type, which is the same as a regular C pointer; P4 is a shared variable of pointer-to-local type.

4.2.3 Execution Model

UPC uses the Single Program Multiple Data (SPMD) execution model. A UPC application spawns a user-specified number of threads at the parallel job startup time. During the entire execution of the UPC job, the number of UPC threads is fixed, i.e., no dynamic threads. Each UPC thread is a logical execution unit with its stream of instructions, a private data space, and a partition of the global address space. To avoid being confused with other definitions of threads (e.g., Pthreads and CUDA threads), "thread" refers to UPC thread in this chapter unless specified otherwise. Different UPC implementations may map UPC threads to either OS processes or low-level threads (e.g., Pthreads). For example, Cray UPC maps each UPC thread to a process while Berkeley UPC has the option to map a UPC thread to either a process or a Pthread.

4.3   A Quick Tour of UPC

The goal of this section is to help users with C programming experience to get started with UPC programming. We assume our readers have basic knowledge of C and hence we will concentrate on the UPC extensions beyond regular C.

It is important to remember that any C program is also a valid UPC program by design because the UPC specification is a superset of the C standard. Therefore, it is common to develop UPC applications by parallelizing existing C programs instead of starting from scratch. In addition, UPC programs can reuse existing libraries written in other programming languages in the same way as sequential C programs.

4.3.1   Self Introspection

For SPMD programming models, it is essential for each thread (or process) to know "How many peers are there?" and "Who am I?". THREADS and MYTHREAD are the UPC language keywords for getting these answers: THREADS gives the number of UPC threads in the current parallel job; MYTHREAD gives the rank of the calling thread, which is from 0 to (THREADS − 1). In MPI parlance, THREADS and MYTHREAD are equivalent to MPI_Comm_size and MPI_Comm_rank for MPI_COMM_WORLD, respectively. Because the current UPC language specification (V1.2) does not support subsets of threads, there is no equivalent of MPI subcommunicators in UPC for the moment. There is ongoing research effort to add support for thread teams in future UPC revisions. Both THREADS and MYTHREAD are constant and thus should be read-only. The following example demonstrates their basic usage.

```
printf("I'm thread %d of %d threads.\n", MYTHREAD, THREADS);
```

4.3.2   Data Layout

The current computer architectural trend of deep memory hierarchies and nonuniform memory access speeds makes data locality an important factor for optimizing performance and energy efficiency. UPC provides users the necessary programming constructs to place data at the right locations. From each UPC thread's perspective, there are three types of memory locations: a private address space, a local partition of the global address space, and remote partitions of the global address space on other threads. The access speeds to these different memory locations usually follow this order:

$$\text{private space} \geq \text{local GAS partition} \geq \text{remote GAS partitions}$$

All variables and data in a UPC program are stored in the private address space by default. To place variables or allocate space in the global address space, the user can express that intention by using the UPC `shared` type qualifier or UPC global memory management functions. In contrast, for most other shared-memory programming models, such as OpenMP and Pthreads, all variables and data are shared by default and thread-private variables need to be specified explicitly. We believe that UPC's "private by default" principle can help users to be more cautious about what data has to be shared in the program and when. It is well-known that over-sharing data can easily cause many correctness and performance problems such as data races and false sharing.

All statically declared shared objects (except shared arrays) reside in Thread 0's partition. To declare a shared variable in the global address space, it simply needs to add a `shared` type qualifier in the variable declaration. For example:

```
shared int x;
shared struct tree t;
```

UPC requires that shared variables must be declared in the global scope, i.e., outside of any function. This is because variables inside a function are commonly stored in a private stack and would be meaningless when a thread is outside of the function scope. Variables in the global address space are visible to all threads at all time. Please note that conventional C global variables are private to each UPC thread and only UPC `shared` variables are stored in the global address space and visible to all threads. The following example shows the distinction between a C global variable and a UPC global address space (shared) variable:

```
int a; // C global variable private to each UPC thread
shared int s; // UPC shared variable visible to all threads
```

Shared Arrays in UPC are stored in a block-cyclic distribution manner, which can be declared by the following syntax:

```
shared [BS] element_type array_name[array_size];
```

Example: `shared [2] int b[16];` on 4 UPC threads

Logical data layout

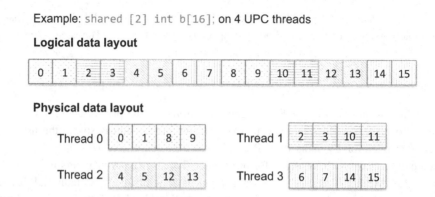

Physical data layout

Figure 4.2: Block-cyclic distribution example of a UPC array. Array elements of the same box pattern have affinity to the same UPC thread.

where `[BS]` is the layout qualifier that specifies the chunk size of each block. The blocking size, `BS`, must be a compile-time constant expression. Of all possible values, the most commonly used layouts are `[0]`, `[1]` and `[*]`.

- `[0]` means indefinite blocking or no blocking—all elements of the array have affinity to the same thread. `shared []` is the same as `shared [0]`.

- `[1]` means cyclic distribution—elements of the array are distributed in a round-robin fashion: the first element is on thread 0, the second element is on thread 1 and so forth. This is the default data layout—`shared` is the short form of `shared [1]`.

- `[*]` means blocked distribution—elements of the array are evenly divided into `THREADS` contiguous blocks and then each block is allocated to the thread with the same rank.

Figure 4.2 depicts an example of a statically allocated shared array. It is important to know that UPC guarantees that the local portion of a shared array is always contiguous. This implies that the user can cast a pointer-to-shared to a regular C pointer and use it to access the entire local part of the shared array without paying the global-to-local address translation overhead for every array element access. This is one of the most effective performance optimization techniques for UPC programs but it is the programmer's responsibilities to ensure that the C pointer only references valid local storage. UPC does not allow up-casting a regular C pointer to a pointer-to-shared.

Elements of multi-dimensional arrays are distributed as if they are laid out linearly in a row-major order. Because UPC currently only supports one-dimensional blocking, users who want to use multi-dimensional blocking (e.g., 2-D block-cyclic distribution) have two options to work around this limitation: 1) map the multi-dimensional array to a one-dimensional array and customize the array indexing functions based on the array element layout; 2) build a directory-based multi-dimensional arrays (also known as "array of arrays" or "array views").

Pointers in UPC are extended to support referencing shared objects in the global address space. Depending on the "shared" property of the object referenced by the pointer as well as the "shared" property of the pointer itself, there are four common types of pointers as follows:

```
shared void *P1; // private pointer to shared object
shared void * shared P2; // shared pointer to shared object
void * P3; // private pointer to private object
void * shared P4; // shared pointer to private object
```

As depicted in Figure 4.1, `P1` is a private variable whose content is a global address. `P2` is a shared variable whose content is a global address. `P3` is a private variable whose content is a local address, i.e., a regular C pointer. `P4` is a shared variable whose content is a local address. `P4` is uncommon because a local address is only valid on the thread that owns its referenced storage and thus it should not be dereferenced on other threads. The usage of the UPC `shared` type qualifier in pointer types is analogous to `const` in C: a pointer-to-constant (`const int* p1`) vs. a constant pointer (`int* const p2`).

UPC programs can query the thread affinity of a shared object by passing its address to the `upc_threadof` function. If the pointer-to-shared is referencing an element in a shared array, it also contains a `phase` property, which is the offset of the referenced element within the block. For shared arrays with indefinite blocking or blocked layout (i.e., only one block per thread), the phase of a pointer is the same as the offset from the beginning of the local part of the array.

```
size_t upc_threadof(shared void *ptr);
size_t upc_phaseof(shared void *ptr);
```

Arithmetics of pointers-to-shared can be defined in terms of the `upc_threadof` and `upc_phaseof` functions.

```
shared [B] Type *p;
upc_phaseof(p + i) = (upc_phaseof(p) + i) % B;
upc_threadof(p + i) =
  (upc_threadof(p) + (upc_phaseof(p) + i) / B) % THREADS;
```

Dynamic global memory allocation   UPC provides dynamic global memory management routines in its core library for allocating and freeing shared arrays. There are three
allocation functions and two deallocation functions.

```
shared void * upc_all_alloc(size_t nblks, size_t nbytes);
shared void * upc_global_alloc(size_t nblks, size_t nbytes);
shared void * upc_alloc(size_t nbytes);
void upc_free(shared void *ptr);
void upc_all_free(shared void *ptr);
```

upc_all_alloc and upc_global_alloc allocate a block-cyclic distributed array
of nblocks blocks with nbytes per block in the global address space, which is the
same as

```
shared [nbytes] char[nblocks * nbytes];
```

The difference between upc_all_alloc and upc_global_alloc is that the function upc_all_alloc is a collective operation that should be called by all threads while
upc_global_alloc is noncollective and should be called by only one thread. The
function upc_alloc allocates an indefinite blocking array in the partition of the calling
thread. Dynamically allocated memory should be deallocated by only one thread calling
upc_free, or collectively with upc_all_free.

4.3.3   Communication

Communication in UPC is one-sided. Expressing data communication in UPC can be done
naturally as assignment statements or by using shared-memory copy functions. Shared data
in the global address space can also be directly referenced by any thread. In the following
printf example, UPC compiler will first *get* the value of the shared variable sa from the
global address space to a local temporary and then output it.

```
shared int sa = 5;
printf("%d\n", sa);
```

For assignment statements, if the left-hand side variable is `shared` and the right-hand side variable is local, then the assignment is equivalent to a "put" operation. If the left-hand side variable is local and the right-hand side variable is `shared`, then the assignment is equivalent to a "get" operation.

In addition to supporting fine-grained accesses to shared objects, UPC includes standard library functions for bulk data transfers. These functions include `upc_memcpy` for moving data within the global address space, `upc_memput` for sending data from local space to global space, and `upc_memget` for retrieving data from global space to local space.

```
void upc_memcpy(shared void * restrict dst,
                shared const void * restrict src,
                size_t n);

void upc_memget(void * restrict dst,
                shared const void * restrict src,
                size_t n);

void upc_memput(shared const void * restrict dst,
                void * restrict src,
                size_t n);
```

Using the bulk memory copy functions can usually achieve higher bandwidth than using fine-grain assignments because the underlying network and memory subsystem are commonly designed to moved data more efficiently in large chunks. Nonblocking versions of the aforementioned bulk data transfer functions are also available to overlap communication with computation or other communication.

4.3.4   UPC Memory Consistency Model

The memory consistency model is a formal specification of the ordering rules of memory operations in a parallel program. Because understanding the memory consistency model of a language is crucial to writing correct and efficient programs, we will review the most important rules in the UPC memory consistency model here.

The UPC memory consistency model supports *strict* and *relaxed* memory operations.[4] Strict memory operations are executed by each thread in the same order as they appear in the program. In addition, all threads observe the same total ordering of all strict memory operations as required by the sequential consistency model [171]. Due to its deterministic behavior, a UPC program using strict memory operations is easier for the programmer to analyze but may restrict many valid optimizations available in modern computers that

---

4. Memory operations include read (load) and write (store) operations.

reorder operations. For example, strict write accesses cannot be reordered even when they are writing to different locations.

Relaxed memory operations can be reordered by the UPC compiler or the underlying hardware as long as there is no data dependency specified in the program. Relaxed memory operations issued from different threads can be executed in arbitrary order unless explicit synchronization is enforced by the programmer. It would cause a *data race* if two threads concurrently access the same location (and one of the accesses is write) without synchronization and the result is nondeterministic. Only relaxed memory operations *issued from the same thread and accessing the same memory location* are executed in the program order. The synchronization primitive, upc_fence, guarantees that all prior memory operations issued from the current thread are completed before the fence returns. Relaxed memory operations cannot be reordered with respect to strict memory operations. It is important to note that a *correctly-synchronized (i.e., race-free)* UPC program should behave as if it were executed in the sequential consistency model because the reordering of operations is not visible in the result of any execution for such programs.

Memory operations in a UPC program are *relaxed* by default for getting better performance. User can change the memory operation type to *strict* by using either the upc strict pragma or the strict type qualifier. For example:

```
#pragma upc strict
strict shared [] double *sa;
```

Here is an example showing the difference in reordering rules between strict and relaxed accesses. Consider the following code snippet to be executed by a UPC thread:

```
shared int A[10];
A[0] = 1;
A[1] = 2;
```

If the memory operation type is relaxed, the UPC implementation may reorder the assignment statements of A[0] and A[1] because they are writing to two different global memory locations. However, if the memory operation type is strict, the UPC implementation must execute these two write operations in their program order deterministically, which causes slower performance.

A general tutorial on memory consistency models can be found in [6] and the complete formal UPC memory consistency model is described in Appendix B of the UPC specification [279].

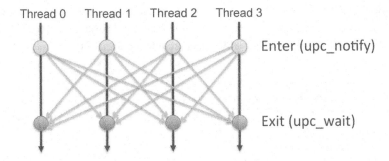

Figure 4.3: Bipartite dependency graph of executing a nonblocking barrier

4.3.5 Synchronization

As in other SPMD programming systems, UPC programs can use *barriers* to synchronize all threads. UPC provides two flavors of barriers: blocking and nonblocking. Blocking barriers can be invoked by using the UPC keyword, `upc_barrier`. No thread can return from `upc_barrier` until all other threads have reached the matching `upc_barrier`. In addition, `upc_barrier` guarantees that all outstanding memory operations would be completed before the barrier finishes.

For advanced users, UPC provides nonblocking barriers that separate the beginning of the synchronization phase from its completion and thus allow overlapping between barrier wait time and other useful work. Nonblocking barriers are started by `upc_notify` and completed by `upc_wait`. The control dependency graph corresponding to a nonblocking barrier invocation is a complete bipartite graph—there is an edge between each pair of `upc_notify` and `upc_wait`. Note that there is no ordering dependency between any pair of `upc_notify`'s nor any dependency between a pair of `upc_wait`'s.

Since UPC supports sharing data in the global address space, it is necessary to have a protection mechanism to avoid data races when multiple threads may access the same address. Similar to Pthread mutex, UPC provides *locks* for serializing the operations in a critical region.

The opaque data type, `upc_lock_t`, can be used for locks in UPC. UPC locks need to be dynamically allocated at runtime and used via a `upc_lock_t*` pointer. Because UPC locks are similar to globally shared variables, it is important to know where the lock is stored as it would take nontrivial amount of communication time (at least a round-trip) to acquire a remote lock. However, the UPC specification does not specify the lock location and leaves it to be implementation specific. For the Berkeley UPC im-

plementation, `upc_global_lock_alloc` allocates the lock on the calling thread while
`upc_all_lock_alloc` allocates the lock in a round-robin fashion, starting from thread
0. The function prototypes for using UPC locks include the following:

```
upc_lock_t *upc_all_lock_alloc(void);
upc_lock_t *upc_global_lock_alloc(void);
void upc_lock_free(upc_lock_t *ptr);

void upc_lock(upc_lock_t *ptr);
void upc_unlock(upc_lock_t *ptr);
int upc_lock_attempt(upc_lock_t *ptr);
```

The two functions `upc_lock` and `upc_unlock` are for acquiring and releasing a lock.
`upc_lock_attempt` tries to acquire a lock without blocking if the lock is unavailable.
A `upc_fence` is implied when calling `upc_lock` and `upc_unlock` functions. As a
performance optimization practice, it is recommended to minimize lock usage, especially
spin-waiting on a remote lock.

4.3.6 Collective Operations

In contrast to the conventional "process-centric" approach for collective operations, UPC
collectives takes a "data-centric" approach in that the "root" of the collective operation is
implicitly specified by the affinity of the input or output buffer. A peculiarity of UPC collectives is that all collective function arguments must be *single-valued*, which means that
all threads should pass in the same argument values when calling the collective function.
The header file `<upc_collective.h>` must be included by all UPC programs using
collective operations.

UPC collective operations have two main categories: data movement (e.g., broadcast)
and computing aggregated results (e.g., allreduce). Commonly used collective functions
for moving data include the following:

```
void upc_all_broadcast (shared void * restrict dst,
                        shared const void * restrict src,
                        size_t nbytes,
                        upc_flag_t flags);

void upc_all_scatter   (shared void * restrict dst,
                        shared const void * restrict src,
                        size_t nbytes,
                        upc_flag_t flags);

void upc_all_gather     (shared void * restrict dst,
```

```
                      shared const void * restrict src,
                      size_t nbytes,
                      upc_flag_t flags);

void upc_all_gather_all(shared void * restrict dst,
                      shared const void * restrict src,
                      size_t nbytes,
                      upc_flag_t flags);

void upc_all_exchange  (shared void * restrict dst,
                      shared const void * restrict src,
                      size_t nbytes,
                      upc_flag_t flags);
```

All collective functions usually take four arguments: the input buffer (src), the output buffer (dst), the data size (nbytes), and the synchronization flags for the operation (flags). Note that each collective function makes a different assumption of the data layouts of the src and dst buffers. Thus, the user must prepare the data buffers as expected by the collective operation, or undefined results would occur. Table 4.1 lists the expected data layouts for various UPC collective functions.

Collective function	Buffer	Expected data layout (T = THREADS)
upc_all_broadcast	src	shared [] char[nbytes]
	dst	shared [nbytes] char[nbytes*T]
upc_all_scatter	src	shared [] char[nbytes*T]
	dst	shared [nbytes] char[nbytes*T]
upc_all_gather	src	shared [nbytes] char[nbytes*T]
	dst	shared [] char[nbytes*T]
upc_all_gather_all	src	shared [nbytes] char[nbytes*T]
	dst	shared [nbytes*T] char[nbytes*T*T]
upc_all_exchange	src	shared [nbytes*T] char[nbytes*T*T]
	dst	shared [nbytes*T] char[nbytes*T*T]

Table 4.1: Expected data layout of the buffer parameters in UPC collective functions

Synchronization flags. Because UPC collective functions use shared arrays for input and output buffers, an early arriving thread may start moving data before other threads enter the corresponding collective function if that does not affect the correctness of the program. The synchronization flags are for the programmer to specify when the participating threads of a collective operation may start moving data and when the data movement must be completed. There are three flags for the function entrance and another three for the exit.

- `UPC_IN_ALLSYNC`: A thread in the collective function must *not* read any input buffer or write to any output buffer until *all* threads have entered the collective operation.

- `UPC_IN_MYSYNC`: A thread may start to read or write to its own buffers after it enters the collective function.

- `UPC_IN_NOSYNC`: A thread may read or write to all threads' buffers as soon as it enters the collective function. This is a flag that should be used with caution because it is easy to cause data races.

- `UPC_OUT_ALLSYNC`: All threads must complete the data movement for the collective operation before any thread may exit the collective operation. This implies that all input buffers can be reused and all output buffers contain the results of collective operation when any thread returns from the collective function.

- `UPC_OUT_MYSYNC`: A thread's own buffers are ready after it exits a collective function.

- `UPC_IN_NOSYNC`: The input and output buffers are not ready until *all* threads have completed the collective operation. In practice, a thread can not touch its own buffers even after exiting the collective function because it does not know if there is another thread still inside the collective function. It requires a later synchronization step (e.g., a barrier) to know if all threads have exited the collective function. Only after that synchronization point, the results of the collective operation are guaranteed to be available in the buffers.

From a practical point of view, the most commonly used synchronization flag combination is (`UPC_IN_MYSYNC` | `UPC_OUT_MYSYNC`), which is equivalent to the semantics of MPI collectives. In our experience of using and implementing UPC collectives, the `NOSYNC` flags are often unable to provide performance improvement due to other restrictions in the program. To fully release the opportunity for overlapping, one should use *nonblocking* collectives, which allow true overlapping between communication and computation.

In summary, UPC collectives provide a convenient mechanism for common communication patterns in global address space. However, it also lacks some popular features such as "communicators" and "vector collectives" as in MPI. Users may also directly use MPI collectives in a UPC program if the underlying UPC and MPI implementations are interoperable.

Due to space limitations here, some features in UPC, such as UPC I/O and computational collectives, have not been covered in this section. The complete set of UPC libraries can be found in the UPC specification or the UPC manual [281]. Finally many UPC compilers may have implementation-specific extensions. For example, Berkeley UPC extensions are available at `http://upc.lbl.gov/docs/user/#extensions`.

4.4 Examples of UPC Programs

4.4.1 Random Access Benchmark

The Random Access benchmark measures fine-grain memory access rates to random locations in terms of giga-updates per second (GUPS). Below are the main pieces of the Random Access benchmark. The statement used to update `Table` in UPC is the same as in sequential C, which illustrates the PGAS productivity advantage of UPC.

```
// Define constants for the update algorithm
#define TableSize (1ULL << 20)
#define NUPDATE   (4ULL * TableSize)
#define POLY      0x0000000000000007ULL

// Cyclically distributed 1-D array (block size is default to 1)
shared uint64_t Table[TableSize];

// Start the random number generator at the Nth step
uint64_t starts(int64_t N);

// The main random access update function
void RandomAccessUpdate()
{
  uint64_t i;
  uint64_t ran = starts(NUPDATE/THREADS*MYTHREAD);

  for (i = MYTHREAD; i < NUPDATE; i += THREADS) {
    ran = (ran << 1) ^ (((int64_t) ran < 0) ? POLY : 0);
    Table[ran & (TableSize-1)] ^= ran; // random access update
  }
}
```

In this UPC Random Access example, the user expresses the algorithm naturally in terms of updating the shared array in the global address space directly. The performance optimization is delegated to the UPC implementation. High-quality UPC compilers often automatically aggregate the updates to achieve better throughput.

4.4.2 Jacobi 5-Point Stencil

In this example, we first show how to build a directory-based 2D array in UPC. The main idea is that each thread will have local directory that stores the pointers to the global storage of the data. An array element access operation can be done by first looking-up the pointer of the corresponding row and then indexing the pointer with the column offset to access the target element.

```
/**
 * Allocate a row-majored M-by-N shared matrix with 1-D row
 * blocking. This is a collective function that should be called by
 * all UPC threads. The data storage of the matrix is globally shared
 * but each thread keeps an local copy of the row pointers for fast
 * accesses.
 */
shared [] double ** alloc_matrix(size_t M, size_t N)
{
  int t;
  size_t i, rows_per_thread;
  shared [] double **matrix;
  shared double *data;

  matrix = (shared [] double **)malloc(M*sizeof(shared [] double *));
  assert (matrix != NULL);
  rows_per_thread = (M+THREADS-1)/THREADS;
  data = (shared double *)upc_all_alloc(THREADS,
                                rows_per_thread*N*sizeof(double));
  assert (data != NULL);

  /* Compute the starting row M1 and the end row M2 for each thread */
  for (t=0; t<THREADS; t++) {
    size_t q, r, M_1, M_2;
    q = M / THREADS;
    r = M - (q * THREADS);
    if(t < r) {
      M_1 = (q + 1) * t ;
      M_2 = (q + 1) * (t + 1) - 1;
    } else {
      M_1 = (q + 1) * r + q * (t - r) ;
      M_2 = (q + 1) * r + q * (t - r + 1) - 1;
    }

    /* Each thread sets up its part of row pointers */
    for (i=M_1; i<=M_2; i++)
      /* Set up the i'th row pointer for the matrix */
      matrix[i] = (shared [] double *)(&data[t])+(i-M_1)*N;
  }

  return matrix;
```

```
}

/**
 * Free the shared matrix allocated by alloc_matrix. It should be
 * called by all threads.
 */
void free_matrix(shared [] double **matrix)
{
  if (MYTHREAD == 0)
    upc_free((shared void *)(matrix[0]));
  free(matrix);
}
```

The `main` function of the 5-point stencil example shows how to use the shared 2D array
that we just built. If the user is interested in further performance optimization, the array
update loop can be changed to use a regular C pointer for accessing local elements and
only use the pointer-to-shared for accessing remote elements in other threads' partitions.

```
int main()
{
  shared [] double **u;
  shared [] double **unew;
  shared [] double **f;

  /* Read in problem and solver parameters. */
  read_params(&ngrid, &maxiter, &tol, &omega);
  n = ngrid - 1;
  h = 1.0 / n;

  /* Allocate memory for shared matrices */
  u = alloc_matrix(ngrid, ngrid);
  unew = alloc_matrix(ngrid, ngrid);
  f = alloc_matrix(ngrid, ngrid);

  init_fields(f, u, n);

  /* Compute the new value of u based on the current values of its
   * top, left, right, bottom neighbors and itself.
   */
  for (int k=1; k<=maxiter; k++) {
    upc_forall (int i=1; i<n; i++; u[i]) {
      for (int j=1; j<n; j++) {
        utmp = 0.25 * (u[i+1][j] + u[i-1][j] + u[i][j+1] + u[i][j-1]
                       - h*h*f[i][j]);
        unew[i][j] = omega*utmp + (1.0-omega)*u[i][j];
      }
    }
    upc_barrier;
  }
}
```

4.4.3 Sample Sort

In this example, we use UPC to implement a variant of the sample sort algorithm. In this example, we will learn about how to use UPC collectives and one-sided data transfer functions. The basic steps of the sample sort algorithm are listed here.

1. Thread 0 takes $C \times$ THREADS samples from the keys to be sorted, where C is usually a small constant.

2. Thread 0 sorts the sample keys and subsamples the sorted set to THREADS-1 splitters for partitioning all keys in a balanced way. The key splitters are broadcast to all threads.

3. Every thread sorts and partitions its local part of the keys into THREADS partitions based on the splitters from the previous step.

4. Every thread sends its ith partition to thread i. This approach is equivalent to using an MPI_Alltoallv operation.

5. Every thread locally sorts its partition of the distributed array

```
#include <upc.h>
#include <upc_collective.h>
#include <stdio.h>
#include <stdlib.h> // for qsort()

#define ELEMENT_T uint64_t
#define RANDOM_SEED 12345
#define SAMPLES_PER_THREAD 32
#define KEYS_PER_THREAD 4 * 1024 * 1024

typedef struct {
  shared void *ptr;
  size_t nbytes;
} buffer_t;

shared [THREADS] ELEMENT_T splitters[THREADS][THREADS];
shared [] ELEMENT_T my_splitters[THREADS];
shared [] ELEMENT_T * shared sorted[THREADS];
shared size_t sorted_key_counts[THREADS];
shared [THREADS] buffer_t all_buffers[THREADS][THREADS];

/* Initialize the keys to be sorted with random numbers */
void init(ELEMENT_T *my_keys, size_t my_key_size);

/* Integer comparison function for qsort */
int compare_element(const void * a, const void * b);
```

```
/* Compute the splitters for partitioning the keys array */
void compute_splitters(shared ELEMENT_T *keys,
                       size_t key_count,
                       int samples_per_thread)
{
  if (MYTHREAD == 0) {
    ELEMENT_T *candidates;
    int candidate_count = THREADS * samples_per_thread;
    int i;

    candidates = (ELEMENT_T *)malloc(sizeof(ELEMENT_T) * candidate_count);
    assert(candidates != NULL);

    // Sample the key space to find the partition splitters
    // Oversample by a factor "samples_per_thread"
    for (i = 0; i < candidate_count; i++) {
      uint64_t s = sfmt_genrand_uint64(&sfmt) % key_count;
      candidates[i] = keys[s]; // global accesses on keys
    }

    qsort(candidates, candidate_count, sizeof(ELEMENT_T),
          compare_element);

    // Subsample the candidates for the key splitters
    for (i = 0; i < THREADS; i++) {
      my_splitters[i] = candidates[i * samples_per_thread];
    }
    // Broadcast the key splitters from Thread 0 to all
    upc_all_broadcast(splitters, my_splitters,
                      THREADS*sizeof(ELEMENT_T),
                      UPC_IN_MYSYNC | UPC_OUT_MYSYNC);

    free(candidates);
  } else {
    // All other threads (MYTHREAD != 0) receive the splitters
    upc_all_broadcast(splitters, my_splitters,
                      THREADS*sizeof(ELEMENT_T),
                      UPC_IN_MYSYNC | UPC_OUT_MYSYNC);
  }
}

/* Re-distribute the keys according to the splitters */
void redistribute(shared ELEMENT_T *keys, size_t key_count)
{
  size_t i;
  int k;
  size_t offset;
  size_t *hist;
  ELEMENT_T *my_splitters = (ELEMENT_T *)&splitters[MYTHREAD][0];
  ELEMENT_T *my_keys = (ELEMENT_T *)&keys[MYTHREAD];
```

```
ELEMENT_T my_new_key_count;

hist = (size_t *)malloc(sizeof(size_t) * THREADS);
assert(hist != NULL);

// local sort
qsort(my_keys, KEYS_PER_THREAD, sizeof(ELEMENT_T),
      compare_element);

// compute the local histogram from the splitters
bzero(hist, sizeof(size_t) * THREADS);
k = 0;
for (i = 0; i < KEYS_PER_THREAD; i++) {
  if (my_keys[i] < my_splitters[k+1]) {
    hist[k]++;
  } else {
    while (my_keys[i] >= my_splitters[k+1] && (k < THREADS - 1))
      k++;
    if (k == THREADS - 1) {
      hist[k] = KEYS_PER_THREAD - i;
      break;
    } else {
      hist[k]++;
    }
  }
}

/* Set up the buffer pointers for the key exchange step later */
offset = 0; // offset in elements
for (i = 0; i < THREADS; i++) {
  all_buffers[MYTHREAD][i].ptr = \
    ((shared [] ELEMENT_T *)&keys[MYTHREAD]) + offset;
  all_buffers[MYTHREAD][i].nbytes = sizeof(ELEMENT_T) * hist[i];
  offset += hist[i];
}

sorted_key_counts[MYTHREAD] = 0;
upc_barrier;
for (i = 0; i < THREADS; i++) {
  sorted_key_counts[MYTHREAD] += \
    all_buffers[i][MYTHREAD].nbytes / sizeof(ELEMENT_T);
}

sorted[MYTHREAD] = \
  (shared [] ELEMENT_T *) upc_alloc(offset * sizeof(ELEMENT_T));
assert(sorted[MYTHREAD] != NULL);
upc_barrier;

/* All threads exchange keys, which is equivalent to an alltoallv
 * operation.
 */
```

```
    offset = 0; // offset in bytes
    for (i = 0; i < THREADS; i++) {
      // Send data only if the size is nonzero
      if (all_buffers[i][MYTHREAD].nbytes) {
        upc_memcpy(sorted[MYTHREAD] + offset / sizeof(ELEMENT_T),
                   all_buffers[i][MYTHREAD].ptr,
                   all_buffers[i][MYTHREAD].nbytes);
        offset += all_buffers[i][MYTHREAD].nbytes;
      }
    }
  upc_barrier;
}

/* Implement the sample sort algorithm */
void sample_sort(shared ELEMENT_T *keys, size_t key_count)
{
  compute_splitters(keys, KEYS_PER_THREAD, SAMPLES_PER_THREAD);

  upc_barrier;

  redistribute(keys, key_count);

  upc_barrier;

  qsort((ELEMENT_T *)sorted[MYTHREAD], sorted_key_counts[MYTHREAD],
        sizeof(ELEMENT_T), compare_element);

}

int main(int argc, char **argv)
{
  size_t my_key_size = KEYS_PER_THREAD;
  size_t total_key_size = KEYS_PER_THREAD * THREADS;
  shared ELEMENT_T *keys;

  keys = upc_all_alloc(total_key_size, sizeof(ELEMENT_T));
  assert(keys != NULL);

  /* initialize the keys with random numbers */
  init((ELEMENT_T *)&keys[MYTHREAD], my_key_size);
  upc_barrier;

  sample_sort(keys, total_key_size);
  upc_barrier;

  return 0;
}
```

4.4.4 1-D FFT

The last example is to compute 1-D FFT of a distributed array, which is also one of the HPC challenge problems. In this example, we will illustrate a few techniques: 1) how to optimize a matrix transpose operation by aggregating fine-grained communication; 2) show a parallel application development strategy—use UPC to express the high-level parallel algorithm and communication patterns while reusing third-party optimized numerical library for local computation.

We use the "six step" FFT algorithm introduced by David Bailey [21].

1. View the input 1-D array of size N as an N_1-by-N_2 matrix stored in C row-major order, where $N = N_1 \times N_2$. Transpose the input data to an N_2-by-N_1 matrix, of which the N_1 dimension is contiguous.

2. Compute N_2 individual N_1-point 1-D FFTs on the N_2-by-N_1 matrix from the previous step in parallel. Because the matrix is partitioned by rows and each row is contiguous, this step does not require communication and can use an optimized local FFT library such as FFTW [115].

3. Multiply the matrix by the twiddle factors W, where $W_{k,l} = e^{-2\pi i k l / N}$ for $\{0 \leq k < N_2, 0 \leq l < N_1\}$ and i is the imaginary unit $\sqrt{-1}$. This step is an element-wise operation and thus does not require communication.

4. Transpose the N_2-by-N_1 matrix from the previous step back to an N_1-by-N_2 matrix

5. Compute N_1 individual N_2-point 1-D FFTs on the matrix from the previous step in parallel.

6. Transpose the N_1-by-N_2 matrix to an N_2-by-N_1 matrix, whose linearization in row-major order is the end result of the 1-D FFT

Readers familiar with FFT algorithms may recognize that this four-step distributed 1-D FFT algorithm is very similar to the row-column algorithm for computing 2-D FFT except the extra step for multiplying the twiddle factor before transposing the matrix.

To simplify the example a little, we further assume that the size of the distributed array is a power of two, $N = 2^M$ and $N1 = N2 = \sqrt{N}$. Next, we first show the main program that is basically a direct translation of the work flow of the "six-step" FFT algorithm:

```c
#include <upc.h>
#include <math.h>
#include <stdio.h>
#include <stdlib.h>
#include <fftw3.h>

#define PI2 6.2831853071795864769252867665590057

typedef struct {
  double re, im;
} complex_t;

typedef shared [] complex_t* dist_array_t;

// Shared arrays
shared dist_array_t In[THREADS], Out[THREADS], Aux[THREADS];

// Local part of the shared arrays
complex_t *l_In, *l_Out, *l_Aux;

// Initialize a local array with random numbers
void init_rand(complex_t *array, int size);

// Multiply the twiddle factors to the local part of the shared array
void mult_twiddle(complex_t *array, int ncols);

// Transpose the "src" shared array to the "dst" shared array
void transpose(shared dist_array_t *src, shared dist_array_t *dst,
               int ncols);

int main(int argc, char *argv[])
{
  fftw_plan plan;
  int m, n, n2;

  if (argc > 1) {
    m = atoi(argv[1]);
    if (m < 2 || m > 15) {
      if (MYTHREAD == 0) {
        printf("The array size (2^%d)^2 is out of range.\n", m);
        printf("Please use (2 <= m <= 15).\n");
        exit(1);
      }
      upc_barrier;
    }
  } else {
    m = 10;
  }
  assert(m <= 15);
  n = 1 << m ;
  n2 = n * n; // This is total size of each 1D shared array.
```

```
    upc_barrier;

    if (MYTHREAD == 0 && n % THREADS != 0) {
      printf("Error: (2^m) should be a multiple of THREADS!\n");
      printf("m = %d, THREADS = %d.\n", m, THREADS);
      exit(1);
    }

    upc_barrier;

    if (MYTHREAD == 0) {
      double total_GB = 3.0 * n2 * sizeof(complex_t) / 1e9;
      double MB_per_thread = total_GB / THREADS * 1e3;
      printf("1D FFT: %d x %d elements, total %.2g GB, %.3f MB/thread\n",
             n, n, total_GB, MB_per_thread);
    }

    In[MYTHREAD] = upc_alloc(sizeof(complex_t) * n2 / THREADS);
    Out[MYTHREAD] = upc_alloc(sizeof(complex_t) * n2 / THREADS);
    Aux[MYTHREAD] = upc_alloc(sizeof(complex_t) * n2 / THREADS);

    l_In = (complex_t *)In[MYTHREAD];
    l_Out = (complex_t *)Out[MYTHREAD];
    l_Aux = (complex_t *)Aux[MYTHREAD];

    assert(l_In != NULL);
    assert(l_Out != NULL);
    assert(l_Aux != NULL);

    upc_barrier;
    if (MYTHREAD==0) printf ("Initialization\n");

    // Every threads initializes the local part of the input array
    init_rand(l_In, n2 / THREADS);

    // Initialize the FFTW plan
    plan = fft_init(l_In, n, n / THREADS);

    if (MYTHREAD==0) printf ("Step 1: transpose 1\n");
    transpose(In, Out, n);

    if (MYTHREAD==0) printf ("Step 2: local fft 1\n");
    fftw_execute_dft(plan, (fftw_complex *)l_Out, (fftw_complex *)l_Out);

    if (MYTHREAD==0) printf ("Step 3: multiply twiddle factors\n");
    mult_twiddle(l_Out, n);

    if (MYTHREAD==0) printf ("Step 4: transpose 2\n");
    transpose(Out, Aux, n);
```

```
    if (MYTHREAD==0) printf ("Step 5: local fft 2\n");
    fftw_execute_dft(plan, (fftw_complex *)l_Aux, (fftw_complex *)l_Aux);

    if (MYTHREAD==0) printf ("Step 6: transpose 3\n");
    transpose(Aux, Out, n);

    upc_barrier;
    return 0;
}
```

In the above `fft_1d` program, all UPC threads execute each of the subroutines in a lockstep fashion. The data initialization and local FFT computation functions are mostly sequential C code. The most interesting part of the implementation is the `transpose` step, which includes UPC one-sided data transfers and a local transpose operation.

```
/* Transpose a local square matrix */
void local_transpose (complex_t *a, int lda,  int size)
{
    int k, l;
    for (k = 0; k < size; k++ ) {
        for (l = 0; l < k; l++ ) {
            complex_t tmp = a[k*lda+l];
            a[k*lda+l] = a[l*lda+k];
            a[l*lda+k] = tmp;
        }
    }
}

/**
 * Transpose a distributed matrix stored in src and output it to dst.
 * And the matrix is assumed to be square.
 */
void transpose(shared dist_array_t *src, shared dist_array_t *dst,
               int ncols)
{
    int i, j;
    int nrows = ncols / THREADS;
    complex_t *l_src = (complex_t *)src[MYTHREAD];
    complex_t *l_dst = (complex_t *)dst[MYTHREAD];

    upc_barrier;

    // Noncontiguous all-to-all to transpose the blocks
    for (i = 0; i < nrows; i++ ) { // i'th row in the block
      for (j = 0; j < ncols; j += nrows ) { // j'th block column
#ifdef USE_NB_MEMCPY
        // dst's j'th thread block's i'th row and MYTHREAD*nrows column
        upc_memput_nbi(&dst[j/nrows][i * ncols  + MYTHREAD * nrows],
                l_src + i * ncols + j, // the start address of l_src(i, j)
```

```
                      sizeof(complex_t) * nrows);
#else
        upc_memput(&dst[j/nrows][i * ncols  + MYTHREAD * nrows],
                   l_src + i * ncols + j, // the start address of l_src(i, j)
                   sizeof(complex_t) * nrows);
#endif
    }
  }

#ifdef USE_NB_MEMCPY
  upc_synci(); // wait for all communication to complete
#endif

  upc_barrier;

  for (i = 0; i < ncols; i += nrows) {
    local_transpose(l_dst + i, ncols, nrows);
  }
}
```

The `transpose` function demonstrates a common strategy in high-performance UPC code—aggregate internode communication and leverage optimized libraries for a single node. Many other numerical linear algebra algorithms can also benefit from similar message aggregation techniques [217].

4.5   Looking Forward

UPC++ [311] is a recent effort to enable the PGAS model for C++ applications. UPC++ was designed with three main objectives: 1) provide an object-oriented PGAS programming model in the context of the popular C++ language; 2) add useful parallel programming idioms unavailable in Unified Parallel C (UPC), such as asynchronous remote function invocation and multidimensional arrays, to support complex scientific applications; 3) offer an easy on-ramp to PGAS programming through interoperability with other existing parallel programming systems (e.g., MPI, OpenMP, CUDA). UPC++ uses a C++ template library implementation strategy (metaprogramming) that minimizes development cost while providing desirable syntactic features and competitive performance. Interested readers may get more details and follow the UPC++ effort on the project website at `https://bitbucket.org/upcxx`.

After more than a decade of its inception, UPC has a growing community and is mature enough to be used in production software. Because programming languages alone cannot deliver application performance, we encourage the broader HPC community to collaborate on getting UPC and UPC++ better. We believe that PGAS languages can help develop new advanced and scalable algorithms that would be otherwise difficult to implement.

5 Global Arrays

Sriram Krishnamoorthy, Pacific Northwest National Laboratory
Jeff Daily, Pacific Northwest National Laboratory
Abhinav Vishnu, Pacific Northwest National Laboratory
Bruce Palmer, Pacific Northwest National Laboratory

5.1 Introduction

Global Arrays (GA) [214] is a distributed-memory programming model that allows for programming in a shared-memory style combined with one-sided communication, to create a set of tools that combine high performance with ease-of-use. GA exposes a relatively straightforward programming abstraction, while supporting fully-distributed data structures, locality of reference, and high-performance communication. GA was originally formulated in the early 1990's to provide a communication layer for the Northwest Chemistry (NWChem) [213] suite of chemistry modeling codes that was being developed concurrently [282]. The goal of the NWChem development was to create a code for performing quantum chemistry calculations that would scale to the largest parallel computers available during that period. At that time, MPI [126] had not yet been released. Furthermore, it became evident that trying to create a large chemistry program based on the exchange of messages using a send/receive protocol would lead to extremely complicated code that was also likely to suffer from poor scalability and uneven distribution of work. To overcome these difficulties, a group of computer scientists and computational chemists, led by the late Jarek Nieplocha, began developing a one-sided communication library based on the concepts of "put" and "get." As a consequence of using one-sided communication, this library was also able to support a global address space (GAS) that allowed users to access parts of large, distributed data sets using a global set of indices, thus avoiding tedious and error-prone index translations that normally accompanied any exchange of data using send/receive communication. Both of these factors combined to dramatically reduce the complexity of parallel programming using GA.

The first implementation of GA was described in 1994 [212] and was created specifically to support two-dimensional distributed arrays representing the matrices that occur in quantum chemistry calculations. It soon became apparent, however, that GA had much wider applicability to a variety of parallel computational problems so the original 2D interface was generalized to support distributed arrays with an arbitrary number of dimensions. Current implementations support arrays up to a maximum of 7 dimensions. Over the years, additional functionality has been added to the library. Some examples include support for ghost cells and ScaLAPACK-style block-cyclic data distributions [36], user control of data mapping to processors, processor groups, nonblocking put and get operations, periodic interfaces, and basic linear algebra operations. All of this has been done while still preserving the functionality in the original 1994 interface.

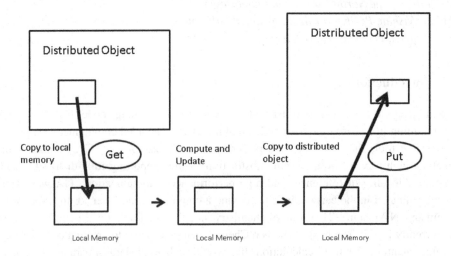

Figure 5.1: Schematic illustration of work flow in a typical GA-based calculation. Data from a globally distributed array is copied to a local buffer, modified by the code and then copied back to another distributed array.

Global Arrays now represents a complete library for developing high-performance parallel programs and has been used to implement parallel programs outside the realm of computational chemistry. These applications include particle-based algorithms such as molecular dynamics [282] and smoothed particle dynamics [226], a host of grid-based algorithms such as fluid dynamics, Darcy-scale subsurface reactive flow modeling, kinetic lattice boltzmann algorithms and manipulation and analysis of atmospheric data. GA is completely interoperable with MPI, allowing users to develop parallel codes using a mixture of GA and MPI. Thus, programs written with GA are still capable of calling subroutines and libraries based on MPI. This allows users to pursue optimal solutions to their computing challenges instead of being force to choose between incompatible alternatives.

5.2   Programming Model and Design Principles

The GA programming model is centered around the notion of "global" data arrays. Users can create data arrays that are visible to all processes. Processes can exchange data between the global data array and local buffers (arrays), through put/get operations to/from specified sections of the global array, without requiring coordination with other processes. This is illustrated schematically in Figure 5.1.

The two core concepts enabled by the GA toolkit are 1) the ability to create distributed arrays that can be referenced through a set of global indices and 2) the ability to copy data to and from the distributed array to a local buffer without involving any processes other then the process making the request. This is a significant simplification over message-passing, which requires programmers to first determine the location of a particular piece of data (i.e., MPI rank). It is often also necessary to determine a local offset within an array on the remote process. These calculations, or at least parts of them, must be performed for each exchange of data. Furthermore, both the sender and the receiver must determine that they are participating in a data exchange and post the appropriate send and receive calls, thereby creating an additional level of synchronization that may be unnecessary and potentially undesirable. This can result in inefficiencies if one process is blocking waiting for another process to become available. One-sided communication, on the other hand, involves only the requesting process, so data exchanges are simpler. Furthermore, because GA supports a global index space, the user can request data by simply using the global indices for that data segment. There is no need to decompose a single request for a large block of data into multiple separate requests to individual processes.

The flip side of using a one-sided programming model is that data consistency, which is generally handled automatically in a message-passing model, must be explicitly managed. This is done through synchronization using fence operations (that flush all outstanding communication from the system), and barriers (that force all processes to reach the same point in the program execution before proceeding further). Such synchronization is used to guarantee that global arrays are in a known, well-defined state before proceeding with the next step in the calculation.

The use of the global index space means that programming using GA is very similar to programming in shared memory. However, GA avoids some of the major pitfalls of shared memory. The first is that although GA looks like a shared memory programming model, it is implemented for fully-distributed data. Thus, GA is not limited by the size of shared-memory platforms and is able to run on the largest available computers [13]. Second, GA supports the concept of data locality and users can determine which data is "local" and which data is "remote." Accessing remote data has higher costs associated with it and programmers can optimize their calculations to rely, as much as possible, on using local data and minimizing both the frequency of accessing remote data and the size of data accessed. In pure shared-memory programming, all data appears flat and the cost of accessing one data element over another is the same. Depending on the actual architecture, this may not be true but the distinctions between different types of data are not supported by a pure shared-memory programming model.

GA itself sits on top of a separate library, Aggregate Remote Memory Copy Interface (ARMCI) [273], that contains the low-level routines used to implement GA. This library is relatively small and compact and contains all the vendor-specific primitives necessary to port GA from one platform to another. The original support model for GA required a port for ARMCI as new platforms came on line. More recently GA has moved towards using runtimes based on functionality available from MPI. The first of these was a compatibility port based on MPI two-sided communication, which ran on any platform that supports the MPI-1 standard. However, it did not scale well beyond a handful of processors [286]. Recent efforts include more sophisticated ports based on the functionality in both MPI-1 and MPI-2 that have much better scaling characteristics [92]. Future development in GA will focus primarily on MPI-based runtimes with the eventual goal of relying entirely on MPI for ports to new platforms.

5.3   Core Functionality

Although GA supports a great deal of functionality, a relatively small number of operations are used to write the bulk of GA-based code. These operations will be discussed in detail in this section. For illustrative purposes, we will use the C interface to describe the core functionality of GA, but interfaces are available in Fortran, C++, and Python [91] as well.

Before calling any other functions or subroutines in GA, the library must be initialized using a call to GA_Initialize. This must occur after a basic parallel runtime has been initialized, usually MPI. After initialization, other GA calls can be made until the end of the program. At that point, the GA library must be shut down by a call to GA_Terminate, followed by a call that closes down the parallel runtime. Terminating the GA library at the end of a program guarantees that the program exits cleanly and that all data generated by the program is exported to the user. In between initialization and termination, several additional GA calls can be used allowing for a rich set of communication capabilities.

Most parallel codes start by determining how many processes are available and what the local process IDs are (GA process IDs are equivalent to MPI ranks). The functions that can be used to find this information are GA_Nnodes and GA_Nodeid. The following program illustrates how these functions can be used to write a simple "Hello World" program:

```c
#include <stdio.h>
#include "ga.h"
#include "macdecls.h"

#include <mpi.h>

int main(int argc, char **argv) {
    int me, nprocs;

    /* Initialize Message Passing library */
```

```
    MPI_Init(&argc, &argv);

    /* Initialize GA */
    GA_Initialize();

    /* Find local processor ID and number of processors */
    me     = GA_Nodeid();
    nprocs = GA_Nnodes();
    printf("Hello world: My rank is %d on %d processes\n", me,
            nprocs);
    fflush(stdout);

    GA_Terminate();

    MPI_Finalize();
}
```

Note several features of this program. The header files ga.h and macdecls.h contain definitions of certain predefined data types and functions in the GA library, and must be included in any file with calls to GA. The GA library is initialized after the communication library is initialized (MPI_Init in this case) and is terminated before the communication library is terminated (MPI_Finalize). The remaining calls to GA all occur between the initialization and termination calls. For this simple "hello world" program, there are only two calls to identify the total number of processes and the unique process identifier.

Once GA has been initialized and some basic configuration data has been obtained, the next step is to create an actual Global Array. There are a number of ways to do this and GAs can have many different attributes including number of dimensions, sizes, data types, and data distributions. However, "simple" GAs can be created by specifying only a few attributes and, for these, a relatively compact set of functions are available. The simplest of these is NGA_Create.

```
int NGA_Create(int type, int ndim, int dims[], char *name, int chunk[])
```

This function allows the users to specify the data type, number of dimensions, and number of elements along each dimension. For most C and Fortran data types, equivalent GA data types exist (e.g., C_INT for the C data type int). The number of dimensions in the array and the number of elements in each dimension are specified using the variables ndim and dims, respectively. The array can also be given a character string name using the parameter name. The dims and chunk arrays both contain ndim elements. The chunk array can be used to control how the array is partitioned among processes. Setting an element of chunk to a positive value tells the partitioning routines in GA to not allow any local block to contain fewer than that number of elements along the corresponding dimension. This is particularly useful for disallowing GA from partitioning an array along a particular dimension. By setting the corresponding `chunk` value equal to the `dims` value, the user is guaranteed to get a partition that keeps all the values of the array along that dimension on the same process. If the user sets a value of the `chunk` array to 0 or -1, the partitioning is left up to the GA library. The return value from this function is a GA handle that can be used to reference this array in future GA operations. Any function that operates on this array will require this handle as an input argument.

The `NGA_Create` command represents the simplest way of partitioning data among processes, but there are many other options. Irregular distribution commands are available to allow users to completely specify how data is partitioned between processes and restricted arrays can provide additional options for mapping data to processes. There are also options for creating arrays with block-cyclic distributions that can be used to create more even distributions of data across processes. These are particularly useful for situations where the work in an array tends to be somewhat localized.

Once all computation using an array is complete, it must be destroyed using the following function:

```
void GA_Destroy(int g_a)
```

The argument to this function is a GA handle. The function releases the memory allocated for this array back to the system and frees up the handle for use in a new global array.

Once a global array has been created, data can be moved in and out of it from local buffers using the commands `NGA_Put` and `NGA_Get`. The `NGA_Put` command has the following syntax:

```
void NGA_Put(int g_a, int lo[], int hi[], void* buf, int ld[])
```

The first argument to the function is the global array handle; the next two arguments are arrays that indicate the low and high indices bounding the block of global array data elements into which data is being copied. Both these arrays contain `ndim` elements. The first element of the local data is given by the pointer `buf` and the data is laid out in the buffer according to the stride array `ld`. Note that `ld` contains `ndim-1` elements and the strides are arranged starting with the second slowest dimension and finishing with the fastest dimension. The pointer `buf` is assumed to point to a contiguous block of memory so users should be careful in C or C++ about allocating `void**` pointers for use as local buffers. The complement of the `NGA_Put` operation for getting data is:

```
void NGA_Get(int g_a, int lo[], int hi[], void* buf, int ld[])
```

This function can be used to move data from a global array into a local buffer. The arguments have the same meaning as NGA_Put, but the direction of data movement is reversed. Another function that is similar to NGA_Put is:

```
void NGA_Acc(int g_a, int lo[], int hi[], void* buf, int ld[], void *alpha)
```

Instead of simply overwriting the data in the block denoted by lo and hi, NGA_Acc scales the data in buf by the value alpha and then adds it to the contents of the global array. This operation is atomic, so multiple processes performing an accumulate operation on the same array element will give the same answer (modulo round-off error) irrespective of the order the operations occur in.

A typical model for using a global array is to first have all processes load data into an array. Then, once the appropriate synchronization is complete, each process grabs data from the global array to do some work locally with the data. When the local computation is complete, the outcome can be written back to the same or another global array. However, the semantics of put and get say nothing about how operations are ordered on other processes. Thus, before data put by a process is visible to other processes, appropriate synchronization needs to be performed. This can be done with the following function:

```
void GA_Sync()
```

This function acts like a barrier in the program execution. No process can return from this function before all processes have entered it. Together with an execution barrier, this function also performs an additional step of flushing all outstanding communication from the network before any process is allowed to return from it. This is sufficient to guarantee that all global arrays are in a consistent state before the calculation proceeds further.

These functions are sufficient to implement the work flow model illustrated in Figure 5.1. The following code fragment illustrates how these calls are used.

```
/* Determine values for ndim, dims_a, dims_b, chunk_a, chunk_b */
int g_a, g_b;
/* Create global arrays */
g_a = NGA_Create(C_DBL, ndim, dims_a, "array_A", chunk_a);
g_b = NGA_Create(C_DBL, ndim, dims_a, "array_A", chunk_a);
/* Perform other functions to set up calculation */
while (/* some condition is true */) {
```

```
/* Evaluate lo and hi arrays for block of data from g_a
 * and create local buffer "buf" and array of strides "ld" */
NGA_Get(g_a, lo, hi, buf, ld);
/* Do some work on the array elements in buf and evaluate
   lo and hi arrays for the location in g_b that receives
   modifications */
NGA_Put(g_b, lo, h, buf, ld);
/* Synchronize system so that g_b is in a known state */
GA_Sync();
/* Do some more stuff */
}
/* Clean up global arrays at end of calculation */
GA_Destroy(g_a);
GA_Destroy(g_b);
```

This code begins by creating some global arrays, g_a and g_b. At the start of a computational cycle, data is obtained from g_a and copied into a local buffer. The contents of buf are then modified locally and the results copied into a block of g_b. GA_Sync is called to guarantee that the contents of g_b are in a known state. After that, more operations may be performed on the data and the cycle repeats.

Additional functions are available that are crucial for allowing users to exploit locality when writing their applications. As mentioned before, GA makes a distinction between local and remote data and assumes that accessing local data is faster than accessing remote data. To determine what data is remote and what data is local, programmers can use the following function:

```
void NGA_Distribution(int g_a, int iproc, int lo[], int hi[])
```

The arrays lo and hi contain the bounding indices of the array elements held locally on process iproc. Any requests for data by process iproc that are bounded by lo and hi will not require data transfer across the network and can be expected to be relatively fast. This information can be used to increase the overall performance of applications by allowing programmers to optimize the amount of locally held data used in their computations and minimizing the amount of remote data required.

Further, if the global array data that is needed for a computation is already held locally, there may be no need for copying the data to a different buffer using get operations. Instead a pointer to the local data can be obtained using the following function:

```
void NGA_Access(int g_a, int lo[], int hi[], void *ptr, int ld[])
```

The arrays lo and hi are the bounding indices for the block of local data for which a
pointer is being requested, ptr is a pointer to the data and ld is an array of strides that
details how the data is laid out in local memory. Once the pointer, ptr, has been obtained,
local elements of the array can be directly referenced through language syntax (e.g., with
C or Fortran syntax).

The semantics of the GA access functions assume that the data is locked when the function NGA_Access is called and that other processors are blocked from accessing or modifying the data (this is not always implemented). Because of this any call to NGA_Access
should be paired with a call to one of the following functions:

```
void NGA_Release(int g_a, int lo[], int hi[])
```

or

```
void NGA_Release_update(int g_a, int lo[], int hi[])
```

If the access is read only, then NGA_Release should be called, and if the data has been
modified then NGA_Release_update should be called. Because locks are usually not
implemented, it is a good idea to not rely on these functions to avoid a data inconsistency,
and use the GA_Sync function instead.

5.4   Process Groups

GA has strong support for the use of collectives on subsets of processes, similar to the use
of subcommunicators in MPI. The equivalent concept in GA is that of a process group.
Collectives on process groups only involve the processes in the group and are ignored by
processes outside the group. In addition, global arrays themselves can be created on a
process group. This allows users the opportunity to divide large calculations into subtasks,
which are themselves parallel. This leads to multiple levels of parallelism, where the highest level of parallelism subdivides the problems into tasks, which are in turn distributed
over multiple processes. A single calculation can potentially be divided into a hierarchy of
tasks containing many levels.

The creation of a process group is straightforward and can be accomplished using the
following command:

```
int GA_Pgroup_create(int *list, int size)
```

Here `list` is an array containing the IDs of the processes in the group and `size` indicates how many processes are in the group. This function is called only by the processes in the group. It returns a handle that can be used to reference the group in other group-aware functions. Similarly, a group can be destroyed using the following function:

```
int GA_Pgroup_destroy(int p_handle)
```

Here p_handle is the handle of the process group to be destroyed. This function returns 0 if the process group is not active.

Although GA is group aware, the number of functions that have explicit group dependencies is fairly small. Collective operations, such as GA_Sync, come with group-aware counterparts (GA_Pgroup_sync) and it is possible to create global arrays themselves by using process-group versions of the create functions:

```
int NGA_Create_config(int type, int ndim, int *dims,
                      char *array_name, int *chunk, int p_handle)
```

Here p_handle is a handle to the group that the array is restricted to. An array that is bound to a process group is distributed only over processes in the group and collective operations are restricted to processes in the group. Most operations involving multiple arrays defined on different process groups will fail. The only exceptions are the GA_Copy and GA_Copy_patch functions that allow users to copy one global array to another. This can be used to copy data between arrays defined on different process groups if one group is completely contained within another.

GA also supports the concept of a default process group, which can simplify using process groups in applications with multiple levels of parallelism. The default process group is the group that the GA library assumes is in effect when executing collective operations. When a program is initialized, the default group is the world group containing all processes. This can be changed in subsequent parts of the code by using the function:

```
void GA_Pgroup_set_default(int p_handle)
```

Once this has been set, all collectives will be restricted to processes in the default group unless explicitly specified using group-aware calls. Global arrays that are created when the default group is set are automatically restricted to processes in that group. The default process group allows users to convert existing parallel code to run on process groups with minimal changes, since most operations remain the same. The following code fragment illustrates how the default process group can be used to implement a code using multiple levels of parallelism:

```
/* create subgroup p_a */
int p_a = GA_Pgroup_create(list, nproc);
GA_Pgroup_set_default(p_a)
Parallel_task(...);
GA_Pgroup_set_default(GA_Pgroup_get_world());

/* create another subgroup within p_a */
void Parallel_task(...)
{
  int p_b = GA_Pgroup_create(new_list, new_nproc);
  /* Store current default group */
  int default = GA_Pgroup_get_default();
  GA_Pgroup_set_default(p_b)
  Parallel_subtask();
  GA_Pgroup_set_default(default)
}
```

This fragment also makes use of some functions that can retrieve the handle to the world group and the current default group.

5.5 Extended Array Structures

GA has many options for laying out data within an array. These include ghost cells, block-cyclic data layouts, and data maps. Arrays created with these options are similar to conventional arrays and many of the GA operations are transparent. However, each has features that may be useful in specific instances.

Ghost cells were originally developed to support the solution of continuum partial differential equations (PDFs) on structured grids. Many PDF solvers perform a rectangular decomposition of the grid cells over processes and then need to periodically update "ghost" cells along the boundary. These cells represent values in the array on neighboring processes. The update operation that fills in the ghost cells with current values is usually highly synchronous and can therefore be optimized. GA has mechanisms for creating global arrays that are padded by a user-specified number of grid cells along each dimension. These cells can be updated via a single GA function:

```
void GA_Update_ghosts(int g_a)
```

All ghosts are updated with data from a neighboring process and periodic boundary conditions are applied to blocks at the the edges of the array. Applications can be nonperiodic but this needs to be enforced at the application level. The data in the ghost cells is invisible to most GA operations (e.g. put, get) but it can be accessed via special commands such as NGA_Access_ghosts and NGA_Get_ghost_block.

Instead of distributing data evenly using large rectangular decompositions, GA also allows users to map out data using block-cyclic distributions. Both a simple block-cyclic distribution and a ScaLAPACK-style distribution are supported [36]. Block-cyclic distributions start by allowing users to specify a block size for each global array (separate arrays can have different sized blocks). The array is decomposed into blocks, depending on the dimensions of the array and each block is mapped to a process. For a simple block-cyclic distribution, blocks are indexed in row-major order and each block is mapped to the process given by the block index modulo the number of processes. The ScaLAPACK distribution requires the user to specify a process grid where the total number of processes is equal to the number of available processes (for example, 12 processors can be decomposed into a 2×6, 4×3, 3×4, or 6×2 grid). The arrangement of blocks within the original array also forms a grid and the indices of the block within this grid are mapped to the process with same grid coordinates, after taking the modulus of each of the block indices with respect to the process grid dimensions. This data layout exactly corresponds to the layout in ScaLAPACK and thus can be used to convert global arrays to a format that can be used inside ScaLAPACK subroutines. Most GA operations are transparent with respect to these options, with the exception of calls that probe data layouts.

GA also allows users to specifically map out how the data decomposition in a global array is mapped to processes. This was originally designed to allow users to place data in a global array on a subset of processes but to allow the data to be visible to a larger set of processes.[1] A side benefit of this functionality was that it also allowed copies of arrays to be made with different mappings to processes. This has turned out to be very useful in implementing fault-resilient algorithms [283].

5.6   Support for Sparse Array Operations

Although GA was original developed to support distributed dense arrays, it has considerable utility for managing distributed sparse data structures as well. This comes about because sparse data structures are frequently stored as a collection of dense one-dimensional arrays. This is also true for unstructured systems such as irregular grids and hierarchical data trees that are also represented as a set of one-dimensional arrays with additional one-dimensional or quasi one-dimensional arrays that are used to store relations between different elements of the data structure. For example, an unstructured grid might be represented as a list of cell centers and another list of vertex elements. A third list might be an

---

1. This is different from process groups where data is only visible to processes within the group.

array of integers with one index running over the cells, and the other index running over the vertices associated with each cell. Similarly, a hierarchical data structure might consist of a list of nodes with other lists defining parental and child relations. Although the data structures themselves can be considered sparse, their representations are often dense and therefore amenable to storage using GA.

GA has several functions that are particularly useful for manipulating such data structures. The most important of these are the GA scatter and gather functions, which are generalizations of the put and get functionality discussed previously. Unlike put and get, which operate on blocks of data defined by their low and high indices, scatter and gather can move random lists of data items into and out of global arrays at arbitrary locations. The interfaces for both functions are similar, with the only significant difference between them being the direction of data movement. The function call for scatter is:

```
void NGA_Scatter(int g_a, void *v, int *subsArray[], int n)
```

The vector `v` is an array of `n` data elements containing the values that are to be moved into the global array and `subsArray` is the array of indices. The number of index sets in `subsArray` is also `n` and the number of indices in each index set is equal to the dimension of `g_a`. There is also a scatter-accumulate form of this function that can be used to add the contents of `v` to the existing values.

The gather function has essentially the same set of arguments except that `v` is the buffer that will receive values coming from the GA:

```
void NGA_Gather(int g_a, void *v, int *subsArray[], int n)
```

These two functions have many applications when dealing with sparse or unstructured data objects, primarily because there are no regular or structured access patterns in many cases. As an example, consider an unstructured grid that is distributed over many processes. Data associated with grid cells may be stored in a set of 1D GAs. Each process is home to a collection of grid cells forming an irregular, but connected, region and possibly representing a contiguous set of data in the GA. However, the ghost cells around the boundary of this domain, which are needed to update various operators defined on the grid, are located at random locations in the distributed array. The scatter and gather operations are very useful in this case for updating this data in the GA or moving this data to local buffers for use in computations.

5.7 Array Collectives

GA supports a large number of collective operations over arrays, which are useful in implementing many algorithms. These collectives include simple operations such as setting all array elements to zero, filling all elements with the same value, scaling all elements by a value, and evaluating the norm of a 1D array. Other collectives include operations that are more selective and operate on portions of an array. These include a collection of operations that can be used to manipulate or extract the the diagonal elements of a square array, operations for scaling individual rows or columns and patch versions of collectives that only act on a user-specified subdomain of the array.

GA also includes some basic linear algebra functionality, including addition and multiplication of two arrays. Multiplication subsumes both matrix-matrix and matrix-vector operations, depending on the dimensions of the arrays involved. Array multiplication is a key functionality in many high-performance computing algorithms and the routines in GA have been highly optimized for performance. Symmetrization of arrays and array transposes are also supported and are important parts of many algorithms.

5.8 Dynamic Load Balancing Idiom

GA has strong support for dynamic load balancing through the use of the read-increment capability. This is supported via the function:

```
int GA_Read_inc(int g_a, int *subscript, long inc)
```

The function will read the value in an *integer* global array at the location specified by `subscript` and then increment the value by `inc`. This operation is atomic, so only one process can perform the read-increment operation on an array element at one time. Read-increment makes it straightforward to create global counters that can be used to dynamically partition tasks in a parallel calculation. The user creates an integer global array with a single element and initializes it to zero. Individual processes can then use the `GA_Read_inc` function to read the current value of the array and increment it by one. The current value corresponds to a task index that can be decomposed into some quantity of work. When the process is finished, it calls the read-increment function again and gets the index for another task. If a process is bogged down by a task that is slow, other processes will grab work from it by making more calls to the read-increment function and executing extra tasks. This load-balancing scheme relies on the ability to define a large calculation as a series of tasks with the assumption that all processes have enough information to execute the task based on a single task index. The code for setting up a simple counter is as follows:

```
int ndim=1,dims=1,chunk=0,zero=0;
int itask;
int g_task;
/* Create global counter */
g_task = NGA_Create(C_INT, ndim, &dims, "counter", &chunk);
/* Initialize counter to zero */
NGA_Zero(g_task);
/* Get first task */
itask = GA_Read_inc(g_task, &zero, 1);
while(itask<NTASKS) {
  /* Execute task itask
      :
   */
  /* Get next task */
  itask = GA_Read_inc(g_task, &zero, 1);
}
```

5.9   Use in Applications

The main driver for developing GA was the NWChem suite. Most packages in NWChem support quantum chemistry calculations of one sort or another and these, in turn, are built around the construction and manipulation of large distributed arrays. Many calculations in quantum chemistry involve the evaluation of multi-index data objects $\langle ij|kl \rangle$, where each element is a multidimensional integral. Higher order methods can generate arrays with even more indices. Much of the work in quantum chemistry computations is focused on the generation of these data objects and this maps very nicely to the GA programming model. The array can be decomposed into a large number of blocks. Data for those blocks can be accessed easily by any process using the put/get semantics and the task of constructing the blocks themselves can be distributed over processes using the dynamic load balancing constructs available in GA.

GA has also been used to parallelize the Subsurface Transport Over Multiple Phases (STOMP) [291, 290] code. This effort made extensive use of the support for ghosts cells in GA to implement neighbor exchanges of data. In addition, global arrays were also used for many I/O routines in this code. The TETHYS hydrodynamic simulation code [240] is also built around GA and implements calculations on unstructured meshes. It uses the gather-scatter functionality in GA to implement neighbor exchanges of data. Both STOMP and TETHYS use the PETSc libraries, based on traditional MPI, for their solvers and matrix/vector data structures so they are good examples of applications in which both GA and MPI are used for communication.

Another significant application of GA is the GridPACK[TM] framework for creating simulations of the electric power grid [227]. Power grid networks are represented as distributed graphs and the scatter-gather functionality can be used to exchange data between graph elements on different processes. Power grid engineers are very interested in contingency-type calculations that consist of multiple calculations of different scenarios. These calculations can make use of the dynamic load-balancing capabilities supported by GA. In addition, GridPACK™ also makes extensive use of the solvers and distributed sparse matrix functionality in PETSc, so it is another example of a mixed GA/MPI code.

6 Chapel

Bradford L. Chamberlain, Cray Inc.

Chapel is an emerging parallel language designed for productive parallel computing at scale. Chapel originated as part of Cray Inc.'s participation in the DARPA High Productivity Computing Systems (HPCS) program, which ran from 2002–2012. At present, Chapel development is focused on transforming the research prototype produced under HPCS into a production-grade implementation. Cray leads the effort of designing and developing Chapel, in collaboration with members of the research and open-source communities.

Chapel supports a multithreaded execution model, permitting the expression of far more general and dynamic styles of computation than the typical single-threaded Single Program, Multiple Data (SPMD) programming models that became dominant in the 1990's. Chapel is designed such that higher-level abstractions, such as those supporting data parallelism, can be built in terms of lower-level concepts in the language, permitting the user to select between various levels of abstraction or control as necessitated by their algorithm or its performance requirements.

This chapter provides a brief introduction to Chapel, starting with a condensed history of the project (Section 6.1). It then describes Chapel's motivating themes (Section 6.2), followed by a survey of its main features (Section 6.3), and a summary of the project's status and future work (Chapter 6.4).

6.1 A Brief History of Chapel

6.1.1 Inception

DARPA's HPCS program was launched in 2002 with five teams, each led by a hardware vendor: Cray Inc., Hewlett-Packard, IBM, SGI, and Sun. The program challenged the teams to develop technologies that would improve the productivity of HPC users in terms of performance, portability, programmability, and robustness. The vendors were encouraged to reconsider all aspects of their system stack with the goal of delivering technologies that would be revolutionary and distinct from their established roadmap. Along with changes to their processor, memory, and network architectures, the vendor teams also proposed new and enhanced software technologies, including novel programming languages.

In 2003, the HPCS program transitioned to phase II, and a programmatic downselect occurred, enabling the Cray, IBM, and Sun teams to pursue their proposed research plans. At the outset of this phase, the initial designs of the new programming languages began to emerge, with the Cray team pursuing the Chapel language, IBM starting work on X10 [76, 246], and Sun (later acquired by Oracle) developing Fortress [10].

Cray's HPCS project was named *Cascade* after the prominent mountain range just east of its corporate headquarters in Seattle. The project was led by Burton Smith, Chief Scientist of Cray at the time. Though he believed that existing HPC programming models were a productivity limiter for high-end systems, Burton was initially hesitant to pursue a new programming language under HPCS, due to skepticism about whether languages designed by lone hardware vendors could be successful. He soon reconsidered this position, however, after an enumeration of well-established programming languages in both HPC and mainstream computing revealed that most of them had originally been developed by a single hardware vendor. In most cases, the key to a language's long-term success involved a transition to a broader, more community-oriented model at an appropriate point in its life cycle. In January–February 2003, the Cascade team announced its intention to pursue a new language at various HPCS reviews and meetings. Work on Chapel began in earnest that year under the leadership of David Callahan.

The Chapel language took its name as an approximate acronym for *Cascade High Productivity Language*, coined by Callahan. The team generally felt lukewarm-to-negative about the name, in large part due to its possible religious implications. However, nobody came up with a preferable alternative quickly enough, and the name stuck. When asked about it, team members would occasionally quip, "We'll wait until we've gotten the language to a point that we're thoroughly happy with it and then switch to a truly great name."

6.1.2   Initial Directions

Chapel's initial design was shaped primarily by four people who set the language on the path that it continues to follow today: David Callahan, its chief architect from Cray Inc.; Hans Zima, an academic partner within the Cascade program representing CalTech/JPL; Brad Chamberlain, a recent graduate from the ZPL project at the University of Washington; and John Plevyak, an independent contractor who joined the Chapel project in late 2003, bringing with him a strong background in iterative flow analysis and type inference [233].

To a great extent, Chapel's feature set reflects a combination of the backgrounds of these four initial architects: David Callahan established the overall vision for the language and, from his extensive experience with the Tera MTA (Multi-Threaded Architecture), brought the notion of a general, multithreaded execution model with lightweight, data-centric synchronization [11]. Hans Zima was a founding contributor to the High Performance Fortran (HPF) language in the 1990s, and brought with him the lessons learned from that high-profile endeavor [161]. Brad Chamberlain's dissertation focused on the benefits of supporting first-class index set concepts in parallel languages [65], so he contributed an alternative model for data parallelism with the goal of improving upon the array abstractions supported by HPF and ZPL. And finally, John Plevyak's experience filled an expertise gap in the group that Callahan correctly believed would be crucial for the language's success—supporting static type inference with the goal of making parallel programming more productive, particularly as a means of supporting generic functions and classes.

With this combined background, the initial team set off to define Chapel. Much of the early brainstorming was guided by explorations of parallel computations that had posed challenges for previous parallel languages. Examples included finite element methods, fast multipole methods, connected components algorithms, n-body simulations, and the like. Draft codes and documents to explain them were circulated, punctuated by marathon design summits where the virtues and flaws of various options were debated, often passionately and at length. In the fall of 2004, David Callahan took on the task of writing an initial draft of the language specification, which served as a straw man for subsequent debate, refinement, and implementation. With that, the Chapel project was off and running.

6.1.3 Phases of Development under HPCS

The Chapel project's history during the course of HPCS can be thought of as falling into three distinct periods: For the first period, from 2003 to early 2006, the project was in a molten state, with team members splashing around and trying to construct a common vision of the language that they could all agree upon and conceivably implement. This period saw the first publication describing Chapel [57], as well as the formation of the initial development team who would get Chapel up and running.

The second period, from 2006–2008, marks the timeframe in which both Chapel's design and the compiler architecture began stabilizing [66], permitting a number of milestones to be achieved at regular intervals: In April 2006, task-parallel Chapel codes were run for the first time. In December 2006, the first release was made available to external users and evaluation teams on a by-request basis. July 2007 saw the execution of the first distributed-memory task-parallel programs. In June 2008, the first data-parallel constructs started working, and by September 2008, the first distributed-memory data-parallel codes were executing. During this period the core Chapel development team at Cray kept their heads tucked down, to move the implementation along as far and fast as possible.

The third period, from 2008–2012, constitutes the time when the Chapel team began to increasingly look outward in an attempt to attract users to Chapel and get feedback on its design and implementation. During these years, Chapel moved to a SourceForge-based open-source control repository, switched to a public release mechanism, started supporting early users, and established a number of collaborations with academics, lab staff, and members of industry outside of Cray. The Chapel team also stepped up its level of outreach during this period, particularly in terms of giving tutorials on Chapel in forums like the annual SC conference series and PRACE community events. All the while, improvements were made to the implementation to flesh out missing features and boost performance in order to make progress and retain the interest of early users.

6.1.4 Life After HPCS

At the time of publication, the Chapel project remains an active and ongoing effort. By the end of the HPCS program in late 2012, Chapel had successfully achieved its programmatic requirements and, more importantly, had sparked substantial interest among HPC users. As a result, the Cray team embarked on a five-year effort to improve Chapel from the research prototype that was developed under HPCS to a production-grade implementation [69]. The goals of this effort are: to improve Chapel's performance and scalability; to address immature aspects of the language; to port Chapel to emerging node architectures involving deeper memory hierarchies and heterogeneous processors; to improve its interoperability features; to nurture the Chapel user and developer communities; and to explore the transition of Chapel's governance to a neutral body external to Cray.

   With this overview of Chapel's history in mind, we now move on to describe some of the motivating themes and concerns that helped shape Chapel's design.

6.2 Chapel's Motivating Themes

To understand Chapel's features, it can be helpful to understand the themes that influenced what would or would not be included in the language. In this section, we provide an overview of these themes to establish a framework for the language features described in Section 6.3.

6.2.1 Express General Parallelism

One of the first and most important themes in Chapel is the concept of supporting general parallel programming. In particular, Chapel's goal is to be a language in which users will never hit a point where they conclude "Well, that was fun while I was trying to do x and y; but now that I want to do z, I'll have to go back to using MPI," (or whatever technology they had been using). This approach is in strong contrast to the host of parallel languages from the 1990s that focused on a specific type of parallelism, to the exclusion of other styles—e.g., HPF and ZPL's overriding focus on data-parallelism to the detriment of task-parallelism and nested parallelism. Chapel's founders believed that while focusing on a single style of parallelism was a prudent approach for an academic project, for a new language to truly be adopted within a field as diverse as HPC, it had to support a wide variety of computational styles.

To this end, Chapel was designed with features to support data parallelism, cooperative task parallelism, and synchronization-based concurrent programming. In addition, these styles were designed so that they could be composed arbitrarily to support nested parallelism.

In addition to permitting diverse styles of parallelism, Chapel was also designed to support general granularities of parallelism, both in the user's program and the target hardware. In practice, algorithms tend to contain parallelism at multiple levels: computational models, function calls, loop iterations, and even individual statements or expressions. Meanwhile, modern hardware typically supports parallelism across multiple machines or cabinets, network nodes, and processor cores, as well as vector operations that support parallelism in the instruction set. Most conventional parallel programming models target only a subset of these software and hardware granularities, and often just one. As a result, programmers must use hybrid programming models that mix multiple concepts and notations in order to take full advantage of all available parallelism in their algorithm and hardware. For example, a parallel program wanting to take full advantage of a petascale system today might use MPI to express executable-level parallelism across the nodes, OpenMP (Chapter 12) to express loop or task parallelism across the processor cores, and CUDA (Chapter 15), OpenCL (Chapter 16), or OpenACC [1] to offload parallel kernels to an accelerator. In contrast, Chapel strives to support the expression of all parallelism in a user's program while targeting all available hardware parallelism with a single, unified set of language concepts.

6.2.2 Support a Multithreaded Execution Model

At the time of Chapel's inception, like today, most of the deployed distributed-memory programming languages and notations exposed programming and execution models based on single-threaded cooperating executables, with SPMD models as a particularly common case. The Chapel team attributes much of the lack of productivity and generality within HPC programming to this restriction since it forces users to take a process-centric view of their computation rather than describing and orchestrating the parallelism as a whole.

Chapel chose instead to adopt a multithreaded execution model in which each process will typically be composed of multiple threads. Users express parallelism within their programs in terms of *tasks* that represent units of computation that can, and should, execute in parallel. These tasks are then executed by the threads, potentially creating additional tasks, either within the same process or a remote one. The result is a programming and execution model that is far more dynamic and general than traditional single-threaded SPMD models.

6.2.3   Enable Global-View Programming

Another way in which Chapel diverges from most adopted HPC notations is by supporting what its designers refer to as a *global view* of data structures and control flow. The concept is to move away from requiring computations on distributed data structures, like arrays, to be expressed in terms of the subarrays owned by each process, as is typical in conventional approaches like MPI or Fortran 2008's *co-arrays*. Instead, the programmer can declare and compute on distributed data structures as they would for a completely local version. Such variables are referred to as *global-view data structures* since they can be declared using a global problem size and accessed using global indices rather than via per-processor extents and local indices. Since large-scale programs are almost always data-intensive, Chapel also supports a wide variety of global-view array types, including multidimensional rectangular arrays, sparse arrays, associative arrays, and unstructured arrays.

Chapel's *global view of control* refers to the fact that a Chapel program begins executing using a single task and then introduces parallelism through the use of additional language constructs. This is in contrast to SPMD programming models in which users write their program with the assumption that multiple copies of main() will execute simultaneously.

It is important to note that while previous languages, like HPF and ZPL, also supported global-view concepts, they did not provide a rich means of escaping these abstractions in order to exert more control over execution details. Recognizing that high-level abstraction is not ideal for every scenario, Chapel was designed such that users could selectively avoid using global-view abstractions and drop down to more explicit local-view constructs. As a specific example, Chapel programmers can choose to write traditional single-threaded SPMD programs using manually-distributed data structures, and even message passing, if they so choose. In summary, providing a global view of computation for programmability should not preclude the expression of more explicit parallelism, since having a greater degree of control can also play a crucial role in productivity.

6.2.4   Build on a Multiresolution Design

The previous section's notion of programming at higher levels of abstraction or greater degrees of control as needed is part of what Chapel refers to as its *multiresolution design philosophy*. The idea is to have the language support higher- and lower-level features, permitting the user to benefit from abstractions like global-view arrays when appropriate, while still being able to do more explicit low-level programming when desired or necessary. Moreover, Chapel was designed such that its higher-level abstractions are implemented in terms of the lower-level ones. This ensures that they are all compatible, permitting users to mix and match between different levels arbitrarily.

As a specific example, Chapel's data-parallel loops and global-view arrays are higher-level features that are implemented in terms of its lower-level features like task-parallelism and explicit control over locality. Another example of a multiresolution feature is Chapel's support for *hierarchical locale models*, which permit advanced users to specify how Chapel is mapped to a target architecture by creating classes representing the processors and memories of a system's compute nodes. The user implements tasking and memory interfaces for these classes which are targeted by the compiler.

6.2.5 Enable Control over Locality

Because Chapel was designed to execute on large-scale systems where locality and affinity are crucial for performance, locality is considered a core concept in Chapel along with parallelism. Chapel's locality features provide control over where data values are stored and where tasks execute so that users can ensure parallel computations execute near the variables they access, or vice-versa.

Chapel supports a Partitioned Global Address Space (PGAS) memory model [288] in which a user's code can refer to any lexically visible variable regardless of whether it is stored in a local or remote memory. If the variable is remote, the compiler and runtime are responsible for implementing the communication that is required to load or store the variable over the network. Users can reason about the location of a variable statically using Chapel semantics, or dynamically using a variety of execution-time queries.

Chapel supports expression of locality using distinct language concepts from those used to introduce parallelism. This contrasts sharply with SPMD programming models in which each copy of the executable serves as both the unit of parallelism and of locality for the program. By separating these concerns into two distinct feature sets, Chapel permits programmers to introduce additional parallelism within a single process, or to execute code on a distinct compute node without introducing parallelism. This orthogonal design results in a clean, natural separation between parallelism ("what should run simultaneously?") and locality ("where should it run?").

6.2.6 Support Data-Centric Synchronization

Another motivating theme in Chapel is the expression of synchronization in a data-centric manner. This has two primary benefits. The first is that by associating synchronization constructs with variables, the locality of the abstraction is well-defined since each variable has a specific location on the target machine. The second is that since most synchronization is designed to guard access to data structures or values, combining the synchronization constructs with the variables being accessed typically results in a more elegant expression of the algorithm.

6.2.7   Establish Roles for Users vs. the Compiler

Chapel has been designed so that the responsibility of identifying parallelism and managing locality rests on the user rather than the compiler. Although Chapel is often characterized (correctly) as being a large and feature-rich language, it was intentionally designed to avoid reliance on heroic compilation or promises that the compiler would automatically manage everything for the user. To this end, Chapel was designed to avoid relying on the compiler to introduce parallelism and manage locality. While nothing in the language precludes an aggressive compiler from performing such transformations automatically, such technology is not expected of a Chapel compiler (and conversely, identifying parallelism and locality *is* expected from users).

Owing to its PGAS nature, one of the main roles of the compiler (and runtime libraries) is to implement the global namespace in a manner that transparently and efficiently transfers data values between their stored location and the tasks that reference them. This communication management forms the Chapel compiler's biggest role, along with traditional compiler concerns of scalar code generation and optimization.

Chapel's multiresolution design also serves to distinguish between different user roles. For example, a parallel programming expert can work at lower levels of the language, implementing parallel loop schedules and distributed data structures that can then be used by an applied scientist who does not need to be exposed to all of the implementation details. Chapel's user-defined *domain maps* are a key example of this philosophy.

6.2.8   Close the Gap Between Mainstream and HPC Languages

When polling students about which programming languages they are most familiar and productive with, responses typically focus on modern languages like Python, Java, and Matlab, along with experience with C and C++ from those who have worked in more systems-oriented areas. Meanwhile, the HPC community uses Fortran, C, and C++ almost exclusively along with technologies like MPI and OpenMP with which most students have no experience. Part of Chapel's goal for improving productivity is to narrow this gap in order to make better use of the graduating workforce while also leveraging productivity advances enjoyed by mainstream programmers.

To this end, the Chapel design team selected features and themes in productive mainstream languages and sought ways of incorporating them into a language suitable for HPC programming. In doing so, the goal was to support features that would neither undermine the goal of scalable performance nor alienate traditional HPC programmers.

Chapel's type inference capability is an example of a mainstream language feature that was customized to support good performance. Chapel chose to support type inference in order to give users the ability to quickly prototype code and benefit from polymorphism in a manner similar to scripting languages like Python and Matlab. However, unlike most scripting languages, Chapel's type inference is implemented in the compiler, resulting in a fixed static type for each variable in order to avoid the overheads of dynamic typing at execution time. The use of type inference is completely optional in Chapel so that programmers who prefer using explicitly-typed languages (e.g., for clarity or robustness in library interfaces) can still program in a more traditional style.

Chapel's object-oriented programming (OOP) capabilities are an example of a mainstream feature that was included in a manner that would keep it palatable to more traditional HPC programmers. In Chapel's early years, the design team spoke with HPC programmers who would offer opinions like "I'm simply not accustomed to using object-oriented features. If I had to rewrite my code in an object-oriented style it would create a lot of work for me because it's not how I've been trained to think." To this end, Chapel supports object-oriented features for all of the productivity and modularity benefits that they provide, yet intentionally avoids basing the language on a pure object-oriented paradigm (as with Smalltalk or Java) so that C and Fortran programmers can opt to ignore the OOP features and write more traditional block-structured imperative code.

6.2.9 Start From Scratch (but Strive for Familiarity)

The decision Chapel's designers made that has probably been called into question most often was the choice to design Chapel from a blank slate rather than as an extension to an existing language. There are many reasons why Chapel took this approach; perhaps the simplest is that all adopted languages carry with them a certain amount of baggage which reflects their original goals of supporting something other than general, large-scale parallel computing. As a result, most extension-based parallel languages tend to be a subset of a superset of a sequential language, making them incompatible with preexisting source code. Moreover, such languages still require a significant learning curve from users who must not only learn the new features that have been added, but also remember which ones have changed. The Chapel team's attitude is that the intellectual effort involved in learning a new parallel language stems primarily from learning the semantics of its parallel constructs, not their syntax. Thus, starting from scratch and designing features that express those new semantics as clearly as possible can have great value when compared to trying to force them into a language that was not originally designed with parallelism in mind.

That said, Chapel has also tried to avoid inventing concepts simply for the sake of it. In designing Chapel, the team studied successful (and unsuccessful) languages in order to learn from them, selecting features that would work well together. Chapel's primary influences include C, Modula, Fortran, C++, Java, C#, CLU [180], Scala [219], ML [134],

Perl, Matlab, ZPL [70, 255], HPF [161], and the Cray MTA™/XMT™ extensions to C and Fortran [241].

Chapel's developers believe that in order to preserve the community's investment in legacy applications and libraries, it is more important to interoperate with existing languages than to extend them. To that end, Chapel directly supports interoperability with C, and has also worked with the Babel project at Lawrence Livermore National Laboratory to support a greater number of languages [234], including Fortran, Java, and Python.

The Chapel team likes to joke that they chose not to extend an existing language in order to offend all user communities equally rather than favoring one at the risk of alienating others. Joking aside, one of the encouraging results of Chapel's approach is that users from diverse language backgrounds—Fortran, C, Java, Python—have described Chapel as being familiar. That so many users find aspects of Chapel that are familiar and comfortable to them, while considering others an improvement over what they are used to, is an indication that the melting pot approach taken by Chapel can help with adoption rather than hindering it.

6.2.10   Shoot for the Moon

Another early criticism of Chapel was that the project bit off more than it could hope to complete under HPCS funding alone. This observation accurately reflects the team's intention. Chapel's founders believed that a truly successful, general parallel language would need to be very broad in its feature set and would need to involve a larger community than simply the Cray Chapel team. To this end, many of the original features were intentionally open research topics as a means of striving for a more productive solution and encouraging collaborations with the broader community. Examples of such features include user-defined data distributions (which are supported today), distributed software transactional memory (which resulted in collaborative research [44, 256] that never made it back into the master branch), and distributed garbage collection (which has not been pursued significantly, due to a lack of interested collaborators combined with a growing sense of skepticism about its value to Chapel).

6.2.11   Develop Chapel as Portable, Open-Source Software

The final theme in this discussion is the choice to develop and release Chapel as portable, open-source software. This decision was made primarily due to the fact that it is nearly impossible to get any new parallel language broadly adopted, let alone one that is not freely and generally available. Making the project open-source has also lowered barriers to involving external collaborators and helps potential users be less wary about what might happen if support for Chapel ends. As a result, the Chapel project is being developed as a GitHub project,[1] and it is implemented and released under the Apache License, version 2.0.[2]

The portability of Chapel—both in terms of the compiler and its generated code—was also considered strategically crucial since nobody would adopt a language that only runs on systems from a single vendor. Moreover, making Chapel's implementation portable permits users to develop parallel programs on their desktops and laptops, and then move them to large-scale machines as the programs mature and resources become available. In order to maximize portability, the Chapel compiler has been developed in ISO C++ and generates ISO C99. All parallelism in Chapel is implemented using POSIX threads, and all communication can be implemented using the portable GASNet communication library's support for one-sided communication and active messages (Chapter 2). As a result of this approach, Chapel runs on most parallel systems, whether custom or commodity.

In Summary. The themes in this section have been crucial to defining the Chapel language and setting it apart from most conventional and competitive technologies. Readers who are interested in more detailed coverage of Chapel's motivating themes and philosophies are referred to various online blog articles [64, 63]. The following sections provide an overview of Chapel's main features, which have been designed with these themes in mind.

6.3   Chapel Feature Overview

This section gives an introduction to Chapel's primary features in order to provide an overview of the language. By necessity, this description only presents a subset of Chapel's features and semantics. For a more complete treatment of the language, the reader is referred to the Chapel language specification [89], materials on the Chapel website,[3] and examples from the Chapel release.[4] This section begins with the base language features and then moves on to those used to control parallelism and locality.

---

1. https://github.com/chapel-lang/chapel (note that the Chapel repository was previously hosted by SourceForge and the University of Washington).
2. http://www.apache.org/licenses/LICENSE-2.0.html (note that earlier versions of Chapel were released under the BSD and MIT licenses).
3. http://chapel.cray.com
4. Located in $CHPL_HOME/examples

6.3.1 Base Language Features

Chapel's base language can be thought of as the set of features that are unrelated to parallel programming and scalable computing—essentially, the sequential language on which Chapel is based. As mentioned in Section 6.2.9, Chapel was designed from scratch rather than by extending an existing language, and the base language can be thought of as those features that were considered important for productivity and for supporting user-specification of advanced language features within Chapel itself. Overall, the base language is quite large, so this section focuses on features that are philosophically important or useful for understanding Chapel code in subsequent sections.

Syntax. Chapel's syntax was designed to resemble C's in many respects, due to the fact that so many adopted languages at the time tended to utilize C syntax to greater or lesser degrees. Like C, Chapel statements are separated by semicolons, and compound statements are defined using curly brackets. Most Chapel operators follow C's lead, with some additional operators added; Chapel's conditionals and while-loops are based on C's; and so forth.

In other areas Chapel departs from C, typically to improve upon it in terms of generality or productivity. One of Chapel's main syntactic departures can be seen in its declarations which use more of a Modula-style left-to-right, keyword-based approach. For example, the following declarations declare a type alias, a variable, and a procedure in Chapel:

```
type eltType = complex;    // 'eltType' is an alias for the complex type

var done: bool = true;     // 'done' is a boolean variable, initialized to 'true'

proc abs(x: int): int {    // a procedure to compute the absolute value of 'x'
  if (x < 0) then
    return -x;
  else
    return x;
}
```

In this example, the `type` keyword introduces a new type identifier, `var` introduces a new variable, and `proc` introduces a new procedure, as noted in the comments. Other declaration keywords are used to create compile-time constants (`param`), run-time constants (`const`), iterators (`iter`), and modules that support namespace management (`module`).

Chapel uses the left-to-right declaration style in part because it better supports type inference and *skyline arrays*—arrays whose elements are themselves arrays of varying size. In addition, adopting a left-to-right declaration style aids productivity by making declarations easier for a nonexpert to read.

Basic Types. Chapel's basic scalar types include boolean values (`bool`), signed and unsigned integers (`int` and `uint`), real and imaginary floating point values (`real` and `imag`), complex values (`complex`), and strings (`string`). All of Chapel's numeric types use 64-bit values by default, though users can override this choice by explicitly specifying a bit width. For example, `uint(8)` would specify an 8-bit unsigned integer. All types in Chapel have a default value that is used to initialize variables that the user has not initialized. Numeric values default to zeroes, booleans to false, and strings to empty strings.

Chapel supports record and class types, each of which supports the creation of objects with member variables and methods. Records are declared using the `record` keyword and result in local memory allocation. Classes are declared using the `class` keyword and use heap-allocated storage. Records support value semantics while classes support reference semantics. For example, assigning between variables of record type will result in a copy of the record members by default. In contrast, assigning between variables of class type results in the two variables aliasing a single object. Records can be thought of as being similar to C++ structs while classes are similar to Java classes.

Chapel also supports tuple types that permit a collection of values to be bundled in a lightweight manner. Tuples are useful for creating functions that generate multiple values, as an alternative to adopting the conventional approach of returning one value directly and the others through output arguments. Chapel also uses tuples as the indices for multi-dimensional arrays, supporting a rank-independent programming style. The following code illustrates some simple uses of tuples in practice:

```
var t: (int, real) = (1, 2.3);    // a tuple 't' with int and real components

var (i, r) = t;                   // de−tuple 't' into new variables 'i' and 'r'

...t(1)...                        // refer to 't's first (integer) component

var coord: (real, real, real),    // a homogeneous 3−tuple of reals
    coord2: 3*real;               // an equivalent way to declare coord
```

Range and Array Types. Another built-in type in Chapel is the *range*, used to represent a regular sequence of integer values. For example, the range "`1..n`" represents the integers between 1 and n inclusive, while "`0..`" represents all of the nonnegative integers. Chapel's ranges tend to be used to control loops, and also to declare and operate on arrays. Ranges support a number of operators including intersection (`[]`), counting (`#`), striding (`by`), and setting the alignment of a strided range (`align`). The following Chapel code illustrates some range values and operators:

```
1..9                    // represents  1, 2, 3,  ..., 9
1..9 by 2               // represents  1, 3, 5, 7, 9
1..9 by -1              // represents  9, 8, 7,  ..., 1
9..1                    // represents  an empty range
1..9 # 3                // represents  1, 2, 3
1..9 # -3               // represents  7, 8, 9
(1..9)[6.. by 2]        // represents  6, 8
lo..hi by 2 align 1     // represents  the odd integers  between 'lo' and 'hi' ( inclusive )
0..#n                   // represents  0, 1, 2,  ..., n−1 (the first 'n' elements in 0..)
```

Chapel has extensive support for arrays, described in greater detail in Section 6.3.3. However, to introduce the concept, the following declarations create three array variables.

```
var Hist: [-3..3] int,          // a 1D array of integers
    Mat: [0..#n, 0..#n] complex,  // a 2D array of complexes
    Tri: [i in 1..n] [1..i] real;  // a 'triangular' skyline array
```

The first example declares a 1D array, *Hist*, whose indices range from -3 to 3, and whose elements are integers. The second declaration creates a 2D $n \times n$ array of complex values, *Mat*, which uses 0-based indexing. The final example is a 1D skyline array named *Tri* that uses 1-based indexing. Each of *Tri*'s elements is a 1-based 1D array of reals whose length is equal to its index in the outer array. This essentially creates a "triangular" array of arrays.

Type Inference.   Chapel supports type inference as a means of writing code that is both concise and flexible. For example, the type specifier of a variable or constant declaration can be elided when an initialization expression is provided. In such cases, the Chapel compiler infers the type of the identifier to be that of the initialization expression. The following code illustrates some examples:

```
param pi = 3.1415;        // '3.1415' is a real, so 'pi' is too
var count = 0;            // '0' is an integer, so 'count' is too
const perim = 2*pi*r;     // if 'r' is a real/complex, 'perim' will be too
var len = computeLen();   // 'len' is whatever type computeLen() returns
```

The first two declarations are fairly straightforward—the type of each initializing literal expression is well-defined by Chapel (`real` and `int`, respectively), so the identifiers being declared have matching type. In the third line, *perim*'s type is based on the type resulting from multiplying r by an integer and a real. If r were a `real`, *perim* would be a `real`; if it were a `complex`, *perim* would be a `complex`; etc. In the final line, *len* will be whatever type the procedure `computeLen()` returns. Note that these final two forms have the advantage of making these declarations flexible with respect to changes in the types of *r* and `computeLen()` at the cost of making the declarations a little less self-documenting—a reader would need to know the types of *r* and `computeLen()` in order to determine the types of *perim* and *len*.

Chapel's type inference also applies to function declarations: a function's argument and return types may be omitted. Omitted argument types are inferred by the compiler by inspecting the function's callsites and adopting the types of the corresponding actual arguments. Such function declarations are generic, and the compiler will create distinct instantiations of the routine for each unique callsite type signature, resulting in a capability much like C++'s template functions. If a function's return type is omitted, it is inferred by unifying the types of the expressions generated by its `return` statements.

As a simple example, consider the `abs()` function shown previously, but written in its type-inferred form:

```
proc abs(x) {          // 'x's type and the return type of abs() will be inferred
  if (x < 0) then
    return -x;
  else
    return x;
}
```

In this version of `abs()`, the formal argument *x* has no type specifier, and no return type is given. As a result, `abs()` may be called with any type that supports less-than comparison against integers and the unary negation operator—e.g., integers, floating point values, or any user-defined type that supports these operators. The compiler infers the return type of `abs()` by noting that both of the returned expressions have the same type[5] as *x*, in which case the return type will match the argument type. If the function is called within a user's program as `abs(3)` and `abs(4.5)`, the compiler would create both `int` and `real` instantiations of `abs()`.

For-loops and Iterators.   Chapel's for-loops are different from C's, both syntactically and semantically. In Chapel, for-loops are used to iterate over data structures and to invoke iterator functions. Chapel's for-loops declare *iteration variables* that represent the values yielded by the *iterand expression*. These variables are local to a single iteration of the loop's body. The following statements demonstrate some simple for-loops:

---

5. . . . assuming that unary negative preserves *x*'s type—if not, the compiler will attempt to find a unifying type that supports both returned expressions and throw an error if it cannot.

```
for i in 1..n do        // print 1, 2, 3, ..., n
  writeln(i);

for elem in Mat do      // double all elements in 'Mat'
  elem *= 2;
```

The first loop iterates over the range "1..n", referring to the individual integer values using the iteration variable *i*. Each iteration of the loop's body gets its own private local copy of *i*, so it cannot be used to carry values across distinct iterations. In addition, a range's iteration variables are constant, and therefore may not be reassigned within the loop body.

The second loop iterates over the *Mat* array, referring to its elements using the iteration variable *elem*, which is once again local and private to the loop body. When iterating over an array, the iteration variable refers to the array's elements; thus, assignments to it will modify the array's values. Here, the loop has the effect of iterating over all of the array's values, doubling each one.

Chapel loops can also be used to iterate over multiple iterands in a lockstep manner, known as *zippered iteration*. As an example, the following loop iterates over the elements of *Hist* and the unbounded range "1.." in a zippered manner:

```
for (elem, i) in zip(Hist, 1..) do
  writeln("Element #", i, " of Hist is: ", elem);
```

In addition to looping over standard data types, Chapel programmers can write their own iterator functions that can be used to drive for-loops. As a simple example, the following declaration creates an iterator which generates the first *n* elements of the Fibonacci sequence:

```
iter fib(n) {              // generates 'n' Fibonacci numbers
  var current = 0,         // 'current' and 'next' store two consecutive values
      next = 1;            //    from the sequence

  for i in 1..n {
    yield current;         // yield the current value
    current += next;       // increment it by the next
    current <=> next;      // swap the two values
  }
}
```

Iterator functions generate results for their callsites using *yield* statements. For example, in the Fibonacci iterator above, each iteration yields its value of *current* back to the callsite.

Execution continues after the yield statement until the iterator returns (either via a `return` statement or by falling out of the function).

Iterator functions are typically invoked using for-loops. For example, the following loop would print out the first *n* Fibonacci numbers:

```
for (i,f) in zip(1..n, fib(n)) do
  writeln("fib(", i, ") = ", f);
```

In this example, the iteration variable *f* takes on the values generated by `fib()`'s yield statements.

Iterators were included in Chapel for their benefit in abstracting loop-nest implementation details away from the loops themselves, providing reuse and customization benefits similar to what traditional functions do for straight-line code. While new users often worry that iterators may incur unnecessary performance overheads, it is important to note that most iterators, like the Fibonacci example above, can be implemented simply by inlining the iterator's body into the loop invocation and then replacing the `yield` statement with the loop body.

Other Base Language Features.   In addition to the features described here, Chapel's base language also supports a number of additional constructs, including: enumerated types and type unions; type queries; configuration variables that support command-line options for overriding their default values; function and operator overloading and disambiguation; default argument values and keyword-based argument passing; meta-programming features for compile-time computation and code transformation; modules for namespace management; and I/O to files, strings, memory, and general data streams.

6.3.2   Task Parallelism

As alluded to in Section 6.2.2, all parallelism in Chapel is ultimately implemented using *tasks*—units of computation that can and should be executed in parallel. All Chapel programs begin with a single task that initializes the program's modules and executes the user's `main()` procedure. This section provides an overview of Chapel's features for creating tasks and synchronizing between them.

Unstructured Task Parallelism.   The simplest way to create a task in Chapel is by prefixing a statement with the `begin` keyword. This creates a new task that will execute the statement and then terminate. Meanwhile, the original task goes on to execute the statements that follow. As a trivial example, the following code uses a `begin` statement to create a task to execute the compound statement while the original task continues with the `writeln()` that follows it.

```
writeln("The original task prints this");
begin {
  writeln("A second task will be created to print this");
  computeSomething();              // it will then compute something
  writeln("The second task will terminate after printing this");
}
writeln("The original task may print this as the second task runs");
```

Because the two tasks in this example can execute concurrently, the final `writeln()` could be printed before the second and third `writeln()`s, between them, or after them, depending on how the tasks are scheduled.

Tasks in Chapel are anonymous, so there is no way to name a task directly. The two ways in which a user can check for task completion are through the `sync` statement or by coordinating through shared synchronization variables, described below.

The Sync Statement. Chapel's `sync` keyword prefixes a statement and causes the task encountering it to wait for all tasks created within the statement's dynamic scope to complete before proceeding. As an example, the use of the `sync` statement in the following code will wait for all the tasks generated by a recursive binary tree traversal to complete before the original task continues.

```
sync { traverseTree(root); }
writeln("All tasks created by traverseTree() must now be done");

proc traverseTree(node) {
  processNode(node);

  if (node.left != nil) then           // If there is a left child ...
    begin traverseTree(node.left);     // ... create a task to visit it

  if (node.right != nil) then          // Ditto for the right child ...
    begin traverseTree(node.right);
}
```

As can be seen, the `sync` statement is a big hammer. For finer-grain interactions between tasks, programmers can use special variable types that support data-centric coordination—Chapel's synchronization and atomic variable types—described in the following sections.

Synchronization Variables. A Chapel *synchronization variable* is like a normal variable, except that in addition to storing its value, it also stores a *full/empty state* that is used to guard reads and writes. As mentioned in Section 6.1.2, this concept was adopted from the similar Tera MTA and Cray XMT features [11, 241]. By default, a read of a synchronization variable blocks until the variable is full, reads the value, and leaves the variable in the empty state. Similarly, a write blocks until the variable is empty, writes the new value, and then leaves it full.

As a simple example, the following code implements a bounded-buffer producer/consumer idiom using an array of synchronization variables to implement the buffer:

```
1   var buff$: [0..#buffsize] sync real;

3   begin producer(numUpdates);    // create a task to run the producer
4   consumer();                    // while the original task runs the consumer

6   proc producer(numUpdates) {
7     var writeloc = 0;
8     for i in 1..numUpdates {
9       buff$[writeloc] = nextVal();   // this write blocks until 'empty', leaves 'full'
10      writeloc = (writeloc + 1) % buffsize;
11    }
12    buff$[writeloc] = NaN;           // write a sentinel to indicate the end
13  }

15  proc consumer() {
16    var readloc = 0;
17    do {
18      const val = buff$[readloc];     // this read blocks until 'full', leaves 'empty'
19      processVal(val);
20      readloc = (readloc + 1) % buffsize;
21    } while (val != NaN);
22  }
```

In this program, line 1 declares an array, *buff$*, whose elements are of type `sync real`. Thus, each element is a synchronized floating point value that carries a full/empty state along with its value. Because the array's declaration does not contain an initialization expression, its elements start in the empty state. Since incorrect accesses to synchronization variables can result in deadlock, Chapel programmers typically name them using a $ by convention, in order to alert readers to their presence and avoid introducing inadvertent reads or writes that may never complete.

Continuing the example, line 3 creates a task to execute the producer while the original task continues on to line 4 where it executes the consumer. The two tasks each sit in a tight loop, writing (lines 8–11) or reading (lines 17–21) *buff$*'s elements, respectively. Note that the typical safety checks required to prevent the producer from overwriting elements or the consumer from getting ahead of the producer are not required in this implementation—the full/empty state associated with each *buff$* element naturally prevents these error cases from occurring.

In addition to the default read/write semantics, synchronization variables support a number of methods that permit other modes of reading/writing their values. For example the `readFF()` method provides a way to read a synchronization variable, blocking until it is full, but leaving it full rather than empty. Similarly, `readXX()` permits the task to peek at a synchronization variable's value regardless of the full/empty state.

In addition to providing a controlled way of sharing data, synchronization variables also play an important role in defining Chapel's memory consistency model. Typical Chapel variables are implemented using a relaxed memory consistency model for the sake of performance, which makes them an unreliable choice for coordinating between tasks. By contrast, loads and stores cannot be reordered across synchronization variable accesses, which also serve as memory fences. This permits synchronization variables to be used as a means of coordinating data sharing for larger, more relaxed data structures.

As an example, the following code fragment hands off a buffer of data (*buff*) between two tasks:

```
1   var buff: [1..n] real;
2   var buffReady$: sync bool;

4   begin {
5     fillBuffer(buff);
6     buffReady$ = true;        // signal the buffer is filled by making buffReady$ 'full'
7   }

9   {
10    const val = buffReady$;   // block until buffReady$ becomes full
11    processArray(buff);       // the implicit memory fence guarantees 'buff's readiness
12  }
```

The first task (lines 4–7) fills *buff* and then signals to the other task that the buffer is ready by filling the synchronization variable *buffReady$*. Meanwhile the original task (lines 9–12) blocks on the *buffReady$* flag until it is full (line 10) and only accesses the buffer once it is. Note that using a normal variable for *buffReady$* would not be guaranteed to work since it would be subject to relaxed consistency and therefore could have its loads/stores reordered with respect to *buff* by either the compiler or architecture. Making *buff* into an array of synchronization variables would also achieve the desired result, but would add significant overhead to every access of *buff*.

Chapel supports a variation of synchronization variables called *single-assignment variables*. They are almost identical except that once their full/empty state is set to full, it can never be emptied. For this reason, default reads of single-assignment variables use the `readFF()` semantics described above.

Single-assignment variables (and synchronization variables, for that matter) can be used to express future-oriented parallelism in Chapel by storing the result of a `begin` statement into them. As an example, consider the following code snippet:

```
var area1$, area2$: single real;

begin area1$ = computeArea(shape1);
begin area2$ = computeArea(shape2);

doSomethingElse();

const totalArea = area1$ + area2$,
      areaDiff = abs(area1$ - area2$);
```

This program creates two single-assignment variables, *area1$* and *area2$*. It then uses `begin` statements to create a pair of tasks, each of which computes the area of a shape and stores the result into its respective single-assignment variable. Meanwhile, the original task goes on to do something else. When it is done, it computes the total area by reading the two single-assignment variables. If the helper tasks have not yet generated their results, it will block due to the full/empty semantics of the single-assignment variables. Due to the single-assignment semantics, the variables can then be read again without blocking, for example to compute *areaDiff*, the magnitude of the difference between the areas.

Atomic Variables.   Chapel also supports data-centric coordination between tasks using *atomic variables*. These are variables that support a set of common atomic operations which are guaranteed to complete without another task seeing an intermediate or incomplete result. Chapel's atomic variables are modeled after those of the C11 standard and benefit from the design work done there.

As an example of using atomic variables, consider the following program which uses atomic variables to compute a histogram in a manner that ensures updates will not be lost due to read-read-write-write ordering issues:

```
var hist: [0..#histSize] atomic int;
forall elem in Mat {
  const bucket = computeBucket(elem);
  hist[bucket].add(1);
}
```

This program uses a forall-loop (to be introduced in Section 6.3.3) to perform a parallel iteration over an array named *Mat*. For each element, *elem*, the corresponding bucket is computed and incremented. The increment is performed using the `add()` method for atomic variables, causing the argument value to be accumulated atomically into the histogram element. Since multiple tasks may update a single bucket value simultaneously, using a normal array of integers and incrementing them using addition may cause two tasks to read the same value before either had written its update, causing one of the updates to be lost. Proper use of atomic variables can guard against such races in a reasonably lightweight manner, given appropriate hardware support.

Structured Task Parallelism. In addition to the `begin` keyword, Chapel supports two statements that create groups of tasks in a structured manner. The first of these is the `cobegin` statement—a compound statement in which a distinct task is created for each of its component statements. The `cobegin` statement also makes the original task wait for its child tasks to complete before proceeding. Note that this differs from the semantics of the `sync` statement in that only the tasks created directly by the `cobegin` are waited on; any others follow normal fire-and-forget semantics. Although the `cobegin` statement can be implemented using `begin` statements and synchronization variables, that approach adds a considerable cost in verbosity for the user and fails to convey the intent as clearly to the compiler for the purpose of optimization.

As a simple example, the producer/consumer tasks from the earlier bounded buffer example could have been created with a `cobegin` as follows:

```
cobegin {
  producer(numUpdates);
  consumer();
}
writeln("We won't get here until producer() and consumer() are done");
```

Chapel's other form of structured parallelism is the *coforall-loop* which is like a traditional for-loop except that it creates a distinct task for each iteration of the loop body. Like the `cobegin` statement, `coforall` has an implicit *join* that causes the original task to wait for all of its children to complete before proceeding.

As an example, the following loop creates a distinct task for each element in an array:

```
coforall elem in Mat do
  processElement(elem);
writeln("We won't get here until all elements have been processed");
```

For very large arrays, coforall-loops tend to be overkill since you would not typically want to create a distinct task for every array element. In such cases, programmers would typically use the data-parallel constructs of the following section instead. In practice, the `coforall` loop tends to be used when the number of iterations is close to the target hardware's natural degree of parallelism, or when true concurrency between iterations is required (e.g., if distinct iterations synchronize with one another).

6.3.3   Data Parallelism

Chapel's task-parallel features support very explicit parallel programming with all the related hazards, such as race conditions and deadlock. In contrast, Chapel's data-parallel features support a more abstract, implicitly parallel style of programming that is typically easier to use. The primary features for data parallelism are forall-loops, ranges, domains, and arrays, described in this section.

forall-loops.   The *forall-loop* is Chapel's data parallel loop construct. Syntactically, it is similar to for-loops and coforall-loops. As a simple example, the following code uses a forall-loop to iterate over a range in parallel:

```
forall i in 1..n do
  A[i] += 1;
```

The net effect of this loop is to increment elements 1 through *n* of array *A* in parallel.

Unlike for-loops, which are executed using a single task, and coforall-loops, which use a task per iteration, forall-loops use an arbitrary number of tasks, as determined by the loop's iterand. For example, in the forall-loop above, the range value "1..n" determines the number of tasks used to execute this loop. For typical iterands, this choice is based on the amount of hardware parallelism available. Many parallel iterators also have arguments that permit the user to specify or influence the number of tasks used to execute the loop. Like all loop forms, Chapel's forall-loops support zippered iteration in which corresponding elements are generated together in parallel.

Because the number of tasks used to implement a forall-loop is not known *a priori*, forall-loops must be *serializable*. That is, it must be legal to execute the loop using a single task. A consequence of this is that there can be no synchronization dependences between distinct iterations of the loop, since there is no guarantee that they would be executed by distinct tasks.

Forall-loops also support an expression-level form, as well as a shorthand syntax that makes use of square brackets. For example, the forall-loop above could have been written:

`[i in 1..n] A[i] += 1;`. The syntactic similarity between this shorthand and array type specifiers is intentional—one can read an array type like `[1..n] string` as "for all indices from 1 to *n*, store a string."

As part of Chapel's multiresolution approach, advanced users can implement their own parallel iterators which can be invoked using forall-loops. This is done by writing parallel iterators that create the tasks to implement the loop and then determine how the iteration space will be divided amongst them. These iterators are themselves implemented using Chapel's lower-level features, such as task parallelism and base language concepts. With this mechanism, users can write very simple iterators that statically partition the iteration space, as well as more complex ones that decompose the iteration space dynamically. The details of authoring parallel iterators are beyond the scope of this chapter; interested readers are referred to published work [68, 32] and the Chapel release for further details and examples.

Domains and Arrays. In Chapel, a *domain* is a first-class language concept that represents an index set. Domains are used to drive loops and to declare and operate on arrays. The following code creates constant domains that describe the size and shape of the arrays declared in Section 6.3.1:

```
const HistSpace: domain(1) = {-3..3},
      MatSpace = {0..#n, 0..#n},
      Rows = {1..n},
      Cols: [Rows] domain(1) = [i in Rows] {1..i};
```

The first line declares a 1-dimensional domain describing the index set from -3 to 3, inclusive. The second and third lines use Chapel's type inference to declare a 2D $n \times n$ domain and a 1D *n*-element domain. The final declaration creates an array of domains, using a forall-loop to initialize each element based on its index.

Given these domains, the original array declarations of Section 6.3.1 could be rewritten as follows:

```
var Hist: [HistSpace] int,
    Mat: [MatSpace] complex,
    Tri: [i in Rows] [Cols[i]] real;
```

The original declarations were equivalent to these ones; they simply resulted in the creation of *anonymous domains*. The benefit of naming domains is that it permits an index set to be referred to symbolically throughout a program, providing readers and the compiler with a clearer indication of the relationships between arrays and iteration spaces. As an example, the following loop can be proven to require no array bounds checks since *HistSpace* is the domain used to declare *Hist*.

```
forall i in HistSpace do
  Hist[i] = 0;
```

In addition to dense rectangular domains and arrays, Chapel supports a variety of other domain types including *associative*, *sparse*, and *unstructured* domains. Associative domains store a set of index values of arbitrary type, such as strings, floating point values, or class object references. An associative array can be thought of as providing a hash table or dictionary capability, mapping the domain's indices to array elements. Unstructured domains have anonymous indices and are designed to represent pointer-based data structures like unstructured graphs. Sparse domains represent arbitrary subsets of a parent domain's index set. Their arrays store an implicit "zero" value for any index that is within the parent domain but not the child.

All of Chapel's domain types support a rich set of operations including serial and parallel iteration, membership tests, and intersection. Regular domains also support operators and methods that permit new domains to be created from them; for example, one such method simplifies the creation of boundary conditions.

Chapel's arrays support a rich set of operations including serial and parallel iteration, random access, slicing, reshaping, aliasing, and reindexing. Arrays can also be logically reallocated by reassigning their domain variables. When a domain's index set is modified, all arrays declared in terms of that domain are logically reallocated to reflect its new index set. Array values corresponding to indices that persist between the old and new domain values are preserved.

Promotion.   In addition to explicit forall-loops, data-parallelism in Chapel can also be expressed using *promotion* of scalar functions and operators. When a domain or array argument is passed to a function or operator that is expecting a scalar argument, the function is invoked in parallel across all of the domain's indices or array's elements. These promotions are equivalent to forall-loops, but often result in a more compact expression of parallelism. As an example, the forall loop shown earlier to zero out *Hist* could be written as `Hist = 0;`—effectively, a promotion of the scalar assignment operator.

When multiple scalar arguments are promoted, the resulting expression is equivalent to a zippered forall-loop. For example, given the standard `exp()` function for exponentiation, the call `exp(A, B)` with conforming arrays *A* and *B* would be equivalent to the following forall-loop expression:

```
forall (a, b) in zip(A, B) do exp(a, b);
```

Note that both standard and user-defined functions and operators can be promoted in this way.

Reductions and Scans. Chapel's other major data-parallel features are *reduction* and *scan* expressions. Reductions can be used to flatten one or more dimensions of a collection of values while scans are used to compute parallel prefix operations. As an example, the following statement computes the largest sum of squares value over corresponding elements of *A* and *B*:

```
var biggest = max reduce (A**2 + B**2);
```

Note that the exponentiation and plus operators are promoted in this example.

Chapel provides a number of standard reduction and scan operators, such as sum, product, logical and bitwise operations, and max/min (with or without location information). Users can also write their own reduction and scan operators by specifying functions to accumulate and combine input and state values. Though this topic is beyond the scope of this paper, our approach can be viewed in the release or read about in published work [95].

6.3.4 Locality Features

Chapel's final feature area permits a programmer to control and reason about locality. At the low level, a Chapel programmer can explicitly specify the system resources on which a task is run or a variable is allocated. At a higher level, Chapel programmers can specify how domains and arrays are distributed across a system, resulting in distributed-memory data-parallelism. This section touches on both styles.

The Locale Type. The core of Chapel's locality features is the *locale* type. Locales represent units of the target system architecture that are useful for reasoning about locality and affinity. For most conventional parallel architectures, a *locale* tends to describe a compute node, such as a multicore or SMP processor. Due to Chapel's PGAS memory model [288], tasks executing within a given locale can access lexically visible variables whether they are allocated locally or on a remote locale. However, Chapel's performance model indicates that variable accesses within a task's locale will be cheaper than remote ones. This approach supports productivity through Chapel's global namespace, while still supporting the ability to obtain scalable performance by being sensitive to where tasks execute relative to the data they access.

When executing a Chapel program, users specify the number of locales on which it should run using an execution-time command-line flag. Within the Chapel source code, these locales can be referred to symbolically using a built-in, zero-based 1D array named *Locales*, which stores *numLocales* locale values. These values represent the system resources on which the program is executing and permit the user to refer to them and query their properties. Like any other array, *Locales* can be reshaped, sliced, reindexed, etc.

As a simple example, the following statement computes the total amount of memory available to the locales on which a Chapel program is running:

```
const totalMem = + reduce Locales.physicalMemory();
```

This idiom uses a `physicalMemory()` method that is supported by the locale type, promoting it across the entire *Locales* array. It then uses a reduction to sum the individual memory sizes into a single value, *totalMem*. Other locale methods support queries such as the number of processor cores, the number of tasks or threads executing, the callstack limit, the locale's name, its ID, and so forth.

On-Clauses.   Chapel programmers specify that a statement should execute on a specific locale using an *on-clause*. The on-clause takes a single operand that specifies which locale to target. If the expression is a variable, the statement will execute on the locale in which the variable is stored. As an example, consider the following statements:

```
on Locales[numLocales-1] do
  writeln("Hello from the last locale");

on node.left do
  traverseTree(node.left);
```

The first statement causes a message to be printed from the last locale on which the program is executing. The second statement specifies that the `traverseTree()` function should execute on whichever locale owns *node*'s left child. In practice, data-driven on-clauses like this tend to be preferable since they make the code more independent of the number of locales on which the program is running.

It is important to emphasize that on-clauses do not introduce parallelism into a program, keeping with Chapel's theme of using distinct concepts for parallelism and locality. However, on-clauses and parallel constructs compose naturally. For example, to launch an asynchronous remote task to traverse the left subtree above, we could have used:

```
begin on node.left do
  traverseTree(node.left);
```

Another common idiom is to launch a task per locale via a coforall-loop like the following:

```
coforall loc in Locales do
  on loc do
    writeln("Hello from locale ", loc.name);
```

This loop effectively generates traditional SPMD-like parallelism.

Within a Chapel program, the locale on which a variable is stored, or a task is running, can be queried. All variables support a *.locale* method that returns the locale in which it is allocated. For tasks, a built-in variable, *here*, can be used to query the locale on which the current task is executing.

Domain Maps, Layouts, and Distributions. Chapel's locales can also be used to create global-view, distributed arrays. Every Chapel domain is defined in terms of a *domain map* that specifies how it, and its arrays, should be implemented. When no domain map is specified (as in the preceding sections), a default domain map is used. It maps the domain's indices and array's elements to the current locale (*here*). Domain maps like these which target a single locale are referred to as *layouts* since they only specify how domains and arrays are stored in local memory. Domain maps can also target multiple locales as a means of storing distributed index sets and arrays; these are referred to as *distributions*.

As a simple example of a distribution, the following redefinition of *MatSpace* from Section 6.3.3 would result in a distributed Block-Cyclic implementation of its index set and of the *Mat* array that was declared in terms of it:

```
const MatSpace = {0..#n, 0..#n}
                 dmapped BlockCyclic(startIdx=(0,0), blocksize=(8,8));
```

This declaration says that *MatSpace*'s domain map should be an instance of the standard *BlockCyclic* distribution. Its arguments specify that 8×8 blocks should be dealt out to the locales, starting at index $(0,0)$. By default, it will target all of the locales on which the program is running, reshaping them into a square-ish virtual array of locales. The user can also pass an optional array of target locales to the *BlockCyclic* constructor as a means of precisely controlling which locales the distribution should target and how they should be arranged logically.

Note that because of Chapel's global namespace and global-view arrays, a change to a domain declaration like this is the only thing required to convert a shared-memory parallel program into one that supports distributed-memory execution. Forall-loops over distributed domains/arrays are typically implemented such that each locale iterates over the indices/elements that it owns locally, providing a natural model for affinity.

User-Defined Domain Maps. As part of Chapel's multiresolution design, advanced users can author their own domain maps as a means of controlling the distribution and layout of domains and arrays, as well as the implementation details of their iterators, accessor functions, etc. Creating a domain map requires creating three descriptor classes, one to represent the domain map itself, a second to represent one of its domains, and a third to represent one of its arrays. These descriptors must support a required interface that the compiler targets when lowering high-level global-view operations down to the per-locale data structures and operations required to implement them. They can also support optional interfaces that the compiler can use for optimization purposes, when present.

Domain maps are considered the highest-level concept in Chapel's feature set because they tend to be written using data parallel features, task parallel features, locality features, and the base language. As an example, the *BlockCyclic* domain map shown above uses on-clauses to create local descriptors on each target locale to represent its individual portion of the global domain or array. It uses local domains, arrays, and data parallel operations to implement each locale's portion of the global array. It uses task parallelism and on-clauses to implement parallel iterators that execute using the target locales. And it uses classes, iterators, generics, and type inference from the base language to do all of this in a productive way.

As part of the project's research goals, all arrays in Chapel are implemented using the same domain map framework that an end-user would. This is done to avoid a situation in which standard "known" domain maps perform well but user-defined domain maps result in a significant performance penalty. Instead the Chapel team has chosen to use the same framework for all arrays as a forcing function to ensure that user-defined domain maps can achieve competitive performance.

A more detailed description of user-defined domain maps is beyond the scope of this chapter. Interested readers are referred to the Chapel release and published work for more information about, and examples of, user-defined domain maps [71, 67].

6.4   Project Status

As mentioned previously, Chapel is an active and ongoing effort. At the time of publication, all of the features described in this chapter are implemented and work correctly, with one exception: skyline arrays as described in Section 6.3.1 are not yet implemented. As a result, today's arrays of arrays must have inner arrays that share a common domain. Workarounds for this feature exist for users who require such data structures today.

The Chapel team creates two Chapel releases per year, each spring and fall. Highlights of recent releases have included adding support for vectorization of forall-loops in cooperation with the back-end compiler; a growing standard library of common operations, including FFTW routines and file system utilities; a *chpldoc* utility for source-based documentation; and improvements to portability and performance. Other nascent efforts include support for an interpreted Chapel environment, a tool for visualizing communication and tasking intensity within Chapel programs, and Python interoperability.

Chapel's performance remains hit-or-miss at present, depending on the scenario. Generally speaking, performance has recently been improving significantly, particularly since the HPCS program wrapped up.[6] For single-locale programs, execution is increasingly competitive with hand-coded C+OpenMP [32]. Multi-locale executions can be more or less competitive with conventional approaches, depending on the computational idioms and target architecture, but have also been improving with time. Generally speaking, more work is required to optimize Chapel's communication, both in terms of applying traditional global-view communication optimizations [255] and simply by reducing the compiler's tendency to insert communication conservatively, which tends to thwart back-end compilers' serial code optimizations.

The user community's reaction to Chapel has been increasingly positive as the project has progressed. Initially, HPC users expressed a great deal of skepticism about the decision to pursue a new language, largely due to lingering disenchantment around HPF's failure in the 1990's [161]. As the community learned more about Chapel and grew to understand its philosophical and practical divergences from HPF, pessimism gave way to curiosity and cautious optimism. At present, many potential users believe that a mature implementation of Chapel would be very attractive to them, and the number of earnest users who are trying it out for their projects has grown markedly with recent releases.

Future Directions.   Although Chapel's primary features are implemented and working, other aspects of the language are still being improved, both in the implementation and specification of the language.

In the base language, a major lack is a capability for handling error conditions in large-scale codes, whether using exceptions or some other feature more specialized for parallel execution. This was a known lack in the original design, but one that was deferred due to resource constraints, and which has become increasingly important as the number of

---

6. http://chapel.sourceforge.net/perf/

Chapel users grows. Other areas for base language improvements include constrained generic interfaces, additional support for interoperability with other languages, and improved constructor/destructor features.

As part of Chapel's task parallel features, we want to add a notion of identifying logical teams of tasks. This capability would give users the ability to identify and operate on subsets of tasks using collective operations such as barriers, broadcasts, reductions, and *eurekas*—the ability for one task to signal that its team members can stop executing. Task teams may also serve as a means of assigning distinct execution policies to tasks, such as "these tasks may be work-stolen and load-balanced" versus "these tasks should be bound to their own threads and run to completion."

Within Chapel's data parallel features, a major lack is support for *partial reductions*, which are crucial for implementing many algorithms effectively, particularly in linear algebra. We would also like to add support for replicated array dimensions similar to ZPL's flood and grid dimensions [94]. At a lower-level, improvements are planned for Chapel's parallel iterator framework to support increased performance and flexibility.

The main effort that is underway in the area of locality is support for *hierarchical locale models* [274]. Chapel's classic definition of locales is very adept at describing *horizontal locality* such as that which exists between nodes of a commodity cluster. However, Chapel programmers have traditionally had no way to target specific processors or memories on compute nodes involving Non-Uniform Memory Access (NUMA) domains or heterogeneous resources. Hierarchical locales are designed to address this, using Chapel's multiresolution philosophy to permit programmers to model their target architectures in terms of objects that support a standard tasking and memory interface. Programmers can then access such sublocales using traditional on-clauses and distributions. At present, this framework is in use within every Chapel program, though ongoing work strives to efficiently target nonflat compute node architectures.

Summary. Overall, the Chapel language and compiler have demonstrated a great deal of promise with respect to general, productive, multiresolution parallel programming. We encourage potential users to give Chapel a try and to report back with feedback and areas for improvement. In evaluating Chapel, we suggest focusing less on what Chapel's current performance happens to be, and more on whether you agree that the language will be able to generate competitive performance as the implementation matures. We believe that a revolutionary and scalable parallel programming language is unlikely to materialize overnight, so urge parallel programmers to exercise patience with new languages like Chapel rather than giving up hope prematurely. Moreover, being an open-source project, we encourage programmers to help become part of the solution rather than simply sitting on the sidelines.

7 Charm++

Laxmikant Kale, University of Illinois, Urbana-Champaign
Nikhil Jain, University of Illinois, Urbana-Champaign
Jonathan Lifflander, University of Illinois, Urbana-Champaign

7.1 Introduction

Parallel programming is more difficult than sequential programming, despite occasional claims to the contrary by some. One needs to worry about additional issues such as race conditions, load imbalance, communication, locality, etc. How can one go about simplifying parallel programming? This is the question that motivated the development of Charm++ in the 1990s [153].

The design of Charm++ was guided by the following three design principles:

1. The first principle, which we sometimes paraphrase as *"no reliance on magic, at least until you have learned the trick,"* is to avoid an approach that depends on a component whose feasibility is not yet proven. This ruled out ambitious projects based on unrealized technologies, such as automatically parallelizing compilers. The basis of this principle was in part pragmatic: we wanted our abstractions to be useful for developing applications *"now"* rather than in the future when the world's dream system has been built. But, in part, it was also based on a skepticism about whether such pie-in-the-sky technologies can extract all the parallelism that a computational problem has (in contrast to the parallelism evident in the corresponding sequential code).

2. The second, related, principle was based on the belief that what one needs is not full automation by "the system" but a good partnership between the parallel programmer and the "system." We sought *an optimal division of labor between the programmer and the system.* Of course, as we developed and tested lower-level abstractions, we recognized that the optimal shifted in the direction of more automation. But we always wanted the development of abstractions to be grounded in efficient implementations.

3. The third principle was that the features and abstractions we design should be motivated by use cases coming from full-fledged "real" applications. Sometimes, there is a tendency among computer scientists to design abstractions based on the intrinsic beauty of an idea. This "platonic" view of design often leads to failure when the idea does not get adopted in the real world, since it does not address the needs of application developers. Of course, basing ideas and abstractions on just one application—an application-centered approach—does not lead to lasting contributions either, because they may be too specialized. This principle of "application-oriented but computer-science-centered research" was enunciated in a position paper [159].

The resultant programming model was characterized by its innovative use of overde-composition, and its then unique execution model. We begin with a description of these foundational features.

7.2   The Charm Programming Paradigm and the Execution Model

7.2.1   Overdecomposition as a Central Idea

Examining "Parallel Programming" as an activity in light of the principle of optimal division of labor, it becomes clear that parallel decomposition (*what* to do in parallel) is something that the programmers can do reasonably well, whereas the tedious details of which processor executes what at which time are good candidates for automation by the system. Especially in science and engineering applications, the parallelism (which typically arises from the physical world being simulated) is relatively easy to identify. This is true even for more abstract mathematical linear algebra algorithms.

Leveraging this observation requires an additional conceptual step: if the programmers can decompose, they can *overdecompose* into a large number of chunks (i.e., logical work-units and data units), rather than decomposing to the physical processors. This idea of *overdecomposition* into natural work units and data units of reasonable granularity was the key to the entire programming paradigm that is at the base of Charm++.

It is useful to recall that this idea arose from our early work in the world of tree-structured computations in parallel logic programming: the divide-and-conquer and state-space-search world [158]. There, it was natural to see that if we let every recursive call become a unit of decomposition and scheduling, the overhead will be overwhelming. This was true even with work-stealing as pioneered by Vipin Kumar et al. [237], and formalized and popularized later in Cilk (Chapter 13): you still had the programmer deciding what a task executes. At the same time, the processor-oriented decompositions appeared unnatural, because you could not easily decompose work to processors a-priori. The right approach seemed to be to let the programmer decide a reasonable grainsize, and turn over the placement and scheduling of the nodes of the tree to the runtime system [157].

As we turned our attention to applications in science and engineering, the same principle of overdecomposition was found to be extremely fruitful: the basic idea is to have the programmer divide the computation into multiple collections of chunks of the right granularity. The right granularity is defined as "as small as possible, as long as it adequately amortizes the overhead," where the overhead is from scheduling, messaging, and from other runtime system "tax" based on the number of chunks. The overhead also comes in the form of extra memory (for example, the increased memory needed for "halos" in stencil computations, when units are overdecomposed). Fortunately, these overheads are relatively small, allowing for a range of grainsizes to be suitable, *and* the grainsizes could easily be set parametrically, often without recompiling the program. Further, the degree of decomposition does not have to be influenced by the number of processors.

The overdecomposed chunks (which can be work-units or data-units or amalgams of the two) can take many forms in different languages within this paradigm. They can be objects, migratable user-level threads, functional "thunks," continuations, and so on. Overdecomposition into chunks still leaves the question of how these chunks interact with each other. Our broad programming paradigm, which we now call the XMAPP model [160], is neutral to that: many possible interaction mechanisms are possible, and we will see the possibilities in a later section on languages within the Charm family. Charm++ [3], which is the major model within this paradigm, uses C++ objects as its chunks: an object is an amalgam of work and data unit. It uses *asynchronous method invocation* as the mechanism by which chunks interact with each other. Thus, Charm++ objects are units of mapping (what gets assigned to a processor) while the asynchronous method invocations are units of scheduling (what to execute next).

7.2.2 Message Driven Execution

A natural consequence of overdecomposition is that there are multiple work and data units mapped to a single processor core. Some arbitration mechanism is needed to decide how control transfers among these units. Here we made another important decision: control will transfer among these units implicitly and cooperatively, under the control of a data-driven user-level scheduler. There is one scheduler on each processor core, which works with a pool of asynchronous method invocations targeted at objects on that core that are awaiting execution. It picks one of these method invocations and transfers control to the scheduling unit associated with it by invoking the method on the object named in the invocation. Control transfers back to the scheduler only when the method returns. This requires that the unit of scheduling must not contain any blocking calls.

Of course, a programming language that is an instance of this programming paradigm (XMAPP) may include blocking constructs; we only expect that the *implementation* of such a language break the computation up in such a way that every scheduling unit it offers to the runtime system is a nonblocking one. If the scheduling unit were to be a user-level thread, this requirement amounts to requiring cooperative multithreading. In the broader paradigm, beyond Charm++, a scheduling unit involves exactly one work-unit or data-unit, and possibly some other data. Thus, it may represent a continuation, or a message, in addition to an asynchronous method invocation.

7.2.3   Empowering Adaptive Runtime System

Overdecomposition, and having the programmer express the parallel computation in terms
of the logical work-units and data-units, begs another question: who is going to assign
the units to processors? Much of the literature in parallel programming that examines
this sort of question assumes that the alternatives are to let the *compiler* do the mapping
or to let the *programmer* provide it. Some go further, and say that the compiler should
provide a mapping but the programmer should be able to override it. But we believe that
there is a alternate choice: the runtime system. A runtime system can assign objects to
processors initially, and, more importantly, can *change* the assignment in the middle of
execution if it so wishes. This becomes possible because the programmer has not been
allowed to use the knowledge of which processor an object is housed on in any way that
will interfere with such migrations. Of course, you can find which processor you are on
during execution of a scheduling unit and print it. But the only interactions are with other
objects via asynchronous method invocation, and that continues to work whether the other
object is local or somewhere else.

   This creates a degree of freedom for the runtime system that turns out to be tremendously
powerful. An *adaptive* runtime system can use its knowledge of the machine, and the
current state of the computation to optimize execution in a variety of ways. We will see
some of those ways in a later section; but for now we just note how consequential and
significant these relatively simple design decisions are! Our research program resulting
from trying to exploit this degree of freedom has kept us occupied for the past decade or
more, while yielding a lot of low-hanging fruit for multiple applications [3].

7.3   Basic Language

In Charm++, the programmer decomposes an application into objects with methods that
can be invoked asynchronously by other objects. Each object is mapped to a processor
by the runtime, and has only one method executing at a time. After it finishes, control is
passed back to the Charm++ runtime, which determines the next method to execute on that
processor depending on the availability of data.

   A Charm++ program is composed of C++ code and an interface file (called a .ci file) that
describes the parallel objects and their corresponding method signatures to the Charm++
runtime. This allows easy integration with previously written sequential C++ code.

7.3.1   Chares: The Basic Unit of Decomposition

C++ objects that are units of parallelism (or units of mapping) are specially designated by
the user, and are called *chares*. Chares are managed by the runtime system (RTS): they

are placed on a processor by the RTS, scheduled for execution by it, load-balanced with other objects, etc. Communication occurs by invoking a method on a chare, which does not require the user to know its location. During the course of the execution, chares can be created and destroyed as the computation progresses.

Execution of a Charm++ application starts with a special chare, called the *main chare*. This chare typically performs setup and the creation of further parallel objects. In the following example interface file, the user defines the main chare and a constructor for it where the execution begins.

```
mainmodule foo {
  mainchare Master {
    entry Master(CkArgMsg* m);
  };
};
```

In the corresponding C++ file, the same object needs to be described with the code that should be executed when the constructor is called:

```
#include "foo.decl.h"
struct Master : public CBase_Master {
  Master(CkArgMsg* m) {
    CkPrintf("Running foo on %d processors\n", CkNumPes());
  }
};
#include "foo.def.h"
```

The files foo.decl.h and foo.def.h are generated by the Charm++ compiler from the interface file, and contain declarations and definitions of the generated classes, respectively. CBase_Master is the underlying generated class for the main chare that is generated by the Charm++ runtime. The user simply extends this class and gains the parallel functionality of the class described in the interface file. CkArgMsg* includes two fields: argc and argv that can be accessed by dereferencing m in this case, e.g., m->argc.

7.3.2 Entry Methods: The Basic Unit of Scheduling

Any C++ object that is described as a chare can have an entry method, which is a normal C++ method, but special (or specially designated) in the sense that it can be invoked remotely and asynchronously by another chare. The parameters passed to the method (by the caller) are serialized, packed into a message, and sent to the called chare. The parameters of an entry method must be serializable so that they can be efficiently packed and unpacked. The Charm++ runtime provides efficient serialization for many common data types in C++ (arrays, vectors, sets, maps, etc.), along with common data types. To enable generation of the serialization code, the entry method signatures must be declared in the interface file. For an example, see Section 7.3.4.

To remotely communicate among chares, a proxy, which is returned when a chare is created, can be used by any object to invoke entry methods on it. An entry method is invoked by instigating a method call on the remote proxy much like a traditional method call in C++. Under the hood, Charm++ packs the parameters and sends a message to the processor where the chare lives.

7.3.3   Asynchronous Method Invocation

Remote invocations on a proxy in Charm++ are asynchronous and nonblocking. Asynchronous method calls cause the description of a chare to be reactive. Each method is a description of the action to perform when a message arrives, i.e., an entry method is invoked.

7.3.4   Indexed Collections of Chares: Chare Arrays

In many applications, a pattern arises where each chare created must obtain proxies to a set of other chares depending on the application's communication. While this approach allows arbitrary networks of chares to be created, the structural setup and bookkeeping requires substantial effort from the programmer. To reduce this effort, Charm++ supports collections of homogeneous chares (i.e., with the same C++ type) that are indexed uniquely within the collection. Every chare can then be addressed using the array proxy and the index within that array. Chare arrays provide further semantic information about the structure of an application, which allows the Charm++ runtime to optimize collective operations between sets of elements in a chare array.

Today's Charm++ applications often create multiple multidimensional chare arrays. If desired, the arrays can be sparse, i.e., only some of the indices within its range are actually populated by a chare. A chare that is a member of a chare array can communicate with other members of the same chare array, as well as members of other chare arrays. Invoking a method on the array proxy, or a section of the array without a specific index, results in a broadcast or a multicast, which is mapped efficiently by the runtime to the hardware considering topology and other architectural parameters.

In the Charm++ interface file, a 1-dimensional chare array of N chares is described with a constructor and one entry method as follows:

```
array [1D] Foo {
  entry Foo(void);
  entry void someMethod(int arg);
};
```

This chare array can then be constructed by calling the Charm++ parallel new operator ckNew, which instantiates the elements and invokes Foo's constructor on each element. The array proxy, CProxy_Foo, that is returned from this creation can then be used internally or externally to invoke an entry method on the entire array, a subset, or one element.

```
int numChares = 100;
CProxy_Foo array = CProxy_Foo::ckNew(numChares);
```

The corresponding C++ code provides the actual code to execute when the runtime calls the constructor or the entry method is invoked by another object.

```
class Foo: public CBase_Foo {
  Foo() { /* array constructor */ }
  void someMethod(int arg) {
    /* do something when someMethod is invoked */
  }
};
```

The array proxy can then be used to broadcast to the entire array a certain entry method, which causes it to be invoked on every array element.

```
array.someMethod(123);
```

By indexing the array proxy, a specific element in the array can be addressed and an entry method executed on just that element.

```
int element = 5;
array[element].someMethod(17);
```

Many-to-one commutative-associative operations (i.e., reductions) among chare array elements are asynchronous; each element deposits its contribution to the reduction when it is ready. Once the reduction is finished, an entry method is invoked by the runtime with the result from the reduction. The contribute call can be augmented with parameters when the reduction has an operator and payload.

```
contribute(CkCallback(CkReductionTarget(X, finished), proxyToX));
```

In the Charm++ interface file, an entry method can be marked as a reduction target, indicating that it can be used to return the final value once the reduction has completed.

```
chare Foo {
  entry [reductiontarget] void finished();
}
```

7.3.5 Readonly Variables

Charm++ supports declaring `readonly` variables that can be read by any parallel object in a certain module. Like a sequential const variable in a C++ class, readonlys can only be set in the main chare's constructor and then are propagated by the Charm++ runtime to all the processors. Readonly variables are declared like this in the interface file:

```
mainmodule foo {
  readonly int bar;
  mainchare Driver { ... }
};
```

In the C++ file, they are declared and can be written only in the main chare's constructor:

```
/* readonly */ int bar;
class Driver : public CBase_Driver {
public:
  Driver(CkArgMsg* m) {
    bar = 1;
  }
};
```

The variable `bar` is then readable by any parallel object in the `foo` module.

7.3.6 Charm++ Objects: User and System view

The left part of Figure 7.1 illustrates the view of a Charm++ application as seen by the programmer: a collection of chare objects, interacting via asynchronous method invocations (shown via arrows). In this picture, we show three *chare arrays*: A is a simple 1D dense array, B is a spare 1D array (some elements in B[0..3] do not exist), and C is a 2D array.

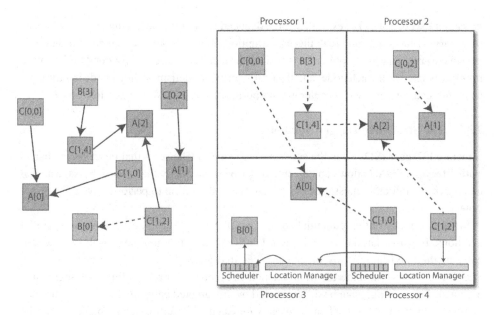

Figure 7.1: User and system view of a Charm++ application.

Note that each element of the chare arrays is a *chare*, a coarse-grained entity visible to the runtime system (in particular, it is *not* an array of scalars).

The diagram on the right shows how the runtime system views the same setup. In this case, we depict a machine with 4 processor cores (on the same or different nodes). In the system view, objects are anchored to specific cores. Communication between chares (i.e., the asynchronous method invocation) is mediated by the runtime system. As an example, we expand the anatomy of the call from chare C[1,2] to chare B[0]. There is a location manager on each processor that finds the processor where the target chare (B[0] in this case) lives. Scalable techniques for location management used by the Charm++ runtime system are described in [172]. The location manager finds that B[0] lives on processor 3, and routes the message to it. After confirming that the object is indeed present on its processor, the location manager on processor 3 enqueues the message in the local scheduler's queue.

In Charm++, a rank is associated with each scheduler that is (typically) assigned to a core, and is called a PE (from the old term "processing element"). The design decision to anchor a chare to a core was taken to enhance locality, and to avoid locking overheads. Locality is enhanced because an object always executes on the same core, unless migrated away by the runtime. No locking is necessary for accessing elements of a chare because no two entry methods can be simultaneously active on the same chare (since only one processor executes it). However, there are advanced features in the language, typically used by library writers, that can break these assumptions in a well-defined manner. Further, it is possible to run Charm++ applications in a mode such that there is only one "PE" (akin to rank) associated with each node, and the (multicore) parallelism within a node is expressed using pthreads or OpenMP. Accelerator support is also provided (see Section 7.6.4).

7.3.7   The Structured Dagger Notation

Structured Dagger (SDAG) is the scripting language in Charm++ that describes a chare's static lifecycle. SDAG allows an object to describe sequentially the flow of message arrival that it expects (all other messages are buffered) and the action to perform given its current state.

SDAG has many of the sequential constructs (`while`, `if`, `for`, etc.) and a few parallel additions. In particular, the `when` keyword in SDAG tells the runtime to wait for a certain entry method and buffers any other messages that arrive for other entry methods. The SDAG code blocks until the `when` is satisfied and then the corresponding code segment is executed. The messages can be differentiated by the targeted entry method and a reference number, which can be set when sending a message. If multiple entry methods can be executed in any order, the `overlap` keyword can be used, which allows multiple `when` clauses to be fulfilled in arrival order. Additionally, the keyword `serial` can be used to indicate a block of sequential C++ code to be executed.

7.3.8   Example: 1-D Decomposed 5-point Stencil Code

The following describes a 5-point stencil on a 2D-grid with a simple 1-D decomposition in Charm++. In this application, there is a main chare that begins the computation by creating a chare array of parallel objects, each one responsible for an equal number of rows of the 2D-grid. Each element in the chare array sends the two boundary rows to its two neighboring chare array elements. For the edge cases, we assume that the 2D-grid is wrapped.

After sending the boundaries, each array element waits to receive its two neighboring elements and then executes the computation kernel that computes the 5-point stencil. The kernel returns a boolean value signifying whether it has locally converged, depending on the error tolerance. These booleans are then ANDed together in a reduction between all the chare array elements, and the target of the reduction is a callback that broadcasts back to all the chare array elements the result. Depending on the result, the elements either all continue or send a message to the main chare that convergence has been reached, causing the main chare to print and call `CkExit()`.

For the stencil, in the basic Charm++ code, an array element will not explicitly wait to receive the neighboring elements; instead it describes reactively the action to perform when it receives a boundary element. For each neighboring element that arrives, it will update its local boundary based on those values, and then if all boundaries have arrived it can start the computation kernel. This requires the object to keep the state of how many neighbors have arrived and then perform a different action (the last will spawn the kernel).

The advantage of this reactive approach is its generality: it allows arbitrary dynamic dependencies to be described. However, when a chare's lifecycle can actually be described statically to the runtime, the buffering and counting of messages can be automatically performed by the runtime, and the appropriate block of C++ code can be executed upon message arrival depending on the state of the object. Hence, the SDAG-based implementation of the same array element explicitly defines the expected messages and their sequential control flow.

The following Charm++ interface file shows the SDAG-based implementation of the array elements for performing a 5-point stencil computation. First, it declares the readonly variables and the main chare. Then, it declares the 1-D chare array, called `Jacobi`, along with the SDAG description of the lifecycle of its objects. Each object, while it has not converged, asynchronously sends messages that contain its boundary rows to update the ghost cells of its neighbors. After the sends, it waits for two updates to arrive, calling the sequential C++ `updateBoundary` code for each boundary arrival. After both the boundaries have arrived, the compute kernel is executed and the array element deposits its convergence value to a reduction. The target of this reduction is a broadcast to the entire array which checks convergence and possibly continues or sends a message to the main chare that the computation is completed.

```
mainmodule jacobi1d {
  readonly CProxy_Main mainProxy;
  readonly int dimX; readonly int dimY; readonly int blockSz;
  readonly int numChares;
  mainchare Main {
    entry Main(CkArgMsg *m);
    entry void done();
  };
  array [1D] Jacobi {
    entry Jacobi(void);
    entry void updateGhosts(int dir, int size, double gh[size]);
    entry [reductiontarget] void checkConverged(bool result);
    entry void run() {
      while (!converged) {
        serial {
          thisProxy(wrapY(thisIndex-1)).updateGhosts(BOTTOM, dimY, t[1]);
```

```
            thisProxy(wrapY(thisIndex+1)).updateGhosts(TOP, dimY, t[blockSz
                ]);
        }
        for (remoteCount = 0; remoteCount < 2; remoteCount++) {
          when updateGhosts(int dir, int size, double buf[size])
          serial { updateBoundary(dir, buf); }
        }
        serial {
          int conv = computeKernel() < DELTA;
          CkCallback cb(CkReductionTarget(Jacobi, checkConverged),
              thisProxy);
          contribute(sizeof(int), &conv, CkReduction::logical_and, cb);
        }
        when checkConverged(bool result) serial {
          if (result) { mainProxy.done(); converged = true; }
        }
      }
    };
  };
};
```

Listing 7.1: Charm Interface file with control flow loop in SDAG for 5-point stencil

In the main chare's constructor, the Jacobi array is created and a call to the entry method, run, is broadcast to the entire array causing each element to execute the run method described above. The rest of the C++ code has the Jacobi constructor and the sequential routines to update the boundary and compute the 5-point stencil.

```
#include "jacobi1d.decl.h"

/*readonly*/ CProxy_Main mainProxy;
/*readonly*/ int dimX, dimY, blockSz, numChares;

class Main : public CBase_Main {
public:
  CProxy_Jacobi array;
  Main(CkArgMsg* m) {
    // read arguments from m, into dimX, dimY, blockSz, numChares
    mainProxy = thisProxy;
    jarray = CProxy_Jacobi::ckNew(numChares); // Chare array creation
    jarray.run(); // Start the computation
  }
  void done() { CkExit(); }
};
```

Listing 7.2: Main chare creates Jacobi chares and begins execution

7.4 Benefits of Overdecomposition and Message Driven Execution

7.4.1 Independence from Number of Processors

Although the code for a 5-point stencil computation, described in the previous section, superficially looks similar to the corresponding MPI code, there are critical differences. The number of chares `numChares` is not the same as the number of cores (or nodes, for that matter). It is a number independent of the processor count, chosen by the programmer to amortize the overhead. A 3D-version of this code, with a 3D-grid decomposed into a 3D-array of chares, illustrates this better. Assuming an equal decomposition along each dimension, the number of processors will need to be a cube in a plain MPI implementation. In Charm+, the number of *chares* needs to be a cube, but the number of processors is unrestricted. One can run them on 173 processors, if one wants.

This ability to decouple decomposition from processors is useful to exploit any machine (or part of the machine) that is available for a job to its fullest extent. Even more importantly, it enables other runtime benefits, such as fault-tolerance strategies, as we will see later. Of course, a programmer can write a multiblock-style MPI code to achieve a similar outcome. However, the lifecycle of each block is not separately expressed in a processor-centric code. Further, the programmer is then assuming responsibility for managing placements of blocks on their own.

7.4.2 Asynchronous Reductions

Reductions in Charm++ are nonblocking operations. Neither the processor nor the chare object participating in it is blocked. First, the contribute operations extends over one chare array. If the application has other chare arrays, they can continue their execution as usual. Secondly, after calling `contribute` to deposit its data into a reduction, a chare object is free to execute other entry methods if it so chooses. In the code shown above, the chares choose to wait for the callback, `checkConverged`. But consider an alternative design (shown in Listing 7.3): we decide that convergence checking every iteration is an overhead, and we should do it every 5 iterations (say). Further, we want to use the result of convergence testing done in iteration $5k + 1$ to be tested 4 iterations later (in iteration $5(k + 1)$). This is easy to accomplish by adding a conditional `if (i % 5 == 1)` (on line 26 of Listing 7.3), and adding another conditional `if (++i % 5 == 0)` on line 29. Essentially, the reduction that starts in iteration $5k + 1$ will continue in the background, and overlap with the computation and communication of the next 4 iterations of the stencil algorithm.

```
serial {
  int c = computeKernel() < DELTA;
  CkCallback cb(CkReductionTarget(Jacobi, checkConverged), thisProxy);
  if (i % 5 == 1)
    contribute(sizeof(int), &c, CkReduction::logical_and, cb);
}
if (++i % 5 == 0) {
  when checkConverged(bool result) serial {
    if (result) { mainProxy.done(); converged = true; }
  }
}
```

Listing 7.3: Stencil code with asynchronous reductions to overlap computation and communication.

Asynchronous collectives, in general, can improve performance significantly, because although the elapsed-time for such collectives is often high, the processor-time occupied by them is relatively small [156].

7.4.3 Adaptive Overlap of Communication and Computation

In Charm++, since multiple chunks are assigned to one processor, no single chunk can block the execution on a processor (unlike, say, a blocking receive in MPI). If one chunk is waiting for its data, another chunk can execute *if* its data (i.e., method invocation) is available. This message-driven execution adaptively overlaps communication and computation without any extra programmer effort.

With a straightforward, but naïve, MPI application, one may strictly separate the compute and communicate phases. This can be optimized further with nonblocking MPI calls, and with techniques that initiate data transfer as early as possible and delay synchronization to as late as possible. This may, for example, reduce the time spent waiting for communication from (say) 20% to 10%. But the fact remains that the network is utilized only 20% of the time, and for the remaining time there are no bytes on the network. This spurt of communication now needs to be supported by the network. It is this sort of application behavior that necessitates an overengineered communication network, expensive and power hungry to boot.

In contrast, overdecompostion in the Charm model naturally creates latency tolerant applications, without extra programming effort. Further, it automatically leads to spreading of the communication over an iteration or time-step, thus utilizing the communication network better. You can live with a "cheaper" lower bandwidth network better, and reduce the chance of communication contention impacting performance.

7.4.4   Compositionality

This is a subtle point, but one very important for modularity. With traditional models such as MPI, it is *very hard* to get two *separately developed independent modules* to interleave their execution on an overlapping set of processors. The term "separately developed" here means that each module cannot reference entities in the other module directly, while the term "independent module" means that there is no data dependency between them and their work can be carried out in any order. Typically, on any individual processor, one of the modules will complete its step, and then the other module can be given control explicitly. Of course, you could use wild-card receives to interleave the execution of the two modules, but this gets "very hard," especially if each module's code has a complex life cycle, with long chain of message receipts.

Why is such interleaving important? Execution of any parallel module may lead to idle time on individual processors. This could be due to communication latencies or load imbalances. With interleaved execution, idle time in one module can be be overlapped with useful computation in the other. With Charm++, such interleaving occurs completely automatically, as a natural consequence of its data-driven execution model, without any programming on user's part.

7.4.5   Software Engineering Benefits: Separation of Logical Entities

In many traditional programs, the processor-centric view leads to unnecessary coupling between modules. Domains of different kinds in the same simulation are typically divided into the same number of chunks, and i^{th} chunk of one module is placed with i^{th} chunk of the other module, simply because they both need to be on the ith processor. Such undesirable coupling arising out of processor-centric programming models is completely eliminated by Charm++: you can decompose different domains into different number of pieces, and leave it to the runtime to decide which chunks co-exist on a processor (say, to minimize communication).

7.5   A Design Example: Molecular Dynamics

As a larger example that illustrates some of the features of Charm++, consider a program to simulate biomolecules. In such an application, atoms in the simulation box are simulated in femtosecond time steps. In the particular algorithm we discuss, atoms are partitioned into cubic *cells*. There are three categories of forces experienced by each atom, and correspondingly, we create multiple chare arrays to calculate them. Each *nonbonded force* calculation object receives coordinates of atoms in two cells within a prespecified cutoff distance from each other, calculates the forces (electrostatic and Van der Waal's) on atoms

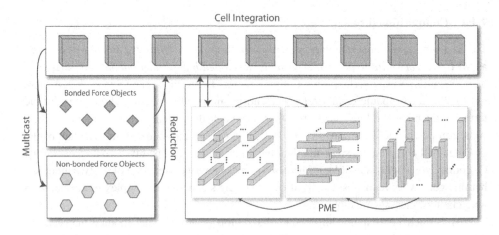

Figure 7.2: Molecular dynamics using multiple chare arrays in Charm++.

in each set due to those in the other set, and sends the resulting forces back to the two cells via reductions. The *bonded force* calculation objects calculate forces due to atoms connected by bonds. The more interesting and complex operation is the calculation of long-range forces using the so-called particle-mesh Ewald algorithm—this involves a forward and backward 3-D FFT. Since this is a fine-grained, yet communication intensive, operation, a pencil decomposition as shown in Figure 7.2 is used. This involves calculating line FFTs sequentially along each dimension, permuting data between phases in order to bring the lines over which FFT needs to be calculated together on a single processor. This can be naturally expressed using *three arrays of chares* consisting of pencils parallel to the X-axis, Y-axis and Z-axis, respectively.

Thus, the natural decomposition of this application involves 6 separate arrays of chares. A Charm++ program expresses the lifecycle of each type of the element of these chares cleanly and separately, without worrying about where (as in, on which processor) each chare object lives. The runtime system decides the placements of various objects onto processors so as to minimize communication, balance load, handle interconnection topology-related optimizations, etc. NAMD [231], the widely-used molecular dynamics simulation code, uses a decomposition that is similar to the one described above.

7.6   Adaptive Runtime Features

A simple reference implementation of Charm++ as described so far can be created relatively easily with a static scheme (e.g., cyclic or block) assignments of chares to processors, a correspondingly simple location manager, a message-driven scheduler, with no migration of chares across processors during execution. The basic benefits of the model, listed in Section 7.4, such as adaptive overlap of communication and computation, and no dependence on processor counts, are still realized with this simple implementation. However, only an implementation that incorporates a more sophisticated *adaptive* runtime system can unleash the full power of the separation of concerns created by the model by ensuring that user's view is not processor-centric. An adaptive runtime can observe and monitor the behavior of the application and the hardware as the computation evolves. Such monitoring is enabled by the fact that the runtime system schedules each chare object, and mediates communication between them. It can then take actions that improve the execution efficiency or reliability of the application. We next describe a few of the capabilities that the current Charm++ implementation supports.

7.6.1   Load balancing Capabilities in Charm++

Load imbalance, especially when it arises dynamically as the application evolves, has the potential to be biggest impediment to high performance and strong scaling of applications. Even for applications with little or no dynamic change, making initial assignment of work to processors can be challenging. Charm++ has several schemes for automatically balancing load.

A large class of schemes in actual use in Charm++ rely on a heuristic principle that we call "principle of persistence": the computational load and communication patterns exhibited by naturally decomposed objects *tend to* persist over time. This is true for a wide variety of applications, including those with dynamic refinements, or slow change in balance (as in the case of particle migrations). When user specifies the use of such strategies, the Charm++ RTS maintains a database of object loads and, optionally, communication graphs. It then uses a (user-specified) strategy, from the Charm++ suite of load balancers, to create a new assignment of objects to processors and then migrates the objects to their new destinations before resuming execution.

The suite of strategies include those that ignore communication, as well as those that focus on reducing communication costs. Some are simple heuristics, while others are based on complex graph algorithms. Some only aim to *refine* an existing assignment, reducing the migration costs, while others seek to rebalance better by ignoring the existing assignments. An application programmer can also write an application-specific (or general-purpose) strategy, and plug it in using a standard interface provided by Charm++. Strategies that utilize graph partitioners, such as METIS, Scotch and Trilinos, are also available. Here, it is important to remember that the graph we are talking about has the chare objects as its vertices. As such, compared with the normal application domain of these partitioners, where they may partition billion element graphs, the target here is much smaller graphs. This is one of the second-order benefits of the Charm++ approach. The domain remains chunked in the same set of partitions, but the assignments of chunks to processors changes. This makes the execution time for creating a new assignment of chares to processors much smaller compared with full-fledged domain decomposition. In rare situations, one can also merge or split existing chares by deleting or inserting new elements in a chare array, although this feature is rarely used.

Leveraging the small size of the graph, many strategies collect the object-graph on one core (or node), and apply the decision-making algorithm sequentially [305, 307]. For very large machines, hierarchical strategies and distributed strategies are also available [306, 199]. If selected, a MetaBalancer scheme monitors execution characteristics and their evolution and selects an appropriate strategy and decides how often to apply it at runtime [198]. This relieves the application users from having to conduct performance fine-tuning experiments and find the optimal load-balancing parameters. In addition, when the application behavior varies dynamically, the automatic selection of load-balancing parameters helps improve performance as the parameters also evolve dynamically with the application. Automatic load balancing is a signature strength of Charm++. Many of our applications have shown benefits of this feature on machines sizes up to $260,000$ cores [35, 243, 132].

Adding Load Balancing to the Stencil Example

Using load balancing in Charm++ is relatively easy. The dominant mode in which it is used is synchronous: all chares call a special (collective-like) function called AtSync() as shown on line 35 of the 5-point stencil code shown in Listing 7.4. The RTS decides a new placement of objects, migrates them, and calls a predesignated entry method, ResumeFromSync, signifying resumption of execution. The object may find itself at another processor at this time; this is inconsequential from the programmer's point of view. To facilitate migration, the object's data must be serialized. Charm++ provides a convenient "PUP" (pack-unpack) interface for chare objects to simplify the specification of serialization code. In addition to this, the programmer must choose the load-balancing strategy on the command line. With this simple change, the code is ready to be automatically load-balanced.

7.6.2   Fault Tolerance

Charm++ supports several fault-tolerance schemes, some in experimental mode and others in fully production versions. The migratable-objects model is an excellent fit for fault tolerance strategies: if we can migrate an object to another processor for load-balancing, we can use the same mechanisms to checkpoint ("migrate") it to the disk, or to another processor's memory. The baseline scheme leverages this ability and allows the application code to create a globally synchronous checkpoint with a single call [310, 142]. The runtime will make sure that all its data structures are faithfully stored. An interesting consequence of the migratable objects model is that this checkpoint can be used to resume execution on a different number of processors, as long as the original program was carefully written to avoid references to actual processors.

A similar scheme is also available to create checkpoints in other processor's memory, instead of the disk [309, 308, 211]. In this case, the system can detect failure and automatically recover the application without killing the job. Each object creates a checkpoint on its current processor, as well as on a buddy processor. On detecting failure, the runtime system restores objects on the nonfailed processors from their own checkpoints; the objects on the failed processor all restored on a spare processor using the checkpoint stored on its buddy.

Both of these schemes require that the job scheduler should not kill the job if one of the nodes crashes. The basic scheme can be used as it is on a dedicated cluster of workstations. On large-scale machines, we have demonstrated the scheme using a fault-injection mechanism that ensures that the job is not killed by the scheduler. The checkpoint overhead can be as low as a few milliseconds for low-memory applications such as molecular dynamics, and only hundreds of milliseconds for large-memory applications [211, 210, 194]. More interestingly, the recovery time, measured from the time that the failure was detected to the point the application resumed execution, is quite low as well.

We have recently extended this work to utilize local storage, such as flash memories, and to reduce the impact of checkpoint time even further by overlapping checkpoint traffic with application execution. More experimental strategies that Charm++ provides are:

(1) Proactive fault tolerance, where the RTS utilizes signals from some external environmental monitoring system that warn it about an impending failure of a node. The RTS reacts by migrating chares away from that node and adjusting runtime structures such as spanning trees to eliminate the dependence on the (potentially) doomed node.

(2) A message-logging scheme that avoids having to rollback all the processors when one node fails. Only the failed node's objects are restored from a checkpoint, and they reexecute their messages (saved at their sender) [191, 192, 190, 193]. This saves energy during recovery [195]. Further, the recovering objects are migrated to multiple processors during recovery, thus parallelizing recovery. This feature allows the system to tolerate faults that happen at a faster frequency than the checkpoints!

```
if (i % lbPeriod == 0) {
  serial { AtSync(); }
  when ResumeFromSync() {}
}
if (i % checkpointPeriod == 0) {
  serial { CkStartMemCheckpoint(CkCallback(CkIndex_Jacobi::finished(),
                                           thisProxy)); }
  when finished() { }
}
```

Listing 7.4: Stencil code with load balancing and checkpoint/restart

Adding Fault Tolerance to the Stencil Example

Utilizing checkpointing and fault tolerance support requires minimal code changes. Leveraging the same PUP interface created for load balancing, all that the programmer has to do is make a call to the runtime at some periodicity to checkpoint their data. The rest is handled by the system! For example, checkpoints can be created in memory by calling `CkStartMemCheckpoint` as shown on line 39 of the 5-point stencil code in Listing 7.4. When the checkpoint has been created, the callback function specified by the user is invoked by the runtime (function `finished()` on line 41 in the Listing 7.4).

7.6.3 Shrinking or Expanding the Set of Processors?

A feature of Charm++ that has been explored extensively in the past, and one that may become important again due to "HPC-in-the-cloud" scenarios, is its ability to change the set of processors assigned to a job at runtime. This is accomplished by migrating objects away from (or in to) the processors that the job scheduler requests from (or assigns to) a running Charm++ job. So, a job running on 10,000 processors can be made to give up 1000 processors, continuing to run on 9000 processors, and later can be given 3000 more processors, as long as the job scheduler is capable of such behavior. We have demonstrated this using a job scheduler of our own design, and we hope that, over time, mainstream schedulers will start supporting such malleable jobs [131]. The utility of such features to maximize system utilization is obvious, and the Charm++ runtime ensures that it can utilize the available processors with the best possible efficiency.

7.6.4 Support for Heterogeneity and Accelerators

Accelerator chips of various kinds are now quite popular in high-performance computing, such as the cell processor, GPGPUs, and Intel's Xeon Phi chips. New features are being added to Charm++ to support and adaptively select accelerated entry methods. Specifically, the user can tag entry methods as "accelerated," and specify whether the method should run only on the host, only on the accelerator or either one. The runtime system balances the load between the host and the accelerator. It also performs heterogeneous load-balancing among accelerated and nonaccelerated nodes, such as those found on the Blue Waters system [109].

7.6.5 Additional Features

In addition to the Structured Dagger notation for describing the life-cycle of a chare, one may also tag an entry method as "threaded." The system creates a user-level thread (much more lightweight than a pthread, and one that is not visible to the native OS) when such a method is invoked. Threaded methods support synchronous method invocations, and can block for a "future" data structure. Any method invocation can also be given a certain priority by the sender, which influences how they are scheduled on the destination processor by the Charm++ runtime.

Charm++ also has support for processor- or node-level entities that allow the creation of collections of objects that have one element on every processor ("Group") or node ("Node-Group"). These collections are often used to optimize algorithms by mapping directly to the machine.

7.6.6 Experimental Feature: Thermal and Energy Management

Several recent research efforts in Charm++ have aimed at reducing cooling energy. These allow the machine operator to use a warmer A/C setting, but creates a risk that some chips will overheat. To avoid such a scenario, the runtime periodically monitors the temperature of each core; for the cores that get too hot, it reduces their frequency a notch using dynamic voltage and frequency scaling (DVFS). Once the overheated cores get cool enough, the RTS bumps up their frequency [249]. These actions may create a load imbalance in HPC applications which will normally make such a scheme impractical. However, Charm++ load balancers can handle different speed ratios between cores, and can thus restore balance after every exercise of a DVFS frequency adjustment [197]. Other strategies for minimizing and constraining some user-specified combination of power, energy, and execution time, are also being currently developed [248, 247].

7.7 A Quick Look Under the Hood

Figure 7.3 shows the overall architecture of the Charm++ runtime system. At the base of the stack, the low-level runtime system (LRTS) abstracts machine details, including the native communication primitives. This layer provides efficient remote communication

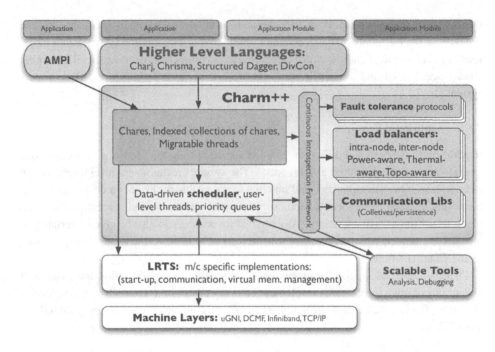

Figure 7.3: Software stack of Charm++ and its family of languages.

among end points in a distributed setup. The next layer (called "Converse") provides data-driven scheduling and user-level threads. In addition to supporting the Charm++ runtime, this layer provides a common interface on top of which other high-level programming frameworks such as MPI can be implemented. Next, the Charm++ runtime provides migratable work and data units (chares), migratable threads, and scalable location managers. It also interfaces to plug-in strategies for load balancing, fault tolerance, and strategies for optimizing specific communication patterns. Many high-level languages have been implemented on top of the Charm++ runtime system. Applications are either written directly in the interface provided by Charm++ or in these high-level languages.

7.8   Charm++ Family of Languages

Charm++ improves programming productivity because of all the features mentioned earlier, including modularity, compositionality, and automation of resource management. Yet, its interaction mechanism is fairly primitive: asynchronous method invocation among objects is akin to message passing and is the only mechanism in Charm++. But, with those features, Charm++ is also an excellent substrate for designing higher-level languages. Any such language will inherit these features from Charm++, and modules written in it will interoperate well with each other. We have developed several such languages which we briefly describe next.

Adaptive MPI (AMPI): Charm++ empowers users with legacy MPI code to take advantage of processor virtualization and overdecomposition with minimal effort. AMPI, Charm++'s interface to MPI, enables developers to run any MPI program using Charm++ as the execution engine. The key advantage of using AMPI is the freedom to choose the number of MPI ranks independent of the processor/core count. Choice of MPI ranks can thus be made from the application perspective which leads to substantial performance gains. Under the hood, MPI ranks are mapped to Charm++ user-level threads. Multiple user-level threads may reside on the same processor and are managed by the Charm++ scheduler. Presence of multiple threads on a processor enables overlap of communication with computation without programming effort. In addition, AMPI users can take advantage of other inbuilt Charm++ functionalities such as object migration, dynamic load balancing, fault tolerance, and communication libraries.

Improved performance has been demonstrated for many MPI applications using AMPI. The execution time of BRAMS, which is an MPI-based weather-forecasting code, decreases by 25% when run on AMPI [244]. The application primarily benefits from overlap in computation and communication and dynamic load-balancing. A comprehensive study of the advantages of AMPI for micro benchmarks such as Jacobi3D, NAS's BT-MZ, and Fractography3D (crack propagation simulation) has also been done [143]. AMPI has also been used to execute, fine-tune and debug programs which require large numbers of MPI ranks, on small systems. For example, Rocstar, which is a solid rocket-motor simulation code, takes advantage of these features on a small system [150].

Charisma only allows static data-flow among Charm++ objects. To understand its motivation, consider a large Charm++ program. The chare classes express the behavior of each type of object in the program. However, the behavior of the program as a whole is not directly visible, and can be thought of as an emergent property of the behavior of individual objects. This detracts from the expressiveness of the application code. For a significant class of applications, the data-flow among the objects does not change across application iterations. The same set of objects exchange the same pattern of messages with each other in each step. Of course, the content and even the size of such messages may be different across iterations. For such applications, Charisma provides an elegant expression: the global flow of control and data among multiple chare arrays is expressed in a script-like language. The sequential methods of each object are expressed in C++, as before. The individual objects themselves only consume and publish values, whereas the charisma code connects the publishers and consumers [149].

Multiphase Shared Arrays (MSA) provide a global address space abstraction for the Charm++ library that allows data to be distributed by the system and accessed by any processor. It is motivated by the observation that for many applications, the accesses to the data arrays will all be in the same mode of operation (read-only, one-writer per element, or accumulate) during distinct phases. Hence, in MSA, the entire array is in one mode at a time and the mode can only be changed through a collective. To enable adaptivity, MSA uses data virtualization by organizing the data into "pages" that are distributed across processors and can migrate depending on runtime access patterns [203].

CharJ is an experimental programming language [29] that demonstrates improved productivity and performance through compiler-level support of the Charm++ parallel programming model. Since we are no longer tied to C++ in Charj, we provide linguistic support for declaring chares, asynchronous methods, and many other constructs in Charm++. Currently, we are continuing this line of research by developing a follow-on language that provides even more concise and powerful constructs that map to Charm++.

7.9   Applications Developed using Charm++

Several highly-scalable applications have been developed using Charm++. One of the earlier, and most well-known, applications developed using Charm++ is *NAMD*. This is an application that was co-developed by a team consisting of Klaus Schulten, Robert Skeel, Laxmikant Kale, and coworkers. NAMD is designed for simulations of biomolecular systems. The main challenge in biomolecular simulation is to do millions (or even billions) of timesteps, where the work available for parallelizing in each timestep is relatively small. NAMD has demonstrated a step time of around 250 microseconds on recent supercomputers [168, 259, 258, 187] and has scaled to machines with more than 600,000 cores. It also shared the Gordon-Bell award in 2002 [231]. It is a widely-used program with over 70,000 users and occupies a significant fraction of cycles on most national supercomputers in the U.S. In Section 7.5, we discussed how NAMD utilizes overdecomposition, load balancing, and topology-aware mapping in Charm++ to achieve scalability.

OpenAtom [46, 34, 167] is an application for simulating electronic structures of materials using the Car-Parinello molecular dynamics algorithm (CPAIMD). Implemented from scratch using Charm++, as a successor to the Piny code, in a collaboration led by Dr. Glenn Martyna of IBM, OpenAtom strives for strong scaling with a finer decomposition of this problem. Although the technical details of the problem or its parallel aspects are beyond the scope of this book chapter, it is worth noting that the logical expression of CPAIMD in Charm++ requires over a dozen different chare arrays (distinct collections of chare objects). Although the computation is relatively static in terms of load patterns, it still requires a strong topology-aware initial load balancing. Most importantly, this application allowed us to exhibit effects of contention induced by the interconnection topology on communication performance on modern machines. The topology-aware mapping that we developed for it reduced execution time by 40% or more [46]. The ability to do this mapping was facilitated by the degrees of freedom created by the object-based decomposition.

ChaNGa is a computational astronomy program developed in a collaboration led by Prof. Thomas Quinn of University of Washington. It supports both gravity and gas dynamics, via a particles-in-tree code. Scaled efficiently for over $500,000$ cores [196, 148], this application demonstrates the utility of dynamic load balancing in Charm++.

Several other applications, such as *Episimdemics* for simulation of spread of contagion in a network of people and places [304] and *ClothSim* for simulation using Asynchronous Contact Mechanics [209], have been developed or ported by the HPC community using Charm++.

7.10 Charm++ as a Research Vehicle

In addition to its use for developing adaptive, scalable parallel applications, Charm++ is a excellent vehicle for facilitating research on various issues of critical importance in high-performance computing, as we move towards exascale.

The load balancing framework in Charm++ provides an easily accessible way to plug-in different load-balancing strategies. Load balancing in the general setting, as well as in specialized settings suitable for different applications, is still an open area of research. Researchers can test their ideas with relatively little effort on various benchmarks and applications in the Charm++ suite.

Similarly, communication between chares can be *delegated* to a user-defined plug-in library. This allows researchers to develop and test alternative algorithms for optimizing communication operations, such as collectives, or message-combining strategies.

With some additional effort, researchers can also leverage the Charm++ infrastructure for developing fault-tolerance strategies. Another area where we hope to have a significant participation by the HPC research community is in developing new languages and frameworks on top of Charm++. The interoperability and compositionality features of Charm++ ensure that such languages will have automatic support for dynamic load balancing, and can interleave execution of modules in novel languages with more traditional modules in Charm++ and MPI. The main benefit of Charm++ here is its powerful backend that makes development of new languages quite easy (of course, beyond any compilation effort that is needed by the language).

7.11   Charm++: History and Current State

Charm++ has evolved over the years, in response to the types of applications we considered and the abstraction needs that we perceived in them. Its precursor, the Chare Kernel, and the early C-based Charm system, were used for combinatorial search applications, and parallel logic programming. By 1993, we developed a C++-based version called Charm++ [155, 154]. As we increasingly focused on applications, many of the modern concepts were added to it. A major application, NAMD, was developed using Charm++ during 1996-98, which led to revamping of many features in Charm++, including the chare arrays with migratable elements [172]. Several applications, including OpenAtom and ChaNGa, were started in the 2003-04 time frame under the support of the NSF ITR program. Adaptive MPI was developed with motivation provided by working the DOE/ASCI supported Rocket Simulation center (CSAR) at Illinois, and the desire of application scientists to continue working within the familiar MPI paradigm. Although the base language has remained the same since about 1998, much effort has been spent on its adaptive runtime system, and refinement of features via application experience.

7.12   Summary

Charm++ is a C++-based parallel programming system based on the ideas of overdecomposition, migratability and asynchrony. These ideas, embodied in the XMAPP family of languages, turn out to empower an adaptive runtime system to do effective resource management. It has been used over the past decade to develop many applications, and to develop and demonstrate adaptive techniques such as dynamic load balancing, communication optimization, automatic fault tolerance, and power/thermal optimizations.

While Charm++ was developed for supporting dynamically-evolving applications, its runtime adaptation techniques as well as the overdecompostion based programming model turn out to be directly useful for the coming era of extreme scale (exascale and beyond) of parallel computing, which is characterized by dynamic variability in the architecture itself. The data-driven task scheduling that is gaining popularity in HPC now, is already a natural part of the Charm++ execution model. Consequently, we expect Charm++ to play an important role in parallel application development in future, both at the extreme scale, and at the broad-industry medium-scale scenarios.

8 Asynchronous Dynamic Load Balancing

Ewing Lusk, Argonne National Laboratory
Ralph Butler, Middle Tennessee State University
Steven C. Pieper, Argonne National Laboratory

This chapter describes what is fundamentally one of the earliest parallel programming models, combined with a new implementation approach that allows it to scale far beyond its original ambitions. The model is the *manager-worker* model, invented early in the history of parallel computing because of its basic simplicity together with the ease with which load balancing—a complex challenge in some parallel programming models—could be achieved. We define here a specific application programmer interface (API), realized as a library callable from conventional programming languages, called ADLB (for Asynchronous Dynamic Load Balancing), and describe a scalable implementation of this library. In addition to the details of the API itself, we present a number of use cases ranging from "demonstration" applications that illustrate simple use of the API to a large production application in nuclear physics that illustrates its power to scale to the largest machines in the world. We also describe how ADLB can be used as the runtime system for a high-level parallel computing language described elsewhere in this book (see Chapter 10).

8.1 Introduction

We will probably never find the single perfect programming system, capable of elegantly expressing every possible type of algorithm and preparing it for efficient execution on all computers, large and small. Not only is the variety of algorithms continually expanding, but the variety of computer hardware to execute them is expanding as well, from the largest supercomputers with millions of processing elements to the tiniest special-purpose processors. Nevertheless, the approach we present here can yield benefits in simplicity of expression while enabling extremely scalable execution in a surprisingly large number of applications.

The structure of this chapter is as follows. In Section 8.2 we describe the load-balancing problem in general and the manager-worker approach to it, with its advantages and disadvantages. In Section 8.3 we describe the ADLB instantiation of this model in detail, presenting the complete API. Section 8.4 describes our scalable implementation of this API, together with two alternative approaches that may prove useful in the long run. Section 8.5 provides examples of use, both plain and fancy.

8.2 The Manager-Worker Model and Load Balancing

In the traditional manager-worker parallel programming model, one process is designated as the *manager* or *master* process, and all the others are *workers*. (This model has also been referred to as the *master-slave* model.) The manager has access to a data structure representing a pool of tasks (which we call *work units*) that can be executed in parallel. We think of them as independent, although nothing in the manager-worker model itself prevents them from communicating or synchronizing with one another. See Figure 8.1.

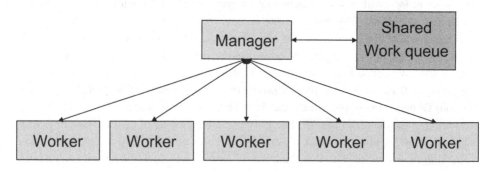

Figure 8.1: Manager Process and Worker Processes

The worker processes request work from the manager, execute the work unit they receive, and return results to the manager, implicitly requesting another unit of work. The manager process executes a loop, processing requests from the workers by selecting an appropriate work unit from the pool of work units and assigning it to the requesting worker. Workers can also create new work units, sending them to the manager to store in the pool. Once the manager determines that the overall computation is completed, either because the pool of work units is exhausted or for some other reason (perhaps one worker has returned what was being searched for in a parallel search), it responds to requests for work with an "all done," and the workers can exit, followed by the manager.

The appeal of this model is that it mirrors a familiar structure of noncomputational parallel processing. A human manager divides a large and complex task into work units that can be performed independently by human workers, who need not be aware of the overall structure, and keeps them busy as they finish tasks and become available for more work. The computational version is completely analogous.

Comparison with other models.   The fundamental aspect of *all* parallel programming models is the decomposition of a problem into work units that can be executed in parallel, together with the management of *dependencies*; some tasks cannot be executed until others have returned results that form their input. In some sense, programming models differ precisely in how they express the definition of these tasks and the dependencies among them. The manager-worker model attains the simplicity of both its concepts and its possible implementations from the fact that it leaves both work-unit definition and dependency specification entirely up to the user of this model, whether end-user, library, or compiler.

Advantages of the manager-worker model. The first advantage of this model is conceptual, as discussed above; it is a straightforward adaptation of concepts we are familiar with from our normal computation world. The second is that it can easily be implemented portably via MPI. The communication between the manager and the workers can be encapsulated in MPI messages; writing an MPI manager-worker program is easy, since the algorithm is straightforward for both the manager (a sequential process of managing dependencies, selecting the next work unit, and optionally storing new work units), and the worker (process the work unit sequentially and return the result). All the complexity of parallel algorithms has been abstracted away. The third advantage is a bit deeper: automatic *load balancing*. We define load balancing to be the process of ensuring that if there is work to be done and a process available to do it, then the work is assigned to the process. The manager-worker model does this automatically: if the work units are of widely varying sizes (in terms of required execution time) or if the computational resources allocated mean that some workers are slower than others, then the manager-worker algorithm smoothly handles this situation, since its sole function is to match available work with available workers. This is its most fundamental difference from other programming models, which must handle the problem of idle processors in some other way.

An additional advantage of this model is the potential for a limited form of fault tolerance. If the manager retains a copy of the data necessary for a work unit until the worker assigned to it reports completion, then a failure of that worker to complete the work unit can be addressed by simply assigning that same work unit to the next worker that asks for work. Of course, if the work units are large, this incurs a memory cost; and for this reason ADLB does not currently implement this approach.

Disadvantages. The primary disadvantage is its lack of generality. Not all algorithms can be efficiently implemented with this approach, although more than one might initially think. A second disadvantage—one that we intend to address with ADLB—is that of *scalability*. In the model as presented thus far, the manager process is responsible for containing in its memory the entire collection of open work units (or being able to generate them as requested by the workers), as well as for communicating with all the workers. Both of these tasks represent scalability challenges. In a computation comprising a large number of work units and a large number of worker processes, the single manager process may run out of memory to hold the entire database of work units, or run out of processing power to handle a large number of incoming requests, or both. It is this combination of challenges that ADLB has been designed to address.

Related work. The basic idea is not new. One of the earliest parallel programming libraries, Linda [8], had many elements in common with what we discuss here, although perhaps its main thrust was as a distributed database. Cilk (Chapter 13) is a compiler-based approach to load balancing in shared-memory C/C++ programs.

8.3 The ADLB Library Definition

The basic idea of ADLB is to abstract away the manager process, since its algorithm is already known. Actually, we have to distribute some of its functionality to the workers, but this distribution can be done. We focus first on the worker algorithm. Each worker executes a simple loop of getting work from the manager, returning results, and (optionally) creating new work and putting it into the pool of work units (see Figure 8.2). The key to implementing this model is to develop a scalable approach for the work pool. Instead of a single manager process to implement it, as described above, we may need multiple processes for scalability. In this section we describe a programming model (and a specific API) for this purpose; in the next section we will describe several possible implementations, including one that has proved effective at extreme scale.

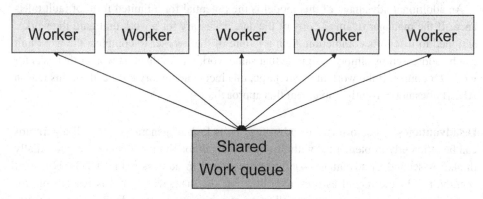

Figure 8.2: Worker Processes without Master

8.3.1 API Introduction

A few aspects of the API assume that the application using ADLB is an MPI application. In particular, we assume that the application has called `MPI_Init` before making any ADLB calls.

The key to abstracting the work pool is to realize that what workers do is to *get* work units from the pool and *put* new work units into it. These will become the fundamental operations of the API. In order for the workers to absorb some of the functionality of the manager (selecting which work unit should be assigned in response to a request) these operations will incorporate a number of arguments by which assorted high-level parallel algorithms can be expressed. Here we define the meanings of these arguments.

First, we define work units. In order to make our library completely general, these are defined by an array of bytes, identified in memory only by an `(address, length)` pair. Addresses are specified in the usual way appropriate to the calling language; the length is a nonnegative integer. The internal structure of this array is left completely to the user. One may associate with each work unit a `type`, which may be used by workers to filter the work they request. Types are specified as integers. Work units are also assigned `priorities`, expressed as integers (possibly zero or negative). In ADLB, priorities are hints, causing the library to prefer assignment of some work units ahead of others, without *requiring* that higher-priority work be given out ahead of lower-priority work. As we will see, strict priority ordering can be managed by using types. Some work units can be given an `answer_rank`, specifying which worker process should be notified when this work unit is completed. It is also possible to specify a `target_rank`, which ensures that a work unit can be retrieved only by a specific application process. These ranks are the MPI ranks of application processes in the MPI communicator returned by the initialization call to the ADLB library.

8.3.2 The Basic ADLB API

The API is modeled on the widely used MPI API; all C functions return return codes as their values; the corresponding Fortran versions are subroutines that return their return codes in an additional last argument. We give here both the C and Fortran language bindings. We leave out details of most of the possible return codes; they can be found in the documentation that comes with the code itself (see Section 8.3.4).

We have already discussed how at its most abstract level the model consists only of *put* and *get* operations, for putting work units into the work pool and getting them out. Here are the formal versions of these operations. We split the *get* operation into two steps in order to allow for explicit memory management. The first one *reserves* work and is told how large the reserved work unit is, so that memory for it can be explicitly allocated in the calling process' memory. Then this work unit (identified by a handle returned by the *reserve*) is retrieved into the allocated memory.

```
int ADLB_Put(void *work_buf, int work_len, int reserve_rank,
             int answer_rank, int work_type, int work_prio)
    ADLB_PUT(work_buf, work_len, reserve_rank, answer_rank, work_type,
             work_prio, ierr)
```

Here work_buf points to the work itself; work_len is the length of the work in bytes, and reserve_rank can be -1 (wild card) if the work is not to be reserved for a particular rank. If reserve_rank is nonnegative ADLB reserves the work for the specified rank. Some applications use answer_rank to indicate which rank is interested in the results of computations from this work. The application sets work_type but it must be one of those registered at the time of ADLB_Init (see below). The application also determines work_prio. ADLB will make a nonexhaustive attempt to assign work of the prescribed types in priority order.

```
int ADLB_Reserve(int *req_types, int *work_type, int *work_prio,
                 int *work_handle, int *work_len, int *answer_rank)
    ADLB_RESERVE(req_types, work_type, work_prio, work_handle,
                 work_len, answer_rank, ierr)
```

The function ADLB_Reserve reserves work but does not retrieve it. This approach is useful for finding out how large a piece of work is and allocating buffer space before the actual retrieval. This call waits until either work is found or ADLB_NO_MORE_WORK is returned as the return code. Here req_types is a vector of types that the worker will accept. ADLB will return the highest-priority work of one of those types that it can find easily. If a work unit of the first type in the list can be found, it will be reserved, and so on down the list. Therefore this mechanism can be used to impose strict priority among types. Specifically, work_type is set to the type of work actually reserved; work_prio is set to the priority of the work reserved; and work_handle is set to a value that is used to retrieve the work later. One can use work_len to allocate buffer space before retrieving the work unit with ADLB_Get_reserved. Although not used by all applications, answer_rank tells which rank to send answers to (i.e., reserve them for).

```
int ADLB_Get_reserved(void *work_buf, int work_handle)
    ADLB_GET_RESERVED(work_buf, work_handle, ierr)
```

The function `ADLB_Get_reserved` uses the handle obtained during a previous `ADLB_Reserve` to retrieve the work.

These three functions, `ADLB_Put`, `ADLB_Reserve`, and `ADLB_Get_reserved`, provide the gist of ADLB; the other functions, while necessary or useful, are in some sense ancillary (e.g., `ADLB_Init`).

A nonblocking version of `ADLB_Reserve` also exists.

```
int ADLB_Ireserve(int *req_types, int *work_type, int *work_prio,
                  int *work_handle, int *work_len, int *answer_rank)
    ADLB_IRESERVE(req_types, work_type, work_prio, work_handle,
                  work_len, answer_rank, ierr)
```

This is the same as `ADLB_Reserve` but returns immediately rather than waiting for work to become available. The return code says whether work of the requested type is available.

Following MPI, we have functions to initiate and terminate use of the library. The arguments to `ADLB_Init` shown here are specific to the production implementation; their meanings will be made clear in Section 8.4. We also leave out here some other arguments relevant to tuning and debugging.

```
int ADLB_Init(int nservers, int ntypes, int type_vect[], int *am_server,
             MPI_Comm *app_comm)
    ADLB_INIT(nservers, ntypes, type_vect, am_server,
              app_comm, ierr)
```

This function must be called by all processes before any other ADLB functions, but after `MPI_Init`. The argument `nservers` indicates how many processes should become ADLB servers. The program must provide to ADLB an integer array of all the types of work that it will put into the work queue. Here `type_vect` contains an entry for each type, `ntypes` provides the length of that vector, and `app_comm` is a new MPI communicator that application processes should use for communication instead of `MPI_COMM_WORLD`. Many programs do not need to perform communication other than making calls to ADLB. Nonetheless, `app_comm` can be used for all MPI calls.

```
int ADLB_Finalize()
    ADLB_FINALIZE(ierr)
```

This function should be called to finalize ADLB operations and print usage statistics prior to calling `MPI_Finalize`.

Processes become ADLB servers (see Section 8.4) by calling the following function.

```
int ADLB_Server(double malloc_hwm, double interval)
    ADLB_SERVER(malloc_hwm, interval, ierr)
```

Processes that are to become ADLB servers invoke this function. The second argument, `interval`, specifies how often, in seconds, we wish to have ADLB log periodic statistics. If the value of this argument is `0.0`, then no logging is done.

In some parallel algorithms, particularly ones that are essentially parallel searches, not all work units in the pool need to be completed for the computation to be finished. The computation can be short-circuited (solution found!) by calling the following:

```
int ADLB_Set_problem_done()
    ADLB_Set_problem_done(ierr)
```

Once this is called, ADLB starts returning ADLB_NO_MORE_WORK return codes for those functions that reserve work.

8.3.3   Optimizing Memory Utilization with Batches

In some cases (as in our flagship application, GFMC) the data for a related set of work units consists of a large section common to all of them together with a much smaller work-unit-specific part. ADLB manages this set of work units with only one copy of the large common section. It does so by means of the *batch put*. The application begins a series of puts with `ADLB_Begin_batch_put`, which specifies the common part of the batch of work units, does a series of `ADLB_Put`s of the individual parts, and then calls `ADLB_-End_batch_put` to terminate the batch.

```
int ADLB_Begin_batch_put(void *common_buf, int len_common)
    ADLB_BEGIN_BATCH_PUT(common_buf, len_common, ierr )
```

This function begins a series of related puts. ADLB will assemble the pieces when work units are retrieved, with the common part first. The length returned by `ADLB_Reserve` will be the sum of the two lengths.

```
int ADLB_End_batch_put()
    ADLB_END_BATCH_PUT(ierr)
```

This function terminates the sequence of related puts that make up a batch.

8.3.4   Obtaining and Using ADLB

ADLB is open source and freely available. The site at [5] contains all the source code and a descriptive paper [182] about the library and its use in a large-scale application. The README file included there contains the API in more detail than described here, including additional tuning and debugging related arguments to ADLB_Init and possible return codes from each function and their meanings. Also described there are additional ADLB functions for debugging and tuning, some of which have behavior specified by arguments to ADLB_Init that were omitted earlier. The distribution also includes the simpler examples described in Section 8.5.

8.4   Implementing ADLB

The ADLB API described above admits of multiple implementations. Here we describe the "production" implementation—*ADLBM*—which has proven to be robust and scalable. We also describe two experimental alternative implementations. The multiple implementations demonstrate the abstractness of the model.

8.4.1   ADLBM Implementation

The overall scheme is shown in Figure 8.3. We divide the collection of MPI processes into ADLB *servers*, which will execute only code in the ADLB library, and *clients*, which will execute application code. This partitioning is done when all MPI processes call ADLB_Init. As described above, one argument to ADLB_Init is the number of MPI processes that will become servers.[1] The remaining processes are formed into a new MPI communicator that is returned by the call. The application is free to use MPI (restricted to this communicator) independent of its use of ADLB, or it may find that ADLB can handle all its communication needs. A flag returned from ADLB_Init indicates whether a process should become a server. Those that become servers do so by calling the function, ADLB_Server; the others proceed with application code. One advantage of having dedicated processes is that they can carry out load-balancing activities in the background, independently of the application processes.

   Figure 8.3 illustrates the basic communication pattern internal to ADLB; each client process is served by a single ADLB server, and this relationship is fixed. Work units are stored on the servers. Put and get operations in the clients are communicated to the client's server, which may be able to satisfy the request locally or may need to involve

---

1. The fraction of processes that should be designated as servers depends on the number and size of the specific ADLB application's work units and must be determined by experimentation. Experience shows that a good initial guess is about 5–10% of the total number of MPI processes.

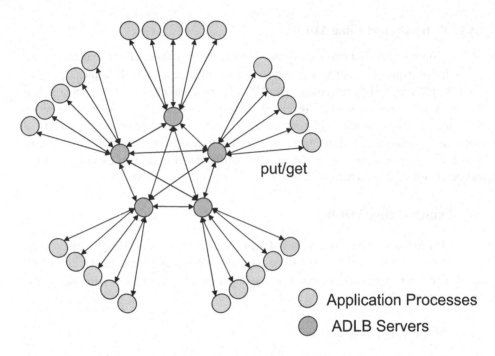

Figure 8.3: ADLB Clients and Servers

other servers. In order to preserve a global view of the entire work pool, each server
maintains data on how many work units of each type are stored on each server. The multiple
copies (one on each server) of this essentially global data structure are kept synchronized
by thinking of the servers as a ring and constantly circulating around this ring a "status
vector" message containing this data, which is updated by each server as the message
passes through. By circulating this message frequently, the local copies in the servers,
which they use to satisfy requests from their clients, are kept approximately accurate. Fall-
back algorithms compensate for the fact that synchronization is not perfect. For example,
a reserve may be unable to be satisfied locally, then redirected, based on status vector
information that has become out of date, to another server that no longer has that type of
work unit. In that case the request will be redirected to another server.

What happens on a put?   ADLB_Put attempts to send a work unit to the client's assigned server. If the server has room for it, the local copy of the status vector is updated
to reflect its presence. As the status vector circulates, its existence and location will even-

tually become known to other servers. If the server is low on available memory, the work unit is directed to another server, based on information in the status vector.

What happens on a get?   ADLB_Reserve sends a request message to the local server. If a matching work unit is present on that server, it is marked as reserved (so that no other client can reserve it); and a handle to it, along with its size, is returned to the client, which can now retrieve it with ADLB_Get_reserved. If a matching work unit is not present, then the status vector is consulted, and the request is sent to a server that does have a work unit conforming to the constraints specified by the ADLB_Reserve. If it still has the work unit it returns the appropriate handle to the client. If not, it forwards the request to another server.

8.4.2   Alternative Implementations

The simplicity of the basic programming model here makes it relatively easy to try other implementations than the one described above, in order to experiment with different approaches. The two implementations described below are on hold at the time of this writing, but they may be further developed in the future.

An Implementation Based on Remote Memory Access

In an effort to eliminate the situation where the status vector became out of date, we implemented a version of ADLB in which a single process was dedicated to maintaining the database describing which work unit of which types are available on which servers (basically the information kept in the status vector of the production implementation). In order to eliminate data transfer costs to and from this process, all movement of work units themselves was done with MPI-2 RMA operations (MPI_Put and MPI_Get) among clients. This approach worked well for small numbers of processes but was ultimately nonscalable because of the single-process bottleneck. It was not that the processing requests overloaded the single process, but rather that the network became congested, even though the messages to and from this process were small.

An Implementation Based on Threads

In another implementation we replaced the server processes with threads running alongside the client processes. This eliminated data transfer costs between client and server (since they share memory) but meant that many more servers had to be kept synchronized; and the status vector, having to circulate among many more servers, became increasingly inaccurate at large scale.

8.5   Examples

In this section we illustrate the flexibility of the manager-worker model, as instantiated in ADLB, by describing some applications, both simple (for demonstration purposes) and complex (as actually used on large-scale machines by "real" applications).

8.5.1   A Simple Batch Scheduler

Suppose one has a collection of sequential jobs to be run on a Linux cluster on which MPI is installed, allowing ADLB to be installed on top of it. Let us also suppose that each job is completely described by a single command line, and these command lines are stored in a file on one of the nodes of the cluster. Then regardless of the varying lengths of the jobs (whose lengths need not be known ahead of time) or the number of nodes in the cluster, we can efficiently schedule the jobs by treating each one as an ADLB work unit. One process reads the file and puts each command line into the work pool. Then all processes just get work units (jobs) from the pool and execute the command lines using the Linux `system` command. The logic is straightforward:

```
ADLB_Init
if (rank = 0)
    Open command file
    For each line
        ADLB_Put the string into the work pool
ADLB_Reserve a command
while success
    ADLB_Get_Reserved(command-line)
    system(command_line)
    ADLB_Reserve
ADLB_Finalize
```

Several refinements could be added to this basic scheme while still relying on ADLB for parallelism and load balancing. For example, this scheduler could be run as an infinite loop, in which command lines are continually added to the end of the input file as new jobs are submitted. Overall times could be improved by giving priority (as an argument to the ADLB_Put) to long jobs if estimated times were submitted along with the command line itself. One could use ADLB's work unit types to implement multiple job queues, say for long and short jobs.

8.5.2   Dynamic Task Creation: A Sudoku Solver

The algorithm shown here is not a good algorithm for solving a Sudoku puzzle, but it illustrates how ADLB can support a particularly simple expression of a generate-and-test algorithm, making use of very large degrees of parallelism through recursive dynamic work unit creation.

The goal of the puzzle is to take a partially filled-in Sudoku 9x9 "board" (we will assume familiarity with the puzzle type) and fill in the blank squares with digits from 1 to 9 in such a way that each row, column and 3x3 box contains all nine digits. Here is a way to do this using ADLB.

```
ADLB_Init
if (rank = 0)
    ADLB_Put(original problem board)
ADLB_Reserve
// note all processes execute this loop
while success (not done)
    ADLB_Get_reserved(a partial board)
    Find first blank square
    if (no such square) // problem solved
        ADLB_Set_problem_done
    else
        check row, column, and box of blank square for illegal values
        for each legal value
            create new board, substituting legal value for blank
            ADLB_Put(new board)
    ADLB_Reserve
ADLB_Finalize
```

Again, improvements can be made even staying within the ADLB framework. Note that this algorithm produces a great deal of parallelism rapidly. One way to assist the search is to give priority to boards that have smaller numbers of blank squares, an approach that leads to a depth-first search. ADLB automatically detects multiple solutions (by optionally continuing past the first solution) and invalid input boards (by detecting when there is no more work and no process is continuing and therefore might produce more work).

8.5.3 Work Unit Types: The Traveling Salesman Problem

The TSP is a classic computer science problem. We give here not necessarily the most efficient solution but one that does illustrate the applicability of ADLB to branch-and-bound search algorithms. In the previous two examples all work units were of the same type; here we illustrate the use of multiple types. We also demonstrate work unit priorities, target ranks, and batch puts.

We start with a graph with weighted edges (like roads connecting cities, with distances assigned to each road segment). The problem is to find the shortest closed path that includes all the nodes of the graph (the path taken by an efficient traveling salesman who visits all his clients and returns home). The pseudocode below shows how we can express this as a branch-and-bound problem using ADLB. The application processes form themselves into a binary tree to facilitate broadcasting of new bounds. Work units of type WORK consist of a partial path leading away from the starting city. Work units of type BOUND UPDATE consist of a new shortest path length (so far) from the starting city back to itself. Doing the work consists of adding the connected cities to the end of this path and putting the new work units back in the pool. When a new bound (length of shortest path so far) is found, it is broadcast by sending it to process 0, which then sends it as a message to its children, who pass it to their children, and so on. Messages are sent by putting them in work units with specific target ranks. The priority of bound-update work units is set to be higher than that of work packets consisting of partial paths, since a new bound may permit work to be trimmed from the search.

```
ADLB_Init
if myrank == 0
    read num_cities and vector_of_distances
(MPI) broadcast num_cities and vector_of_distances
if myrank == 0
    ADLB_Put WORK // starting city
compute parent, lhs_child, rhs_child        // form broadcast tree
while not done
    ADLB_Reserve (BOUND_UPDATE or WORK)
    ADLB_Get_reserved
    if BOUND_UPDATE
        if bound in the update < current bound
            current_bound = bound in the update
            ADLB_Put BOUND_UPDATE with target_rank = lhs_child_rank
            ADLB_Put BOUND_UPDATE with target_rank = rhs_child_rank
    else // WORK
        ADLB_Begin_batch_put
        for city in cities
            if city is not in path already
                path = path + city
                if path contains all cities
                    if path's dist < best_path_so_far
                        best_path_so_far = path
                else
                    if path < current_bound
                        ADLB_Put WORK     // path to extend further
        ADLB_End_batch_put
        if best_path_so_far < current_bound
            ADLB_Put BOUND_UPDATE with target_rank = 0 // for broadcast
    if myrank == 0
        print current_bound info
ADLB_Finalize
```

8.5.4 GFMC

ADLB was motivated by an application in theoretical nuclear physics called GFMC (for Green's Function Monte Carlo) [293]. GFMC provides *ab initio* calculations of properties of light nuclei by solving the many-body Schrödinger equation using realistic two- and three-nucleon interactions. It is generally recognized as the most reliable method for nuclei with 6 to 12 nucleons. More details can be found in [182] and [62].

The ADLB implementation has evolved over the years as GFMC has been run on ever larger computers. Originally designed to provide balancing of processing loads, ADLB has been augmented to balance memory usage and, more recently, network message traffic as well. In some recent calculations, GFMC/ADLB has scaled to more than 250,000 MPI ranks on an IBM Blue Gene/Q.

GFMC uses a pattern of problems generating subproblems, each of which must be solved (its answer computed) before the originating problem is complete. In this case, a work unit generates its subparts as additional work units and puts them in the pool with `ADLB_Put`, specifying its own rank as the `answer_rank`. Then it enters a loop of asking for work of either the subproblem type or its answer, until it has all the answers and can complete. Since it is also working on the subproblems itself, it cannot starve.

8.5.5 Swift

Swift is a parallel scripting language, described in Chapter 10 of this book. ADLB, with some extensions, is used as its execution engine. Details can be found in [294] and [18].

8.6 DMEM: A Helper Library for Dealing with Large Data

In our current implementation of ADLB all work units are stored on the servers. Thus the number of servers needed in an ADLB application depends not only on the processing requirements[2] but also on the maximum storage requirements of the application for work units at any one time. Since increasing the number of servers decreases the number of MPI processes available for the application computation itself, finding the right balance is important, though difficult.

We implemented DMEM, a small distributed-memory library, to relieve the ADLB servers of the responsibility for storing work units. Instead, application processes *put* work units into DMEM and manipulate them via a *handle* that encodes the location and size of a work unit. DMEM runs as a separate thread on all application processes and can store work

---

2. we have found using 5–10% servers adequate for GFMC runs of more than 100,000 MPI ranks as long as the work units are not too large

units on any of the application processes where it can find appropriate memory. ADLB is then free to manage only the handles instead of the work units themselves. In order to enable work units to be larger than 2 GB, the size is an `MPI_Aint`, typically an 8-byte integer on large systems.

Reducing the size of the ADLB work units, and hence the number of ADLB servers needed, has multiple benefits. First, more MPI processes are available for application computing. Second, a given server is more likely to be able to accept an `ADLB_Put` without redirecting it to another server. Third, a given server holds (the handles of) a larger number of work units and hence is more likely to satisfy an `ADLB_Reserve` without communicating with the other servers.

The DMEM API in C is straightforward.

```
int DMEM_Init(MPI_Comm user_comm, MPI_Aint init_memsize,
              int num_irecvs_to_post)

int DMEM_Finalize()

int DMEM_Put(void *pkg_addr, MPI_Aint pkg_len, DMEM_handle dh)

int DMEM_Get(DMEM_handle dh, void *buf_addr)

int DMEM_Copy(DMEM_handle orig, DMEM_handle *copy)

int DMEM_Get_part(DMEM_handle dh, MPI_Aint offset, MPI_Aint len,
                  void *buf_addr)

int DMEM_Update(DMEM_handle dh, MPI_Aint offset, MPI_Aint len,
                void *buf_addr)

int DMEM_Free(DMEM_handle dh)
```

Some debugging and tuning functions also are available. The Fortran interface, following MPI and ADLB, can be deduced from the C interface: the Fortran versions are subroutines and have an extra integer argument as their last argument, in which a return code is returned. DMEM is available at the same web site as ADLB [5].

8.7   Summary and Future Directions

We have presented ADLB, a library whose implementation provides scalability for the traditional manager-worker programming model. ADLB is fundamentally simple, while unusual features such as work unit types, priorities, and targets enable the expression of algorithms that go beyond simple queue-of-tasks applications. ADLB is working well now for GFMC, its motivating application, and will be aided further by coming improvements to DMEM, its helper. Both libraries remain under development, but production-ready versions are available now.

9 Scalable Collections of Task Objects

James Dinan, Intel

Applications that exhibit irregular, dynamic, and unbalanced parallelism are growing in number and importance in the computational science and engineering communities. Irregularity in the computation often arises from the simulation of fundamentally irregular and sparse physical systems or from the processing of datasets that capture nonuniform or time-evolving phenomena. Current computational modeling efforts across a variety disciplines continue to harness increasing amounts of sparsity and adaptivity to improve efficiency by focusing the computation on the most interesting regions of the data [303]. In such applications, the size of individual work units that comprise the computation is often irregular and varies across data sets, introducing significant challenges to the efficient parallel decomposition and distribution of the workload. Because of these properties, it is challenging for these programs to achieve high levels of efficiency and scalability on large-scale, high-performance systems.

Over the past two decades, one-sided and global address space (GAS) programming models have gained popularity as a means for providing the programmer with a global view of distributed, shared data. These programming models are discussed in detail throughout this book and include the GASNet (Chapter 2), and MPI one-sided models (Chapter 1), as well as the Global Arrays (Chapter 5), and UPC (Chapter 4) partitioned global address space (PGAS) programming models. While there are many differences among the approaches taken by each model, all of them provide the programmer with asynchronous, one-sided access to data regardless of its physical location in the system. Data in one-sided and global address space models is distributed across the memories of multiple nodes and, for any given node, can be logically partitioned into local patches that have low access cost (i.e., high *affinity*) and remote patches that have a high access cost due to communication. An important consequence of these models compared with two-sided message passing is that they allow the programmer to access nonlocal data without participation from the remote process. Because these systems allow flexible and asynchronous access to the data, they are attractive solutions for supporting irregular and dynamic applications on distributed memory systems.

In spite of the flexible data models provided by the one-sided and GAS models, most still require the programmer to explicitly partition the computation into a process-centric execution. However, irregularity in the data access pattern often results in irregularity in the computational intensity and dynamically evolving parallelism, which can lead to load imbalance and loss of computational efficiency. Thus, utilizing such parallelism requires sophisticated techniques to manage the workload. Such infrastructure, however, is not provided by most one-sided and GAS models. Thus, programmers have often resorted to simple but inefficient strategies to manage their parallelism.

The Scalable Collections of Task Objects (Scioto) [98, 97] programming model addresses this gap between the flexible one-sided and GAS data models and rigid process-centric computation model by introducing a task parallel approach for expressing the computation. Task parallel programming is a technique for expressing and managing parallelism by decomposing a computation into a dynamic collection of tasks that can be executed concurrently. Tasks in this collection can be automatically scheduled and executed by the runtime system to improve load balance, optimize for data locality, and provide resilience in the presence of faults. In addition, the task model is able to support computations that exhibit dynamic parallelism where additional parallelism is uncovered as the computation progresses or where the structure of the parallelism may be data-driven.

9.1   The Scioto Task Parallel Execution Model

Scioto extends process-centric execution models with task parallel regions. Scioto tasks operate on data stored in globally accessible locations; Scioto is agnostic of the particular global data space and the execution model is compatible with a variety of global address space (GAS) and one-sided data systems. Our discussion in this chapter focuses on the Scioto+GA implementation of the Scioto execution model that utilizes the Global Arrays (GA) toolkit for distributed shared multidimensional arrays [215]. GA pairs well with the Scioto execution model because several computational science applications that utilize GA suffer from poor parallel performance because of fundamental irregularities present in th atomic and quantum mechanical systems under simulation.

Scioto addresses a programmability gap that is present in many GAS models: a highly flexible, asynchronous, global data space is provided, however the computation is still expressed in terms of a static, process-centric execution model. Thus, data can be readily moved to a given piece of computation, but the computation is stationary and can not be easily moved to the data. Scioto extends the flexible global address space with an interface for specifying computation through individual units of work, called *tasks*. The inputs and outputs of these tasks are stored in the global address space. Thus, Scioto tasks can be executed on any resource in the system that has access to the global data store, allowing the runtime system to perform automatic load balancing of the computation.

Tasks provide a concise, but powerful, abstraction that allows the programmer, compiler, or automated tool to express the units of work in computation. A task-parallel programming model defines the data-sharing and execution semantics for tasks. In Scioto, the parallelism is expressed by creating task objects to represent work units; adding them to a shared *task collection*; and then collectively processing the task collection in a task-parallel execution region. During a task-parallel region, the runtime system takes control of the execution and automatically schedules and executes tasks. The task-parallel phase ends when all tasks, including those created dynamically, have completed execution. This

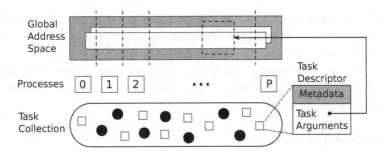

Figure 9.1: Scioto execution model: A collection of tasks is shared by P processes and tasks operate on data stored in the global address space. Tasks are represented by descriptors, which contain metadata as well as task arguments that can reference data in the global address space.

model effectively creates a layer of virtualization between the computation and the available resources. Thus, when processing a task collection the runtime system has many opportunities to automatically perform load balancing and optimize task execution by utilizing data locality.

Scioto's programming interface is centered around *task collections*, shown in Figure 9.1 which are distributed containers of tasks. Multiple task collections can be created and collections can span different groups of processes. An initial set of tasks must be added to the collection and the programmer can optionally specify an initial assignment of tasks to processes. Once one or more tasks have been added, the tasks are automatically scheduled and executed during a collective task parallel phase of the program. During this phase, tasks can spawn additional subtasks to utilize dynamic parallelism.

9.1.1 Task Objects

A Scioto task object is represented by a *task descriptor*, which is a contiguous data object containing task metadata and immediate arguments. Metadata is used internally by Scioto to track task information, including locality information that can be used to reduce communication overheads. The arguments portion of a task object contains user-supplied data, which will be available to the task when it executes. This contiguous data segment can contain any data the user wishes to provide to the task and a structure or array is often declared to define the layout of this data. References to global data can be included in the task arguments and such references must be *portable*, or valid for use on all processes participating in a given task collection.

The *task class* metadata field of a task object contains a portable task class identifier, which is used to identify the characteristics and implementation of a given task. Task classes must be collectively registered with a task collection before tasks of that type can be created. The task class specifies the size of the arguments segment of the task object as well as the *task execution callback function* which will be used by the Scioto runtime system to execute the given task.

9.1.2   Task Input/Output Model

In the Scioto model, tasks read from and write to globally accessible data. Many different mechanisms for asynchronous data sharing on distributed memory systems are available and the Scioto execution model is designed to be compatible with a variety of one-sided and global address space models. At a minimum, the global address space must provide primitives for allocating globally accessible regions of memory, and performing one-sided read and update operations. Many provide additional capabilities to synchronize accesses to shared data and some provide wait-free synchronization mechanisms such as atomic swap and accumulate that allow for high degrees of concurrency in the global address space. Higher level languages and tools such as UPC [280], CAF [218], or Global Arrays [215] allow the user to create high-level shared data structures—such as distributed multidimensional arrays or trees—and to interact with distributed global data objects through uniform or partitioned mechanisms.

Scioto's task model was designed to support any of these data sharing mechanisms by allowing the user to include portable references to global data objects (e.g., global array handles and indices or UPC shared pointers) as a part of the task's arguments. For example, under many one-sided models for communication, a portable shared pointer is the tuple $\langle process, address \rangle$ where $process$ refers to the process that has the data and $address$ is address of the data in $process'$ shared address-space.

Access to Local Data

In a base SPMD execution, the static data segment is common across all execution contexts and data located in this memory (e.g., global variables) can be accessed from within a task. This mechanism may not be sufficient to meet programmers' needs, so Scioto also provides a *common local object* (CLO) store that can be used to provide access to local objects. Common local objects are local data items that are globally available, or present at every process participating in a task collection. CLOs are registered collectively and the registration returns a portable handle, which can be used at any process to query the given object—this handle can be included in the input data to a given task.

Common local objects can be used to access input and output data buffers without going through the global address space. For constant input data, communication overheads can be avoided by replicating data on every node. Similarly, for output data, which the application will gather or reduce, results can be accumulated locally, avoiding synchronization in the global address space. For some models, such as MPI-RMA or ARMCI, which do not use portable references to global allocations, common local objects can be used to generate portable references to allocation handles that will be used when accessing the global data store.

9.1.3 Task Execution Model

Scioto provides a "bag of tasks" execution model in which the programmer first *seeds* a task collection with an initial set of tasks; the user may optionally specify an initial assignment of tasks to processes and load balancing will only be performed if the initial assignment is unbalanced. Initial task placements can be especially useful when integrating Scioto with existing task-partitioning strategies. Next, the task collection is collectively *processed* by all attached processes, as shown in Algorithm 1. During the processing phase, the Scioto runtime system dynamically schedules and executes tasks.

Algorithm 1 Task parallel execution model.

  { Let T_p be a task collection }
$T_p \leftarrow \{initial\_tasks...\}$
while $t \leftarrow next\_task(T_p)$ **do**
    $execute\_task(t)$
end while

Tasks may spawn new subtasks during their execution and the task parallel region completes only after all tasks and subtasks have completed. Tasks are processed from the task collection in LIFO order (Last In First Out) according to the work-first principle [39]. For tasks which dynamically create subtasks, this yields a depth-first traversal of the task tree and bounds the space requirements of the task collection as proportional to $O(T_{depth})$. An example task tree is shown in Figure 9.2. This example shows a dynamic parallel computation where new sub-tasks have been spawned during the task parallel phase.

Scioto utilizes a *ready-tasks* execution model where, once a task has been added to the collection, it is assumed that all of its dependencies have been satisfied and that it is ready to execute. Thus, tasks are assumed to be *nonblocking* in the sense that, once started, they must be able to run to completion irrespective of the order and concurrency with which other tasks are executed. Because of this semantic, it is invalid for a task to wait for another task to produce data or to make a matching synchronizing call (e.g., send/receive).

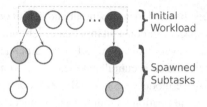

Figure 9.2: Example dynamic parallel task tree. Completed tasks are black, running tasks are shaded, and available nonstarted tasks are white.

This model was chosen to ensure scalability and performance by avoiding overheads from live task migration, task sequencing, and asynchronous task-execution progress.

Data flow between Scioto tasks can be accomplished through two mechanisms: phase-based execution and ancestor-child dependence. Multiple Scioto task collections can be created and, during execution, tasks can add new tasks to a second task collection. Once tasks in the current collection have completed, the second collection can be processed, allowing for task-parallel phases where the output of one task parallel phase is an input to a following phase. Similarly, when new tasks are added to the current task collection, data produced before the child task was added will be available as an input to that task. The programmer can track any data or control dependencies through the global address space and spawn tasks when their dependencies have been met.

9.2   Multilevel Parallel Task Collections

Each partitioning of a problem into multiple subproblems that can be processed in parallel is referred to as a level of parallelism. A majority of parallel programs use a single level of parallelism. However, many problems do not expose enough parallelism after a single partitioning and multiple levels of parallelism may be used to achieve better resource utilization. A common example of multilevel parallelism involves performing a coarse partitioning of the problem into chunks of work and then assigning each chunk to a group of processors or a group of cores on an SMP node. This chunk of work is then divided into smaller units of work that are processed in parallel by the group of processors. One distinct advantage of this strategy is that execution teams can leverage a high degree of locality and utilize algorithms that may be challenging to scale to higher degrees of parallelism.

Many important applications from computational science and engineering utilize multilevel parallelism. Programs that utilize coarse-grain distributed-memory parallelism coupled with finer-grain shared-memory parallelism have become commonplace. In addition, a variety of parallel solvers and libraries (e.g., PETSc [25], ScaLAPACK [37]) provide multiprocessor parallel routines that programmers can use in the implementation of a task. In order to accommodate the benefits of multilevel parallelism, tasks can be configured to execute on groups of processes rather than on a single process.

9.2.1 Scioto Execution Teams

Task scheduling on arbitrary resources is a challenging problem, for which no lightweight, fully distributed strategy is known. In order to avoid the complexity associated with dynamic resource management and scalability challenges of scheduling tasks on arbitrary resources, Scioto defines a simpler model which uses fixed-size task-execution groups. In this model, the programmer partitions processes into execution teams before entering a task-parallel phase. During the task-parallel phase, teams remain fixed and tasks are executed in parallel by these teams. This model is sufficient for a majority of HPC applications and its simplicity allows for an efficient and scalable implementation by avoiding complexity involved in dynamic group-formation and scheduling of tasks with varying resource requirements.

During task-parallel execution, Scioto designates a process from each execution team as the team leader. The leader manages task execution for the entire team and is responsible for participating in dynamic load-balancing. Once the leader acquires a task it broadcasts the task descriptor to the team and the team collectively executes the task. Collective operations are permitted within the execution team. However, collectives between teams are not permitted (collectives are also not permitted when no teams are in use). When the task parallel region has completed, the leader broadcasts a termination message and processes return to the base model.

9.3 Scioto+GA Programming Interface

Scioto+GA programs begin and end in the SPMD execution model used by Global Arrays and collectively enter into *task-parallel regions* when processing a task collection. This model presents the programmer with a global view of a distributed collection of tasks referred to as a *GA task collection* (GTC). The task collection is physically distributed and each task is assigned an affinity with respect to a particular process. When selecting tasks for execution, tasks with the highest affinity to a given process or execution group are processed first and tasks with lower affinity are given lower priority. When load balancing is performed, low-affinity tasks are given the highest priority to be transferred.

9.3.1 Core Programming Constructs

A Scioto+GA task collection is identified by a portable gtc_t reference, which can be copied via simple assignment and included as a task argument. This can be useful when using multiple task collections to provide multiple task-parallel phases; tasks can be placed into a second task collection while executing the first task collection.

Every task object is associated with a *task class* that defines the properties of its task instances, including the size of the task object's argument segment and how the task should be executed. When a task class is registered, a portable task class identifier for the task type, task_class_t, is returned. This identifier will be used when creating instances of that type of task. Because it is a portable reference, it can also be included as a task argument. Such functionality is useful when tasks may create subtasks of a different type from the parent.

Scioto's CLOs are also represented using portable handles that can be used to look up a given object in the CLO dictionary. These references, called clod_t, can be passed as arguments to tasks and used on any process to look up the local copy of the common local object.

9.3.2 Implementing a Scioto Task

A Scioto task object is implemented by a function with the following prototype:

```
void task_fcn(gtc_t gtc, task_t *descriptor);
```

This function is registered with Scioto when a task class is created and will be called by the runtime system when a task is executed. When the task is executed, it receives a portable reference to the current task collection as well as a local pointer to the task descriptor that contains the task's metadata and arguments. The task collection reference can be used to interact with Scioto, for example, to create subtasks.

A task descriptor is an opaque object and is accessed using the GTC API. Task descriptors are contiguous objects, which eliminates the need for marshalling when transferring a task during load balancing. As shown in Figure 9.3, the task body contains task arguments in a contiguous segment of the task descriptor and the layout of this data can be specified through the creation of a struct.

```
typedef struct {                         typedef struct {
  /* Task Metadata (Scioto Data) */        /* References to GAs */
  task_class_t task_class;                  int   A, B; /* Input GA references  */
  int          created_by;                  int   C;    /* Output GA references */
  int          affinity;
  ...                                       /* Indices of C block:  (C = A*B) */
                                            int   block[3];
  /* Task Arguments (User Data) */        } mm_task;
  uint8_t      args[0];
} task_t;
```

Figure 9.3: Scioto's internal task descriptor implementation that incorporates metadata and arguments into a contiguous task object (*left*). An example user-defined task argument layout for a blocked matrix-matrix multiplication task (*right*).

9.3.3   Example: Matrix-Matrix Multiplication

Listing 9.1 shows an example Scioto+GA program that performs blocked matrix-matrix multiplication to solve $C = A \cdot B$. Parallelization is performed in terms of blocks of the output C matrix. A block of the C matrix is computed by the function mm_task_fcn().

In this example, all processes first collectively register the mm_cls task class for the mm_task_fcn() task callback. This function takes, as input, a task with an mm_task body that contains portable references to the input and output arrays (integers under GA) and the indices of the blocks to multiply. Next, the task collection is collectively created and an instance of the mm_cls task class is created on each process. The task arguments are populated with references to the global arrays being multiplied.

After this, all processes seed the task collection with the multiplication tasks. Each processor creates only the tasks corresponding to patches of the output array that are local by calling the user-defined function, get_owner(), and comparing the result with its own process id. After the task has been added, the data in the task buffer has been copied into the task collection and the buffer is reused by calling gtc_task_reuse(). Finally, the task collection is processed and all tasks are executed.

9.4   The Scioto Runtime System

A variety of techniques and algorithms can be used to create a dynamic task-scheduling runtime system suitable for executing a Scioto task-parallel phase. Here, we describe the implementation of Scioto+GA, which is built using GA's ARMCI one-sided communica-

```
void mm_task_fcn(gtc_t gtc, task_t *task) {
  mm_task *mm = gtc_task_args(task);

  /* Perform multiplication on the given block */
  Multiply_Block(mm->A, mm->B, mm->C, mm->block[0], mm->block[1],
                 mm->block[2]);
}

void main(int argc, char **argv) {
  gtc_t           gtc;       /* Task collection handle */
  task_class_t    mm_cls;    /* Task class pointer */
  task_t          *task;     /* Task descriptor pointer */
  mm_task         *mm;       /* Task arguments pointer */
  int             A, B, C;   /* Global array handles */

  GA_Initialize();
  /* Initialize global arrays A, B, and C (code not shown) */

  mm_cls = gtc_task_class_register(sizeof(mm_task), mm_task_fcn);
  tc     = gtc_create(sizeof(mm_task), MAX_TASKS);
  task   = gtc_task_create(mm_cls);
  mm     = gtc_task_args(task);

  mm.A = A;
  mm.B = B;
  mm.C = C;

  /* Enumerate tasks add tasks with local affinity to my portion of the task collection */
  for (i=0; i < NUM_BLOCKS; i++)
    for (j=0; j < NUM_BLOCKS; j++)
      for (k=0; k < NUM_BLOCKS; k++)
        if (get_owner(i,j,k) == me) {
          mm.block[0] = i;            /* Setup task arguments */
          mm.block[1] = j;
          mm.block[2] = k;
          gtc_add(gtc, me, task); /* Add the task to the task collection */
          gtc_task_reuse(task);    /* Reuse the task buffer to create the next task */
        }

  /* Collectively execute all tasks */
  gtc_process(gtc);

  gtc_destroy(gtc);
  GA_Terminate();
}
```

Listing 9.1: Task-parallel blocked matrix-matrix multiplication using Scioto+GA. The task argument layout, mm_task, is defined in Figure 9.3.

tion library and uses work stealing to perform dynamic load balancing. Additional details and discussion of scalability and efficiency techniques can be found in [98, 99, 97].

This Scioto runtime system maintains a *deque*, or double-ended queue, on every process. The deques are preallocated with a fixed size and stored in the ARMCI shared segment, enabling asynchronous, one-sided access by all processes to every deque. When tasks are added to the collection, they can be enqueued on either the head or the tail of a specific process' deque. When processes execute tasks, they are taken from the head of the queue and when tasks are moved for load balancing, they are taken from the tail of the deque. This head/tail usage allows the runtime system to provide simple task priorities that can be used to prioritize tasks with high locality for the local process by adding them to the head of the queue.

9.4.1 Shared Task Queue Approach

Scioto+GA task collections are implemented by preallocating contiguous arrays of task descriptors in ARMCI shared space on each process. These arrays are treated as a contiguous circular queues and `head` and `tail` indices are maintained to mark the front and back of the queues. Each queue contains a process' current pool of available work and we refer to the aggregation of all queues as the task collection.

Processes can push and pop tasks to and from the head or tail of their local queue. Processes are also able to manipulate remote queues using ARMCI one-sided operations. Because queues are contiguous arrays, several tasks can be simultaneously pushed onto or popped off of a remote queue using a single one-sided communication operation. During an operation on a remote queue, the queue must be locked to prevent updates from colliding. This synchronization leads to a reduction in concurrency that can adversely affect the performance of the local process as it can end up waiting for thousands of cycles while a remote process manipulates its queue. In [99] we describe a technique for splitting the queue into private and shared portions to reduce overheads of interacting with shared queues.

9.4.2 Dynamic Load Balancing Approach

As the computation progresses, processes may exhaust the work available in their work queue. When this happens, dynamic load balancing must be performed in order to obtain more work. Scioto uses a locality-awareness enhanced version of the work-stealing-based dynamic load-balancing algorithm [39]. Under work-stealing, processes that have exhausted their local work must search among their peers for surplus work. This is done by randomly selecting a peer and performing remote operations on its patch of the task collection to steal surplus work if any is available.

Locality-awareness is implemented by prioritizing the queue such that tasks with high local affinity are placed toward the head of the queue and tasks with low affinity to the local process are placed toward the tail. Steal operations are then performed with respect to the tail of the queue and local task processing is performed with respect to the head of the queue. Thus, tasks with high affinity are most likely to execute on the local process and tasks with low affinity will be the first to be stolen when load balancing is performed.

Work Stealing

Under work-stealing, when no work is available, processes steal tasks from the tail of another process' deque. The process that initiates the steal operation is referred to as the *thief* and the process that is targeted by the steal is referred to as the *victim*. Because the thief is responsible for initiating load-balancing requests, work stealing is a *receiver-initiated* load-balancing algorithm and the total volume of load-balancing operations performed will therefore be proportional to the load imbalance. In addition, given an appropriate work division scheme, it has been proven that the load imbalance under work-stealing is bounded, making it a *stable* load-balancing algorithm [205, 31].

Scioto performs dynamic load balancing using random work-stealing. When a process has exhausted all of its local work, it becomes a *thief* and selects a peer process at random. The deque on this *victim* process is then accessed and a portion of the work is transferred from the victim to the thief. In the ARMCI implementation of Scioto, the steal operation is performed using one-sided operations that lock the victim's deque and dequeue a chunk of work from the tail of the deque.

Scioto's steal size is configurable and the default behavior is to steal half of the tasks available on the victim. This strategy estimates that each task contains the same amount of work and attempts to evenly divide the victim's workload. In addition, it also enables a thief to become a work source for other thieves, resulting in a logarithmic diffusion time for computations that expand from a small set of tasks.

9.4.3   Termination Detection

In order to determine when the computation has completed, processes must detect when all processes are idle and no more work is available. The process of detecting this stable global state is referred to as *termination detection*. Many schemes are possible, ranging from centralized schemes using shared counters and termination-detection servers to fully distributed schemes. A wave-based algorithm similar to that proposed by Francez and Rodeh [113] was initially used by Scioto+GA. In spite of the low latency of this approach, the invalidation protocol became too difficult to maintain in the presence of sophisticated task-spawning and load-balancing schemes. In place of this wave-based scheme, a four counter algorithm was selected, which also detects termination in $O(logN)$ communication steps [185]. This simpler approach essentially performs a sequence of two nonblocking allreduce operations to find the total number of tasks created and the total number completed. When these numbers are equal across both operations and the same values are observed twice, the computation has terminated.

9.5 Conclusion

Scioto [98, 99, 97] defines a task-parallel execution model that extends process-centric parallel programming models with task-parallel regions. Scioto tasks operate on data that is stored in a one-sided or global address space and the Scioto model is agnostic of the particular global data mechanism that is used. This model addresses a gap present in many one-sided and GAS programming models by complementing the flexible, asynchronous data model with a flexible, dynamic view of the computation. Scioto is especially well matched with applications that exhibit irregular and dynamic parallelism. It provides convenient interfaces and mechanisms for expressing dynamic parallelism and provides opportunities for a runtime system to automatically perform load balancing and other optimizations to mitigate imbalance that can occur with these types of parallelism.

Scioto+GA is discussed as an instance of the Scioto model that utilizes the Global Arrays data model. The Scioto+GA runtime system is constructed using multiple distributed queues to store the contents of the task collection. Individual processes operate with respect to work located in their own queue, which is sorted to improve locality. Dynamic load balancing is achieved using a highly scalable work-stealing engine.

10   Swift: Extreme-scale, Implicitly Parallel Scripting

Timothy Armstrong, The University of Chicago
Justin M. Wozniak, Argonne National Laboratory and The University of Chicago
Michael Wilde, Argonne National Laboratory and The University of Chicago
Ian T. Foster, Argonne National Laboratory and The University of Chicago

Scientists, engineers, and data analysts frequently find themselves needing to execute a set of application tasks hundreds—or even millions—of times, for example to optimize a design simulation or to process large collections of data records. Such activities can be intellectually and administratively arduous, due to the need to orchestrate many data movements and application execution tasks, and to track the resulting outputs, which themselves often serve as inputs to further applications. Further complicating these activities is the frequent need to leverage distributed and parallel computing resources in order to complete computations in a timely manner.

Task-parallel programming models allow existing code (libraries or programs) to be rapidly developed into scalable applications. However, they generally do not capture the high-level *workflow structure* of the overall application. Concepts like iteration, recursion, and reduction are lost if the user must coordinate tasks with the task-parallel library. It is difficult to compactly express these abstractions in the event-handling style required by the master-worker model. Additionally, data management is lost, and data dependencies must be encoded in an ad hoc manner.

The Swift parallel scripting language represents a unique approach to this problem. Swift transparently *generates* an task-parallel ADLB program (cf. Chapter 8) from a high-level script, which contains data definitions, data dependencies, and links to external native code (i.e., C/C++/Fortran). This program can then be run on an MPI-based high-performance computer.

Like other scripting languages, Swift allows programmers to express computations via the linking together of existing application code by, for example, specifying that the output of program A be provided as input to tasks B and C, the outputs of which are then consumed by task D. This approach has the advantages of allowing for rapid application development and avoiding the need to modify existing programs. Swift supports concurrency implicitly, so that in our example, if tasks B and C have no other dependencies, they can both execute in parallel as soon as A completes. As described in the following, Swift is not limited to directed acyclic graph (DAG) dependency expressions.

Additionally, Swift introduces a powerful data model that allows for typical scalars (integers, floats, strings), arrays, structs, and so on. Swift also supports an unformatted byte array (called a *blob* for "binary large object"), which can hold arbitrary native data for messaging from one task to the next. Furthermore, Swift represents external files as variables, which can also be the subject of data dependent operation (similar to Makefiles). These features together can reduce greatly the costs of developing and running computations such as those referred to above.

In this chapter, we introduce the Swift programming model and execution model. We aim to provide enough information to allow the reader to write a Swift program. We first use simple examples to introduce key Swift concepts and then introduce the language syntax, demonstrating its broad applicability to highly productive large scale computation. We finally describe the distributed architecture that is used to run applications on even the largest parallel computers.

10.1   A First Example: Parallel Factorizations

We use a simple example to introduce the Swift language, computing the factors of all numbers, up to N, in parallel, and then produce a histogram of the popularity of each factor.

Swift script file: **factors.swift**

```
1   int N = parseInt(argv("N"));
2   bag<int> M[];
3   foreach i in [1:N] {
4     int factors[] = factorization(i);
5     foreach f in factors {
6       M[f] += 1;
7     }
8   }
9
10  foreach b,i in M {
11    printf("%i: %i", i, bagSize(b));
12  }
```

Swift usage in the shell:

```
1   > swift-t factors.swift -N=10 | sort -n
2   1: 10
3   2: 5
4   3: 3
5   4: 2
6   5: 2
7   6: 1
8   ...
9   10: 1
```

Figure 10.1: Swift example: Factorization

The Swift script is shown at the top of Figure 10.1 as `factors.swift`. This Swift program has one link to an external function, `factorization()` (line 4), which could be implemented in native code. This function returns all factors of a given integer, e.g.,

$$\texttt{factorization(12)} \rightarrow \texttt{1,2,3,4,6,12.}$$

The program begins by obtaining `N` from the user (line 1), then looping (line 3) from 1 to `N` *concurrently*. Swift internally uses the Asynchronous Dynamic Load Balancing (ADLB) model (Chapter 8) for task management. In this example, each loop iteration is implemented as an ADLB task, executing somewhere in the system.

Each `factorization(i)` call then executes as a task (line 4), returning the array of factors. Each factor must increment its count. This count is maintained in the *bag* for that factor, i.e., `M[f]` is incremented each time `f` occurred as a factor (line 6). `M[]` is thus defined as an array of bags, each containing integers (line 2). This structure should be recognizable as a MapReduce pattern; in fact, Swift can elegantly represent MapReduce [93] and various of its generalizations [7, 103].

Swift execution is shown at the bottom of Figure 10.1. For `N=10`, the factor 1 appears 10 times, 2 appears 5 times (once for each even value of `i`), and so on. The output is piped through `sort` because the `printf()` statements (line 11) execute in load-balanced, system-defined order.

10.2 A Real-World Example: Crystal Coordinate Transformation

We use a second example to show how the Swift language can be used to analyze data: in this case, to apply an data transformation to a 3D dataset. This example builds on the concepts in the previous example, with only slight additional complexity.

This scientific use-case is from X-ray scattering at the Advanced Photon Source at Argonne National Laboratory. The task is to perform a coordinated transform on a three-dimensional pixel array, converting the data from detector coordinates to real coordinates. Each chunk of the input data contributes to some set of output chunks, but the precise mapping is not known in advance. Thus, the transform function returns the list of output chunk identifiers as part of its output. Figure 10.2 shows an example use in two dimensions. The diamond-hashed chunks (input chunks 3, 6, 8, 12, and 13) contribute to output chunk 2. The transformed data from each is put in a bag and then merged into the output chunk. This application also clearly has MapReduce-like behavior.

This pattern is represented in the Swift script in Figure 10.3. The program has four external functions, implemented in C++, each prefixed with `cctw_`. (The C++ version is runnable as a stand-alone program, parallelized for a multicore machine with the Qt Concurrent library. Swift enables this same code to run across multiple nodes.) For each input chunk `i`, the input HDF file is read (line 3), obtaining the hyperslab corresponding to chunk ID `i`: represented by a Swift blob. Then, the chunk is transformed (line 6), producing arrays of output chunks and output IDs. For each output pair `j` (line 7), the

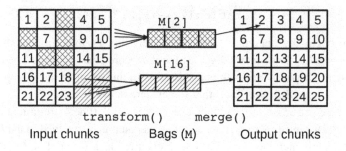

Figure 10.2: Crystal coordinate transformation dataflow pattern.

chunk is appended to the corresponding bag (line 9). Thus, in this application, each bag contains blobs (not integers as in the previous example).

Once each transform has completed, the blobs for each bag can be merged via a simple weighted addition (line 13). Then, the output chunks can be written to the corresponding HDF hyperslabs (line 14).

As in the factorization example, each call to an external function is run as concurrently as possible, limited only by data dependency. This approach allows Swift to make good use of massively parallel computers, without the direct use of lower-level libraries. Thus, we see how existing program components (C++ components, in this case) can be used to create a high-performance task-parallel computation through the use of a high-level script. Note also how Swift's bag, array, and blob features make it easy to distribute and compute over binary data on parallel computers.

10.3 History of Swift

The original implementation of Swift (called *Swift/K* because it is based on a runtime system called Karajan) was designed for coordination of large-scale distributed computations that make use of multiple autonomous computing resources distributed over varied administrative domains, such as clusters, clouds, and grids. Swift/K focused on reliability and interoperability with many systems at the expense of performance: execution of the program logic is confined to a single shared-memory *master* node, with calls to external executable applications dispatched to execution resources as parallel tasks over an execution provider such as Coasters [135] or Falkon [236]. Even in favorable circumstances with a fast execution provider executing tasks on a local cluster, at most 500–1000 tasks can be dispatched per second by Swift/K. This rate is insufficient for applications with more demanding performance needs such as a high degree of parallelism or short task duration.

```
 1   bag<blob> M[];
 2   foreach i in [1:n] {
 3     blob inputChunk = cctw_input("xray-data.hdf", i);
 4     blob outputChunks[];
 5     int outputIds[];
 6     (outputIds, outputChunks) = cctw_transform(i, bl);
 7     foreach chunk, j in outputChunks {
 8       int outputId = outputIds[j];
 9       M[outputId] += chunk;
10     }
11   }
12   foreach g in M {
13     blob b = cctw_merge(g);
14     cctw_write(b);
15   }
```

Figure 10.3: Swift example: Crystal coordinate transformation

Optimizations to the language interpreter, network protocols, and other components could increase throughput, but a single-master architecture ultimately limits scaling and is unsuitable for applications with tasks with durations of hundreds of milliseconds or less or with a high degree of parallelism (more than several thousand parallel tasks) [225]. Thus, in order to address the needs of many demanding parallel applications, the current Swift implementation, sometimes called *Swift/T* (because it is based on a runtime system called Turbine [296], which uses ADLB), achieves high-performance by parallelizing and distributing script execution and task management across many nodes.

The current Swift language's syntax and semantics are derived from, and remain close to, the original Swift/K language. Swift focuses on enabling a *hierarchical* programming model for high-performance fine-grained task parallelism, orchestrating large-scale computations composed of external functions with in-memory data, computational kernels on GPUs and other accelerators [164], and parallel functions implemented in lower-level parallel programming models—typically threads or message-passing. These functions and kernels are integrated into the Swift language as typed *leaf functions* that encapsulate computationally intensive code, leaving parallel coordination, task distribution, and data dependency management to the Swift implementation.

Swift can be rigorously analyzed and enhanced by a range of compiler optimization techniques to achieve high efficiency and scalability for a broad range of applications on massively parallel distributed-memory computers. Its design is motivated by the limitations of current programming models for programming extreme-scale systems and addressing emerging problems such as programmability for nonexpert parallel programmers, abstraction of heterogeneous compute resources, and the composition of heterogeneous task types into unified applications.

We next provide an overview of Swift syntax and semantics. We then present the design and implementation of an efficient and scalable runtime system for this execution model, and techniques for efficiently compiling Swift for this style of runtime system, including compiler optimization techniques that allow applications developed in Swift to execute efficiently on massively parallel distributed-memory systems.

10.4   Swift Language and Programming Model

The main features that characterize Swift are:

- A **hierarchical programming model** where computationally intensive code is written in various other programming languages and parallel coordination is written in Swift.

- **Implicit parallelism** and relaxed execution ordering constraints: program statements can execute out-of-order, whenever input data is available.

- Control structures, including conditional if/switch statements and loop constructs, that are **semantically related to the equivalent imperative constructs**, but are adapted for implicit parallelism and monotonic data.

- Use of data types such as single-assignment variables with the property of *monotonicity*, which can ensure that results of computations are deterministic even with nondeterministic scheduling of tasks.

Swift can guarantee deterministic execution even with implicit parallelism because its standard data types are *monotonic*; that is, they cannot be mutated in such a way that information is lost or overwritten. A monotonic variable starts off empty, then incrementally accumulates information until it is *frozen*, whereupon it cannot be modified further. Programs that attempt to overwrite data will fail at runtime (or compile time, if the compiler determines that the write is definitely erroneous). If write operations that modify monotonic variables are *commutative*, then writes can be reordered without changing the final result.

If reads to Swift data types are constrained so that transient states are not observable, then we can achieve deterministic computation even with nondeterministic ordering of operations. Swift programs using futures-based data types with these restrictions on reads are deterministic by construction, up to the order of side-effects such as I/O. For example, the output value of an arbitrarily complex function involving many data and control structures is deterministic, but the order in which, say, print statements execute depends on the nondeterministic order in which tasks run. Further nondeterminism is introduced only by non-Swift code, such as the implementation of builtins (the library function rand()), and external functions (written in native code).

Basic Swift variables are single-assignment I-vars [216] (sometimes alternatively called futures), which are frozen when first assigned. All basic scalar primitives in Swift are semantically I-vars: ints, floats, booleans, and strings. Files can also be treated as I-vars, with an I-var in the language mirroring a file in the file system to which it is *mapped*. Assigning a mapped file variable in Swift then results in a file appearing at that path.

Composite data types can be incrementally assigned in parts but cannot be overwritten. The only composite data types that Swift originally supported were structs and associative arrays [292], both of which are monotonic futures-based data types. The *associative array* is the most complex and heavily used of the two. Integer indices are the default, but other index types including strings are supported. The array can be assigned all at once (e.g., int A[] = f();), or in parts (e.g., int A[]; A[i] = a; A[j] = b;). An array lookup operation on A[i] will return when A[i] is assigned. An incomplete array lookup does not prevent progress; other statements can execute concurrently.

The Swift language guarantees that variables are automatically *frozen* when the implementation is sure that no more writes will occur. This allows Swift code to refer directly to properties such as the size of arrays and ensures that reads of nonexistent array keys will eventually fail. The implementation of automatic freezing in Swift requires both compiler analysis and runtime support.

We introduce the Swift language here through a series of examples that illustrate its syntax and semantics. The examples use version 0.8.0 of Swift.[1]

10.4.1 Hello World

We begin with the Swift version of the classic "Hello, World" program in Figure 10.4, which needs two lines of code: the import statement that imports the builtin io module, then the call to the printf function from the io module to print a string.

```
1 | import io;
2 | printf("Hello World");
```

Figure 10.4: Swift example: Hello World.

Adding another printf in Figure 10.5 adds an interesting twist related to Swift's implicit parallelism (the following examples omit import statements to the Swift standard

---

1. http://swift-lang.org/Swift-T

library). In Swift, the statements are allowed to run in any order because there is no data dependency between them: the program might print `Hello World` *after* `Goodbye World`.

```
1   printf("Hello World");
2   printf("Goodbye World");
```

Figure 10.5: Swift example: Hello/Goodbye World.

10.4.2   Variables and Scalar Data Types

Variables in Swift are strongly and statically typed: each variable's type is known at compile time and automatic conversion between types happens in few cases. The basic data types in Swift, which are treated as scalar values, are: `int` (64-bit integer), `float` (double-precision floating point), `string` (unicode string), `blob` (binary string), `boolean` (boolean value), `void` (no value: used for signaling), and `file` (file variable representing filesystem entry). Scalar variables are single-assignment I-vars: once a variable is declared, it can be assigned at most once; a second assignment leads to a runtime error. Figure 10.6 demonstrates various modes of declaration and assignment of variables.

```
1    //  Declaration then assignment
2    int x;
3    x = 0;
4    printf(x);
5
6    //  Combined declaration and assignment
7    float y = 2.0 + toFloat(x);
8
9    //  Use before assignment is valid (dataflow is resolved at runtime)
10   string z;
11   printf(z);
12   z = "The quick brown fox jumped over the lazy dog";
```

Figure 10.6: Swift example: data types.

Variables can be assigned without being explicitly declared. If an variable name that has not previously been declared is assigned, Swift creates a new variable in the current scope with a type matching the expression on the right hand side of the assignment. This technique can be used in many but not all cases. For example, in Figure 10.7, automatic declaration can be used for `x` and `condition`, but `y` requires an explicit declaration because the assignments are both in inner scopes.

```
1   // x is automatically declared as a string variable
2   x = "Hello" + " " + " World";
3
4   // x is automatically declared as a boolean
5   condition = true;
6
7   if (condition) {
8      y = x;
9   } else {
10     y = "";
11  }
12  // Error! y is not defined in this scope
13  printf(y);
```

Figure 10.7: Swift example: Automatic declaration.

10.4.3   Dataflow Execution

As mentioned earlier, Swift is implicitly parallel, with program execution ordered by data dependencies. Thus, any two operators, function calls, or other parts of a Swift program can execute in parallel if there is no direct or indirect data dependency between them.

In Figure 10.8, the two calls to f can execute in parallel because neither depends on data produced by the other. The call to g, however, cannot execute in parallel with either f call because it depends on the data produced by both of them.

```
1   x = f(0);
2   y = f(1);
3   z = g(x, y);
4
5   printf("%i %i %i", x, y, z);
```

Figure 10.8: Swift example: dataflow parallelism between statements.

Different subexpressions of the same expression can also be evaluated in parallel. For example, Figure 10.9 implies the same pattern of parallelism as the previous example, despite the calls to f and g being embedded in the same expression.

```
1   printf("%i", g(f(0), f(1)));
```

Figure 10.9: Swift example: dataflow parallelism among expressions.

10.4.4 Conditional Statements

Conditional execution is supported by the `if` and `switch` statements. We omit discussion
of `switch` statements here for the sake of brevity. The `if` statement's syntax is identical
to that used in many imperative programming languages, such as C, but it executes in a
data-dependent manner consistent with the rest of Swift. The condition of an `if` statement
is evaluated in parallel with other statements in the enclosing block. Once the value of the
condition is computed, the appropriate branch of the `if` statement is executed.

To illustrate how the `if` statement behaves in an implicitly parallel context, consider the
code in Figure 10.10, which executes two computationally intensive simulation functions
in parallel. After they finish, it compares the results and prints a message depending on
the outcome. The programmer does not have to write code to explicitly synchronize and
gather the results from the two parallel computations. Rather, the required synchronization
happens automatically as part of the evaluation of the `if` statement condition, so that the
message is printed once the outcome is known.

```
 1 | float f1, f2;
 2 |
 3 | f1 = simulationA();
 4 | f2 = simulationB();
 5 |
 6 | if (f1 > f2) {
 7 |   printf("Simulation A won!")
 8 | } else {
 9 |   printf("Simulation B won!")
10 | }
```

Figure 10.10: Swift example: conditional execution with `if` statement.

10.4.5 Data-dependent Control Flow

The Swift `wait` statement and `=>` chaining operator can be used to sequence statements
by introducing explicit dependencies into a program. Either construct can be used to make
a second statement depend explicitly on data produced by a first expression or statement,
so that the second executes only after the data produced by the first is frozen, even if the
second statement does not consume its value. This capability can used to add delays to a
program, sequence messages reporting progress, or accommodate side effects in external
functions. Note that, for these constructs to work, the statement that is to be waited on must
produce some output. Most Swift functions have at least one output argument; if they do

not, then it is straightforward to add a `void` output argument to signal when the function finishes executing. Figure 10.11 demonstrates the use of these features.

```
1    //  Chaining of multiple statements
2    printf("Going to sleep") =>
3       sleep(1) =>
4       printf("Woke up") =>
5       sleep(1) =>
6       printf("Woke up again");
7
8    x = compute_something();
9
10   //  The following forms are equivalent:
11   x => printf("Done!");
12
13   wait (x) {
14      printf("Done!");
15   }
```

Figure 10.11: Swift example: data-dependent control flow.

The two constructs differ subtly in several ways. `=>` waits on a statement, while `wait` waits on the expression supplied as its argument. Only statements that produce some kind of output variable support chaining. `=>` can have any statement on its right hand side, while `wait` must be followed by a block enclosed in curly braces.

10.4.6 Foreach Loops and Arrays

Foreach loops are tied closely with Swift arrays, so we introduce both constructs simultaneously.

Arrays in Swift are associative arrays: finite maps of keys to values. The value type can be any Swift type. The default key type is `int` and other scalar key types such as strings are supported. Associative arrays with integer keys can also be viewed as *sparse* arrays: arrays with integer keys that do not need to be contiguous. There are multiple ways to declare and initialize arrays, as shown in Figure 10.12.

The workhorse control-flow construct in most Swift programs is the `foreach` loop for parallel iteration over members of Swift data structures, including arrays. Iterations of a foreach loop are independent and execute in parallel, provided that data dependencies allow. Iteration over an array constructed with the [*begin*:*end*:{*step*}] syntax is the idiomatic way to iterate over a range of integers. In general, this syntax instructs Swift to construct an array literal. However, when it is used in a loop iteration construct, Swift avoids construction of the intermediate array and thus the idiom comes with no perfor-

```
 1  //   Two equivalent ways of declaring an array A mapping integers to strings
 2  string A[int];
 3  string A[];
 4
 5  //   Declaration of an array mapping strings to integers
 6  int A2[string];
 7
 8  //   Equivalent statements that initialize an array with the numbers from 1 to 4
 9  B = [1, 2, 3, 4];  //   List of values (keys 0-3 are implied)
10  B = [1:4];  //   Integer range (keys 0-3 are implied)
11  B = [1:4:1];  //   Integer range with explicit step of 1
12  B = { 0: 1, 1: 2, 2: 3, 3: 4 };  //   Explicit keys
13  //   Assigning piece-by-piece
14  B[0] = 1;
15  B[1] = 2;
16  B[2] = 3;
17  B[3] = 4;
18
19  //   Declaring two-dimensional nested array
20  string C[][];
21  C[0][0] = "top-left";
22  C[0][1] = "top-right";
23  C[1][0] = "bottom-left";
24  C[1][1] = "bottom-right";
```

Figure 10.12: Swift example: array declarations.

mance penalty. To illustrate, Figure 10.13 shows code that builds an array by iterating over a range of integers and then iterating over the constructed array.

The loop iterations in Figure 10.13 may execute in any order and thus the results will likely not print in ascending order. In-order printing can be achieved by combining `for` loops (a construct distinct from `foreach`) with explicit data-dependent control flow (Section 10.4.5).

10.4.7   Swift Functions

So far we have only shown examples with Swift code at the top level of the program. Swift code can also be enclosed in functions for encapsulation and reuse. Swift functions must declare types and names of their input and output arguments. Functions return values by assigning the output arguments in the function body. Recursive function calls are allowed and tail recursion is supported in Swift: tail recursive calls of unlimited depth will not cause Swift to run out of stack space. Figure 10.14 illustrates Swift functions through different implementations of the factorial function.

```
1    //  Get command-line argument n, default value of 100
2    int n = parseInt(argv("n", "100"));
3
4    float harmonic[];
5
6    //  Compute the harmonic series.
7    //  Note that this literally instructs Swift to construct an array containing
8    //  integers 1 to n, then iterate over the constructed array.  However, Swift/T
9    //  always optimizes this to iterate over the range without building the array.
10   foreach i in [1:n] {
11     harmonic[i] = 1 / toFloat(i);
12   }
13
14   //  Iterate over values and indices
15   foreach x, i in harmonic {
16     printf("H[%i] = %f", i, x);
17   }
18
19   printf("sum = %f", sum(harmonic));
```

Figure 10.13: Swift example: basic `foreach` loops.

Function bodies can begin executing as soon as the function is called, regardless of the state of their input and output arguments. In Figure 10.15, assignment of each function input is delayed by a different amount. The `printf` calls in the function will execute at approximately one-second intervals once inputs are assigned.

10.4.8   External Functions

Swift is designed as a language for parallel coordination and scripting: the performance-critical sequential computation work is typically outsourced to code written in other languages. Thus, Swift provides rich support for integration with external functions written in programming languages including C, C++, Fortran, Python, R, Julia, Tcl, alongside the command-line applications traditionally supported by Swift [292]. These functions can be called from Swift code by declaring an *external function* with Swift input and output argument types.

All external functions in native code (C/C++/Fortan) are called via bindings generated with SWIG [28]. The Swift compiler automatically generates all necessary code to manage data-dependent execution and marshal the input and output arguments.

Swift provides a high-level interface for Python, R, Tcl, and Julia, by providing builtin functions that call to the appropriate interpreter, which may be optionally linked with Swift at configure time [297]. These interpreters may, in turn, call language extensions written

```
1   x_val = parseInt(argv("x", "5"));
2
3   f1, f2 = fact2(x_val);
4
5   printf("fact(%i) = %i", x_val, f1);
6   printf("fact_tail(%i) = %i", x_val, f2);
7
8   // Recursive implementation of factorial.
9   (int result) fact(int x) {
10    if (x == 0) {
11      result = 1;
12    } else {
13      result = x * fact(x - 1);
14    }
15  }
16
17  // Tail-recursive implementation of factorial.
18  (int result) fact_tail(int x, int accum) {
19    if (x == 0) {
20      result = accum;
21    } else {
22      result = fact_tail(x - 1, accum * x);
23    }
24  }
25
26  // Compute factorial in two ways, illustrating multiple output arguments
27  (int r1, int r2) fact2(int x) {
28    r1 = fact(x);
29    r2 = fact_tail(x, 1);
30  }
```

Figure 10.14: Swift example: basic Swift functions computing factorials.

```
1   print_three(string x, string y, string z) {
2     printf("%s", x);
3     printf("%s", y);
4     printf("%s", z);
5   }
6
7   a = "Now";
8   sleep(1) => b = "Later" =>
9   sleep(1) => c = "Even later";
10
11  print_three(a, b, c);
```

Figure 10.15: Swift example: delayed assignment of Swift function arguments illustrating execution of Swift function body before arguments are all assigned.

in native code, creating a powerful hierarchical programming model. Figure 10.16 shows a simple external function implemented in Tcl.

Swift also supports native-code parallel libraries written in MPI that accept a communicator on which to execute [298]. When provided with such a function, Swift dynamically creates a subcommunicator and runs the user code on it.

```
1   //  Declaration of log to arbitrary base via Tcl
2   @pure @dispatch=WORKER
3   (float o) my_log (float x, float base) "mypkg" "0.1"
4   [ "set <<o>> [ expr log(<<x>>)/log(<<base>>) ]" ];
5
6   printf("log10(100) = " + my_log(100, 10));
```

Figure 10.16: Swift example: declaration of a external Tcl function. The Tcl fragment is the string literal between the square brackets. Swift variables o, x, and base are marshaled to and from Tcl with the angle bracket syntax. The syntax "mypkg" "0.1" loads the Tcl package mypkg, version 0.1, allowing additional Tcl libraries and/or extensions (native code libraries with Tcl bindings) to be referenced from the Tcl fragment.

The @pure function annotation, used in Figure 10.16, is used to assert that the function is deterministic and has no side-effects. This annotation allows the Swift optimizer to reuse results of the function instead of recomputing them, if needed. The function annotation, @dispatch=WORKER, tells Swift that the function may take a little while to run and should always be executed as an independent task. Other annotations are documented in the Swift user guide [263].

10.4.9 Files and App Functions

Swift supports files as a first-class data type that can be treated similarly to a scalar value in the program. It also supports *app functions*: command-line programs that are wrapped as typed Swift functions. Thus, scripts manipulating files and invoking command-line applications can be expressed with regular Swift variables and function calls, as shown in Figure 10.17. This feature means that Swift can be used to develop file-based workflows, as with Makefiles, with extreme scalability. For example, one user who wanted to test a C compiler under a wide range of tuning parameters used Swift to distribute runs over distributed-memory systems.

```
1   app (file out) cat (file inputs[]) {
2     "/bin/cat" inputs @stdout=out
3   }
4
5   file inputs[] = glob("*.txt");
6   file joined <"joined.txt"> = cat(inputs);
```

Figure 10.17: Swift example: Concatenating all text files in a directory.

10.5   The Swift Execution Model

We briefly describe here Swift's execution model for *data-driven task parallelism*. The execution model provides a foundation for the semantics of the Swift programming language. An important property of the model is that, subject to reasonable constraints, the result of a computation in the execution model is deterministic even when tasks are executed in a nondeterministic order or in a concurrent manner with interleaved reads and writes while accessing a shared data store.

As mentioned earlier, Swift is runs on the Turbine distributed runtime system, which is well suited for massively parallel distributed systems. The core component of Turbine is ADLB; Turbine provides additional features to make it an attractive compiler target for the Swift compiler (STC), providing a small set of primitives that enable Swift to run.

In data-driven task parallelism, all computation is performed by *tasks*, which are abstracted as mathematical functions that take input values and compute outputs of various kinds. Once executing, tasks run to completion and are not preempted. Tasks communicate by reading and writing *shared data* that resides in a data store. A task declares a set of shared data items that it will read and the computed output of a task includes a set of write operations on shared data items. Shared data is also the main means of synchronization: execution of a task can be made dependent on shared data so that the task does not run until that data is available.

To visualize the execution model, we will use a graphical notation for *trace graphs* that show the tasks, shared data, and dependencies that arise during execution. A trace graph, such as Figure 10.18, illustrates a single runtime execution of a program. Note that a single static graph cannot always serve as a specification of the data-driven tasks program because dependencies emerge dynamically at runtime. Tasks may selectively read, write, or spawn based on values computed at runtime: the tasks and relationships between tasks may vary between different executions of the same program, e.g., if the input data is varied. A trace graph never has cycles: in the case of deadlocks, deadlocked tasks will have fewer in-edges than data dependencies.

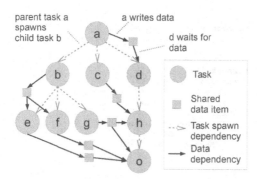

Figure 10.18: Trace graph showing task and data dependencies at runtime in data-driven task parallelism, forming a spawn tree rooted at task a. Data dependencies on shared data defer execution of tasks until the variables in question are frozen. Thus, for example, task h cannot execute until a data item is written by task c.

Figure 10.19: Task spawning two children that synchronize on an item of data.

Each task can spawn asynchronous *child tasks*, resulting in a *spawn tree* of tasks, as in Figure 10.18. In practice, tasks can be implemented through a set of parameterized *task definitions* that make up a program: at spawn time a task definition's parameters are bound to specific values by the parent to produce a child task. This allows parent tasks to pass data directly to their child tasks. For example, this could be small data such as numbers or short strings, along with references to arbitrary shared data. Shared data items can be read or written by any task that obtains a *reference* to the data. Shared data items provide for coordination between multiple tasks. For example, a task A can spawn two tasks, B and C, passing both a reference to a shared data item, which B writes and C reads, as shown in Figure 10.19. *Data dependencies*, which defer the execution of tasks, are the only way to synchronize between tasks. The execution model permits a task to write (or not write) any data it holds a reference to, allowing many runtime data dependency patterns beyond static task graphs.

Figures 10.20 and 10.21 use an example to illustrate how Swift may be translated into the execution model. The example application, an amalgam of several real scientific applications, runs an ensemble of simulations for many parameter combinations. The code

```
 1  blob models[], res[][];
 2  foreach m in [1:N_models] {
 3    models[m] = load(sprintf("model%i.data", m));
 4  }
 5
 6  foreach i in [1:M] {
 7    foreach j in [1:N] {
 8      //  initial quick evaluation of parameters
 9      p, m = evaluate(i, j);
10      if (p > 0) {
11        //  run ensemble of simulations
12        blob res2[];
13        foreach k in [1:S] {
14          res2[k] = simulate(models[m], i, j, k);
15        }
16        res[i][j] = summarize(res2);
17      }
18    }
19  }
20
21  //  Summarize results to file
22  foreach i in [1:M] {
23    file out<sprintf("output%i.txt", i)>;
24    out = analyze(res[i]);
25  }
```

Figure 10.20: Swift code for the data-driven task trace graph of Figure 10.21.

(Figure 10.20) executes with implicit parallelism, ordered by data dependencies. Data dependencies are implied by reads and writes to scalar variables (e.g., p and m) and associative arrays (e.g., `models` and `res`). Swift semantics allow functions (e.g., `load`, `evaluate`, and `simulate`) to execute in parallel when execution resources are available and data dependencies are satisfied. This example illustrates the additional expressivity of the execution model over some common alternatives such as static task graphs or dataflow networks. Simulations are conditional on runtime values: data-driven task parallelism allows dynamic runtime decisions about what tasks to create. The task graph (Figure 10.21) shows an optimized translation to data-driven task parallelism. An unoptimized version would comprise more variables and tasks.

10.6   A Massively Parallel Runtime System

The Turbine runtime system enhances the ADLB load-balancing library, by supporting arbitrary user data, data dependencies, and miscellaneous builtin functions and other tools to support Swift.

Early prototype versions of Turbine extended ADLB with required functionality, such as a distributed data store and data-dependent task release [295]. Since then, we have further extended and enhanced Turbine to produce a complete and scalable distributed language runtime for Swift. This work includes task queue performance and scalability

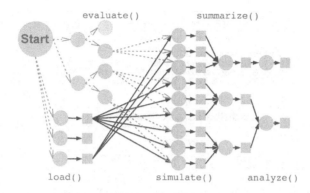

Figure 10.21:   Visualization of optimized parallel tasks and data dependencies for the program of Figure 10.20, for parameters $M = 2, N = 2, S = 3$.

enhancements, work stealing to rebalance work between servers, richer data functionality, and support for garbage collection through reference counting.

10.7   Runtime Architecture

The Turbine/ADLB runtime is a distributed system that allows many *workers* to cooperate in executing massively parallel applications. It enables coordination between workers through three core services that are implemented efficiently and scalably: a *distributed data store* to store shared data, a *distributed task queue* to distribute work, and a *distributed dependency engine* that tracks data dependencies of tasks. Figure 10.22 illustrates the interactions between these services. These services provide operations that support distributed execution of Swift.

Task operations support adding and removing tasks from the distributed task queue. The *payload* of each task is arbitrary binary data that can be interpreted in an application-dependent way. The task operations support adding tasks: enqueuing a task in the dependency engine or for immediate execution. "Get" operations remove a task from the queue of the desired *type*. Different Get variations support nonblocking gets of tasks useful when a worker can execute multiple tasks in parallel or when a programmer wants to overlap task execution with task gets.

A model of differentiated task types is used to support GeMTC GPU tasks [164], task dispatch to multiple worker types when integrated with the NAMD molecular dynamics software [230], and integration with Coasters for execution of remote command-line applications [135]. Parallel tasks have many applications, such as running ensembles of the OSUFlow particle tracing application [298]. The use of task priorities to prioritize criti-

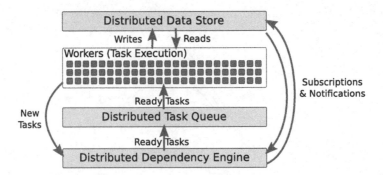

Figure 10.22: A view of the Swift distributed runtime (Turbine/ADLB) as distributed services enabling coordination between workers. Tasks created by code running on workers are passed to the dependency engine. The dependency engine holds tasks until required input data are available, and then passes the tasks to the task queue. Tasks are then sent from the task queue to workers to be executed. While executing, tasks can read and write the distributed data store. Writes to the distributed data store can trigger notifications to the dependency engine if the dependency engine has subscribed to that data.

cal tasks (e.g., tasks that are longer-running or on the critical path of the application) can significantly improve system utilization and reduce time-to-solution [14, 17]. Rank and node-level targeting—both `Hard` and `Soft`—have found applications in data-intensive applications where data is stored locally on the compute node and the cost of remotely reading data is significant [100, 299].

Runtime data operations allow creating, reading, writing, subscribing to, and reference counting of shared data items in the data store.

In order to implement the three distributed services provided by the runtime system, MPI processes are divided into two roles: *workers* and *servers*. Figure 10.23 shows a common way of distributing servers: one server per node. The system can be scaled up arbitrarily by proportionally adding processes of both types. Worker processes can execute any program logic, coordinating with each other using the data and task operations provided by distributed services. The distributed services are implemented by the server processes and accessed with remote procedure calls (RPCs).

Implementation of an efficient and scalable task queue hinges on two key features: efficient task-matching algorithms and data structures to maximize throughput per server, and scalable work-distribution algorithms to handle load imbalances between servers. Task matching only solves the problem of matching work on an individual server to that server's own workers. If a server runs out of work, then it must somehow acquire more work from another server to prevent its workers from sitting idle. Such load imbalances are common

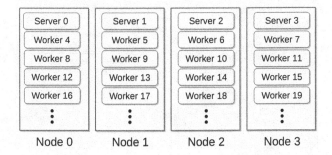

Figure 10.23: Runtime process layout on a distributed-memory system. Worker and server processes are mapped onto multicore systems.

in practice, and thus moving work from overloaded to underloaded servers efficiently is critical. Novel work stealing enhancements were used to address this problem [15].

The runtime's data store implements a distributed data store with semantics based on the abstract data store described below. Data store keys are 64-bit integers and the key space is partitioned between servers in a round-robin manner. Multiple placement strategies are possible when a worker calls `Create`. The current strategy used is to place the data on the nearest server, which improves data locality, but can lead to problems with load imbalance. Each data store key has an associated type tag. For compound data structures, additional type information about members is stored in various ways.

Garbage collection and automatic freezing are supported by a reference counting mechanism. Data-dependent task release is based on a key/path pair becoming frozen. Release is implemented efficiently through a subscription mechanism: any process in the system can subscribe to a key/path pair. Subscriptions are tracked by the server to which the key maps, and when the frozen state is entered, a notification message is set to the subscriber.

Efficient memory management is challenging in a distributed context, especially in the highly dynamic execution model of data-driven task parallelism, because references to a data item may be held by many processes at any given time. The classic memory management problem is generally formulated as the problem of detecting when no direct or indirect references to a data item are held by the executing program. The variable freezing problem can be formulated similarly: detecting when no `Write` references are held.

We tackle both problems with *automatic distributed reference counting*. We give each shared data item two reference counts (*refcount*), one for read references and one for write references. When a data item's write refcount drops to zero, it is frozen and cannot be written; when both refcounts drop to zero, the data can be deleted. Single-assignment variables do not require special treatment, but for variables such as arrays, where multiple

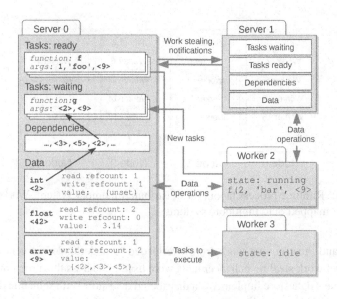

Figure 10.24:   Runtime architecture showing distributed worker processes coordinating through task and data operations. Ready/waiting tasks and shared data items are stored on servers, with each server storing a subset of tasks and data. Servers must communicate to redistribute tasks through work stealing, and to request/receive notifications about data availability on other servers.

assignments are possible, refcounts must be correctly incremented and decremented to track the number of tasks and data structures with references to a key. A well-known weakness of reference counting is that it cannot handle cycles of references. The Swift data model does not permit such reference cycles, which avoids the problem.

10.8   Performance

Large-scale experiments were performed on the Blue Waters supercomputer [109] using Swift. Figure 10.25 shows our scalability and task throughput results obtained by running an embarrassingly parallel Swift program that exercises task matching and work stealing. Swift achieved a peak throughput of 1.47 billion tasks/s on 524,288 cores running the Sweep benchmark [16]. Tasks of 1 ms or more achieve high efficiency; the servers are lightly loaded and queuing delays are minimal.

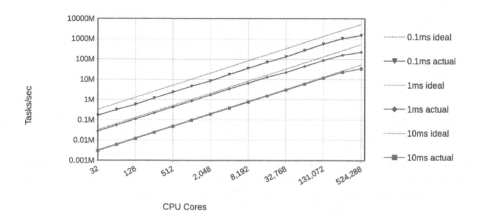

Figure 10.25: Throughput and scaling of runtime system for varying task durations.

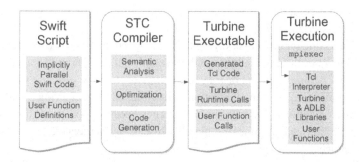

Figure 10.26: The STC compiler is in the middle of the Swift toolchain and translates high-level Swift code into execution code for the Turbine runtime.

10.9 Compiling Swift for Massive Parallelism

STC is a whole-program optimizing compiler for Swift that compiles high-level Swift code to run on the distributed runtime described in Section 10.6. STC generates code in the Tcl scripting language that can execute on the distributed runtime system; the runtime exposes ADLB and supporting libraries via Tcl bindings, enabling ease in the usage and debugging of the generated code. Figure 10.26 illustrates how STC fits into the Swift toolchain. STC implements optimizations aimed at reducing communication and synchronization without loss of parallelism. An intermediate representation captures the execution model, allowing optimization to reduce synchronization and runtime task/data operations involving shared

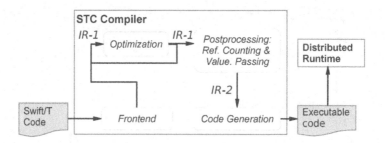

Figure 10.27: STC compiler architecture. The frontend produces IR-1, which is increasingly optimized by successive passes. Postprocessing adds intertask data passing and reference counting information to produce IR-2 for code generation.

data. It enables garbage collection by reference counting which is further optimized. We briefly survey the effectiveness of the compiler optimizations on several benchmarks. Further details of the compilation process can be found in an earlier paper [16] and Armstrong's Ph.D. dissertation [15].

To optimize a wide range of data-driven task parallelism patterns, we need compiler optimization techniques that can understand the semantics of task parallelism and monotonic variables in order to perform major transformations of the task structure of programs to reduce synchronization and communication at runtime, while preserving parallelism. Excessive runtime operations impair program efficiency because tasks waste time waiting for communication; they can also impair scalability by causing bottlenecks in the data store or task queue services.

The STC compiler uses a medium-level intermediate representation (IR) that captures the execution model of data-driven task parallelism. The tree structure of the intermediate representation can be mapped to the spawn tree of tasks, and dependencies through single-assignment data types are a first-class part of the IR. Two IR variants are used in STC, as shown in Figure 10.27. IR-1 is generated by the compiler frontend and then optimized. IR-2 includes additional information for code generation: explicit bookkeeping for reference counts and data passing to child tasks.

Detailed measurements and a comparison to related compilation and optimization work have been presented in prior publications [16, 15].

10.10   Related Work

Ousterhout [224] has written eloquently about the rationale and motivation for scripting languages, the difference between programming and scripting, and the place of each in the scheme of applying computers to solving problems.

Coordination languages such as Linda [8], Strand [110], and PCN [111] support the composition of implicitly-parallel functions programmed in specific languages and linked with the systems. In contrast, Swift coordinates the execution of what are typically legacy applications coded in various programming languages. Linda defines primitives for concurrent manipulation of tuples in a shared "tuple-space". Strand and PCN, like Swift, use single-assignment variables as their coordination mechanism. Linda, Strand, PCN and Swift are all dataflow-driven: processes execute only when data are available.

Swift has its origins in the Virtual Data Language (VDL) [112] developed within the Grid Physics Network (GriPhyN) project for management of large-scale data analysis computations. The term virtual data is intended to indicate that program rules define how data is to be produced; required computations are then performed when the user calls for the final data product.

Execution models and runtime systems combining task parallelism with data dependencies for HPC applications have been explored by several groups [104]. Tarragon [79] and DaGuE [49] implement efficient parallel execution of explicit dataflow DAGs of tasks from within an MPI program. ParalleX [152] provides a programming model through a C++ library that encompasses globally-addressable data and futures, with the ability to launch tasks based on dataflow. StarPU [20] and OmPSS [56] both provide lower-level library and pragma-based interfaces for executing tasks with data dependencies on CPUs and accelerators on distributed-memory clusters.

Habanero Java [264] and Habanero C [77] support asynchronous task parallelism with data dependencies on shared-memory nodes. Extensions to Habanero C support some inter-node parallelism with integration between MPI primitives and Habanero C, although this falls short of providing transparent task migration between nodes. X10 supports asynchronous task parallelism, but synchronization is based on a finish statement and termination detection algorithms, instead of data-dependencies [265].

The Asynchronous Dynamic Load Balancer (ADLB) [182], the basis of our runtime system, is highly scalable and has been successfully used by large-scale physics applications. However, its initial version did not support shared global data and the task queue performance was significantly extended through its integration into Swift.

Scioto (Chapter 9) is a library for distributed memory dynamic load balancing of tasks, similar to ADLB. Scioto implements work stealing among all nodes instead of the server-worker design of ADLB. Scioto's efficiency is impressive, but it does not provide features required for Swift such as task priorities, work types, and targeted tasks.

Recent work on systems such as Sparrow [225], CloudKon [245], and Apollo [50] has attempted to improve throughput of task schedulers in cloud computing to enable workloads composed of "tiny tasks" on large clusters. These systems must deal with problems such as unreliability of workers and the need to enforce scheduling policies for shared resources. As a result of this and other implementation choices, they are unable to achieve anywhere near the efficiency of our runtime system: typical per-task overhead is tens to hundreds of milliseconds.

The MATRIX task scheduler [289], like Swift, seeks to implement high-performance distributed task scheduling with policies such as data-aware scheduling. However, MATRIX is built on a general-purpose key-value store. Our work shows that special-purpose data structures for task matching are required to achieve high performance given scheduling policies such as location-awareness and priorities.

10.11 Conclusion

We have described a hierarchical programming model for massively-parallel computing, which uses a high-level implicitly parallel language, Swift, to orchestrate computational tasks implemented in a range of other programming languages. This approach is a promising direction for addressing future systems challenges of unreliability and heterogeneity while making it substantially easier for nonexpert programmers to construct highly scalable parallel applications.

Swift's distributed Turbine runtime system faces many challenges, some of which—scalable synchronization, task matching, and task distribution—have been addressed with algorithms and data structures that address the problems of implicitly parallel dataflow-based programming models. These new approaches enabled great improvements in runtime performance and made the programming model performant and scalable enough to be attractive for many applications that fit the execution model.

Our experience with Swift provides strong evidence that that a combination of runtime algorithms and compiler techniques can enable high-level implicitly parallel code to drive fine-grained task-parallel execution at massive scales, rivaling the efficiency and scalability of hand-written parallel coordination code for common patterns of parallelism at scales from tens of cores to half a million cores and for a range of task-parallel application patterns including iterative optimization, tree search, and parallel reductions.

The system described in this chapter has been used for production science applications running on over 100,000 cores in production and over 500,000 cores in testing. Application of both compiler and runtime techniques was essential to reaching this scale. The Swift programming model offers a combination of ease of development and scalability that has proven valuable for developers who need to rapidly develop and scale-up applications, and do not have the time, expertise, or need to implement, optimize and debug applications in a lower-level distributed-memory programming model like MPI. Applying Swift to new and different problems will reveal further strengths, weaknesses, and opportunities.

Swift is an open source project with documentation, source code, and downloads for Swift/K and Swift/T available at `http://www.swift-lang.org`.

Acknowledgments

This research was supported in part by NSF grants OCI-721939 and OCI-0944332 and by the U.S. Department of Energy under contract DE-AC02-06CH11357. Computing resources were provided by the Argonne Leadership Computing Facility, XSEDE, Open Science Grid, the UChicago/Argonne Computation Institute's Beagle supercomputer, and the Amazon Web Services Education allocation program.

We gratefully acknowledge the contributions of current and former Swift team members, collaborators, and users: Glen Hocky, Hemant Sharma, Jun Park, Jon Almer, Ray Osborn, Guy Jennings, Jonathan Ozik, Sarah Kenny, Allan Espinosa, Zhao Zhang, Luiz Gadelha, David Kelly, Milena Nokolic, Jon Monette, Aashish Adhikari, Marc Parisien, Michael Andric, Steven Small, John Dennis, Mats Rynge, Michael Kubal, Tibi Stef-Praun, Xu Du, Yadu Nand Babuji, Ketan Maheshwari, Joshua Elliott, Zhengxiong Hou, and Xi Li. The initial implementation of Swift was the work of Yong Zhao and Mihael Hategan; Karajan was designed and implemented by Hategan under an effort led by Gregor von Laszewski. Swift/T is the work of Justin Wozniak and Timothy Armstrong, with contributions by Yadu Nand Babuji.

11 Concurrent Collections

Kath Knobe, Rice University
Michael G. Burke, Rice University
Frank Schlimbach, Intel

11.1 Introduction

With multicore processors, parallel computing is going mainstream. Yet most software is still written in traditional serial languages with explicit threading. High-level parallel programming models, after decades of proposals, have still not seen widespread adoption. This is beginning to change. Systems like MapReduce are succeeding based on implicit parallelism. Other systems like NVIDIA CUDA (see Chapter 15) are partway there, providing a restricted programming model to the user but exposing many of the hardware details. The payoff for a high-level programming model is clear—it can provide semantic guarantees and can simplify the analysis, debugging, and testing of a parallel program.

The Concurrent Collections (CnC) programming model is quite different from most other parallel programming models in several important ways. It is a programming model specifically for coordinating among potentially parallel chunks of computation and data. As such it is a coordination language, and so must be paired with a separate language for computation. In addition, CnC is declarative. It specifies the required orderings among chunks of computation code, but does not, in any way, indicate how those requirements are to be met. In particular, it is not some syntax for connecting with a specific runtime. CnC runtimes might be characterized by how they determine: the grain of data and computation; the placement of data and computation across the platform; and the schedule across time within a component of the platform. Instances of CnC implementations have determined all three dynamically, all three statically and various combinations. Most of the current implementations fix the grain statically but allow for dynamic choice of mapping across the platform and across time. We will address the current implementations in more detail in Section 11.5.

The CnC programming model is a high level, declarative model built on past work with TStreams [163]. CnC falls into the same family as dataflow and stream-processing languages—a program is a graph of kernels, communicating with one another.

A CnC graph can execute along with its environment, a program written in a sequential or parallel language. A CnC graph indicates what input it expects from the environment and what output it returns to the environment. This is all the CnC graph needs to know about the environment. But a CnC graph may play fundamentally different roles in different applications, depending on the relationship of the graph to its environment. Sometimes we think of the environment of a CnC graph as basically "main." It is written in some computation language. Its entire purpose might be to manage a CnC graph execution. In this case, it creates a graph (see Section 11.3.1), inputs data to the graph, and indicates that it is done putting input. (For finitely executing CnC graphs, the program cannot know when it is finished unless it knows that there will be no more input.) The environment waits until the graph execution completes and then gets output data from the graph. Above, we describe a single execution of a single CnC graph. The environment might be much more complex. In particular, most of the application might be in the environment. A single instance of the graph as described above might, for example, be in a loop. Then the same graph might execute multiple times with different inputs. In addition, the environment may have many distinct CnC graphs at separate places in the code. The environment itself might be a parallel program. This would allow for the distinct dynamic instances of a given graph and/or instances of distinct graphs to execute in parallel.

11.2 Motivation

Both, explicitly parallel and explicitly serial languages are overconstrained, though in different ways. CnC avoids both forms of unnecessary constraints. A CnC program is an implicitly parallel program that avoids unnecessary constraints and thereby maximizes the scheduling freedom in executing the program for a given target (efficiency) and also among distinct targets (portability).

The domain expert writing a CnC program focuses on the meaning of the application, not on how to schedule it. CnC isolates the work of the domain expert (interested in finance, chemistry, gaming) from the tuning expert (interested in load balance, locality, scalability). This isolation minimizes the need for the domain expert to think about all the complications of parallel systems. In the CnC domain language, no particular category of machine is assumed. This isolation also minimizes the need for the tuning expert to know about the application domain.

"Old World" languages impair communication between the programmer and the compiler. They introduce arbitrary serial constraints due to the serial ordering of statements and to avoid overwriting of variables (resulting in complicated antidependencies and output dependencies). Program analysis and transformations are then required to expose the true dependencies. In these languages the domain and tuning codes are intertwined. The programmer has to be aware of one when modifying the other, complicating both tasks. Also the programmer writing the domain code has to commit to the form of parallelism that the application will use when targeted to a parallel architecture. CnC is neutral to the form of parallelism, supporting different forms of parallel applications.

11.2.1 Foundational Hypotheses

1. User specification of the semantically required constraints, rather than the parallelism, is simpler and leads to comparable, if not better, performance.

2. Separation of computation from coordination simplifies these activities and supports reuse.

3. Separating the specification of the semantics from the specification of the tuning simplifies both activities.

4. Starting with too much asynchronous parallelism and providing a separate, simple and effective way to control it is easier and more effective than starting with a serial program and adding parallelism.

5. Dynamic single assignment (DSA)/determinism eliminates race conditions, making programs less error prone, easier to reason about and debug. The apparent increase in memory usage can be adequately addressed.

CnC is broader than other parallel programming models along one dimension and narrower along another. CnC is provably deterministic with respect to a program's output (not the schedule). Although this makes it easier to use, it also limits the scope of applications it supports.[1] Some applications are inherently nondeterministic. On the other hand, it allows a wider range of parallel execution styles than other systems. It supports both static and dynamic forms of task, data, loop, pipeline, and tree parallelism.

11.3   CnC Domain Language

11.3.1   Description

The CnC domain specification indicates computations of a program, and the control and data dependencies among these computations. These relationships impose constraints on the execution order. These are the only constraints imposed by the domain specification. There is no arbitrary serial ordering of statements, only the partial ordering based on the dependencies. These constraints are based on the application logic, and are independent of the target architecture.

The CnC domain language coordinates among computation steps. These computation steps are written in a sequential or parallel programming language. For example, Intel ® CnC for C++, supports C++ programs. Other existing systems have Java, C with OpenMP, Scala, Haskell, Python, Habanero Java, and a subset of MATLAB, as the computation language. The data model is based on tuple spaces.

A computation step instance that produces a data item must execute before the computation step instance that consumes that data. A computation step instance that produces a

---

1. We are experimenting with adding controlled nondeterminism to extend the range of applications supported without losing the ease-of-use advantages.

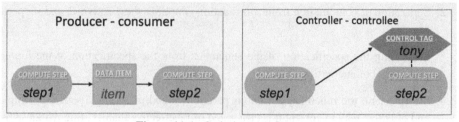

Figure 11.1: Ordering requirements

control tag must execute before the computation step instance controlled by that control tag. These entities and relationships form the nodes and edges of a graph as illustrated in Figure 11.1.

This graphical description includes the computation steps (in circles), the data items (in squares), the control tags (in hexagons) and the producer/consumer relations among them (arrows, dotted in the case of control dependencies). The inputs and outputs are shown as data items produced by the environment and data items consumed by the environment. This facilitates composability of graphs. The graph may be cyclic.

In the remainder of the chapter we use our textual notation instead of the graph notation described above. We represent step, items and tag collections using syntax $(stepName)$, $[itemName]$ and $< tagName >$. Arrows are used for producer and consumer relations. The control relation represented as a dotted line in the graph becomes : : in the text. More than one relation can appear in a statement. A " ; " is used to end a statement.

CnC specification graph.   The three main constructs in a CnC specification graph are *step collections*, *data collections*, and *control collections*. These collections and their relationships are defined statically. But for each static collection, a set of dynamic *instances* is created as the program executes.

A step collection corresponds to a specific computation, and its instances correspond to invocations of that computation with different input tags. A control collection is said to *control* a step collection—adding an instance to the control collection *prescribes* one or more step instances i.e., causes the step instances to eventually execute when their inputs become available. The invoked step may enable other step executions by adding instances to other control collections, and so on.

Steps also dynamically read (get) and write (put) data instances. The execution order of step instances is constrained only by their producer and consumer relationships, including control relations. A complete CnC specification is a graph where the nodes can be either step, data, or control collections, and the edges represent producer, consumer, and control relationships.

A whole CnC program includes the specification, the step code and the environment. Step code implements the computations within individual graph nodes, whereas the *environment* is the external user code that invokes and interacts with the CnC graph while it executes. The environment can produce data and control instances. It can consume data instances and use control instances to prescribe conditional execution.

Collections indexed by *tags*. Within each collection, control, data, and step instances are each identified by a unique *tag*. Tags may be of any data type that supports an equality test and hash function. Typically, tags have a specific meaning within the application. For example, they may be tuples of integers modeling an iteration space (i.e., the iterations of a nested loop structure). Tags can also be points in nongrid spaces—nodes in a tree, in an irregular mesh, elements of a set, etc. Collections use tags as follows:

- A data collection is an associative container indexed by tags. The contents indexed by a tag i, once written, cannot be overwritten (dynamic single assignment). In a specification file a data collection is referred to with square-bracket syntax: [x:i,j].

- A step begins execution with the tag indexing that step instance. The tag provides access to (optional) input data. The next input tag may be a function of the data found in the first input tag, and so on. So the first input tag serves as a seed value for computing the tags of all the step's input and output data. For example, in a stencil computation a tag "i, j" would be used to access data at positions "i+1, j+1", "i-1, j-i", and so on.

- A control tag collection specifies which step instances are to execute. Each tag in a control tag collection is a tuple which controls the execution of a corresponding instance of the controlled computation step. A *tag function* indicates which step instance corresponds to a control tag instance. Tag functions also indicate the relationships between step instances and input and output data item instances, as well as step instances and output control tags.

  Each computation step collection is controlled by exactly one control tag collection. A given control tag collection may control more than one computation step collection. A producer produces the control tags and data items. In either case, the producer might be a computation step or the environment, as shown in Figure 11.1.

Below is an example snippet of a CnC specification:

```
// control relationship : myCtrl prescribes instances of step
<myCtrl> :: (myStep);
// myStep gets items from myData, puts tags in myCtrl and items in myData
[myData] -> (myStep) -> <myCtrl>, [myData];
```

The CnC specification can indicate tag functions:

```
[myData: i] -> (myStep: i) -> <myCtrl: i+1>, [myData: i+1];
```

11.3.2 Characteristics

- **DSA:** Each data instance, that is a name/tag pair, is associated with a unique value. That is, the items obey DSA.

- **Determinism:** The step instance as a whole has no side effects and is a pure function of its input data. A combination of this and the DSA property ensures that the CnC specification is deterministic. The same specification with the same input can run on a thousand cores or on a single core (if it fits), and will produce the same results.

  Determinism in the domain specification means the code produces the same output collections on every execution. These collections are sets so the ordering is not relevant but the names, tag values and contents must be identical.

- **No false dependencies:** A CnC domain specification has implicit asynchronous parallelism. The only required orderings are specified semantic dependencies, not arbitrary orderings.

- **Platform Independence:** The domain specification is independent of the target platform. In particular, it does not make any assumptions about the memory model. Data is identified by tags and is treated as values and not as memory references. This makes it possible to use the same domain specification on shared and distributed memory without changing the step code. In many cases the separate tuning specification alone can handle the platform differences. In Section 11.4 we will show how a CnC runtime can handle distributed memory efficiently.

  Based on tag functions, DSA, determinism and ordering constraints that are due only to true dependencies, the CnC domain language simplifies analysis and transformations such as loop interchange, loop splitting and distribution (local vs. distributed tag component).

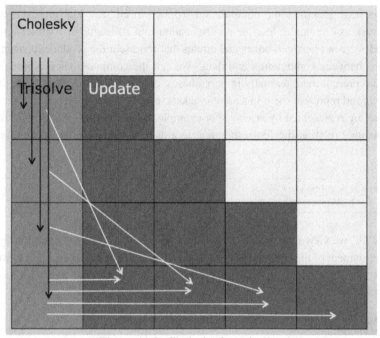

Figure 11.2: Cholesky factorization

11.3.3 Example

Cholesky factorization takes a symmetric positive definite matrix as an input and factors it into a lower triangular matrix and its transpose. The computation can be broken down into three CnC step collections. The step (*cholesky*) performs unblocked Cholesky factorization of the input symmetric positive definite tile producing a lower triangular matrix tile. Step (*trisolve*) applies a triangular system solve on the result of the step (*cholesky*). Finally, the step (*update*) is used to update the underlying matrix via a matrix-matrix multiplication. Figure 11.2 shows the dependencies between tiles of (*cholesky*), (*trisolve*), and (*update*). For more detail, see [55].

Here we describe the four stages for developing a CnC domain specification for an application. It starts at a "whiteboard" level, which does not provide sufficient information for execution. The remaining stages provide the missing information. We use Cholesky factorization as our example.

- **Stage 1**: The whiteboard description.

This stage identifies the computations (drawn in circles), and the data (drawn in boxes), as one might describe an application to a colleague at a whiteboard. It includes arrows between boxes and circles that represent the producer/consumer relations between computation and data. We call the computations *computation steps* and represent them textually in parentheses, e.g., $(trisolve)$. We call the data *data items* and represent them in square brackets, e.g., $[X]$. Producer and consumer relations are represented by arrows. For example, $(trisolve) \rightarrow [X]$. A full producer/consumer relationship (corresponding to a data dependence) would be represented as:

```
(trisolve) -> [X ]
[X ] -> (update)
```

In CnC, we view input/output as instances of producer/consumer relationships. The environment of the CnC graph produces and consumes data items. This is written as $env \rightarrow [X]$ or $[X] \rightarrow env$. The environment can also produce and consume control instances.

- **Stage 2**: Distinguish among the computation instances.

In the whiteboard description, a computation is processing some stream of input over an indefinite length of time. However, there will be distinct instances of the computation, and each takes place somewhere on the target machine at some point in time. The programmer distinguishes among these instances by associating each instance with a distinct tag. In the case of $(trisolve)$, the instances are identified by a tag that is a $row, iter$ tuple. Thus, we write $(trisolve : row, iter)$. The instances of $[X]$ are distinguished by row, column and iteration. We write $[X : col, row, iter]$.

The tuples such as $< column, iteration >$ or $< row, col, iteration >$ are called tags. Tags are used to identify instances and distinguish among them. The term *collection* indicates that a static computation step, say $(trisolve)$, is a collection of dynamic instances and a static data item, say $[X]$, is a collection of dynamic instances.

- **Stage 3**: Identify the instances to be executed.

We can now distinguish among the instances of $(trisolve)$ by tags of the form $row, iter$. But this does not tell us if $trisolve(52, 4)$ will be executed. Each step collection is controlled by one control collection that determines which step instances will execute. We represent control collections in angle brackets. A control collection holds a set of tuples. In our example, $(trisolve : row, iter)$ is controlled by

$< tagRowIter : row, iter >$. The relationship is represented by $::$. We say $< tagRowIter : row, iter > :: (trisolve : row, iter)$. The meaning of this relationship is that every tuple in $< tagRowIter >$ controls the execution of a corresponding instance of $(trisolve)$. During its execution it has access to the value of its tag.

In the Cholesky application, each of the three computation steps is controlled by its own control collection. In many applications, a control collection may control more than one computation's step collections. Imagine an application that processes video frames. A control collection containing $frameIDs$ might control more multiple computations that are to be performed on each frame.

- **Stage 4**: Indicate how the control collections are produced.

In the case of Cholesky, the control instances are statically known. So in this case the control collections are produced by the environment. We write this as $env \rightarrow < tagIter : k >$, and similarly for the other control collections. In general, however, one computation may determine if another will execute. This is a controller/controllee relation (corresponding to a control dependence). For example, we might say:

```
foo( ) -> <barTag: tag>
<barTag: tag> :: bar( )
```

At this point we have the entire representation of the CnC coordination graph for the Cholesky application. The CnC domain specification for Cholesky:

```
env -> [X];
[X] -> env;

<tagIter: k> :: (cholesky: iter);
<tagRowIter: row, iter > :: (triSolve: row, iter);
<tagColRowIter: col, row, Iter> :: (update: col, row, iter);

[X: iter, iter, iter] ->
    (cholesky: iter) ->
        [X: iter, iter, iter +1];
[X: iter, iter, iter+1], [X: iter, row, iter] ->
    (triSolve: row, Iter) ->
        [X: iter, row, iter +1];
[X: col, row, iter], [X: row, col, iter] ->
    (update: col, row, iter) ->
        [X: col, row, iter +1];
```

11.3.4   Execution Semantics

During execution, the state of a CnC program is defined by *attributes* of step, data, and control instances. These attributes are not directly visible to the CnC programmer. Data instances and control instances each have an attribute *Avail*, which has the value *true* if and only if a `put` operation has been performed on it. A data instance also has a *Value* attribute representing the value assigned to it where *Avail* is true. When the set of all data instances to be consumed by a step instance and the control instance that prescribes a step instance have *Avail* attribute value *true*, then the value of the step instance attribute *Enabled* is set to *true*. A step instance has an attribute *Done*, which has the value *true* if and only if its execution is complete.

Instances acquire attribute values monotonically during execution. For example, once an attribute assumes the value *true*, it remains *true* unless an execution error occurs, in which case all attribute values become undefined. Once the *Value* attribute of a data instance has been set to a value through a `put` operation, assigning it a subsequent value through another `put` operation produces an execution error by the single assignment rule. The monotonic assumption of attribute values simplifies program understanding, formulating and understanding the program semantics, and is necessary for deterministic execution.

Given a complete CnC specification, the tuning expert maps the specification to a specific target architecture, creating an efficient schedule. Tag functions provide a tuning expert with additional information needed to map the application to a parallel architecture, and for static analysis they provide information needed to optimize distribution and scheduling of the application.

Strategies for Implementing the Execution Model

They key challenge for every CnC implementation is the execution model of CnC. The currently available runtimes all use dynamic strategies to schedule the execution of steps. The most interesting aspect is how a runtime detects steps to be *enabled*, particularly in absence of tag-functions. It is a trivial task to determine when a step is *prescribed* (e.g., when the tag is put), but knowing when it is fully *inputs-available* is generally impossible without tag-functions. Hence different strategies have been developed to achieve a correct step execution. All approaches have advantages and disadvantages. They make different tradeoffs between what limitations they induce, how much overhead (memory and/or computation) they imply and how visible they are to the programmer.

To avoid the loss of generality, usually, increased overhead is accepted with some probability. Steps can be executed "speculatively" until a needed data item is found unavailable. When this happens several actions can be taken.

- Roll-back step execution and replay after the item became available.

  This solution implies memory overhead and, depending on the implementation language, the programmer must be aware of this behavior to some degree.

- Block thread until the unavailable item becomes available.

  This requires special attention to deadlock prevention like creating a new thread. As thread (or even process) creation is a relatively costly feature, the overhead in computation and memory is significant.

- Halt step execution and resume after item becomes available.

  Continuations require features that are not available in the common languages (yet). This solution promises to keep the computation overhead very low, but the effects on memory consumption are currently unclear.

Runtime performance can be maximized by making certain assumption about and limiting generality. The known approaches which fall into this category do not support data-dependent gets (e.g., require data-tags which depend on data and not only the step-tag). As mentioned above, full tag function availability (or equivalent information) provides the necessary information. An alternative approach limits the scope even further by requiring that the control and corresponding data are produced at the same place.

11.3.5 Programming in CnC

Expressing the Domain

As a coordination language and programming model, CnC must be paired with one or more programming languages to let the developer define the actual step computations. There are two approaches to connecting the rules for coordination with the actual computations. One possibility is to specify coordination and computation in the same programming language via a CnC specific API. The other is to define a new language whose only function is exactly to express the coordination and let a compiler generate the CnC glue in a computation language. Both approaches have (mostly software engineering related) pros and cons. Using a single language has two apparent advantages: it keeps the tool-chain needed to create an application short and, more importantly, it can be fully based on existing industry-standards. However, it also binds the language-independent semantics to a specific language (or even implementation). In our CnC domain language, step-collections are identified with putting their name in parenthesis (e.g., (step1)), data-collections are put in square brackets (e.g., [data1]) and control-collections are represented in angle brackets (e.g., <control1>). The types of data and control tags precede the collections name.

```
(step1);                          step_collection< s1 > step1;
(step2);                          step_collection< s2 > step2;
[double data1 <int>];             item_collection< int, double > data1;
<int control1>;                   tag_collection< int > control1;
(step1) -> [data1];               step1.produces( data1 );
(step2) <- [data1];               step2.consumes( data1 );
control1 :: (step1),              control1.prescribes( s1 );
            (step2);              control1.prescribes( s2 );
(step1) -> <control1>;            step1.controls( control1 );
```

Figure 11.3: CnC semantics expressed in a CnC domain syntax and in a C++ representation

The data-tag follows the data-collection name in angle-brackets. Figure 11.3 shows side by side equivalent declarations in the domain syntax and a C++ representation, where the collections are represented as simple template classes. Both express the combined graph of Figure 11.1.

The CnC domain language expresses producer/consumer relations with arrows ($\rightarrow$) and the control relation is expressed with double colons ($::$). The C++ API uses methods in the collections for equivalent functionality. It is clear from Figure 11.3 that both representations are equivalent and that trivial transformations exist to get from one to the other.

Example: Cholesky

Domain Specification of Cholesky. As an example, the full CnC domain specification for Cholesky could look like this:

```
# step collections
(cholesky: iter);
(trisolve: iter, row);
(update: iter, row, col);
# data collection
[double X <iter, row, col>];
# control collections
<int tagIter>;
<pair tagRowIter>;
<triple tagColRowIter>;
# I/O
env -> [X: iter, row, col],
       <tagIter: iter>,
       <tagRowIter: iter, row>,
       <tagColRowIter: iter, row, col>
env <- [X: iter, row, col];
# control relations
<tagIter: iter>                    :: (cholesky: iter);
```

```
<tagRowIter: iter, row>          :: (triSolve: iter, row);
<tagColRowIter: iter, row, col> :: (update: iter, row, col);
# producer/consumer relations
[X: iter, iter, iter] -> (cholesky: iter) -> [X: iter, iter, iter +1];
[X: iter, row, iter], [X: iter+1, iter, iter]
    -> (triSolve: iter, row)
    -> [X: iter, row, iter+1];
[X: iter, row, col], [X: iter+1, row, iter], [X: iter+1, col, iter]
    -> (update: iter, row, col)
    -> [X: iter+1, row, col];
```

In the C++ API, a CnC graph is defined within a so called `context`. For Cholesky, such a context could look like the following:[2]

```
// The context class
struct cholesky_context : public CnC::context< cholesky_context >
{
    // Step Collections
    CnC::step_collection< cholesky_step > cholesky;
    CnC::step_collection< trisolve_step > trisolve;
    CnC::step_collection< update_step >   update;
    // Item collections
    CnC::item_collection< triple, tile_const_ptr_type > X;
    // Tag collections
    CnC::tag_collection< int > tagIter;
    CnC::tag_collection< pair > tagRowIter;
    CnC::tag_collection< triple > tagColRowIter;
    // The context class constructor
    cholesky_context( int _b = 0, int _p = 0, int _n = 0 )
        : cholesky( *this ),
          trisolve( *this ),
          update( * this ),
          X( *this ),
          tagIter( *this ),
          tagRowIter( *this ),
          tagColRowIter( *this )
    {
        // I/O relations
        ENV.produces( X );
        ENV.consumes( X );
        ENV.controls( tagIter );
        ENV.controls( tagRowIter );
        ENV.controls( tagColRowIter );
        // control relations
        tagIter.prescribes( cholesky, *this );
        tagRowIter.prescribes( trisolve, *this );
```

---

2. The current implementations are evolving. Some of the facilities described here are not available at the time of this writing.

```
        tagColRowIter.prescribes( update, *this );
        // producer/consumer relations
        cholesky.produces( X );
        cholesky.consumes( X );
        trisolve.produces( X );
        trisolve.consumes( X );
        update.produces( X );
        update.consumes( X );


    }
};
```

There are several possibilities to express tag functions in the C++ API. One is to describe them in a separate interface, like:

```
template< class T >
void tuner::depends( const triple & tag, my_context & c, T & dC ) const
{
    dC.depends(X, tag);
    if( tag.col == tag.row ) {    // Diagonal tile .
        dC.depends(X, triple(tag.iter+1, tag.col, tag.iter);
    } else {    // Nondiagonal tile .
        dC.depends(X, triple(tag.iter+1, tag.col, tag.iter);
        dC.depends(X, triple(tag.iter+1, tag.row, tag.iter);
    }
}
```

A Sample Step. Once the CnC semantics are specified, the actual computation needs to be provided. To let the runtime call the steps, it has to conform to a given interface that is defined by the corresponding CnC implementation. Here we show examples which closely follow the conventions as defined by the Intel C++ implementation. Different implementations vary in how strictly they enforce the CnC rules, such as steps having no side effects and items being immutable. Languages like C/C++ provide less capabilities to actually enforce such rules than, for example, Java or even Haskel. In C++, capabilities for disallowing side-effects are already exhausted with requiring steps to be "const." The input arguments to a step are its tag and the collections it has relations with. In the C++ implementation every step has access to the entire graph through the second `context` argument. As an illustration, the following shows the step-body of the update step of the Cholesky example:

```
// Performs symmetric rank—k update of the submatrix.
int update_step::execute(const triple & tag, cholesky_context & c) const
{
    // init local vars
    const int k = tag[0], j = tag[1], i = tag[2];
    tile_const_ptr_type A_tile, L2_tile, L1_tile;

    c.X.get(triple(k,j,i), A_tile); // Get the input tile .

    if( i==j ) {     // Diagonal tile , i=j, hence both the tiles are the same.
        c.Lkji.get(triple(k+1,j,k), L1_tile);
        dsyrk( L1_tile, A_tile, ... );  // computation
    } else {          // Nondiagonal tile .
        c.X.get(triple(k+1,i,k), L2_tile); // Get the first  tile .
        c.X.get(triple(k+1,j,k), L1_tile); // Get the second tile .
        dgemm( L1_tile, L2_tile, A_tile, ... ); // computation
    }

    c.X.put(triple(k+1,j,i), A_tile);   // output for the next iteration
}
```

This code has no side-effects other than putting a new tile into the data-collection: it uses only local variables, it has no status and does not overwrite data. In principle, the computation follows the pattern "consume (get) input $\rightarrow$ compute $\rightarrow$ produce (put) output". More interestingly, this code illustrates that relations in CnC can be conditional. Different instances of this step consume different numbers of data items: when computing the diagonal it depends on only two input tiles, while on nondiagonals three inputs are consumed. Even though this example puts a condition only on the consumer relations, producer and controller relations can also be conditional.

The Environment.   The environment in a CnC program is responsible for instantiating the actual CnC-graph instance and producing initial data control. The latter is done with the same interfaces as used by steps. Between consuming the output and producing input and control, the environment can do arbitrary computation. A simplified environment code for Cholesky could look like this:

```
// Create an instance of the context class which defines the graph
cholesky_context ctxt;
// produce input matrix
for(int i = 0; i < N; i++) {
    for(int j = 0; j <= i; j++) {
        ctxt.X.put( triple(0,j,i), init_tile(j,i) );
    }
}
```

262   Chapter 11

```
// produce control tags
for(int k = 0; k < N; k++) {
    ctxt.tagIter.put( k );
    for(int j = k+1; j <= N; j++) {
        ctxt.tagRowIter.put( pair(k,j) );
        for(int i = k+1; i <= j; i++) {
            ctxt.tagColRowIter.put( triple(k,j,i) );
        }
    }
}
// Wait for all steps to finish (optional)
ctxt.wait();
// get result
for (int k = 0; k < N; k++) {
    for (int j = k+1; j < N; j++) {
        tile_const_ptr_type tile;
        ctxt.X.get( triple(j+1,j,i), tile );
        do_something( tile );
    }
}
```

Distributed Memory

A CnC domain specification never refers to a particular place (e.g., an address) or time (e.g., now). However, it explicitly identifies all entities needed to map the program execution to distributed memory: control instances identify what needs to be computed and data instances identify the data needed for the computations. Moreover, through gets and puts, a CnC program has explicit hooks at all places in the code relevant for distribution and so does not require explicit message handling. The runtime knows exactly which data and control instances are needed; there is no need to infer this information indirectly like other approaches, such as virtual shared memory systems or Cluster OpenMP.

Intel Concurrent Collections for C++ allows any legal CnC application to run on distributed memory. For this, only minimal additional coding is needed. Besides a trivial initialization variable, only marshaling capabilities for nonstandard data types need to be provided. The latter is a limitation of the underlying programming language, C++, because it does not provide marshaling features at the language level. Still, marshaling in this system is very simple and requires the developer to only provide the marshaling functionality. The runtime will take care of using it at the appropriate places.

Distributed evaluation is available in two modes, automatic and user-guided. In nontrivial cases, automatic distribution requires tag-function and their analysis to achieve acceptable efficiency. In the general case, the runtime can work in distributed memory environments even when no tag functions are available. This default behavior requires significant bookkeeping and overhead. When a step is executing, the runtime cannot know where (e.g., on which process) an unavailable item was or will be produced. As a consequence, it needs to synchronize data between processes, leading to broadcast-like communication patterns (or worse). Nevertheless, applications with few data-dependencies between steps can still perform well with the automatic distribution feature.

As an example for distributing the computation, the following code would partition a two-dimensional space (like a matrix) in a row-cyclic manner:

```
int tuner::compute_on( int row, int column ) {
    return row % numProcs();
}
```

The runtime will distribute rows cyclically across the processes and all computations within the same row will be computed on the same process. For column-cyclic distribution one would use something like:

```
int tuner::compute_on( int row, int column ) {
    return column % numProcs();
}
```

For experiments with different distribution plans and/or to make more dynamic decisions, one could also provide several options and decide, on the fly, which distribution to use. Unlike with explicit message-passing approaches, changing the distribution plan does not require any changes to the step-codes.

Tag-functions significantly simplify changes to the distribution. The consumer-steps can be determined by the tag-functions. With this information the runtime uses compute_on to compute the address space where the consuming step-instances will be executed. This mechanism is very convenient because it allows changing the distribution plan only for the computation and the runtime will automatically send the data to where it is needed.

In theory, tag-function analysis allows computing good distribution plans automatically and research on this is in progress. Much of the existing literature on automatic loop transformations and automatic data distributions applies. There are several other differences. For example, DSA makes our problem easier than the general case.

11.3.6   Futures

There are several related topics for future work. The first is a hierarchical domain specification. In such a specification, what looks like a step at one level might actually be a CnC graph at the level below. The inputs/outputs from/to the environment of the lower-level graph would look like inputs/output to/from the higher level step.

Another potential area of future inclusion is support for reuse or libraries of existing subgraphs. This might involve hooking up an input of one subgraph to the output of another or it might be accomplished by using hierarchy. In this case the reused subgraph would be the lower level implementation of what looks like a step at the level above.

Commonly used abstract patterns like tree walks, reductions, joins, streams are also being investigated for future inclusion. The user would need to supply some missing information to make each abstraction concrete.

CnC is deterministic. Some applications are inherently nondeterministic, for example, any that depend on a random number or have a "choose any" component. Support for nondeterminism, but in a controlled way, is also planned. For example, we might be able to continue to support our guarantees but only for a subgraph of the graph of the whole program.

Standard static analyses based on CnC domain specifications will be implemented. They are easier and more effective in CnC. Also an application-specific CnC attribute graph can serve as a base for more aggressive static analysis.

11.4   CnC Tuning Language

The CnC tuning language is separate from the CnC domain language. The tuning specification for an application is indicated by a high-level declarative language. The CnC tuning specification and domain specification are distinct specifications written in distinct, but related, high-level declarative languages. The tuning specification cannot violate the constraints of the domain specification. The domain specification is written by a domain expert. This is a person with expertise in finance, graphics, chemistry, etc. The tuning specification is written by a tuning expert. This tuning expert might be the same person as the domain expert or a different person with expertise in tuning, a static analyzer, an auto-tuner, etc.

Since the domain specification indicates constraints based only on the application, a single domain specification may be used for a wide range of scenarios (distinct architectures, configurations, or goals). There are two caveats. First, the appropriate grain may vary among targets. That may simply be reflected in a parameterized grain. But if the appropriate grains are very different, the static graphs may have to be different. Second, if the target machines are too different, different algorithms might be needed. Even with these caveats, multiple tuning specifications may be used with the same domain specification. So conceptually they must be distinct specifications. But the tuning specification makes reference to collections in the domain specification and may add additional collections and additional relations (constraints). Together, they form a single tuned CnC specification.

The domain specification exposes the potential parallelism in the application. Since it only indicates the semantic constraints, there is typically more than enough parallelism exposed. The tuned application must obey the constraints provided by the domain specification but that leaves many possible legal executions (an execution is a mapping across the platform and through time). The application will execute on a specific architecture, with a limited capacity and its own performance characteristics. The job of the tuner, then, is to improve performance of the application for a specific platform by guiding execution away from or actually eliminating some semantically legal executions that result in poor performance. A primary tuning focus is to improve temporal and spatial locality.

The separation of domain and tuning concerns isolates the domain expert from the tuning facility. This isolation allows the tuning language to provide strong capabilities for control and flexibility without complicating the work of the domain expert. From the tuning expert's perspective, the value of this isolation is that he/she does not have to wade through application code.

11.4.1   Description

The tuning specification refers to the step, item, and control collections in the domain specification. Although separate specifications are written for domain and tuning, some mechanism, such as a build model, is used to integrate the two specifications into a single specification. This integration supports the use of the domain collections and their instances in the tuning specification. The tuning specification generates tags of its own and adds steps of its own, basically extending the application.

The basic concept of the tuning language is the *affinity collection*, a set of computations (collection of steps) that the tuner suggests should be executed closely in space and time. We sometimes refer to an affinity collection as a *group* of step collections. Affinity collections could be generated by static analysis. The next basic concept is a hierarchy of these collections: *hierarchical affinity collections* (HACs). HACs allow the specification of relative levels of affinity with tighter affinity at lower levels. Computations that touch the same data will not benefit from locality if they are too far apart in space or time. HACs are the tuning mechanism for indicating computations that must be proximate in both time and space. This is the highest concern. The tuning language provides additional separate mechanisms for each of space and time.

Hierarchical Affinity Collections

Consider the CnC graph in Figure 11.4. An option for a hierarchical affinity collection for this graph is shown in Figure 11.5. Assume, for our examples, that all step collections in Figure 11.5 form an outer affinity collection. A second grouping option would to be

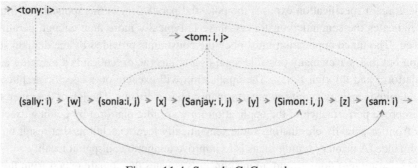

Figure 11.4: Sample CnC graph

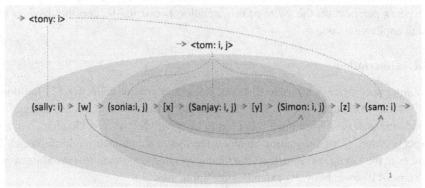

Figure 11.5: Affinity graph

have a single inner affinity collection made up of the step collections (*sonia*), (*sanjay*), and (*simon*). A third option would be to have step collections (*sonia*), (*sanjay*), and (*simon*) form an affinity collection within the outer affinity collection and step collections (*sonia*) and (*sanjay*) form an affinity collection within that one. The domain specification does not imply a particular affinity grouping. This decision is the work of the tuning expert and may depend on the target architecture, configuration, characteristics of the data set, goal (e.g., power vs. speed) etc.

Below, we show the tuning language textual representation for the HAC for Figure 11.5. We use curly brackets to show the hierarchical nesting of affinity collections:

```
{(sally)
 (sam)
    {(sonia)
        {(sanjay)
         (simon)
        }
    }
}
```

Affinity collections have names:

```
{groupa:
        (sally)
        (sam)
        {groupb:
                (sonia)
                {groupc:
                        (sanjay)
                        (simon)
                }
        }
}
```

We need a mechanism to indicate the dynamic instances of affinity collections. In the domain language, steps are used to control conditional execution of step instances. In the tuning language, these collections are prescribed to control which specific instances of the collection will exist.

```
<tony: i> ::
        {groupa:  (sally: i)
                  (sam: i)
                    <tom: i, j> ::
                        {groupb:        (sonia: i, j)
                             {groupc:   (sanjay: i, j)
                                        (simon: i, j)
                             }
                        }
        }
```

The above example illustrates the prescription of affinity collections. Recall that step collections are a static construct and we indicate the instances of a step by a prescribing control collection. An instance in the prescribing control collection corresponds to a step instance that will be executed. Here an affinity collection is a static construct and an instance in the prescribing control collection corresponds to a collection instance that will be

Form	Example
Distribute across *level*	Distribute across sockets
Distribute across *level* via *function*	Distribute across sockets via F(j, k)
Replicate across *level*	Replicate across address_spaces

Figure 11.6: Space-specific mapping options

created. So this specific statement means that for each instance of a tag $< tony : i >$ there will be a corresponding instance of the affinity collection $\{groupa : i\}$.

We will also use prescription to indicate when the tuning actions associated with an affinity collection will take place. The affinity collection action is controlled by a control collection.

Time- and Space-specific Mappings

HACs enable the tuning expert to express affinity within space-time. It is important to provide this general way of expressing locality without requiring a distinction between space and time. But, of course, a tuning expert may want to distinguish spatial and temporal locality. These specific controls are presented here.

Space. The tuning expert has access to the facilities in Figure 11.6 to express specific distributions in space. For example:

```
<groupTag: j> :: {groupOuter: j  replicate_across address_spaces}
```

Here, for each tag in the control collection $< groupTag >$, the corresponding instance of $\{groupOuter\}$ will eventually be executed on all address spaces. $replicate\_across$ is a keyword. $address\_spaces$ derives from the description of the platform tree.

```
<groupTag> :: {groupOuter   distribute_across sockets
        {groupInnerA}
        {groupInnerB}
        {groupInnerC}
        {groupInnerD}
}
```

	Ordered	Unordered
Non-overlapping	serial/barrier	exclusive
overlapping	priority	arbitrary

Figure 11.7: Time-specific mapping options

Here the four inner affinity collections are distributed among the nodes in the tuning tree holding sockets. *distribute_across* is a keyword. *sockets* derives from the description of the platform tree. In the previous example, the components to be placed in space were dynamic instances of the same static affinity collection. In this example, the components are statically distinct affinity collections. The distribution annotation distributes the (static or dynamic) components of the annotated affinity collection according to user functions.

```
<groupTag: j> :: {groupOuter: j distribute_ across address_spaces via f(j)}
```

Here when a tag j arrives in $< groupTag >$, the corresponding affinity instance is placed on the queue associated with address space $f(j)$.

Time.   The tuner may indicate that the set of components in an affinity collection should execute in an order specified by a priority or that they are unordered. The set of components of an affinity collection may be required to run one at a time (or at most N at a time). These two possibilities for each of two traits result in four possible situations, as seen in Figure 11.7.

If the set of components is to be executed in an arbitrary order and they may overlap, they are additionally not constrained with respect to time. If they are to start according to a priority and they are not to overlap, then they execute serially with a barrier between them. (Notice that the component may itself be an affinity collection that executes in parallel.) The other two are the interesting cases. Consider image processing where frames are entering the system. We want the processed frames to exit in order. Here we will have a priority order for starting the work on a frame but we do not want to require that there is a time-consuming barrier between them. This is the ordered/overlapping case. The other interesting case, unordered but nonoverlapping, might be used for components with a large memory footprint. In this case we want to run one at a time but we may not care about the specific order. This case can be generalized from one at a time to N at a time.

11.4.2 Characteristics

1. The CnC tuning specification is declarative.

2. It is isolated from the domain specification.

3. Determinism remains intact, although the tuning language can be used to specify different mappings of data and computation in time and space, in accordance with differing architectures and goals.

4. The HAC mechanism guides, but does not force, specific orderings. It does not explicitly say what goes on in parallel, or that this computation executes before that—just that they execute closely in space and time.

5. It provides time- and space-specific mechanisms that provide more control than the basic HAC.

11.4.3 Examples

Here we describe the four stages for developing a CnC tuning specification for an application. We again use Cholesky factorization as our example.

- **Stage 1**: Whiteboard.

  In the case of tuning, the whiteboard level is simply an indication of the affinity hierarchy. There are a variety of possibilities for tuning Cholesky. For this example we create an inner affinity group that includes $(trisolve)$ and $(update)$. An instance of $(trisolve)$ is used with many of the instances of $(update)$. We call this inner group $groupTU$. We choose for $(cholesky)$ to have a weak affinity with that inner group since an instance of $(cholesky)$ is used with many instances of it. We will call this $groupC$. In this tuning specification we have two distinct HACs, $groupC$ and $groupTU$. Further we can define them as: $groupC(cholesky)$ and $groupTU(trisolve), (update)$.

- **Stage 2**: Distinguish among the computation instances.

  As with steps, groups also have instances. We need to distinguish instances so we can map and schedule distinct instances independently. Instances of $groupC$ will be distinguished by the tag $iter$, so we write $groupC : iter$. Instances of $groupTU$ are distinguished by the tag $row, iter$ so we write $groupTU : row, iter$.

- **Stage 3**: Identify the instances to be executed.

These two steps have two different sets of instances, so they will require different control collections. In this case the required control collections already exist in the domain specification. There is an instance of *groupC* for each tag in $< CholeskyTag >$ and there is an instance of *groupTU* for each instance of $< TrisolveTag >$, so these are the two control collections.

- **Stage 4**: Indicate how the control collections are produced.

  The control collections are produced in the domain specification, so there is no reason to produce them again here. These two specifications will exist together in the full CnC specification.

For this example, we have added affinity collections but the control, item and step collections all exist in the domain specification. This is often the case but, in general, we can augment the domain specification with additional control, item, and step collections that are purely in support of tuning and have no semantic impact. Suppose, for example, we want to create super-tiles to form affinity groups. (The individual step instances may be tiled, of course, but this would create groups of those step tiles that would execute closely in time and space.) In this case the tuning specification may input a problem size, tile size, platform configuration size, and/or a goal (power or time). From this input, a new step might generate the number of rows and columns within a super-tile and/or the number of rows and columns of super-tiles. This process would include additional, step, item and control collections. These can then be referenced within the tuning specification. For this example, the control collection controlling an affinity collection would be a newly computed control collection that identifies the super-tiles. These new collections might have constraint relationships among them and there might be constraint relationships from the domain collections to these new tuning collections. In addition, the tuning specification might even include new constraint relationships among the domain collections. None of these would have semantic implications for the domain applications but the new orderings would be enforced as part of the tuning process.

As we have seen, there can be a variety of tuning specifications for Cholesky. Let us examine the following tuning specification:

```
//  iters  have no  affinity  with each other
    <CholeskyTag: iter> :: {GroupC: iter
                //  all the work for a given  iteration  has  a weak  affinity
                (cholesky: iter)
                <TrisolveTag: row, iter> :: {GroupTU:  row, iter
                    //  the work for a given  iter  and row has  a strong  affinity
                        (trisolve: row, iter)
                        (update: col = (iter+1 .. N), row, iter)}}
```

At the outermost level, there is an affinity collection, $\{groupC\}$, for each value of $iter$. The distinct instances of $\{groupC\}$ are not components of any collection, so there is no affinity among them. But inside a single instance of $\{groupC : iter\}$, the multiple components have an affinity with each other. One is the instance of $(cholesky)$ for this value of $iter$. The others are instances of the $\{groupTU\}$ affinity collection for this value of $iter$ and for multiple values of row. The set of $row, iter$ instances is determined by tags in the control collection $< TrisolveTag >$ from the domain specification. Within an instance of the $\{groupTU : iter\}$ affinity collection, there are multiple components: $(trisolve : iter)$ and $(update : col = (iter + 1..N), row, iter)$. The value of $iter$ referenced by these components is that of their parent instance $\{groupC : iter\}$. One component is $(Trisolve)$. There are multiple $(Update)$ components. The exact number is a function of the values of $iter$ and N. There is reuse here in that this instance of $(Trisolve)$ produces a result that is used by each $(Update)$ instance in the same row. Note the scoping of the tag components. Since $(cholesky : iter)$ is within $\{groupC : iter\}$, the values of $iter$ are the same. Since $\{groupTU : iter\}$ is within $\{groupC : iter\}$, the values of $iter$ are the same.

The tuning specification above for Cholesky is an example of an iterative style specification based on control collections. We anticipate that this will be a commonly used style. Another option is a recursive style. The following tuning code for Cholesky uses a recursively defined affinity collection.

```
<iter= 1> :: {OneIter: iter
            {tri-first: iter
                (cholesky: iter)
                (trisolve: iter+1, iter)
                (update: iter+1, iter+1, iter)
                // recursive definition of {OneIter}
                {OneIter: iter+1}}
            <trisolveTag: row, iter> and row > iter+1 ::
                {tri-up-rest: iter
                    (trisolve: row, iter)
                    (update: col = (iter+1 .. N), row, iter)}}
```

The $\{tri - first\}$ affinity collection processes the three top tiles: $(cholesky)$, the top $(trisolve)$, and the one $(update)$ to the right of that $(trisolve)$. Then it recurses to the next $iter$. The rest of the $(trisolves)$ and $(updates)$ are a second component. The first component corresponds to the critical path, along the main diagonal of the matrix. The first component cannot complete its recursions without some of the results from instances of the second components. These constraints are part of the domain specification and do not need to be repeated here. The control tags for $\{oneIter\}$ are not from the domain specification. They are defined explicitly in the tuning specification. They begin at $< iter = 1 >$ and recurse via the statement $\{OneIter : iter + 1\}$.

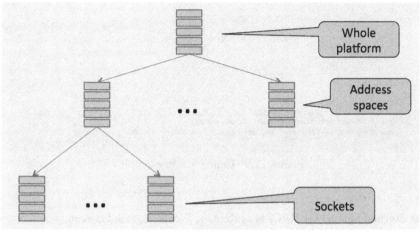

Figure 11.8: Tuning tree

One more possible tuning for Cholesky would be tiling. Most tiles would be two dimensional rectangles, a set of instances for the same iteration and for a neighborhood of rows and columns. Tiles along the diagonal would be triangular. For this tuning specification, prescriptions identify tiles. There is no concept of a tile in the domain specification. The tuning specification has to create a new control collection that identifies tile instances. This will involve new step collections that compute the tile tags. These tags, steps and items are in the language of the domain specification but are not part of the domain specification. They belong to the tuning specification, and will differ among tuning specifications. For instance they were not used in our initial version of Cholesky, nor in the recursive version. We have shown three distinct tunings for Cholesky. The first followed the loop structure of the naïve code and focused on reuse of the result of the $(trisolve)$ computation. The second was recursive. The third was tiled. The domain specification remained untouched for all three.

11.4.4 Execution Model

An execution model is needed to implement the higher-level tuning language. Here we describe one such execution model. Other execution models are possible.

The foundation of the execution model is a representation of the target platform. We assume only that the platform is hierarchical. A description of this hierarchy is used as the foundation of the tuning commands. The platform description names each level, for example, $Level1$, $Level2$, etc., or it might be $address\_space$, $socket$, $core$, etc.

```
<choleskyTag: iter> :: {groupC: iter
  (Cholesky: iter)
  <trisolveTag: row, iter> :: {groupTU: row, iter
            ...
  }
}
```

The action {groupC: iter} is defined as {

  insert the dynamic step instance *(Cholesky: iter)* on some child
  insert the static group *<trisolveTag: row, iter> :: {groupTU: row, iter}* on some child
}

Figure 11.9: Tuning action example

The execution model for HACs is as follows. We distinguish between two components of the CnC runtime: the tuning component and the domain component. The tuning component serves as a staging area for the execution of step instances in the domain component. All tuning actions belong to the tuning component.

The tuning component consists of four parts.

- Tuning actions: one for each affinity collection. These specify the low-level processing for that collection in the tuning tree. The tuning actions control the flow of work to the domain runtime.

- Event handlers: one for each control collection in the tuning specification. These control which instances of the tuning actions take place. When a tag in the normal domain execution becomes available, the handler for that event will cause some dynamic action instances to be instantiated.

- Queue manager: one for each queue. These control when to remove items from the queue and execute them.

- The tuning tree (see Figure 11.8): same shape as the platform tree. There is a work queue associated with each node in the tuning tree. The items in the queue are either static affinity collections/steps or dynamic instances of affinity collections/steps. Each queue contains work that is ready for an action to be performed (such as moving down the tree) and work that is not ready. An instance is *ready* when its associated tag is available. The tuning runtime system selects from a queue the ready work item(s) that are nearest to the head of the queue.

Large static outer affinity collections start at the top of the tuning tree. As an affinity collection is moved down a level in the tree, it will be decomposed into its components.

Since components of a collection at some node only move to children of that node (there is no work stealing), they have a tendency to remain close in the platform, in that nodes in the tuning tree correspond to nodes in the platform tree. To the extent possible, affinity collections are moved down from a node in order of their arrival, so the components of a collection have a tendency to remain close in time. Of course, there is a significant opportunity here for interesting policies (not addressed here) and for the tuning expert to be more specific about when affinity collections are moved and where to. For example, the static outer level affinity collection, $Cholesky$, can have an action defined where an instance of $Cholesky$ is moved down to a child node and the static affinity collection, $groupTU$, is unpacked and moved down to a child node. See Figure 11.9, which shows pseduo-API code for an action on the Cholesky static affinity collection. An action defined on a leaf node can move instances of a static affinity collection or dynamic affinity instances into the domain runtime for execution.

Control Tags

In the previous examples, we have used control collections from the domain specification to prescribe collections. We use tags in the execution model to determine when the actions on those instances are to be performed.

Recall that instances of steps, items and tags from the domain specification acquire attributes as the program executes. We also associate attributes, representing state changes, with affinity collection instances. Collections are similar to steps. Instances of affinity collections can be prescribed (their control tag is true). They can also be executed in the domain runtime. Although steps have an attribute $inputs\_available$, affinity collections currently do not.

Strategies for Implementing the Execution Model

The key to efficient execution on distributed memory is how data and work are distributed and/or shared across address spaces. Hence the system allows the developer (e.g., the tuning expert) to specify a distribution plan which defines how data and work is mapped to the address spaces. In the spirit of separating the domain from tuning, this plan is defined in a tuning layer which is separate from the step code. In a structure called "tuner" the programmer specifies where data- and step-instances should be placed. Tuners are separate objects attached to collections when they are initialized. Whenever the runtime needs this information it will call the respective tuning callback and take the required actions.

11.4.5   Futures

When using prescription for steps, the prescription not only determines which instances will execute but also has some influence on when (some time after the prescribing tag is produced). For prescribing steps, the question of "when" is secondary. In the case of prescribing affinity collections, the control of "when" is a major goal of tuning. We can provide the tuning expert with more control over when affinity collection actions occur so that the tuning process can be more effective in controlling when computations are fed to the domain runtime.

The state of instances can be used to refer to points in the partial order of execution, e.g., $(foo : i).executed$, and also to identify new points in the partial order, e.g., $(foo : i).executed$ and $[x : i + 1].available$. That is, the partial ordering on instance/attribute pairs is used to indicate a "time" within the execution of a domain specification. We can also allow the tuning specification to refer to these attributes for better control of when tuning actions should be performed. The action associated with an affinity collection can take place when the attribute expression associated with the collection holds. With this mechanism, for an affinity collection instance to be ready to execute, its attribute expression must hold.

Step instances have an attribute $inputs\_available$ and cannot execute until this attribute evaluates to true. Affinity collection instances can also have an attribute $inputs\_available$ as part of the mechanism to control when they execute.

11.5   Current Status

CnC implementations currently include those with computation languages such as C++ (based on Intel ® Threading Building Blocks), Hababero Java (based on Java Concurrency Utilities), and .NET (based on .NET Task Parallel Library). Other existing implementations have Java, C with OpenMP, Scala, Haskell, Python, Habanero Java, and a subset of MATLAB as the computation language. An implementation of the tuning runtime described above is under development at Rice University.

11.6   Related Work

Table 11.1 is used to guide the discussion in this section. This table classifies programming models according to their attributes in three dimensions: *Declarative*, *Deterministic* and *Efficient*. A few representative examples are included for each distinct set of attributes. The reader can extrapolate this discussion to other programming models with similar attributes in these three dimensions.

Parallel prog. model	Declarative	Deterministic	Efficient
Intel TBB	No	No	Yes
.Net Task Par. Lib.	No	No	Yes
Cilk	No	No	Yes
OpenMP	No	No	Yes
CUDA	No	No	Yes
Java Concurrency	No	No	Yes
Det. Parallel Java	No	Hybrid	Yes
High Perf. Fortran	Hybrid	No	Yes
X10	Hybrid	No	Yes
Linda	Hybrid	No	Yes
Asynch. Seq. Processes [61]	Yes	Yes	No
StreamIt	Yes	Yes	Yes
LabVIEW [276]	Yes	Yes	Yes
CnC	Yes	Yes	Yes

Table 11.1: Comparison of several parallel programming models.

A number of lower-level programming models in use today—e.g., Intel TBB, .Net Task Parallel Library [275], Cilk (see Chapter 13), OpenMP (see Chapter 12), NVIDIA CUDA (see Chapter 15), Java Concurrency [228]—are nondeclarative, nondeterministic, and efficient. Here a programming model is considered to be efficient if there are known implementations that deliver competitive performance for a reasonably broad set of programs. Deterministic Parallel Java [43] is an interesting variant of Java; it includes a subset that is provably deterministic, as well as constructs that explicitly indicate when determinism cannot be guaranteed for certain code regions, which is why it contains a "hybrid" entry in the *Deterministic* column.

The next three languages in the table—High Performance Fortran (HPF) [161], X10, Linda [122]—contain hybrid combinations of imperative and declarative programming in different ways. HPF combines a declarative language for data distribution and data parallelism with imperative (procedural) statements, X10 contains a functional subset that supports declarative parallelism, and Linda is a coordination language in which a thread's interactions with the tuple space is declarative.

Linda was a major influence on the CnC domain language design. CnC shares two important properties with Linda: both are coordination languages that specify computations and communications via a tuple/tag namespace, and both create new computations by adding new tuples/tags to the namespace. However, CnC also differs from Linda in many ways. For example, an in() operation in Linda atomically removes the tuple from the tuple space, but a CnC get() operation does not remove the item from the data collection. This is a key reason why Linda programs can be nondeterministic in general, and why CnC programs are provably deterministic. Further, there is no separation between tags and values in a Linda tuple; instead, the choice of tag is implicit in the use of wildcards. In CnC, there is a separation between tags and values, and control tags are first class constructs like data items.

The last four programming models in the table are both declarative and deterministic. Asynchronous Sequential Processes [61] is a recent model with a clean semantics, but without any efficient implementations. In contrast, the remaining three entries are efficient as well. StreamIt [123, 124] is representative of a modern streaming language, and LabVIEW [276] is representative of a modern dataflow language. Both streaming and dataflow languages have had major influence on the CnC design.

The CnC semantic model is based on dataflow in that steps are functional and execution can proceed whenever data is ready. However, CnC differs from dataflow in some key ways. The use of control tags elevates control to a first-class construct in CnC. In addition, data collections allow more general indexing (as in a tuple space) compared to dataflow arrays (I-structures). CnC is like streaming in that the internals of a step are not visible from the graph that describes their connectivity, thereby establishing an isolation among steps. A producer step in a streaming model need not know its consumers; it just needs to know which buffers (collections) to perform read and write operations on. However, CnC differs from streaming in that put and get operations need not be performed in FIFO order, and (as mentioned above) control is a first-class construct in CnC. Further, CnC's dynamic put/get operations on data and control collections serves as a general model that can be used to express many kinds of applications that would not be considered to be dataflow or streaming applications.

Most of the existing parallel programming constructs address time. Data parallel constructs, both fine-grained vector constructs and the coarser parallel-for constructs such as those found in OpenMP, indicate a set of operations that can occur at the same time. Fork-join constructs such as a Cilk spawn/sync or Habanaro Java's async/finish or parallel sections are all of this flavor. They indicate when the forked work can start and when the join work can proceed. Task graphs indicate a more general partial ordering.

These approaches indicate when computations take place. Some of these languages have distinct constructs for indicating where a computation is to take place, for example, Habanero Java has the Hierarchical Place Tree (HPT) [302]. But the constructs for time and for space are distinct and unrelated. HPF provides facilities, for coarse-grain and array language constructs, for defining the decomposition and placement of data for distribution across processors and address spaces.

HACs provide a mechanism that allows the programmer to specify locality, while allowing, but not requiring, her to distinguish between spatial and temporal locality. The programmer can optimize the space-time locality, at times trading off temporal and spatial locality. Allowing the programmer to specify space-time locality is a novel contribution.

11.7   Conclusions

CnC is a programming model for parallel systems. Instead of providing facilities for the domain expert to describe the parallelism explicitly, it provides facilities for describing execution order constraints. Subject to these constraints, computations can potentially execute in parallel. This depends only on the application. This approach creates a partial ordering of computations and typically supplies more than ample parallelism. There is a separate language for writing CnC tuning specifications. The central component of the tuning language is HACs. These provide a mechanism that allows the programmer to specify locality, while allowing, but not requiring, her to distinguish between spatial and temporal locality. This is a novel contribution. The programmer can optimize the space-time locality, at times trading off temporal and spatial locality. The tuning facility enables the tuning expert to remove some of the less efficient possible mappings of the parallelism provided by the domain specification. Without the tuning language, CnC has already achieved comparable performance with other parallel models/tools.

12 OpenMP

Barbara Chapman, University of Houston
Deepak Eachempati, University of Houston
Sunita Chandrasekaran, University of Houston

12.1 Introduction

OpenMP [221] is an application programming interface (API) for expressing parallelism for shared-memory architectures in C, C++, and Fortran programs. It consists of a set of compiler directives, library routines, and environment variables for prescribing how the program should execute in parallel. OpenMP provides a *portable* model for parallel programming across a range of shared-memory architectures, including single multicore processors, larger cache-coherent NUMA machines, and heterogeneous node architectures consisting of a host and accelerator devices. OpenMP has been designed from the beginning to support the development of software used for technical and scientific computing. Originally intended to be used for parallelizing loop-centric algorithms, recent versions have extended the scope to algorithms exhibiting a much wider range of parallel patterns. Support for OpenMP is provided by many commercial and open-source compilers, and it is widely available on parallel systems in use today. Although the OpenMP specification can be downloaded from the web, it is not intended to be a guide for the application developer. The goal of this chapter is to discuss some of the most important features of OpenMP and how they may be used to create parallel programs on current architectures.

The OpenMP API is an agreement among the members of the hardware and software vendors that are members of the OpenMP Architecture Review Board (ARB). The ARB is a nonprofit corporation comprised of members from industry and academia that owns the OpenMP brand and manages the OpenMP specification. Their work was originally based on a set of compiler directives for writing parallel programs in Fortran which was developed in the late 1980s. In 1997, the newly formed ARB introduced the first OpenMP specification for use with Fortran and early OpenMP compilers soon followed. Bindings for C and C++ were subsequently defined. The feature set has since grown considerably; version 4.0, the most recent version, was ratified in 2013.

OpenMP enables application developers to create programs that will be executed by a group of cooperating threads with shared access to data. It allows the programmer to take a high-level view of parallelism and leave the lower level details of managing concurrency to the compiler. In other words, OpenMP does not require the programmer to explicitly decompose data and control flow to produce parallel computation. OpenMP is not a new programming language, but is a notation that can be added to a sequential code written in Fortran, C or C++ to describe how the work is to be shared among threads that will execute on different processors or cores and to order accesses to shared data as needed. With the insertion of OpenMP directives, the programmer can specify what portions of sequential code should be executed in parallel. To a non-OpenMP compiler, the directives look like comments and are ignored. By observing a few rules, many codes can be written to be correct when executing as a sequential or parallel program, which is quite useful in development and testing. Another benefit is the ability to incrementally apply OpenMP constructs to create parallel programs from existing sequential codes. Rather than start from scratch, the programmer can insert parallelism into a portion of the code and leave the rest sequential, repeating this process until the desired speedup is realized.

A Brief History

A group of vendors joined together during the latter half of the 1990s to provide a common means for programming a broad range of shared-memory parallel architectures that had, at the time, recently been introduced into the market place. They established the OpenMP ARB which reviewed earlier directive-based APIs for parallel programming, notably work from the Parallel Computing Forum (PCF) [271]. The ARB introduced the first version of OpenMP for Fortran in 1997. The set of directives defined in OpenMP were highly suitable for programming multicore systems. Today, OpenMP is a widely supported portable programming interface facilitating shared-memory parallel programming on virtually all computing platforms. The membership of the OpenMP ARB has been steadily growing. Initially consisting of vendors that provide OpenMP on their platforms, it has expanded to a broad, international membership today including government labs and academic institutions.

The OpenMP ARB published its first API specification, OpenMP for Fortran 1.0, in October 1997 [220]. In October, the following year, the ARB released the C/C++ specification. Version 2.0 specifications for Fortran and C/C++ were released in 2000 and 2002, respectively. In 2005, version 2.5, which was a combined specification for C/C++ and Fortran, was released. Originally designed to target loop-centric algorithms, the specification released in 2008, version 3.0, introduced the ability to define explicit tasks that may be executed concurrently. In July 2011, version 3.1 was released with additional features such as min and max reductions in C/C++. Support for accelerators, sequentially-consistent atomics, error handling, thread affinity, task extensions, user-defined reduction, and SIMD support was included in version 4.0 that was released in July 2013.

The OpenMP ARB's goal has been to ensure that OpenMP remains relevant as computer technology evolves. OpenMP is under active development and features continue to be proposed for inclusion.

12.2 Overview

The OpenMP API defines directives, library routines, and environment variables for expressing the parallelism desired in a given program. Directives may include various clauses to provide further information on the behavior expected from the OpenMP implementation. Directives for C and C++ begin with `#pragma omp`. Directives in Fortran can begin with `!$omp` when using free source form, but other options are available when using fixed source form.

12.2.1 Terminology

Some terms are fundamental to understanding OpenMP, and we review them here:

- **directive**: A pragma in C/C++ or a comment in Fortran that specifies program behavior. A directive may be either *declarative* or *executable*.

- **construct**: An OpenMP executable directive, as well as the lexical extent of any associated statement, loop nest, or structured block, not including any code in routines called from the construct, and (for Fortran) the paired `end` directive if it exists.

- **region**: All code encountered during the execution of an OpenMP construct, including code from called routines or code implicitly generated by the compiler implementation. A region also has a *data environment*, which is the set of variables associated with the region.

- **device**: A logical execution engine, which may consist of one or more processors, defined by the implementation. An OpenMP program begins execution on a *host* device, and it may offload computation and data to one or more *target* devices during program execution.

- **thread**: An execution entity with a stack and associated static memory which is managed by the OpenMP runtime system. Threads bind to a given device, meaning they may not migrate from one device to another.

- **contention group**: The initial thread on the device and all of its descendent threads.

- **team**: A set of one or more threads participating in the execution of a `parallel` region. Each thread in the team has an assigned thread number, ranging from 0 to `num_threads-1`. Every team has a `master` thread, which created the team upon encountering a parallel construct, and it is assigned the thread number 0.

- **league**: A set of one or more thread teams participating in the execution of a `teams` region. A league of teams may only be created on a target device.

- **task**: An instance of executable code and its associated data environment which is executed by a thread residing on some device. All executing code is part of an `implicit` or `explicit` task.

OpenMP requires well-structured programs, and, as described above, constructs are associated with statements, loops, or structured blocks. In C/C++, a "structured block" is defined to be an executable statement, possibly a compound statement, with a single entry at the top and a single exit at the bottom. In Fortran, it is defined as a block of executable statements with a single entry at the top and a single exit at the bottom. For both languages, the point of entry cannot be a labeled statement, and the point of exit cannot be a branch of any type.

Most OpenMP directives are clearly associated with a region of code, usually the dynamic extent of the structured block or loop nest immediately following it. A few (barrier and flush) do not apply to any code. Some features affect the behavior or use of threads. For these, the notion of a binding thread set is introduced. In particular, some of the runtime library routines have an effect on the thread that invokes them (or return information pertinent to that thread only), whereas others are relevant to a team of threads or to all threads that execute the program. We will discuss binding issues only in those few places where it is important or not immediately clear what the binding of a feature is.

12.2.2 Managing the Data Environment

Each task in an OpenMP program has its own data environment which comprises all variables it uses. This may include variables declared in the application which are visible to the task region, or *internal control variables* (ICVs) used by the OpenMP implementation. A variable within the data environment may be either `shared` or `private`. A shared variable is accessible to all tasks executing on threads in the current thread team or (for a `teams` region) to each team in a league of teams. A private variable is a copy that is local to a thread in a `parallel` region or a team in a `teams` region. There is another type of variable, called `threadprivate`, which exists in the static memory of a particular thread on the host device and may only be accessed by tasks executing on that thread. Accessing threadprivate variables on a target device is not allowed.

A target device has its own data environment, called a *device data environment*. The program may declare particular global variables as part of a target device's data environment. It may also *map* additional variables into this data environment. This mapping can be viewed as a link between the original variable within the host device's memory and the target device's data environment. It may involve creating a new copy for the variable in the target device's memory, or (in the case of *unified memory* architectures) the original variable may itself be added to the device data environment, transparent to the program. OpenMP provides mechanisms for synchronizing the values of variables in the device data environment with their original copy.

A programmer can explicitly specify whether a variable in a data environment should be shared or private using data clauses on various constructs which create tasks. Otherwise, OpenMP has its own rules for implicitly determining whether a variable should be shared or private. For example, when a team of threads executes a parallel loop, each thread needs its own value of the iteration variable. This case is so important that the compiler enforces it by making the iteration variable private by default. If the private variable needs to be initialized by the value of the corresponding variable immediately prior to the construct, the variable should be designated `firstprivate`. If the last value of a private variable is needed after the construct completes, the variable can be designated as `lastprivate`. Variables may also be designated as reduction variables with an associated operator. These variables will be used privately by each thread to perform its share of the work and then combined according to the operator as each thread completes its chunk of work.

OpenMP also has a feature called flush, to synchronize memory. A flush operation makes sure that the thread calling it has the same values for shared data objects as does main memory. Hence, new values of any shared objects updated by that thread are written back to shared memory, and the thread gets any new values produced by other threads for the shared data it reads. In some programming languages, a flush is known as a memory fence, since reads and writes of shared data may not be moved relative to it.

12.2.3   Brief Tour of OpenMP Concepts

Parallel regions.   Parallel programs written in OpenMP use the *fork-join* parallel pattern. Conceptually, the program starts executing sequentially and forks additional threads for executing parallel regions as they are encountered. Parallel regions are specified with a `parallel` construct—an `omp parallel` directive with an accompanying structured block of code. It refers to all program statements (including from called procedures) encountered during the execution of this code block. Parallel regions are allowed to be nested as well, so that threads executing a parallel region may create their own parallel regions. Each parallel construct designates whether data should be treated as private or shared. Data that is accessed by threads executing the parallel region will be shared among them by default, unless the application developer instructs the compiler to assign them private copies. There is also a clause, `proc_bind`, to specify the thread affinity between threads in the thread team (i.e., whether threads should be spread out across the processing cores or reside close to each other).

Synchronization. OpenMP defines several *synchronization* mechanisms which allow the programmer to explicitly control execution ordering among threads. These include the `barrier` construct, the `critical` construct, the `atomic` construct, the `ordered` construct, the `taskwait` and `taskgroup` constructs, and routines for locks. Synchronization is especially important for shared-memory programming where threads can access the same data. Incorrectly synchronized programs may result in data races, causing the program to emit incorrect or inconsistent output.

Worksharing. Various constructs may be used within parallel regions to coordinate its multithreaded execution. Such constructs may occur lexically within an enclosing parallel construct or be encountered during the execution of the parallel region but outside its lexical extent (in the latter case, they are called *orphaned* constructs). All of a parallel region's threads will redundantly execute its code. When the threads encounter a `worksharing` construct, the computation to be performed will be partitioned among the threads. Examples of worksharing constructs in OpenMP include the loop constructs `for` (C/C++) or `do` (Fortran), the `sections` construct, and the `single` construct. Worksharing constructs by default end with an implicit synchronizing barrier, meaning every thread must wait until all threads complete execution of its portion of the computation.

Task parallelism. Constructs for explicit *task parallelism* were added in version 3.0. Tasks are code regions that are executed by a single thread within the enclosing parallel region's thread team. By default, each thread executes an implicit task region. A `task` construct is used to explicitly create a task region. This task may be executed immediately by the thread that encountered the `task` construct, or its execution may be deferred and executed at a later point by some thread in the thread team. The `taskwait` construct will cause the enclosing task to suspend until all task regions it created have completed execution. The `taskgroup` construct ensures that all tasks created within the associated taskgroup region, as well as all their descendent tasks, finish execution.

Vectorization. Version 4.0 added support for *single instruction, multiple data* (SIMD) parallelism with the `simd` and loop `simd` (`for simd` or `do simd`) constructs. These constructs help the compiler to safely vectorize loops, indicating that loop iterations may be distributed across SIMD lanes within a thread, or across both threads and SIMD lanes within each thread.

Accelerator support.   A major enhancement that has been added to version 4.0 is support for offloading computation to *target devices*, or accelerators [33]. The `target` and `target data` constructs are used to offload the associated code regions to a specified target device and to define the data environment on the target device, respectively. The `target update` directive is available for synchronizing values of specified data in host memory with their mapped locations in target memory. Additional parallelism constructs for use specifically on target devices are also available. The `teams` construct can be used to create a *league of thread teams* on the target device. The `distribute` construct will distribute iterations of an associated loop among the created teams. Each thread team by default executes with a single thread, but the `parallel` construct may be used to have multiple executing threads per team. OpenMP allows for these constructs to be combined in several ways, providing a flexible means for exploiting data parallelism using a target device. For example, the combined construct `target teams distribute parallel for simd` can be used to offload computation for an associated loop to a specified target device, distributing iterations across SIMD lanes of each thread, across threads of each thread team, and across multiple thread teams in a league (hence, in total, three levels of parallelism).

Region cancellation.   Another newly added feature in OpenMP is *region cancellation*. Sometimes it can be useful to end the execution of a region early, due to the occurrence of an error condition or for search algorithms where an answer is arrived at in a nondeterministic manner. The `cancel` construct may be used to *activate cancellation* in an enclosing specified region (parallel, sections, loop, or taskgroup). The `cancellation point` construct allows other executing tasks to immediately complete execution of a specified region if they detect that cancellation has been activated for the region.

Declarative directives.   OpenMP includes a number of *declarative directives* for declarations of variables and/or procedures in the program. The `threadprivate` directive is used for a list of variables, indicating that they must be replicated with every thread having its own copy. The `declare reduction` directive allows the declaration of *user-defined reductions*. The `declare simd` directive is used to instruct the compiler to generate SIMD versions of a specified procedure, so that it may be called from within a `simd` or `loop simd` construct. Finally, the `declare target` directive is used to map procedures or global variables (not including threadprivate variables) to target devices.

Controlling the runtime environment.   OpenMP also specifies how a programmer may interact with the runtime environment. The API defines a set of ICVs for controlling the execution at runtime. These include controlling the number of threads in a thread team, enabling nested parallelism, specifying the scheduling of iterations in loop constructs, and much more. These ICVs may be accessed by setting environment variables or using runtime library routines. In some cases, the ICV may be set with a clause in the appropriate directive.

12.3   OpenMP Features

In this section, we take a closer look at some of the OpenMP feature set. We provide here informal descriptions of most of the major constructs and present illustrative examples. To simplify the discussion, we describe here the OpenMP constructs available for C/C++ programs. The reader may refer to [221] for a full description of the OpenMP API for Fortran programs.

12.3.1   Parallel Regions

A parallel region is an instance of executable code that is executed by one or more threads in parallel. The entire program can be viewed as enclosed within an implicit parallel region (no associated parallel construct) which has a team of one thread. Such a parallel region is also called an *inactive* parallel region. The `parallel` construct is the basic mechanism used in an OpenMP programs to specify the use of multithreaded parallelism in an *active* parallel region. Without the use of a parallel construct, OpenMP programs will only execute with a single thread on the host device.

Let us take a closer look at the components of a parallel construct:

```
#pragma omp parallel [clause [[,] clause] ...]
structured-block
```

The *structured-block* may be a single statement or a block of statements (enclosed by {}s) with a single entry at the top and a single exit at the bottom. The `#pragma omp parallel` directive indicates that this structured block should be executed by one or more threads in parallel. This is achieved by forking a team of threads, where the thread executing the task that encountered the construct will assume the role of *master* thread in this team with the thread number 0. The other threads in a team of `nt` threads will be assigned thread numbers 1 through `nt - 1`. The directive may optionally include a list of clauses on the same line as well. These clauses may be used to specify:

- how many threads should be used to execute the parallel region:
  `if (scalar−expression), num_threads (integer−expression)`

- the data-sharing and initialization attributes of variables referenced within the construct:
  `default(private|firstprivate|shared|none)`,
  `private(`*list*`)`, `firstprivate(`*list*`)`, `shared(`*list*`)`,
  `copyin(`*list*`)`, `reduction(`*reduction−identifier*`:`*list*`)`

- the thread affinity policy of the threads:
  `proc_bind(master|close|spread)`

Multithreaded Execution

OpenMP implementations will adhere to the same procedure to determine how many threads will execute a particular parallel region. If the `if` and `num_threads` clauses are absent, then the number of threads is determined by the values of several internal control variables. In the typical case, where dynamic adjustment of the number of threads is not enabled, there is no enclosing active parallel region, and the maximum limit of threads allowed by the implementation is sufficiently high, the number of threads is determined by the *nthreads-var* ICV. This may be set using the `OMP_NUM_THREADS` environment variable or the `omp_set_num_threads()` library routine. If the `if` clause is given and its argument evaluates to *false*, then the parallel region is executed with only a single thread. Otherwise, if the `num_threads` clause is given, then the number of threads will be given by its argument (so long as it does not exceed the maximum limit of threads allowed by the implementation).

Once the number of threads, `nt`, is determined, the encountering task will suspend until the parallel region completes execution. The thread that was executing this task along with `nt - 1` other threads will each execute the parallel region as implicit tasks. The parallel region is essentially a single program, multiple data (SPMD) code region. Each thread may query its own thread number, using the `omp_get_thread_num()` function, and use this to determine its own execution path for the parallel region. If the programmer does not control the flow of execution based on the executing thread's thread number and does not make use of worksharing constructs, the computation within the parallel region will be executed redundantly by all threads.

The `master` construct may be used to specify that a structured block of code should only be executed by the master thread of the team:

```
/* parallel region */
...
#pragma omp master
{
    /* this code is executed by the master thread */
    ...
} /* ––– end of master construct ––– */
```

Nested Parallel Regions

If a task executing inside an active parallel region encounters a parallel construct, it will suspend and a new team of one or more threads will be created for the execution of that construct, with the suspended task's thread becoming the master of the new team. Whether or not the new team consists of multiple threads depends on a several factors. If the *nested-var* ICV is not set (by default, it will not be), then the nested parallel region will only execute with the master thread and no additional threads. To set *nested-var*, either the OMP_NESTED environment variable or the omp_set_nested() function may be used. Otherwise, if the number of enclosing active parallel regions already equals the value of the *max-active-levels-var* ICV (set using OMP_MAX_ACTIVE_LEVELS or a call to omp_-set_max_active_levels(), but never exceeding what is supported by the implementation), then again the nested parallel region will only execute with the master thread. Otherwise, the rules for determining the number of threads to use is as described in the preceding section.

Nested parallelism offers a means to exploit multiple levels of parallelism, which may be helpful to increase scalability. We note that the frequent starting and stopping of parallel regions may introduce a nontrivial performance penalty, so nested parallel regions should be used with discretion. Another caveat is that the values of threadprivate variables is not guaranteed to persist across two different *nested* parallel regions. The programmer should also be aware that some implementations may not allow nested, active parallel regions if they do not support more than one active level. The program can check how many active levels are allowed using the omp_get_max_active_levels() function, and it may check the current active level using the omp_get_active_level() function.

Controlling Thread Affinity

In addition to controlling the number of threads to use to execute a parallel region, the program can also specify the thread affinity, or *where* the threads should execute in relation to each other [102]. Thread affinity can have a dramatic effect on the performance achieved using parallel regions, depending on the underlying processor and memory architecture, the

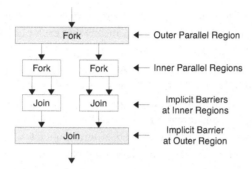

Figure 12.1: Example of nested OpenMP parallel region

nature of the computation being executed by the threads, and the data access pattern of the tasks running on the threads.

The goal of thread affinity is to bind threads participating in the execution of a parallel region to a set of *places*. Conceptually, a device consists of places described with the *place-partition-var* ICV which may be set using the OMP_PLACES environment variable. The place partition describes a list of places available for executing OpenMP threads. A place partition may be defined using an explicit list of places, each described with a set of nonnegative numbers. Each of these numbers represent an execution unit on the device, typically a hardware thread. Suppose for a particular device there are a total of 16 available hardware threads, and the OpenMP implementation assigns numbers 0 through 15 to them. For this, we show examples below of place partitions consisting of 4 "places" of 4 hardware threads each, which may be defined using OMP_PLACES. The interval notation, which can be used to more compactly describe the place partition, is in the format ⟨*lower-bound*⟩:⟨*length*⟩:⟨*stride*⟩, where a unit stride is implied if ⟨*stride*⟩ is not given.

```
fully expanded list:
    "{0,1,2,3},{4,5,6,7},{8,9,10,11},{12,13,14,15}"
each place uses interval notation:
    "{0:4},{4:4},{8:4},{12:4}"
places and the partition itself uses interval notation:
    "{0:4}:4:4"
```

Alternatively, OpenMP provides a way to specify a place partition using an abstract name. This can be achieved using the format abstract_name[(num-places)]. Implementations are required to support at least threads, cores, and sockets as abstract names. Here, threads means that each place should be treated as a single hardware thread, `cores` means that each place should be treated as a single core consisting of one or more hardware threads, and `sockets` means that each place should be treated as a single socket consisting of one or more cores. Using an abstract name without a *num-places* argument leaves it to the implementation to decide how many places to create in the place partition. For a device consisting of 4 cores, each with 4 hardware threads, we could achieve an equivalent place partition as above by setting OMP_PLACES to `cores(4)`.

For a given place partition, thread affinity can be controlled by setting the value of the *bind-var* ICV to *true* or to a list of thread affinity policies which may each be one of: `master`, `close`, or `spread`. This ICV may be set using the OMP_PROC_BIND environment variable. When the ICV is set to *true*, threads will bind to the places they start execution on, though the mapping of threads to places is implementation defined. If set to a list of affinity policies and there is no `proc_bind` clause, the first policy in the list is used for the parallel region. Otherwise, the value given by the `proc_bind` clause is used to set the affinity policy for the parallel region. The implicit tasks which form the new parallel region will each have their *bind-var* within their respective data environments, based on its parent implicit task's *bind-var*. If the value of the parent's *bind-var* is *false*, *true*, or a thread affinity policy list of length 1, then the new implicit tasks get the same value for their *bind-var*. Otherwise, it is set to the thread affinity policy list given by the parent's *bind-var*, minus the first policy.

If the thread affinity policy for the parallel region is `master`, all threads in the team will bind to the same place as the master thread, which is the thread that encountered the parallel construct. If set to `close`, threads will be assigned consecutive places from the place list, wrapping around if necessary. If the number of threads in the team exceeds the number of places, then multiple threads at a time will be assigned to each consecutive place, in order of thread number. For both the `master` and `close` thread affinity policies, the generated implicit tasks will retain the same place partition as the parent implicit task (i.e., the implicit task from the enclosing parallel region running on the thread which encountered the parallel construct). The `spread` thread affinity policy has each thread bind to places in the place partition such that the assigned places are evenly "spread out". Typically a spread affinity policy would be used when the number of threads is less than the number of places. The original place partition is divided into T subpartitions, where T is the number of threads in the new team. The *place-partition-var* ICV for each new implicit task is then set to its corresponding subpartition.

Setting up the Data Environments

Before the implicit tasks for the parallel region can begin execution, their data environments must be set. This involves determining whether each task should have its own copy of a variable or a shared copy, based on a set of data-sharing rules. When a variable is shared for a parallel region, this means that each implicit task's data environment directly references the encountering task's copy of that variable. Global and static variables, unless declared as threadprivate, will be shared by default within a parallel region. Local variables that are part of the encountering task's data environment will also be shared by default within a parallel region. Local variables that are not in the encountering task's data environment will be private within a parallel region by default. Finally, variables that are declared as threadprivate will be private to each thread executing a parallel region. We will run through a short example to illustrate how this works.

```
int x0; /* a global declaration */
int u0; /* a global, threadprivate declaration */
#pragma omp threadprivate(u)

f()
{
    int x1;
    static int u1;
    #pragma omp threadprivate(u1)

    #pragma omp parallel
    {
        int x2;
        static int u2, z2;
        #pragma omp threadprivate(u2)
        g();
        ...
    }
}

/* g may be executed as part of f's parallel region */
g()
{
    int x3;
    static int u3, z3;
    #pragma omp threadprivate(u3)
    ...
}
```

In the example above, the implicit tasks executing the parallel region initially each include variables $x0$, $u0$, $x1$, $u1$, $x2$, $u2$, and $z2$ in their data environments. Of these, variables $x0$, $x1$, and $z2$ are shared among the tasks, and variable $x2$ is private to each task. Variables $u0$, $u1$, and $u2$ are threadprivate, meaning that they are allocated in a static memory reserved for each thread, and their values may persist across tasks executed by the same thread. This persistence is guaranteed for tasks from the same parallel region, and it may be guaranteed for implicit tasks across two consecutive parallel regions, subject to certain constraints. While the implicit tasks are executing g, variables $x1$, $u1$, $x2$, $u2$, and $z2$ go out of scope and hence are no longer part of their data environments, while variables $x3$, $u3$, and $z3$ come in scope and are added to the data environments. In this portion of the parallel region, variable $x3$ is private to each implicit task, variable $z3$ is shared across the implicit tasks, and variable $u3$ is threadprivate. Upon returning from g to f, the data environments are restored.

The `default` clause will change the default attribute for variables that are not thread-private and are part of the encountering task's data environment. The available defaults are `private`, `firstprivate`, and `shared`, which will treat all variables in its argument list as private, firstprivate, and shared, respectively, in the parallel construct. A firstprivate variable is private to each implicit task and initialized with the value of the corresponding variable from the encountering task's data environment, while a private variable's initial value is undefined. The `copyin` clause accepts only threadprivate variables in its argument list. For each variable in the list, the value of the variable belonging to the master thread (same as value of the variable in the encountering task's data environment) is copied to the threadprivate variable belonging to each other thread in the team. Finally, the `reduction` clause will create private copies of the variables in its argument list for each implicit task's data environment. Then, at the end of the parallel region the values of these variables will be *combined* using the specified reduction operator and stored into the corresponding variable in the encountering task's data environment.

12.3.2 Synchronization

As described in the prior section, tasks that are executed within a parallel region may contain *shared* variables in their data environments. When two tasks reference the same shared variable in a manner that is not ordered with respect to each other, the potential for a data race can arise.

To understand the issue more clearly, we will take a brief look at OpenMP's memory model [140]. OpenMP provides a *relaxed-consistency* memory model. Shared variables reside in a memory location that may be accessible by multiple threads. Additionally, each thread has its own temporary view of the shared variable, as it may access it from a copy stored in cache or in a register. OpenMP allows the program to enforce consistency between the executing thread's temporary view and the memory location where the shared variable ultimately resides using the `flush` directive:

```
/* x is a shared variable in the enclosing parallel region */
while (x != 0) {
      #pragma omp flush
}
```

In the above example, the while-loop is executed by a thread, waiting for the shared variable x to be nonzero. The `flush` directive here will "flush" the value of x from its location in memory to the thread's temporary view of x. Without the use of `flush` here, the thread may miss any update to x's memory location made by another thread.

Synchronizing threads in a parallel region to prevent a data race entails not only ordering accesses to a shared variable in some specified manner, but also performing the necessary flush operation to ensure values written by one thread are visible by another. To support this behavior, there is an implicit flush for nearly all the synchronization constructs in OpenMP, and many other constructs that do much more than synchronization. In the remainder of this section, we describe some thread-level synchronization constructs. Synchronization for tasks is covered in more detail in Section 12.3.4.

Barriers

A barrier in a parallel region will cause a thread to suspend execution of its implicit task until all implicit tasks for the region reach the same barrier, and all work to be performed prior to the barrier in the parallel region has completed. As mentioned above, there is also an implied flush, so that the latest updates made by any threads to shared variables prior to reaching the barrier will be visible to all the threads after the barrier. Barriers are perhaps the most common method of synchronization in OpenMP. By default, all worksharing constructs have an implicit barrier at the end of their execution, and a barrier is also implied at the end of any parallel construct (ensuring the master thread does not continue until all threads complete execution of the parallel region). A program may explicitly insert a barrier using the `barrier` construct:

```
/* --- parallel region in progress --- */
...

/* all threads executing the parallel region must reach this point */

#pragma omp barrier

/* all work prior to barrier completed, and all shared variables flushed */

...
```

There is no code specifically associated with the barrier construct; it is a standalone directive. It ensures that all threads reach the barrier, that all work (program code and OpenMP constructs) that precedes the barrier in the enclosing parallel region has completed, and that all threads have the same view of shared variables coming out of the barrier.

For performance reasons, barriers should be used carefully to avoid idle threads. The worksharing constructs all have an optional `nowait` clause to disable the ending implicit barrier. The task construct, described later in this chapter, provides a means for threads to dynamically pick up work to execute while waiting at a barrier.

Critical Sections

The `critical` construct may be used to ensure that only one OpenMP thread in a contention group is executing a section of code with a given name at a time. The format of the critical construct is:

#pragma omp critical [(name)]
     `structured-block`

All constructs defined without a *name* parameter have the same, unspecified name, so naming a critical construct is a good practice to allow concurrent execution of critical sections referencing distinct data. A flush is implied at both the entry and exit of a critical construct. Also, unlike the barrier construct, the synchronization implied here is not limited only to threads in the same team, but rather to all threads in the same contention group. On the host device, this is all threads with the same initial thread as an ancestor.

Atomic Construct

The `atomic` construct is used to ensure that a shared variable is accessed *atomically* by threads in the same contention group. There are several types of atomic constructs that may be used depending on how a variable is being accessed, whether the original value or resulting value needs to be "captured", and whether the construct needs to be executed in a *sequentially consistent* manner. Sequentially consistent atomic regions include an implied flush, whereas atomic regions that are not designated as sequentially consistent do not.

The following examples show typical ways in which an atomic construct may be used in accessing a shared variable x. The `seq_cst` clause may be used to make the atomic operations sequentially consistent. This should be used for cases where all threads need to perform atomic accesses to a variable with same ordering of updates visible to all threads.

```
#pragma omp atomic read
t = x;

#pragma omp atomic write
x = t;

#pragma omp atomic update
x++;

#pragma omp atomic capture
v = x++;
```

12.3.3 Worksharing

OpenMP provides a number of *worksharing* constructs that may be used within a parallel region. These constructs contain a directive with an optional list of clauses, followed on the next line by a statement or block of statements. The construct distributes the work to perform in these statements across all the threads in the team executing the enclosing parallel region. Generally, worksharing constructs should be encountered by all threads in the team, or by none of them. Consequently, all threads will execute the same number of worksharing constructs in a parallel region (unless cancellation occurs for the region—see Section 12.3.7). There are four types of worksharing constructs available:

- loop construct

- `sections` construct

- `single` construct

- `workshare` construct (Fortran only)

Loop Construct

Loop constructs are used to exploit *loop-level parallelism* in an OpenMP program. Since a significant amount of work occurs in loops, loops constructs are perhaps the most commonly used mechanism for parallelizing a program with OpenMP. For a C or C++ program, the loop construct takes the following form:

```
#pragma omp for [clause [[,] clause] ...]
loop-nest
```

The loop nest under the directive must be in a *canonical* form. This means that the total number of iterations for associated loops must be computable before the execution of the outermost loop. Also, the number of iterations in the loop must be countable with an integer and use a fixed increment. Hence, only for-loops in C/C++ and do-loops in Fortran are permitted. Some rewriting of the loop may be necessary to expose parallelism.

The loop directive instructs the OpenMP implementation to distribute the execution of iterations of the associated loops in the loop nest among the encountering threads. The use of such a directive generally implies that the loop iterations are independent; i.e., the program does not depend on the order in which they are executed. The clauses that are allowed with the loop directive may be used to control:

- how loop iterations are to be scheduled onto threads:
  `schedule` (*kind[, chunk_size]*)

- collapsing of multidimensional iteration spaces:
  `collapse`(n)

- synchronization while executing the loop region:
  `ordered`, `nowait`

- data privatization and reductions:
  `private`(*list*), `firstprivate`(*list*), `lastprivate`(*list*),
  `reduction`(*reduction−identifier*:*list*)

Loop Scheduling

Loop scheduling refers to the scheduling of loop iterations onto threads. The particular schedule to use may be specified using the `schedule` clause. Five kinds of schedules are permitted—`static`, `dynamic`, `guided`, `auto`, and `runtime`—and optionally a chunk size may be specified for the static, dynamic, and guided schedules as well. If no `schedule` clause is present, the schedule is implementation-dependent; a static schedule is the common default.

The `static` schedule will divide the iterations into chunks of size `chunk_size` (except for the last chunk, which may be smaller). Then each chunk will be assigned to the threads, in order of thread number, in a round-robin fashion. When no chunk size is given in the clause, each thread will get a single chunk of consecutive iterations, where the chunk size for each thread is approximately equal in size. A static schedule requires no runtime overhead for determining which iterations will execute on a given thread. However, efficient use of threads with a static schedule generally requires that each iteration have a similar amount of work to perform.

The `dynamic` schedule will cause each thread to dynamically request and then execute a chunk of iterations at a time. Upon completing one chunk, another chunk will be requested, and so on until no more chunks are available. If the chunk size is specified on the clause, then the size of the chunks will be determined as with the static schedule. Otherwise, threads will request a chunk of 1 iteration at a time. A dynamic schedule entails a runtime overhead in assigning each chunk of iterations to a requesting thread while ensuring no two threads are assigned the same iteration. Hence, it should generally be used only if there is a significant amount of work to perform per chunk relative to the scheduling overhead and the amount of work to perform in each chunk is not predictable.

The `guided` schedule is similar to a dynamic schedule—each thread will dynamically request a chunk of iterations, execute them, request another of iterations, and so on. The difference is in how the sizes of the iteration chunks are determined. The chunk size assigned to a thread will be proportional to the number of remaining iterations left to execute divided by the number of threads in the executing thread team. Once this number is less than the specified chunk size or less than 1 if a chunk size is not given, the behavior of a guided schedule becomes that of a dynamic schedule. Compared to a dynamic schedule, a guided schedule essentially tunes the chunk size based on the number of iterations left to execute, lessening the scheduling overhead while maintaining a good load balance.

The `auto` schedule will simply instruct the implementation, that is the compiler and/or runtime, to determine how to distribute the iterations among the threads. A compiler may analyze the underlying loop nest to select the most appropriate schedule and/or pass program information to the runtime so that it may perform the selection.

The remaining supported schedule kind is `runtime`. This tells the implementation to use the *runtime-sched-var* ICV in the current data environment, which may be set to a static, dynamic, guided, or auto schedule. This can be set with the `OMP_SCHEDULE` environment variable or by using the `omp_set_schedule(kind, modifer)` function (where the second argument is used to specify the chunk size). To get the schedule kind that would be used for a `runtime` schedule, the `omp_get_schedule(*kind, *modifier)` function may be used.

Collapsing Multidimensional Iteration Spaces

The `collapse(n)` clause, where n is a constant, positive integer, may be used to parallelize the outer n loops of the loop nest, so long as there is no intervening code between the loops (i.e., they are perfectly nested). A `collapse(1)` clause would be the same as having no collapse clause at all. Consider the following code:

```
#pragma omp for collapse (2)
for (i1 = 0; i1 < n1; i1++)
    for (i2 = 0; i2 < n2; i2++)
        ...
```

The directive instructs the implementation to schedule iterations from this 2-dimensional iteration space onto the encountering thread team. In effect, the compiler will "collapse" the loop nest so that it is equivalent to the following:

```
i1 = 0;
i2 = 0;
#pragma omp for private (i3)
for (i1i2 = 0; i1i2 < n1*n2; i1i2++) {
    ...
    i2++;
    if (i2 == n2) {
        i2 = 0;
        i1++;
    }
}
```

The collapse clause will increase the number of iterations that will be mapped to the threads in the team, while reducing the granularity of the work to be performed per iteration. It can be used to obtain a more scalable sharing of work (benefitting from the use of more threads).

Synchronization for Loop Constructs

OpenMP loop constructs typically are used for loops where each iteration is independent. If the iterations are not independent, then OpenMP provides a means for the loop to still be partially executed in parallel using the `ordered` clause. This clause indicates that a portion of the loop body (contained in an `ordered` construct) should execute in iteration order:

```
#pragma omp for ordered
for (i = 0; i < N; i++) {
    ...
    #pragma omp ordered
    {
        /* computation to be executed in iteration order */
        ...
    }
    ...
}
```

By default, loop constructs end with an implicit barrier. This prevents any thread in the executing team from continuing execution after the loop until all iterations of the loop have completed. The `nowait` clause may be used on loop constructs to remove this barrier synchronization.

Data Privatization and Reductions

Variables referenced in a loop construct that are shared in the enclosing parallel region may be privatized using one of the `private`, `firstprivate`, or `lastprivate` clauses. If the variable has already been privatized in the enclosing parallel region (i.e., the implicit tasks executing on the threads have their own copy of the variable in their respective data environments), then it may not be appear as a list item for these clauses on the loop construct. The `private` and `firstprivate` clauses operate similarly here to their use on the parallel construct. The `lastprivate` clause will privatize variables in its list, and additionally the value of the original variable after the loop construct will be assigned the value of the private copy belonging to the thread executing the last iteration. Note that the loop iteration variables of all associated loops in the construct will be treated implicitly as private.

Reductions are common operations performed by loops. Just as for parallel constructs, a `reduction` clause may specified for a loop construct, but it must be *shared* in the enclosing parallel region. The following code shows a typical example:

```
#pragma omp for reduction(+:sum_a)
for (i = 0; i < N; i++) {
    sum_a = sum_a + a[i];
}
```

The first N elements of array `a` are added together and the result will be in variable `sum_a` after the loop completes execution. Each thread will compute a partial sum using a compiler-generated temporary copy of `sum_a` that is initialized to some operator-specific value (e.g., 0 for sum reductions). Each of these copies are then combined into the original `sum_a`.

Sections Construct

The `sections` construct is used to assign distinct code sections each to a thread in the thread team. The format of the sections construct is:

```
#pragma omp sections  [clause [[,]  clause ]  ...]
{
[#pragma omp section]
     structured-block
[#pragma omp section
     structured-block]
     ...
}
```

The code under the `sections` directive may consist of one or more code sections in the form of structured statement blocks, demarcated by the `section` directive. For the first code section, the `section` directive is optional. Each code section is executed by a single thread in the thread team, and the mapping of sections to threads is implementation-dependent. In the code example below, up to three threads from the thread team executing the enclosing parallel region may execute the functions `func_a`, `func_b`, and `func_c` concurrently.

```
#pragma omp sections
{
#pragma omp section
     (void) func_a();
#pragma omp section
     (void) func_b();
#pragma omp section
     (void) func_c();
} /*—— End of sections  block ——*/
```

The clauses that may be used on the `sections` directive are a subset of the clauses accepted for the loop construct, namely `private`. `firstprivate`, `lastprivate`, `reduction`, and `nowait`. The use of the clause `lastprivate` for this construct means that the value in the private copy held by the thread that executes the lexically last code section will be written back to the original variable shared by the implicit tasks belonging to the enclosing parallel region. The rest of the clauses have similar behaviors as when used with the loop construct.

Because the `sections` construct contains a fixed number of code sections that may execute in parallel, it is not well suited for exploiting a large number of threads. However, like the loop construct, the programmer may use the `nowait` clause to allow threads not participating in the execution of the defined code sections to continue execution of its implicit tasks following the sections construct.

Single Construct

The `single` construct may be used to limit the execution of the enclosed statement block to a single thread. The programmer can not specify which thread will execute the statement block with this construct. It may be the first thread to encounter the construct, or it may be determined by the OpenMP implementation in some other manner. A single construct may privatize variables referenced within its statement block using the `private` or `firstprivate` clauses. As with the other worksharing constructs, variables being privatized must be shared in the enclosing parallel region. There is also the `copyprivate` clause, which is unique to the `single` construct. It can be used to broadcast the resulting value of a private variable associated with the thread that executed the structured block to the private copies associated with the other threads.

```
/* x is private in the enclosing parallel region */
. . .
#pragma omp single copyprivate (x)
{
    /* code that updates private copy of x */
    . . .
} /* ––– end of single block ––– */

/* all private copies of x now have the same value */
```

The `single` constructs also accepts the `nowait` clause, as by default there is an implicit barrier executed by all threads at the end of the construct. However, `nowait` may not appear if the `copyprivate` clause is used. This will ensure that all threads have the same value for variables that were copyprivate after executing the single construct.

Workshare Construct

The `workshare` construct is available only for OpenMP programs written using Fortran as a base language. The format of the construct is:

```
!$omp workshare
    structured-block
!$omp end workshare [nowait]
```

This construct will decompose the statements within the structured block into units of work that are distributed among the encountering threads for execution. Unlike worksharing in a loop construct, where correct usage requires that the iterations are independent or explicitly synchronized with the `ordered` directive, the statements within the workshare construct need not be independent of each other. The execution of the statements will proceed in a manner that preserves any dependences that may exist among them. The workshare construct has an implicit barrier at the end which may be eliminated using the nowait clause, as with the other worksharing constructs.

The structured block has several restrictions on the type of statements that are permitted. Basic scalar assignments may occur, where each such assignment will be executed by a single thread. Next, array assignments are allowed, which is a shorthand method in Fortran for performing element-wise assignments from or to arrays. These assignments are executed in parallel using the threads from the encountering team. Also allowed are the Fortran WHERE and FORALL statements/constructs, which entail element-wise array operations as well and are amenable to parallelization in the same manner. The transformational array intrinsic functions available in Fortran (e.g., MATMUL, DOT_PRODUCT, SUM, PRODUCT, etc.) may also appear, and their evaluation will be cooperatively executed by the threads. The atomic construct can appear, and the atomic access operation will be executed by a single thread. However, the execution of any array intrinsics that may also occur for the statement in the atomic construct may be workshared among the threads, as described above.

A workshare construct may contain occurrences of the critical construct, and each such occurrence would be executed by a single thread only. Finally, a parallel construct may also occur, in which case a single thread from the enclosing thread team will form a new thread team to execute it, as if the construct is encountered by only its implicit task.

Combined Worksharing Constructs

The loop, sections, and workshare constructs described above each have a corresponding combined construct which serves as a shortcut for specifying a parallel construct with the worksharing construct nested immediately inside of it.

For example, the combined parallel loop construct is:

```
#pragma omp parallel for [clause [[,] clause]  ...]
loop-nest
```

These combined constructs accept the same clauses as the parallel and worksharing constructs, except the nowait clause is not allowed. Using combined worksharing constructs can be a convenient shorthand. However, because of the cost of creating a parallel region and the required barrier at the end of each parallel region, the programmer should be judicious in their use.

12.3.4 Task Parallelism

Up to this point, we have described tasks as executable code with an associated data environment which executes on a thread. In an OpenMP program, tasks may be generated implicitly or explicitly. Implicit tasks are generated by an implicit parallel region (e.g., the one that surrounds the entire program) or upon encountering a parallel construct. Explicit tasks are generated upon encountering a `task` construct, which has the following syntax:

```
#pragma omp task [clause [[,] clause] ...]
structured-block
```

A generated task is executed by some thread in the current thread team. Clauses on the task directive will determine when a task may begin execution, how the data environment for the task should be set up, whether the task will be tied to the thread it begins execution on, and whether the task's descendents should all be *included* (i.e., executed immediately and completed before the encountering task may resume). The list of clauses on the `task` construct are:

- when the generated task should execute relative to other tasks:
  `if` $(scalar-expression)$, `depend` $(dependence-type:list)$

- the data-sharing and initialization attributes of variables referenced within the construct:
  `default(private|firstprivate|shared|none)`,
  `private`$(list)$, `firstprivate`$(list)$, `shared`$(list)$

- whether the generated task will be untied to a thread:
  `untied`

- overhead of task creation:
  `final, mergeable`

A task construct can be nested inside other OpenMP constructs such as worksharing constructs or inside another task region. It may also be present outside any explicit parallel construct, though in this case it would be restricted to execution on the program's initial thread. Completion of a task can be guaranteed using various task synchronization constructs: an encountered `barrier` or `taskwait`, an enclosing `taskgroup`, or a subsequently encountered `task` with a `depend` clause.

A thread may suspend a currently executing task region at a task scheduling point to execute a different task. Instances of common task scheduling points include (but are not limited to): (1) the point immediately following the generation of an explicit task, (2) the point of completion of a task region, (3) in a `taskwait` region, (4) in an implicit or explicit barrier region, and (5) at the end of a `taskgroup` region. The `taskyield` directive may also be used to explicitly define a task scheduling point in the program.

A task can either be tied or untied. By default, an explicit task is a tied task, which means if the task were to be suspended it must resume execution on the same thread. An untied task, in contrast, can resume execution on any thread in the team. Beyond this difference, tied tasks will impose some additional scheduling constraints. For example, a tied task may not be scheduled for execution on a thread if there exists other suspended tasks that are tied to the thread and not suspended at a barrier, unless it is a descendent of all such tasks. While untied tasks impose less scheduling constraints, they are unsafe to use if they contain code that is thread-dependent (e.g., reference `threadprivate` variables or the execution relies on the thread number of the executing thread).

Using Explicit Tasks

The use of parallel regions and worksharing constructs are ideal for parallelizing structured code with fixed units of parallelism (e.g., iterations of a loop with fixed bounds or statically partitioned code sections). In contrast, explicit tasks are well suited for cases where the code is more dynamic and/or unstructured. Codes containing unbounded while-loops or recursion are prime candidates that are difficult to parallelize using the worksharing constructs described in Section 12.3.3. For example, consider the code below, which depicts the traversal of a linked list using a loop construct:

```
while (p != NULL) {
    p = p->next;
    count++;
}

p = head;
for(i=0; i<count; i++)
{
    parr[i] = p;
    p = p->next;
}
#pragma omp parallel
{
    #pragma omp for schedule( static ,1)
    for(i=0; i<count; i++)
        process_work(parr[i]);
}
```

Parallelizing this code without the use of explicit tasks involves calculating the number of nodes in the list followed by the transformation of the linked list into an array at runtime. With the use of a worksharing loop construct, we can then distribute the work in parallel across the for-loop iterations. However, this is expensive and can be avoided using explicit tasks.

The following code shows the same linked list traversal using explicit tasks:

```
#pragma omp parallel
{
    #pragma omp single
    {
        p=head;
        while (p) {
            #pragma omp task firstprivate (p)
            process_work(p);
            p = p->next;
        }
    }
}
```

A thread team is created with the `parallel` construct. The `single` construct is used to make the implicit task of one thread within the team responsible for generating the explicit tasks, while the remaining implicit tasks suspend at the implicit barrier. The explicit tasks are generated sequentially using a while-loop. Each generated task will invoke the routine `process_work` on some node p in the list. The pointer p is necessarily firstprivate, since it is updated by the implicit task as it generates each task. The execution of the generated "child" tasks is deferred. This means that the generating task can continue execution until it suspends at a synchronization point, where it will then wait for the completion of its generated tasks. The generated tasks may be scheduled for execution on any thread in the thread team. Once all the tasks have completed execution, the threads may resume execution of their respective, suspended implicit tasks.

Data Scoping Within Tasks

The task directive accepts the `private`, `firstprivate`, `shared`, and `default` clauses to influence the data environment. The default scoping for variables referenced in a task construct, but not declared within the construct, is usually `firstprivate`, because the task may not be executed until later (and variables may be out of scope). However, if a variable is determined to be shared in all enclosing constructs up to and including the innermost parallel construct, it will be considered `shared`, as seen in the code below where A is `shared`, B is `firstprivate` and C is `private`.

```
#pragma omp parallel  shared(A)  private (B)
{
    . . .
    #pragma omp task
    {
        int C;
        compute (A, B, C);
    }
}
```

Undeferred and Included Tasks

An OpenMP program may specify when a task should execute in relation to its generating task. By default, explicit tasks are deferred. An undeferred task causes its generating task to suspend until it has completed execution. An `if` clause may be used on a task directive to specify whether the generated task should be deferred or undeferred. If the scalar value expression in the clause evaluates to *false* the task is undeferred; otherwise it is deferred. Such an undeferred task will execute immediately by some thread in the team, unless some other scheduling constraint prohibits this (e.g., the task depends on the completion of a previously generated task).

An included task is an undeferred task that, furthermore, executes immediately by the encountering thread. An OpenMP program can make use of included tasks in situations where the costs of scheduling a task becomes prohibitive. This is accomplished, indirectly, by using the `final` clause on the task directive. When the scalar expression argument for the final clause evaluates to true, it becomes a final task. All child tasks generated by a final task will themselves be final and included. Hence, by generating a final task, an OpenMP program essentially "cuts off" the generation of any nonincluded descendant tasks that may be submitted to the task scheduler.

The following code illustrates the usage of the `if` and `final` clauses.

```
void foo ( )
{
    int i;
    /* this generated task is undeferred */
    #pragma omp task if (0)
    {
        /* this generated task is a deferred task */
        #pragma omp task
        for (i = 0; i < 3; i++) {
            /* this generated task is a deferred task */
            #pragma omp task
                bar ();
```

```
            }
        }

        /* this generated task is a deferred task */
        #pragma omp task final (1)
        {
            /* this generated task is included */
            #pragma omp task
            for (i = 0; i < 3; i++) {
                /* this generated task is also included */
                #pragma omp task
                bar();
            }
        }
    }
```

Supposing some task T is executing `foo`, it will suspend execution upon encountering the first task construct with the `if(0)` clause. The generated undeferred task may in turn generate deferred tasks. The suspended task T resumes without waiting for the completion of these generated deferred tasks. It will then encounter the task construct with the `final(1)` clause. Here T suspends again, generating a deferred (but final) task. This task eventually executes on some thread in the team, and all of its descendent tasks will execute immediately on the same thread as they are generated.

Task Synchronization

There are several ways in which an OpenMP program may specify synchronization between tasks. The `taskwait` construct will cause the encountering task to suspend until all of its child tasks have completed execution. A barrier (whether explicit via the `barrier` construct or implicit such as the one that occurs on worksharing constructs), will cause the encountering threads to suspend the executing task until all explicit tasks generated by the thread team have completed. Note that while a `taskwait` requires only child tasks to complete, a `barrier` will ensure completion of all generated tasks.

The `taskgroup` construct provides another means for waiting on task completion.

```
#pragma omp taskgroup
structured-block
```

It specifies a wait on the completion of all child tasks generated in the taskgroup region, as well as all of their descendant tasks. The end of the `taskgroup` region is a task scheduling point. The task executing the construct will suspend there until tasks generated from within the region have completed.

The `taskwait`, `barrier`, and `taskgroup` constructs allow a task to wait on the completion of its descendent tasks. Task dependencies provide a means for waiting on the completion of prior sibling tasks, where two tasks are siblings if they were generated by the same task (i.e., have the same parent). The optional `depend` clause on a task construct specifies additional constraints on the scheduling of tasks by establishing dependencies among sibling tasks. This clause consists of a dependence type with one or more list items that refer to the storage locations of variables or array sections. The dependence type can be either `in`, `out`, or `inout`. If a task construct has a `depend` clause containing a list *l*, the generated task will not execute until all previously generated sibling tasks, with an `out` or `inout` dependence of at least one item from *l*, have completed. The reader may observe from this description that the `out` and `inout` dependence types are semantically equivalent. At present this is true, but different behaviors may be added in the future.

Consider the following code snippet:

```
/* in a parallel region */
int x = 1;

for (int i = 0; i < N; i++) {
    /* Task 1 created for this iteration */
    #pragma omp task shared(x) depend(out: x)
    preprocess_some_data(&x);

    /* Task 2 created for this iteration */
    #pragma omp task shared(x) depend(in: x)
    do_something_with_data(x);

    /* Task 3 created for this iteration */
    #pragma omp task shared(x) depend(in: x)
    do_something_independent_with_data(x);
}

/* synchronize here and ensure all created tasks have completed execution */
#pragma omp barrier
```

A specific ordering of task execution is enforced using task dependencies, wherein, for each iteration, a value for x is produced in *Task 1* and consumed in *Task 2* and *Task 3*. The variable x in the generated tasks is made shared, since it would be firstprivate, by default. *Task 1* must complete before *Task 2* and *Task 3* from the same iteration can start execution. Moreover, *Task 1* in the next iteration must wait for the completion of *Task 2* and *Task 3* in the current iteration. Note that *Task 2* and *Task 3* can execute in parallel, in any order, with respect to each other.

12.3.5 Vectorization

OpenMP programs may use SIMD constructs to exploit a platform's vectorization support for a given loop nest. Conceptually, each OpenMP thread will consist of one or more SIMD lanes. A program may generate SIMD instructions that execute statements from multiple iterations of a loop nest concurrently across the SIMD lanes of an OpenMP thread. The set of iterations that are concurrently executed are referred to as a SIMD chunk. While compilers may be able to automatically vectorize a code to some degree, using the SIMD constructs can improve the quality of the vectorized code by asserting various properties of the associated loops.

We start with the `simd` construct:

```
#pragma omp simd [clause [[,]  clause ]  ...]
loop-nest
```

The `simd` directive instructs the implementation that the associated loops within the loop nest may be vectorized using SIMD instructions. The encountering thread will execute all the iterations of the loop, with iterations in each SIMD chunk being executed concurrently. The clauses on the directive can specify:

- a nondefault byte alignment for referenced data:
  `aligned`(*list[:linear-step]*)

- collapsing of multidimensional iteration spaces:
  `collapse`(n)

- maximum distance between iterations within a SIMD chunk:
  `safelen`(*length*)

- data privatization and reductions:
  `linear`(*list:linear$-$step*) `private`(*list*), `firstprivate`(*list*),
  `lastprivate`(*list*), `reduction`(*reduction$-$identifier:list*)

The `simd` construct does not explicitly specify which iterations belong to the same SIMD chunk—this is implementation defined. However, the `safelen` construct can indirectly influence how the loop is "SIMDized," ensuring that no two iterations which have a distance (in the logical iteration space) greater than the parameter *length* are in the same SIMD chunk. This is useful for a code such as the following, where there is a loop-carried dependence of distance m which the program asserts will not be less than 16:

```
#pragma omp simd safelen(16)
for (i = m; i < N; i++)
    a[i] = a[i-m] * b[i];
```

In the code above, the compiler may generate $\frac{N-m+1}{16}$ SIMD chunks, each performing 128-bit vector load, multiply, and store instructions. Variables a, b, and m will be shared and the loop index variable i privatized to each SIMD lane. Unlike in the standard loop constructs, the value of i on the last iteration will be copied back to the original i at the end of the SIMD construct.

The compiler will assume that arrays accessed within a SIMD construct are aligned to an implementation-defined byte boundary for its generated vector instructions. The program may explicitly specify the alignment of arrays using the `aligned` clause.

The `linear` clause is used to specify a special type of privatization for variables referenced within the construct. Each SIMD lane receives a copy of the list item, which is initialized to the value of the original variable plus the logical iteration number (0 to N-1 for N total iterations for all associated loops) multiplied by the *linear-step* parameter (which must be loop-invariant). Moreover, the value of the list item on the logically last iteration will be copied to the original variable, as in the case of a lastprivate list item. The following code shows an example of its usage:

```
j = 0;
#pragma omp simd linear(j:k)
for (i = 0; i < N; i++) {
    a[i] = a[i] * b[j];
    j += k;
}
```

The remaining clauses for the `simd` construct behave similarly to the corresponding clauses on the standard loop constructs, except with respect to SIMD lanes rather than threads.

The loop `simd` construct combines the functionality of a standard worksharing loop construct with the `simd` construct. That is, the loop iterations are distributed among the encountering threads, and the set of iterations assigned to each thread is further subdivided into SIMD chunks for vectorized execution. Consider the following simple example:

```
#pragma omp for simd
for (i = 0; i < N; i++) {
    a[i] = a[i] * b[i];
}
```

The iterations of the loop will be distributed across all threads executing the enclosing parallel region and across the SIMD lanes of those threads. All of the clauses permitted on the loop construct and `simd` construct described above may be used on a loop `simd` construct, with identical meanings and restrictions. The exception is that the `ordered` clause may not be used. The loop `simd` construct may also be combined with the `parallel` construct to form the `parallel` loop `simd` construct (e.g., `parallel for simd` for C/C++, `parallel do simd` for Fortran).

Sometimes a loop that may be vectorized contains calls to functions for which SIMD instructions may be generated. By adding the `declare simd` directive above the declaration and definition of such routines, the compiler can be instructed to generate SIMD versions which may then be inlined into a `simd` or loop `simd` construct. The reader may refer to [222] for examples of its usage.

12.3.6 Support for Accelerators

Support for accelerators in OpenMP is provided through a set of device constructs and related runtime functions. The accelerator model makes a distinction between a host device, from which execution begins, and one or more target devices onto which target regions—executable code intended for execution on a target device—may be offloaded. The model treats each of these devices as having their own memory, such that code that executes on any such device will have its own data environment which resides within the device's memory.

For making use of target devices with OpenMP, the following steps are needed:

1. Create a "mapping" between data residing in the host device's memory and data allocated in a target device's memory.

2. Define when and in what direction data is to be synchronized between the host memory and their respective mapped objects in a target device's memory.

3. Specify code regions intended for execution on a target device, called target regions.

4. Distribute work in a target region across teams, across threads in a team, and/or across SIMD lanes in a thread.

OpenMP provides several different constructs, including combined constructs, for performing the above steps. In the remainder of this section we will describe the usage of these constructs.

Data Mapping and Data Synchronization

Global (i.e., file or namespace scope) variables and functions may be mapped to target device(s) for the duration of the program using the `declare target` and `end declare target` directives. For example:

#pragma omp declare target

/∗ global variable declarations ∗/
`int` x, y, u[100];

`int` foo();
#pragma omp end declare target

All the variables and functions with declarations or definitions between the `declare target` and `end declare target` directives will be mapped to corresponding variables/functions in the data environments for all target devices for the duration of the program.

In order to dynamically map data to a target device, OpenMP provides the `target data` construct which has the following form:

#pragma omp target data [clause [[,] clause] ...]
`structured-block`

Data can be mapped to a target device (which is an implementation-defined default device, if not explicitly specified) for the duration of execution of the associated structured block using the `map` clause. The clauses allowed on this construct specify:

- mapping of data from the host to the target device memory:
  `map` ($[map-type :]list$)

- which device to map data to:
  `device` ($integer-expressoin$)

- conditional disabling of the mapping:
  `if` ($scalar-expression$)

The list items on the map clause may refer to variables or contiguous array sections. If a list item in a map clause already exists in the device memory (e.g., it was either mapped using the `declare target` directive or in an enclosing `target data` region), then the map clause is ignored. Otherwise, the list items on the `map` clause may have the alloc, to, from, and tofrom map types. The alloc map type will cause objects to be allocated in device memory with uninitialized values. The to map type will cause objects to be allocated and initialized with values from the host memory. The from map type may be used to allocate data that is uninitialized and then to copy back its values to host memory at the end of the target region. Finally, with the tofrom map type, the data will be allocated and initialized as with the to map type, and additionally, the values will be copied back to the host memory at the end of the target data region. Note that the to, from, and tofrom map types, in addition to creating a mapping between an original variable or array section on the host device to a corresponding variable or array section on the target device, prescribe a data synchronization between the two devices at the boundaries of the target data region.

The target update construct is a standalone directive for specifying data synchronization:

```
#pragma omp target update clause [[[,] clause] ...]
```

Like the target data construct, it accepts a device clause to specify a target device to synchronize with. This directive accepts two "motion" clauses: to(*list*) and from(*list*). For every list item appearing in the to clause, its value in the host data environment will be copied to the corresponding variable on the target device. Likewise, for every list item appearing in the from clause, the value of the mapped variable in the target device's data environment will be copied back into the data environment of the task executing on the host device. If a list item appearing in either motion clause has not already been mapped into the device's data environment, the behavior is unspecified.

Offloading Computation

In order to offload actual computation to a target device, the host must generate a target region. This can be accomplished using the target construct, which has the following syntax:

```
#pragma omp target [clause [[,] clause] ...]
structured-block
```

The target construct subsumes the functionality provided by the target data construct, and additionally the associated structured block is expected to execute on the target device. The clauses used for this construct are identical to those used on the target data construct. The task on the host device that encounters the target construct will suspend until the target region has completed execution on the target device. If the system can not execute the target region on a separate target device, than it may instead execute on the host device. There is an implicit `tofrom` mapping for any variables referenced in the structured block of the construct that are not declared in the construct and are not already mapped to the target device data environment. Any functions called within the target region must have already been mapped to the target device using the `declare target` directive. Likewise, any global variables referenced from the target region, but not within the construct, must have been mapped using the `declare target` directive.

Exploiting Parallelism on Target Devices

The target region generated with the `target` construct will, by default, execute on a single thread on the device, as if enclosed by an implicit task within an inactive parallel region. OpenMP provides three types of parallelism that may be utilized on a target device: parallelism across teams, parallelism across threads, and parallelism across SIMD (or vector) lanes.

To enable parallelism across multiple teams, a `teams` construct may be used. The `teams` construct should be nested closely within a `target` construct, such that no code exists within the target construct but outside the teams construct. The syntax for this construct is:

#pragma omp teams [clause [[,] clause] ...]
`structured-block`

The allowed clauses may be used to specify:

- the number of teams to create:
  `num_teams` ($[scalar-integer-expression]$)

- the maximum number of threads that will participate in each team:
  `thread_limit` ($[scalar-integer-expression]$)

- the data-sharing and initialization attributes of variables referenced within the construct:
  `default(private|firstprivate|shared|none)`,
  `private`($list$)`, firstprivate`($list$)`, shared`($list$)`,
  `reduction`($reduction-identifier:list$)

While the construct may assign multiple threads per team, based on the `thread_limit` clause, initially each team executes with a single thread as if enclosed in a parallel region with team size 1. The remaining threads may be "activated" when the team's initial thread encounters a `parallel` construct or combined worksharing construct. The data-sharing clauses and rules for the `teams` construct work similarly to the `parallel` construct, except they define data sharing, privatization, and reduction with respect to teams rather than threads.

For specifying loop-level worksharing across teams, the `distribute` construct may be used. Consider the following code:

```
#pragma omp target  ...
#pragma omp teams num_teams(T) ...
#pragma omp distribute  dist_schedule ( static , m) private (...)   firstprivate  (...)   collapse (k)
for (i = 0; i < N; i++) {
    for (j = 0; j < N; j++) {
        ...
    }
}
```

In the above code snippet, the `target`, `teams`, and `distribute` constructs are used to execute the iterations of a k-level loop nest across T teams on the target device. The `private`, `firstprivate`, and `collapse` clauses function as they do for the standard loop construct. The `dist_schedule` clause behaves similarly to the `schedule` clause on the standard loop construct, except that only static schedules may be specified.

As mentioned above, when a `parallel` construct is encountered within a teams region by a team's initial thread, it will enable additional threads (not exceeding the thread limit, if specified) in the team to participate in the execution of the parallel region. If the construct occurs in a target region but outside a teams region, then its behavior is as described in Section 12.3.1.

Target devices are often well suited for vectorization and, to take advantage of this, OpenMP programs may incorporate SIMD constructs into target regions. This can be done in a number of ways. A loop distributed across teams using the `distribute` construct may include a nested `simd` or loop `simd` construct. The program may also distribute iterations across teams and SIMDize iterations for each team's master thread with the `distribute simd` construct. Additionally, a program may nest a SIMD construct within a `parallel` construct nested inside a `teams` construct, to take advantage of all three levels of parallelism on the target device.

Combined Target Constructs

OpenMP provides several shortcuts for combining the aforementioned constructs in various ways. Combined construct for use in a target region include:

- `teams distribute`

- `teams distribute simd`

- `teams distribute parallel` loop

- `teams distribute parallel` loop `simd`

Combined constructs that generate a target region and may be used in a task executing on the host device include:

- `target teams`

- `target teams distribute`

- `target teams distribute simd`

- `target teams distribute parallel` loop

- `target teams distribute parallel` loop `simd`

Runtime Library Support

The OpenMP API includes a few library functions for supporting the use of accelerators. The `omp_get_num_devices()` function may be used to query the number of target devices available. Each target device is identified by a unique integer. The function `omp_-get_default_device()` will return the integer corresponding to the default target device, and `omp_set_default_device` may be used to change this default device. An OpenMP program will attempt to use the default target device when executing a target construct if no `device` clause is given. A program may use the `omp_is_initial_-device()` function to determine whether or not the current task is executing on the host device. The `omp_get_num_teams()` function will return the number of teams executing in the current `teams` region. Each team has a designated number, from 0 to `omp_-get_num_teams()-1`. The function `omp_get_team_num()` returns this number when called within a teams region, and it returns 0 otherwise.

12.3.7   Region Cancellation

OpenMP includes features to cancel execution of OpenMP regions of a specified type, based on conditional cancellation at cancellation points. The `OMP_CANCELLATION` environment variable should be set to *true* in order to use this feature, and its value may be queried from the program using the `omp_get_cancellation()` function. The `cancel` construct activates cancellation of the innermost enclosing region of the type specified:

#pragma omp cancel construct−type[[,] if (scalar−expression)]

The available construct types for the `cancel` construct are `parallel`, `sections`, `for` (or do in Fortran), and `taskgroup`. A thread or task requesting cancellation does not lead to the immediate cancellation of the region's execution for other threads or tasks in the identified construct. Instead, they will only cancel their execution of the region once they have reached a cancellation point. The program is responsible for releasing locks or similar data structures that might cause a deadlock when a `cancel` construct is encountered and blocked threads cannot be cancelled. An `if` clause may be used, which will prevent cancellation when its scalar expression argument evaluates to *false*. A `cancel` `taskgroup` construct may result in any task generated within the enclosing taskgroup region to be discarded if they have not yet started execution.

When a task executing within the construct reaches a designated "cancellation point", it may then skip to the end of the region if it is determined that it has been cancelled. Cancellation points are implied at implicit barriers, `barrier` constructs, and `cancel` constructs. An explicit cancellation point may be specified using the `cancellation` `point` construct:

#pragma omp cancellation point construct−type

When a thread encounters the `cancellation point` construct with the construct types `parallel`, `sections`, or `for` (do), it checks if cancellation of the innermost enclosing region of that type has been requested. If so, it will skip to the end of the construct and resume execution from there. A `cancellation point taskgroup` construct must appear in a task generated from within the taskgroup region, and it results in the task immediately completing.

Region cancellation support in OpenMP may be used to write parallel programs that recover gracefully from encountered error conditions. Another example would be algorithms that spawn many tasks in search of a particular answer. This may be written using a `taskgroup` construct, with tasks within the construct using the `cancel` and, optionally, the `cancellation point` directives to exit the taskgroup region once one of the tasks arrives at the answer.

12.4   Performance Considerations

We describe here a few performance considerations when writing OpenMP programs. For more information, the reader may refer to [75].

Optimize the sequential portions.   It is important to also optimize the sequential portions of an OpenMP program. This often involves, among other techniques, reorganizing array accesses in loops and removal of redundant code which may not be done by the compiler. Once an efficient sequential code is obtained, OpenMP constructs can be added incrementally.

Limit overhead of `parallel`.   It is generally a good practice to limit the number of `parallel` constructs used in a program, enclosing as much code as possible. This is particularly important for short running parallel programs. The reason is that the usage of `parallel` can be expensive since it involves creation and management of thread teams. This may include creation and termination of threads, implicit task creation, and the barrier synchronization implied at the end of the construct. All these may add up to a significant portion of the total execution time of program.

Load balancing versus scheduling overhead.   The workload characteristics of a program can have a major influence on loop scheduling. Typically work can be either distributed uniformly, statically (not necessarily uniformly), dynamically, or using guided workload distribution schedules. Choosing the right scheduling technique and a smaller grain size can help to improve load balance, thereby increasing parallel efficiency of the loop execution. However, if the grain size is too small, the load balance can come at the cost of substantial scheduling overheads. For loops where the iterations are not performing a uniform amount of work, it is recommended to experiment with dynamic or guided loop schedules and various chunk sizes to negotiate these two competing issues.

Avoid false sharing.   False sharing can significantly impact performance when (a) shared data is modified by multiple threads, (b) the program's access pattern is such that multiple threads are modifying the same cache line or more than one cache line, and (c) (often exacerbating the issue) these modifications are happening in rapid succession. Careful code inspection can help avoid false sharing. While array padding can help prevent false sharing, a better solution is to avoid the conditions in which false sharing will occur. The goal is to ensure that those variables that cause false sharing are spaced far enough in memory such that it is unlikely they will reside on the same cache line(s). Yet another way for the programmer to address this issue is to use thread-local copies. Programming patterns such as privatization can be used to copy shared data to local memory. This data can be processed (read, modified, updated) without interfering with the other threads. Upon completion the thread may copy the data back to the shared memory and make the data accessible to other threads.

Reducing data movement between devices.   While the `target` construct may also be used to dynamically map data into a target device data environment, for performance reasons it is generally recommended to perform mappings using the `declare target` or `target data` constructs, and to then generate `target` regions from within a `target data` region. In this way, the mappings may persist across the target regions. It is easy to forget that data referenced in a target construct, which does not have an explicit mapping, is implicitly given a `tofrom` mapping. By establishing the mapping in an enclosing `target data` construct, the program may reduce the cost of creating the data mappings and, more importantly, perform data synchronization across devices only at the beginning and end of each encountered `target` construct.

12.5   Correctness Considerations

Some bugs in shared-memory programming can be subtle and difficult to find. One such bug, the data race condition, involves the silent corruption of data during execution, and is hard to detect as it may only manifest itself a small fraction of the time. A data race condition occurs when multiple threads concurrently access the same shared data with at least one of the threads attempting to modify the data. Since there is no guarantee of the order in which the threads access data, this may lead to an incorrect result. Data race conditions may result from the lack of proper synchronization, like using a `nowait` incorrectly or neglecting to enclose such data access in a `critical` construct.

By privatizing variables that do not need to be shared, data race conditions and other issues can be avoided. Since variables are often shared by default in a parallel region, overlooked variables may be unintentionally shared. For example, in a Fortran loop the index variables are always treated as private, but they are only private for the loops associated with a loop construct in C/C++. So in C/C++, the index variable of an inner loop will be shared, if not explicitly privatized. Overlooking such cases are a common source of data race conditions.

A common mistake is neglecting to consider which constructs have an implied barrier. In many cases, the `single` and the `master` constructs may be used for the same purpose. However, the former has an implied barrier and the latter does not. When using the `master` construct, the user should realize that no synchronization is implied, and an explicit barrier may be needed afterwards, whereas for the `single` construct it would not be needed. Where the programmer does not intend the use of a barrier, the `single` construct may be used with the `nowait` clause to disable the unnecessary barrier.

Barriers may lead to the program hanging or a deadlock if they are not used correctly. An explicit barrier must be executed by all threads in the current thread team. If any thread does not reach the barrier, the remaining threads will not be able to progress past the barrier. Another source of deadlocks is the improper nesting of explicit locks. Deadlocked code will appear to be executing work, but will never finish.

The above are just a few common ways in which bugs can be inadvertently introduced in an OpenMP program. For more discussion on this, the reader may refer to [75, 261].

12.6   Summary and Future Directions

OpenMP has evolved significantly since its beginnings where it was used primarily for parallelizing loops. Through all these major changes, the basic philosophy behind the design of OpenMP has remained. The programmer should be able to take existing sequential codes and, with minimal changes, make use of OpenMP to effectively parallelize it. With the use of compiler directives, runtime functions, and environment variables, OpenMP may be used to express loop-level parallelism, task parallelism, vectorization, and offloading of computation to target accelerator devices. OpenMP provides a variety of mechanisms to establish how data should be shared or privatized with respect to SIMD instructions, thread teams, and across thread teams. It also provides a number of synchronization facilities. These include higher-level constructs such as barriers, critical sections, and containers for ensuring completion of a collection of tasks (i.e., `taskgroup`). And, if necessary, it includes low-level mechanisms which may potentially serve as building blocks for custom synchronizations, such as `atomic` and `flush`.

The OpenMP ARB is actively considering new features to add to or enhance the current API, deliberating on changes frequently being proposed by members of the OpenMP language committee. This includes changes to the API that are acceptable to all vendors on all platforms. The challenge they face is to keep the API small enough to be relatively easy to use, yet robust enough to offer sufficient expressivity for exploiting parallelism in an application. Proposals under consideration include error handling mechanisms, support for performance tools, tasking extensions, support for expressing affinity between data and threads/tasks, and enhanced capabilities for programming heterogeneous platforms.

13 Cilk Plus

Arch D. Robison, Intel
Charles E. Leiserson, MIT

13.1   Introduction

Cilk Plus is a parallel extension of C and C++ for exploiting regular and irregular parallelism on modern shared-memory multicore machines. The "Cilk" part targets multithreading, and the "Plus" part targets vectorization. Except for the "array notation" syntax in "Plus," the syntactic extensions can be ignored by plain C and C++ compilers, and the program still compiles as a valid serial program.

For example, consider an operation $C \leftarrow C + A \times B$ on dense matrices. The usual elementary serial algorithm has three nested loops. The following code shows one such algorithm, parallelized with Cilk Plus:[1]

```
#include <cilk/cilk.h>

void MulAdd0() {
    cilk_for (int i=0; i<N; ++i)
        for (int j=0; j<N; ++j)
#pragma simd
            for (int k=0; k<N; ++k)
                C[i][k] += A[i][j]*B[j][k];
}
```

The code is essentially serial code, except the outermost and innermost loops contain syntactic markups that permit parallelism.

- The `cilk_for` keyword designates a `for` loop in which iterations are permitted to run in parallel. The parallelism is implemented foremost by multithreading, and the compiler is allowed to apply vectorization, too.

- The compiler directive `#pragma simd` specifies that iterations may be vectorized. For example, suppose the target machine has vector registers of length V. The generated code can execute $\lceil N/V \rceil$ iterations, where each of N iterations updates V elements of matrix C. If N is not a multiple of V, one last iteration finishes off a partial vector of iterations.

Cilk Plus permits parallelism but never mandates it. The lack of mandatory parallelism is crucial to efficiency: whenever all processors are busy, the system is free to execute a piece of code serially, and not pay the cost of running additional threads.

---

1. For brevity, subsequent examples assume that `<cilk/cilk.h>` has been included. Programs using `cilk_spawn`, `cilk_sync`, or `cilk_for` must include this header, which defines those identifiers as tokens reserved by the compiler. For example, `cilk_spawn` is a macro for `_Cilk_spawn`.

Matrix multiplication can be formulated recursively too, as a divide-and-conquer algo-rithm, which might run faster[2] on large matrices than the loop-based parallel algorithm, for reasons explained in Section 13.6. The following code shows Cilk Plus code for the divide-and-conquer algorithm. The "Cilk" part enables multithreading of the recursion. The "Plus" part enables vectorization of the base case.

```
// Compute C[ib:n][jb:n] += A[ib:n][jb:n] × B[jb:n][kb:n].
void MulAddR(int ib, int jb, int kb, int n) {
    const int threshold = 16;
    if (n<=threshold) {
        // Base case
        for( int i=ib; i<ib+n; ++i )
            for( int j=jb; j<jb+n; ++j )
                C[i][kb:n] += A[i][j]*B[j][kb:n];
    } else {
        // Recursive case — divide each matrix into quadrants.
        int m = n/2;
        assert(2*m==n);
        // Loop iterates twice, for a total of 8 sub—multiplications
        for (int j=jb; j<jb+n; j+=n/2) {
            cilk_spawn MulAddR(ib  , j, kb,   m);
            cilk_spawn MulAddR(ib+m, j, kb,   m);
            cilk_spawn MulAddR(ib  , j, kb+m, m);
            MulAddR(ib+m, j, kb+m, m);
            cilk_sync;
        }
    }
}

// Compute C += A × B.
void MulAdd1() {
    MulAddR(0, 0, 0, N);
}
```

The base case could use `pragma simd`, but for exposition it uses array notation, an-other feature of Cilk Plus that permits vectorization. The notation `[kb:n]` denotes a section of an array with n consecutive elements, starting with the element at index `kb` and ending at index `kb+n-1`. The statement in the innermost loop reads a section of n consec-utive elements starting at `B[j][kb]`, multiplies each element of the section by the scalar `A[i][j]`, and updates each corresponding element in the section starting at `C[j][kb]`. Section 13.2.1 explores array sections in more detail.

2. Or maybe not. Since dense matrix multiplication of large matrices is a popular benchmark, serial compilers often have aggressive optimizations for it, such as converting the flat algorithm into a cache-friendly "blocked" form. Furthermore, memory prefetchers in hardware can do better with the flat form. Nonetheless, dense matrix multiplication serves well for exposition, because most readers know the plain serial code like an old nursery rhyme.

The recursive case is like serial divide-and-conquer code, with a few annotations that permit parallelism. The `cilk_spawn` notation permits the caller to continue without waiting for the callee to return. The `cilk_sync` notation says that execution of the current routine must wait for all callees to return. Hence, by spawning three calls and continuing without waiting to run the fourth call, the code permits four instances of `MulAddR` to run in parallel. The potential four-way parallelism grows exponentially as 4^d for d levels of recursion, thus giving the Cilk Plus system plenty of permitted parallelism to exploit as needed.

The rest of this chapter provides a more in-depth introduction to Cilk Plus. Sections 13.2 and 13.3 detail the extensions for vectorization and multithreading, respectively. Section 13.4 explains the theoretical performance model behind the Cilk portion and the Cilkview scalability-analysis tool which uses the performance model to estimate the scalability of programs. Section 13.5 covers correctness issues regarding races, including the Cilkscreen tool for verifying that a program has no races. Section 13.6 advises about practical usage of the Cilk Plus parallel extensions. Section 13.7 gives a brief history of Cilk Plus, and Section 13.8 summarizes the benefits of using this technology.

13.2   Vector Parallelism

There are two ways to express vector parallelism in Cilk Plus:

array notation specifies operations across sections of arrays.

pragma SIMD marks a loop as suitable for vectorized execution.

The choice between them is largely a matter of taste. Array notation may have more appeal to programmers familiar with Fortran 90 array expressions or APL-style programming [147], and provides a concise notation for clerical tasks such as initializing or copying an array. Pragma SIMD may have more appeal to programmers familiar with OpenMP. There is also a portability issue: the pragma can be ignored by compilers that do not understand it, whereas array notation introduces syntax that makes a program uncompilable if encountered by compilers without the array notation extensions.

While, in principle, the vector parallelism can enable multithreading too, current implementations shy away from doing so because vector operations that are long enough to benefit from the multithreading usually exhibit poor cache behavior.

13.2.1   Array Notation

Array notation consists of specifying array sections and operations on them. The most general section specification has the form $p[i : n : k]$ where p is an expression with pointer type and i, n, and k are expressions with integral type. This expression denotes a section with n elements starting with subscript i and with stride k. The section can be pictured as a vector:

$$p[i], \ p[i+k], \ p[i+2k], \ ...p[i+(n-1)k]$$

The expression p can have array type as well as pointer type, since by C/C++ rules, an array used in an expression decays into a pointer to its zeroth element. The value of k can be positive, negative, or zero. For instance, the section q[n-1:n:-1] contains n elements of q in reverse order, and the section p[3:n:0] is a section with p[3] replicated n times.

Two shorthands exist:

- The expression $p[i:j]$ is equivalent to $p[i:j:1]$. This form is the most common in practice.

- The expression $a[:]$ is equivalent to $a[0:n:1]$, where a must have array type and n is the length of that array type.

Multidimensional sections are allowed. For example, A[0:m][0:n] denotes the upper left m×n submatrix of matrix A. The number of dimensions of a section is called its **rank**. The **shape** of a section is a tuple of the lengths of each dimension. A scalar has rank 0 and an empty tuple as its shape. Examples:

Expression	Rank	Shape
A[0:5][0:8][0:9]	3	(5,8,9)
A[0:5][0][0:9]	2	(5,9)
A[0:5][0][0]	1	(5)
A[0][0][8]	0	()

The type of A does not have to be a three-dimensional array. It could be a composition of array and pointer types, as long as it admits three subscripts. For example, the preceding examples would also work if A was declared as int *(*A)[8] and suitably initialized.

Scalar arithmetic operations apply elementwise to sections. Shapes of all operands must match or be zero. For example:

```
y[10:8] += a*x[20:8];
```

is a parallel equivalent of:

```
for (int i=0; i<8; ++i)
    y[i+10] += a*x[i+20];
```

Function calls work similarly:

```
z[0:8] = atan2(y[0:8], x[0:8]);
```

computes `atan2` elementwise for 8 elements. Subscripting applies elementwise, too:

```
a[i[0:8]] = b[j[0:8]]
```

is the parallel equivalent of:

```
for( int k=0; k<8; ++k )
    a[i[k]] = b[j[k]]
```

If array `i` has a duplicate subscript m, the value of `a[m]` is unspecified after the assignment.

Because array notation statements do not create temporary arrays, care must be taken to not overlap the left and right sides. For example, consider the following:

```
a[0:n] = (a[-1:n]+2*a[0:n]+a[1:n])*0.25f;  // Undefined in Cilk Plus for n>1
```

The equivalent in APL or Fortran 90 is well defined, because those languages require that execution behave as if the right side is fully evaluated before updating the left side. In Cilk Plus, the example is undefined. Just as with structure assignments in C/C++, partial overlap of the left and right sides is undefined, but *exact* overlap is permitted. For example, both of the following statements have the same well-defined meaning:

```
a[0:n] += 1;
a[0:n] = a[0:n] + 1;
```

The prohibition against overlap exists because experience showed that with the APL/-Fortran 90 semantics, compilers often had to introduce unnecessary temporary arrays that significantly hurt performance, and made space demand hugely unpredictable because the number of array temporaries depended on the compiler implementation.

Array notation provides reduction operations for common cases, such as the operation `__sec_reduce_add` for summing a section, and provides a general reduction operation for user-defined operations. The following code sets `S` to the inner product of vectors `X` and `Y`:

```
S = __sec_reduce_add( X[0:N]*Y[0:N] );
```

The intrinsic __sec_implicit_index(k) returns a relative index for the *k*th axis of an implied section. For example,

```
c[0:n][0:n] = __sec_implicit_index(1)-__sec_implicit_index(0);
```

is a parallel equivalent of

```
for (int i=0; i<n; ++i )
    for (int j=0; j<n; ++j )
        c[i][j] = i-j;
```

Limited support for masking exists via using an array section as a control expression in an if, like this:

```
if (a[0:n]%2!=0)
    a[0:n] = a[0:n]*3+1;
else
    a[0:n] /= 2;
```

This code halves each element of a[0:n] that was even, and triples-plus-1 each element of a[0:n] that was odd. Semantically it executes *both* the "then" clause and the "else" clause, each under control of a mask.

APL programmers are fond of puzzling each other with loopless one-line programs. In that spirit, this introduction to array notation ends with a puzzle. What does the following statement do?

```
C[0:N][0:N] = [](int i, int j){
    return __sec_reduce_add(A[i][0:N]*B[0:N][j]);
} (__sec_implicit_index(0),__sec_implicit_index(1));
```

The notation [](...){...} is a C++11 lambda expression [151].

13.2.2 Pragma SIMD

The `pragma simd` directive is the other way to specify vector parallelism in Cilk Plus. When put on a `for` loop, the pragma says that the loop iterations can be executed in SIMD fashion. For example,

```
#pragma simd
for (int i=0; i<n; ++i )
    y[i+10] += a*x[i+20]);
```

permits (but does not require) the compiler to generate code that evaluates multiple iterations at a time using SIMD hardware. It is up to the programmer to determine if the loop is safe to execute in SIMD fashion.

The `pragma simd` directive permits structured control flow inside the loop—even another loop! For example, consider the following:

```
#pragma simd
for (int i=0; i<n; ++i )
    while( a[i]>=1 ) {
        a[i]/=2;
        b[i]++;
    }
```

The pragma permits the compiler to execute, SIMD-wise, a chunk of iterations of the i loop. For each chunk, the `while` loop executes until $a[i] < 1$ for all i in the chunk. If $a[i] \geq 1$ for only some i in the chunk, execution is suppressed ("masked") for the other values of i.

The `pragma simd` directive allows reduction variables, which must be specified in a reduction clause.

```
s = 0;
#pragma simd reduction(+:s)
for (int i=0; i<n; ++i )
    s += a[i]*b[i];
```

The reduction feature sets it apart from the historically popular pragma `ivdep` recognized by many compilers. The summation order is not necessarily the same as the serial code. For example, if the hardware has vector registers of length 8, the generated code might accumulate 8 separate sums, with the kth sum holding $\sum_{i \bmod 8 == k} a_i$, and finish the final sum after the loop finishes. In general, effective vectorization of reductions requires both reassociating and recommuting operands.

13.2.3 SIMD-Enabled Functions

SIMD-enabled functions are a feature of Cilk Plus that enable efficient SIMD execution of functions applied in an elementwise context. The programmer annotates a callee to tell the compiler to generate a version of the callee customized for a particular context, in addition to the usual version of the callee.

For example, consider the following two functions:

```
// Return magnitude of (x+yi) and store phase in *angle.
float Polar(float* angle, float x, float y) {
    *angle = atan2(y,x);
    return sqrt(x*x+y*y);
}

void Foo(float r[], float a[], float u[], float v) {
#pragma simd
    for (int i=0; i<100; ++i)
        r[i] = Polar(&a[i], u[i], v);
}
```

The body of Foo might also be written using array notation instead of with pragma SIMD like this:

```
r[0:100] = Polar(&a[0:100], u[0:100], v);
```

With ordinary calling conventions, the code generated for Foo must call Polar 100 times in either case *if* the compiler cannot see the definition of Polar when it compiles Foo.

If the target machine has SIMD hardware with a vector length of 4, a programmer seeking high performance could be motivated to rewrite it to make the SIMD hardware evaluate four calls at a time, like this:[3]

```
// Like Polar, but computes result for four values of x in parallel.
void VectorPolar(float magnitude[4], float angle[4], float x[4], float y) {
    angle[0:4] = atan2(y,x[0:4]);
    magnitude[0:4] = sqrt(x[0:4]*x[0:4]+y*y);
}

void Foo(float r[], float a[], float u[], float v) {
```

---

3. An assembly-level programmer could be even more aggressive, by passing x[0:4] by value in a vector register, and returning magnitude[0:4] in a vector register. Because arrays cannot be rvalues in C/C++, expressing this notion at the source level would entail the obfuscation of wrapping the vector in a struct.

```
#pragma simd
    for (int i=0; i<100; i+=4)
        VectorPolar(&r[i:4], &a[i:4], &u[i:4], v);
}
```

Here, `VectorPolar` is written specifically for the case that within the calling SIMD loop:

- x is different for each invocation.

- y is *uniform* for each invocation.

- The pointers `magnitude` and `angle` increase in a *linear* fashion with unit stride for each invocation.

Manually writing these vectorized callees for each possible context can become tedious.

SIMD-Enabled functions let the programmer tell the compiler to do the tedious work. Instead of writing `VectorPolar`, the programmer annotates the declaration of `Polar` like so:

```
__declspec(vector(linear(angle),uniform(y)))
float Polar(float* angle, float x, float y);
```

The annotation tells the compiler to generate an additional routine like `VectorPolar` when it compiles `Polar`, and that the variant can be used at call sites. Specializations are distinguished by "name mangling" in the generated code, like that used by C++ compilers for resolving overloads at link time.

The markup for SIMD-enabled functions has additional features. See the language specification [83] for how to specify nonunit strides, specific vector lengths, and support for masking.

Optimization Note

A key issue with array-based parallelism is fusing array operations. Executing each array operation separately is often less efficient than fusing them all together, particularly when the arrays are so big that they do not fit in fast inner-level cache. Furthermore, array notation may incur the need for an explicit temporary array that would not be needed with the equivalent pragma SIMD code. Pragma SIMD often performs better than array notation in such a situation.

For example, consider the following loop using pragma SIMD:

```
#pragma simd
for( int i=0; i<n; ++i ) {
    T t = a*y[i];
    y[i] = x[i]-t;
    x[i] = x[i]+t;
}
```

The equivalent array notation is:

```
T t[n];
t[:] = a*y[0:n];
y[0:n] = x[0:n]-t[:];
x[0:n] = x[0:n]+t[:];
```

This code must execute "as if" each statement completes before the next one starts. Each of the three assignments has an implied parallel loop. A compiler may or may not be a be able to fuse the loops, depending upon what it can prove about the aliasing relationships for x and y. Worse yet, the code requires a temporary array, which may or may not be eliminated by the compiler, thus making stack space requirements less predictable.

On the other hand, there is much to be said about thinking about a problem at the high level of section operations, and occasionally cases pop up by circumstance where separate loops are actually faster. In this case, array notation is ahead by default, and the compiler must work to prove that the pragma SIMD loop can be fissioned into multiple loops. On the whole, however, those can be viewed as exceptions that prove the rule.

13.3   Thread Parallelism

The Cilk portion of Cilk Plus lets the programmer express where multithreaded execution is permitted. It enables writing deterministic multithreaded programs, without using locks or thread-local storage. Like the MIT Cilk system [260, 117] and Cilk++ [176], the Cilk portion of Cilk Plus is a faithful linguistic extension of C and C++, which means that parallel code retains its serial semantics when run on one processor. The Cilk extensions to C++ consist of just three keywords, as shown in the opening example. Except for the array notation, routines `MulAdd0` and `MulAddR` in Section 13.1 would be ordinary C++ code if the keywords `cilk_spawn` and `cilk_sync` were elided and `cilk_for` replaced by `for`.

Parallel work is created when the keyword `cilk_spawn` precedes the invocation of a function. The semantics of spawning differ from a C++ function (or method) call only in that the parent can continue to execute in parallel with the child, instead of waiting for the child to complete as usual in C and C++. The "work-stealing" scheduler in the Cilk Plus system takes care of scheduling the continuation onto an idle thread if one is available.

A function cannot safely use the values returned or written by its children until it executes a `cilk_sync` statement. The `cilk_sync` statement is a local "barrier," not a global one as, for example, is used in message-passing programming [200, 201, 202]. For example, consider this routine for parallel recursive summation:

```
float RecursiveSum(float* a, size_t n) {
    if( n<1024 ) {
        // Reduce on a single strand
        return __sec_reduce_add( a[0:n] );
    } else {
        // Fork—join
        float x = cilk_spawn RecursiveSum(a,n/2);
        float y = RecursiveSum(a+n/2,n-n/2);
        cilk_sync;
        return x+y;
    }
}
```

Without the `cilk_sync`, the x+y might execute before the spawned call to sum has computed the value of x. The example also illustrates a point of good Cilk style. The second recursive call could be spawned, but is not, because spawning it would just add overhead for running its do-nothing continuation in parallel with the call.

In addition to explicit synchronization provided by the `cilk_sync` statement, every function syncs implicitly before it returns, thus ensuring that all of its children terminate before it does. Thus, in routine MulAddR on page 324, the `cilk_sync` before the return is technically unnecessary.

The `cilk_for` construct is syntactic sugar for a divide-and-conquer loop. The compiler turns instances of it into a recursive routine that divides and conquers its iteration space in parallel, and each leaf loop can be executed using vector parallelism. Hence, a `cilk_for` enables both thread and vector parallelism. A `cilk_for` is grammatically restricted so that the iteration space is computable before iterations commence, using straightforward arithmetic. The language specification [83] details the restrictions.

Though, technically, only functions and function objects ("functors") can be spawned, a statement can be spawned by wrapping it in a C++11 lambda expression that turns the statement into a functor. The following fragment uses this technique to compute a and v in parallel.

```
cilk_spawn [&]{a = 4*pi*r*r;}();
v = 4*pi*r*r*r/3;
cilk_sync;
```

The () after the lambda expression is just the usual argument list for a spawned function.

13.3.1 Reducers

Many serial programs use nonlocal variables, which are variables accessible outside of the scope of a single function, method, or class. If a variable is bound outside of all local scopes, it is a global variable. Nonlocal variables are sometimes considered a problematic programming practice [301], but they often make programs easier to write, because they can be accessed at the leaves of a call tree without the overhead and complexity of passing them as parameters through the entire call tree. Programmers would cringe, for example, if writing to stderr required passing it as a parameter all the way down from main! In parallel computing, nonlocal variables may inhibit otherwise independent parts of a multithreaded program from operating in parallel, because they introduce races. This section describes Cilk Plus reducer hyperobjects [114], which can mitigate races on nonlocal variables without creating lock contention or requiring code restructuring.

As an example of how a nonlocal variable can introduce a data race, consider the problem of walking a binary tree to make a list of those nodes that satisfy a given property. Cilk Plus code to solve the problem follows.

```
1  #include <cilk/reducer_list.h>
2  cilk::reducer_list_append<Node*> OutputList;
3  extern bool HasProperty(Node*);

5  void Walk(Node* x) {
6      if (x) {
7          if (HasProperty(x))
8              OutputList.push_back(x);
9          cilk_spawn Walk(x->left);
10         Walk(x->right);
11     }
12     // implicit cilk_sync
13 }
```

If the node x is nonnull, the code checks whether x has the desired property in line 7, and if so, it appends x to the list stored in the global variable OutputList in line 8. Then it recursively visits the left and right children of x in lines 9 and 10.

The code is essentially serial logic with two small changes:

- Serial code would declare `OutputList` as a `std::list` on line 2.

- Serial code would not have the `cilk_spawn` on line 9.

The Cilk Plus code is remarkable in that it can actually update `OutputList` in parallel and always generate the same list from a given tree—one that is *identical* to the list that the serial equivalent would generate.

A classic threading approach would use the lock to serialize updates to `OutputList`. Such a solution would not only lose parallelism, but also determinism because the order of items in the list would reflect the temporal order in which threads acquired the lock. Another classic threading approach would be to eliminate global variable `OutputList` altogether, and change `Walk` to return a sublist for the part of the tree it walked. Though rewriting the call tree in a tiny example is easy, it can become awkward in a large piece of legacy production code.

The Cilk Plus code declares the variable `OutputList` as a ***reducer hyperobject*** [114]. A reducer hyperobject is a linguistic construct that allows concurrent threads of execution to coordinate in updating a shared variable or data structure independently by providing them different but coordinated views of the same object. Thus, reducers preserve the advantages of parallelism without forcing the programmer to restructure the logic of his or her program.

The coordination in the example takes advantage of the fact that list appending is associative. That is, appending list L_3 to list L_2 and appending the result to L_1 produces the same final list as does appending L_3 to the result of appending L_2 to L_1. Either way, the result is the concatenation of L_1, L_2, and L_3 in that order. As the Cilk Plus runtime system load-balances this computation over the available processors, it ensures that each branch of the recursive computation has access to a private view of the variable `OutputList`, eliminating races on this global variable without requiring locks. When the branches synchronize, the private views are reduced (combined) by concatenating the lists, and Cilk Plus carefully maintains the proper ordering so that the resulting list contains the identical elements in the same order as in a serial execution. Section 13.5 says more about views.

Cilk Plus provides predefined reducers for common cases, such as the one in the example and `reducer_opadd` for summation, and it offers a way for programmers to define their own reducers. For C programmers there is an alternative macro-based syntax for reducers.

Reducers can go beyond "pure" mathematical operations like summation and list concatenation. Cilk Plus provides a `reducer_ostream`, which is like a `std::ostream`, but with reducer semantics that make output deterministic. The idea is similar to the `reducer_list`, but with an important optimization. Instead of concatenating all output as one big string and outputting it when the program terminates, the `reducer_ostream` performs output as eagerly as possible, deferring output items only when there are earlier items not yet output. For example, given the following code, calling `Iota(0,100)` always outputs 0 through 99 in order on `stderr`, despite the parallelism within routine `Iota`.

```
#include <iostream>
#include <cilk/reducer_ostream.h>
cilk::reducer_ostream Out(std::cerr);

void Iota(int i, int j) {
    if (j>i+1) {
        int m = i+(j-i)/2;     // m ≈ halfway between i and j
        cilk_spawn Iota(i,m);
        Iota(m,j);
    } else if (j>i)
        Out << i << std::endl;
    // implicit cilk_sync
}
```

A `cilk_for` interacts with reducers in a way that preserves serial semantics. For example, given the definition of `Out` from the previous fragment, the code:

```
cilk_for(int k=0; k<100; ++k)
    out << i << std::endl;
```

can execute iterations in parallel, and yet it always produces 0 through 99 in order in the output.

Exception Handling

Exception handling is an area where Cilk Plus necessarily introduces nondeterminism. If an exception is thrown out of a spawned function, the exception is deferred until the corresponding `cilk_sync`, at which point the `cilk_sync` rethrows the exception. If more than one exception reaches the `cilk_sync`, the one that would have been thrown earliest for serial execution is rethrown and any other exceptions reaching that `cilk_-sync` disappear. When a spawned function throws an exception, the continuation of the spawning function may or may not be cancelled and resume at the sync point. That is, the only "cancellation points" [262] occur immediately after spawning a function.

The following example illustrates exception handling in Cilk Plus:

```
int A[3] = {0,0,0};

void F(int i) {
    A[i] = 1;
    throw i;
}

void G() {
    cilk_spawn F(0);
    cilk_spawn F(1);
    F(2);
    cilk_sync;
}
```

Suppose array A is initially zero and function G() is invoked. There are exactly three possible outcomes for array A:

$$A = \{1, 0, 0\}$$
$$A = \{1, 1, 0\}$$
$$A = \{1, 1, 1\}$$

The first outcome occurs when the continuation after line 9 is cancelled and is identical to serial execution. Indeed, this outcome is the only one possible when there is a single thread. The second outcome occurs when the continuation after line 9 executes and spawns F(1), but the continuation after line 10 is cancelled. The third outcome occurs when no cancellation occurs. It can occur only if there are at least three threads, because it takes a third thread to start F(2) while two other threads march F(0) and F(1) to their eventual throw.

Regardless of how many continuations run in the example, the exception 0 rethrown from the cilk_sync is always 0. The other two exceptions 1 and 2 disappear. The exception that escapes from G() is by design identical to that for sequential execution of g.

The example also shows how from a practical perspective, the possibility of nondeterminism must be allowed if an exception is thrown. If determinism were required regardless of exception behavior, a continuation could not commit any updates to memory until it was known that the spawned routine returned normally.[4]

---

4. Given the current lack of support for fast unbounded transactional memory, guaranteed determinism, even in the presence of potential exceptions, seems problematic.

13.4   Reasoning about Parallel Performance

The Cilk Plus runtime system contains a scheduler based on provably efficient work-stealing [42, 117], which scales application performance linearly with processor cores, as long as the application has sufficient parallelism and the processor architecture provides sufficient memory bandwidth. Furthermore, performance is composable—components may be composed serially, in parallel, or in a nested manner, and the performance of the composition is theoretically predictable, knowing only a few parameters about the components, not their internal structure.

This section explains the rigorous theoretical model of parallelism, the relevant parameters for a component, and how to apply it to Cilk Plus programs. It also describes a small departure from theoretical optimality for the sake of compatibility with legacy calling conventions.

Dag Model

The dag (directed acyclic graph) model of multithreading [40] views the execution of a multithreaded program as a set of instructions (the vertices of the dag) with graph edges indicating dependencies between instructions. (See Figure 13.1.) An instruction x precedes an instruction y, sometimes denoted $x \prec y$, if x must complete before y can begin. Two instructions x and y are in parallel if neither $x \prec y$ nor $y \prec x$. Figure 13.1, for example, shows $1 \prec 2$, $6 \prec 12$, and $4 \parallel 9$.

The dag model of multithreading can be interpreted in the context of the Cilk Plus programming model. A `cilk_spawn` of a function creates two dependency edges emanating from the instruction immediately before the `cilk_spawn`: one edge goes to the first instruction of the spawned function, and the other goes to the first instruction after the spawned function. A `cilk_sync` creates dependency edges from the final instruction of each spawned function to the instruction immediately after the `cilk_sync`. A `cilk_for` can be viewed as divide-and-conquer parallel recursion using `cilk_spawn` and `cilk_sync` over the iteration space.

The dag model permits a precise definition of measures that allow us to define parallelism precisely, as well as to provide important bounds [125, 52, 101, 41] on performance and speedup.

Work Law

The first important measure is work, which is the total amount of time spent in all the instructions. Let T_P be the fastest possible execution time of the application on P processors.

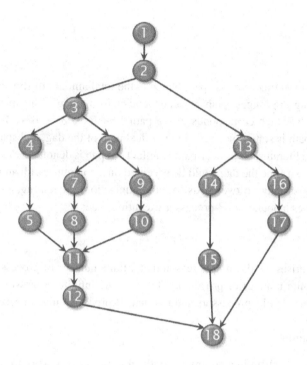

Figure 13.1: DAG representation of a program.

The work is T_1, because it is equivalent to the execution time on 1 processor. The work is an important measure, because it provides a lower bound on P-processor execution time:

$$T_p \geq T_1/P . \tag{13.1}$$

This *Work Law* holds in the dag model, because each processor executes at most 1 instruction per unit time, and hence P processors can execute at most P instructions per unit time. Thus, with P processors, to do all the work, it must take at least T_1/P time.

The Work Law in Inequality 13.1 is a fundamental limit for the speedup on P processors, which in our notation is T_1/T_P. The speedup is how much faster the application runs on P processors than on 1 processor. An application that obtains speedup proportional to P is said to exhibit linear speedup. If it obtains speedup equal to P, it has perfect linear speedup. The Work Law says that is the best speedup possible, since it implies that $T_1/T_P \leq P$. Doing better is called superlinear speedup, which the Work Law precludes in the dag model, but which can happen in models that incorporate caching and other processor effects.

Span Law

The second important measure is span, which is the total amount of time spent executing instructions along the longest path of dependencies in the dag. The span of the dag in our example is 9, which corresponds to the path $1 \prec 2 \prec 3 \prec 6 \prec 7 \prec 8 \prec 11 \prec 12 \prec 18$. This path is sometimes called the critical path of the dag, and span is sometimes referred to in the literature as critical-path length. The span is denoted as T_∞, since it is the theoretically fastest time the dag could be executed on a computer with an infinite number of processors (assuming no overheads for communication, scheduling, etc.). Like work, span also provides a bound on P-processor execution time:

$$T_P \geq T_\infty .\qquad\qquad(13.2)$$

This *Span Law* arises for the simple reason that a finite number of processors cannot outperform an infinite number of processors, because the infinite-processor machine could just ignore all but P of its processors and mimic a P-processor machine exactly.

Parallelism Bounds

The amount of parallelism in a program is defined as the ratio of work to span, or T_1/T_∞. Parallelism can be viewed as the average amount of work along each step of the critical path. Perfect linear speedup cannot be obtained for any number of processors greater than the parallelism T_1/T_∞, otherwise the system would be performing above average work along every step of the critical path. More formally, if $P > T_1/T_\infty$, then the Span Law implies the speedup $T_1/T_P \leq T_1/T_\infty < P$. Since the speedup is strictly less than P, it cannot be perfect linear speedup.

For example, the parallelism of the dag in Figure 13.1 is $18/9 = 2$. That means that there is little point in executing it with more than 2 processors, since additional processors will be surely starved for work.

As a practical matter, many problems have considerable parallelism. For example, dense matrix multiplication of 1000×1000 matrices is highly parallel, with a parallelism in the millions. Many problems on large irregular graphs, such as breadth-first search, generally exhibit parallelism on the order of thousands. Sparse matrix algorithms can often exhibit parallelism in the hundreds.

The bounds discussed so far have been lower bounds on parallel running time. The Cilk Plus work-stealing scheduler provides an upper bound, too, within the assumptions of the dag model. Specifically, for an application with work T_1 and span T_∞ running on a computer with P processors, the Cilk Plus work-stealing scheduler achieves an expected running time (proved in [42]) of

$$T_P \leq T_1/P + O(T_\infty) \,. \tag{13.3}$$

If the parallelism T_1/T_∞ exceeds the number P of processors by a sufficient margin, this bound guarantees near-perfect linear speedup. To see why, assume that $T_1/T_\infty \gg P$. Equivalently, we have $T_\infty \ll T_1/P$. Thus, in Inequality 13.3, the T_1/P term dominates the $O(T_\infty)$ term, and thus the running time is $T_P \approx T_1/P$, leading to a speedup of $T_1/T_P \approx P$.

It is worth contrasting the bounds with Amdahl's law. Amdahl's law says the speedup of a program has an upper bound T_1/T_{serial}, where T_{serial} is the serial portion of the program. In Figure 13.1 the serial portion consists of vertices 1, 2, and 18. Assuming each vertex takes unit time, Amdahl's Law says the speedup is limited to $18/3 = 6$, a much looser bound than the work-span bound of $T_1/T_\infty = 18/9 = 2$. Work-span analysis not only provides a tighter lower bound on parallel running time, it provides an upper bound (Inequality 13.3), too.

Composable Performance

The execution of a program can engender a complicated dag. Furthermore, some portions of that dag might be subdags from "black box" components with unknown structure. Fortunately, the work and span have simple composition properties. In particular, the work and span for a routine can be estimated from its structure and the work and space of its callees without knowing anything more about the dag structures of the callees.

For example, consider the following serial composition:

```
void A() {
    B();
    C();
}
```

The work of A is the sum of the work of B() plus C(), plus any instructions in A itself. Likewise, the span of A is the sum of the spans of its constituents. Now consider parallel composition:

```
void D() {
    cilk_spawn B();
    C();
    cilk_sync;
}
```

The work of D is almost the same as for serial composition of A and B, with a small additional cost of spawning B instead of calling it. The span of D is the maximum of the span of B and C, plus any instructions before the spawn or after the sync.

The precise definition of work, span, and parallelism admits asymptotic analysis in a manner similar to analyzing the time complexity of serial programs. Consider the following concise parallel quicksort:

```
#include <algorithm>
#include <functional>

template <typename T>
void Quicksort(T* begin, T* end) {
    using namespace std;
    if (begin != end) {
        T* middle = partition(begin, end, bind2nd(less<T>(),*begin));
        cilk_spawn Quicksort(begin, middle);
        Quicksort(max(begin+1, middle), end);
        cilk_sync;
    }
}
```

Of course, a production-quality quicksort would do a more careful job of choosing the partition key, as well as combine recursion and iteration to limit stack growth. But the parallelization would still come down to the matter of spawning recursive calls.

Since the speedup for the average case is a bit tricky to analyze [80], we shall settle here for merely analyzing the best possible speedup possible, in the "lucky" case where middle is always halfway between begin and end. Let n be the number of items to be sorted, that is end − begin. The asymptotic recurrences for work and span in the lucky case are:

$$T_1(n) = T_1(n/2) + T_1(n/2) + \Theta(n) \qquad T_1(0) = \Theta(1)$$
$$T_\infty(n) = \max(T_\infty(n/2), T_\infty(n/2)) + \Theta(n) \qquad T_\infty(0) = \Theta(1)$$

Note the similarity of the two lines: work is a *sum* and span is a *max*, because the subsorts run in parallel. The solutions of these recurrences are:

$$T_1(n) = \Theta(n \lg n)$$
$$T_\infty(n) = \Theta(n)$$

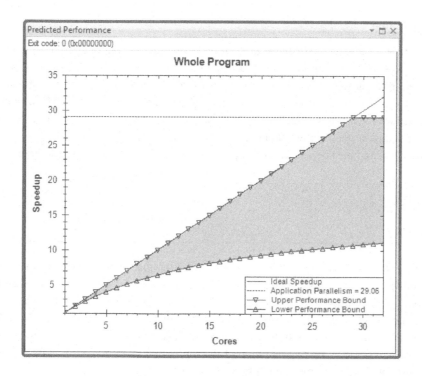

Figure 13.2: Plot from Cilk View

The parallelism, $T_1/T_\infty = \Theta(\lg n)$. Hence using more than $\Theta(\lg n)$ processors will gain little additional speedup. See [80, Chapter 27] for sorting algorithms with more parallelism.

Cilk View Analyzer

Cilk View is a tool that automatically computes the work and span of a Cilk Plus program, for a given input data set and plots bounds based on the previously discussed laws. Figure 13.2 shows an example. The linear diagonal is implied by the Work Law. The top roofline bound is implied by the Span Law. The lower bound is computed using a variation of Inequality 13.3 that uses burdened span, which accounts for estimated scheduling overhead. [136]

Of course, the program speedup may be worse than the estimates if the speedup is limited by a resource beyond the dag model, such as memory bandwidth or latency. Indeed such a shortfall is often a strong hint that memory effects, and not parallelism, is a problem.

Space Bound

Performance is not just a matter of time. A program that runs out of space is not of much use. The Cilk Plus runtime system also bounds stack space. Specifically, a Cilk Plus program running with P workers consumes at most P times the stack space of a single-processor execution, plus a constant amount of space per worker. The bound holds because a worker with a nonempty stack never waits on another worker, and every nonempty stack corresponds to a stack that would have occurred in a sequential execution.

To understand the importance of this property, consider the following code fragment:

```
for (int i=0; i<1000000000; ++i) {
    cilk_spawn foo(i);
}
cilk_sync;
```

This code specifies one billion invocations of `foo` that operate logically in parallel. Executing on one processor, however, this Cilk Plus code uses no more stack space than a serial C++ execution, that is, the call depth is of whichever invocation of `foo` requires the deepest stack. On two processors, it requires at most twice this space, and so on. This guarantee contrasts with that of more naive schedulers, which may create a work-queue of one billion tasks, one for each iteration of the subroutine `foo`, before executing even the first iteration, possibly blowing out physical memory.

Trade Off on Theoretical Efficiency Versus Link Compatibility

Cilk Plus departs from its Cilk forebears in one important aspect: it is fully link-compatible with C/C++ code. Previous implementations of Cilk used a different calling convention than C/C++ that involved nonlinear "cactus stacks," and so calling Cilk code from C/C++ was not allowed or required special hooks. Cilk Plus eliminates the difference—a routine using Cilk Plus uses the normal C/C++ calling convention.

The link compatibility comes at the cost of using some more stacks internally, and theoretically limiting speedup when the stacks run out. In practice, however, this suboptimality seems to be not noticeable, and the practical advantage of link compatibility overwhelms these concerns, making Cilk Plus easy to integrate with existing code bases.

A fascinating alternative that preserves both the theoretical guarantees and link compatibility is Cilk-M [175], which maps multiple virtual address spaces onto the same physical address space, in a way that each processor can use a linear calling convention even though the system is using a cactus stack underneath. The Cilk-M runtime is link compatible with code generated by Intel's implementation of Cilk Plus.

13.5   Reasoning about Races

Nondeterminism arising from race conditions is a terror for parallel programmers. This
section describes two strong defenses against nondeterminism that Cilk Plus offers: a way
to incorporate and reason about parallelism hierarchically and an efficient tool for detecting
potential races. This section also sketches how to reason about reducers.

Strands

A strand is a sequence of instructions executed serially with no intervening spawn or sync.
A strand corresponds to sequence of vertices in the dag model where all but the first vertex
has exactly one incoming edge, and all but the last vertex has exactly one outgoing edge.
A data race [208] exists if logically parallel strands access the same shared location, the
two strands hold no locks in common, and at least one of the strands writes to the location.
Note that this definition of a race is independent of the number of physical processors.
Whether a program has a race is a property of the program, not its execution environment.

Cilk Plus makes reasoning about the absence of races straightforward, because there is
no "dangling parallelism" where parallel activity created by a call continues after the call
returns. For example, consider:

```
void Bar() {
    A();
    cilk_spawn B();
    C();
    // implicit cilk_sync;
}
```

Define the readset and writeset of x, respectively, as the sets of memory locations read
and written by routine x. To analyze whether routine Bar has a race, you need to know
only:

- the readset and writeset of B and

- the readset and writeset of C,

and then apply the definition of a race. This might sound obvious, but is not true of all
parallel models. For example, if A were allowed to create parallel threads of control that
remained running after A returns, then the readset and writeset of those threads would need
to be known, too, and checked for racy overlap with the sets for B and C. Because Cilk
Plus has an implicit sync at the end of every routine, it enforces a "single thread in; single
thread out" discipline.

From a caller's viewpoint, a race-free call acts the same as if it were implemented serially. Thus, a program can be designed to be race free by building it bottom-up and reasoning about race freedom at each level in the hierarchy.

Cilk Screen Race Detector

For better or for worse, large-scale software is sometimes beyond human reasoning, even in a hierarchical fashion, particularly when components are written by different authors or involve legacy and third-party serial code. Fortunately, the reasoning is simple enough to be done by a tool, called Cilk screen, if the program is ostensibly deterministic, which means it is written using pure Cilk Plus, without locks and without thread-local storage. For an ostensibly deterministic program, Cilk screen always reports a race bug if the race bug is exposed: that is, if two different schedulings of the parallel code would produce different results. If Cilk screen finds no races for a given input, the application is surely deterministic for that input, even if different result never happened during testing. The theory behind Cilk screen, and weaker guarantees for programs using locks, are elaborated in [107, 78].

Hence, best use of Cilk screen requires a test suite that ensures good path coverage of an application, but the test suite need not have the ability to detect that a race occurred. Indeed, Cilk screen runs the application serially, using dynamic instrumentation [181, 54] to intercept every load and store executed at the user level. Metadata in the Cilk Plus binaries [82] identifies the parallel control constructs in the executing application precisely. Because Cilk Plus enforces a series-parallel discipline, Cilk screen race detector can use provably good algorithms [106, 78, 30], developed originally for MIT Cilk, which enables it to detect races efficiently and accurately.

Cilk Plus also works in conjunction with the Intel Parallel Inspector race detector, which is useful when checking programs that combine Cilk Plus with other threading mechanisms, and thus need more general (albeit theoretically less efficient) race detection technology. [27]

Hyperobject Views

The notion of a strand also enables reasoning about views of a hyperobject. The state of a hyperobject as seen by a strand of execution is called the strand's "view." A strand can access and change any of its view's state independently, without synchronizing with other strands. Throughout the execution of a strand, the strand's view of the reducer is private, thereby providing isolation from other strands. When two or more strands join at a cilk_sync, their different views are combined according to a system- or user-defined method, reduce(). It is sometimes useful to know when two strands are guaranteed to see the same view. Consider the following example that uses same hyperobject for doing different reductions in parallel.

```
1  #include <cilk/reducer_opadd.h>

3  float Sum[N], D[N][N];
4  cilk::reducer_opadd<float> Tmp;

6  void SumRows() {
7      cilk_for( int i=0; i<N; ++i ) {
8          Tmp.set_value(0);
9          cilk_for( int j=0; j<N; ++j )
10             Tmp += D[i][j];
11         Sum[i] = Tmp.get_value();
12     }
13 }
```

How can the programmer know that line 11 accesses the same view as line 8 and that view has stabilized despite other ongoing iterations of the i loop?

Two strands s_1 and s_2 see the same view of a hyperobject if they are ordered (or identical) and there is no strand s_3 that is parallel to one and not the other. Formally:

$$(s_1 \not\parallel s_2) \wedge (\forall s_3 \in S : s_1 \parallel s_3 \Leftrightarrow s_2 \parallel s_3)$$

where S be the set of all strands in the execution.

These conditions hold when s_1 is the strand for line 8 and s_2 is the strand for line 11. Strands in other iterations of the i loop are parallel to both s_1 and s_2, and strands in the same iteration of the i loop are ordered with respect to both s_1 and s_2.

13.6   Practical Tips

Cilk Plus provides just a few simple, but general, concepts. How to use them is up to the programmer. Though asymptotic theory is a useful guide for design, constant factors do matter. This section gives tips on using Cilk Plus to squeeze out better performance.

Vectorization

Array notation and pragma SIMD are not magic. They give permission to vectorize, but if the hardware lacks the necessary vector instructions, they do little good. Thus, it pays to have some idea of the vector capabilities of the target machine:

- For what data types does the machine have vector instructions?

- Can the machine do strided loads, or does data have to be contiguous? Even if it does, it likely handles contiguous data faster.

- Can the machine deal with vector subscripts for loads ("gather") and/or for stores ("scatter")? If it has both, is one faster? A general rule of thumb is that if you need to choose between using a gather or a scatter, go with the gather.

Good vectorizing compilers typically have options for generating vectorization reports, and reading these reports can be valuable. An old joke in the compiler community is that vectorizing compilers are not good at vectorizing all code automatically, but are good at training programmers to write easily vectorizable code.

Parallel vs. Serial Cutoffs for Recursion

Serial recursive algorithms typically have a "cutoff" where they switch to an iterative algorithm. For example, quicksort implementations often switch to another kind of sort for sorting short subsequences. Parallel recursive algorithms sometimes benefit from having a second cutoff where they switch from parallel to serial recursion. For example, a subsort may be too small to be worth parallelizing, but still worth doing recursively. Because Cilk Plus makes spawning cheap, the need for the second cutoff is less common in Cilk Plus than systems with heavier tasking, but nonetheless, spawning is not free and sometimes the second cutoff can be beneficial.

Where Cilk Plus shines relative to other tasking systems is recursive algorithms where quickly estimating the amount of remaining work is impractical, and thus there is no way to determine when the algorithm should switch to serial recursion. In those cases, Cilk Plus's low overhead for spawning usually puts it ahead of systems with heavier tasking.

Cache-Oblivious Algorithms

Getting good speed out of modern processors often requires efficient use of the memory hierarchy. A cache hit can be hundreds of times faster than a cache miss. A page miss carries an even bigger penalty. A blocked algorithm improves cache reuse by operating on cache-sized blocks of data. Each block is brought into cache and processed before moving on to the next block. For example, a blocked matrix multiply would multiply subblocks of the matrices. Typically each key loop becomes two loops: one over blocks and one over elements within a block. For instance, the usual triply-nested loop for matrix multiplication has a six-deep nesting in its blocked form. A blocked algorithm gets even more complicated when multiple levels of cache are considered, and requires tuning to optimize the block size. Having too big a block size can be as bad as not blocking at all.

An alternative is to use cache-oblivious algorithms, which exploit all possible levels of cache that might exist. The general approach is recursive blocking—subdivide the data set recursively. Eventually the data set becomes small enough to fit in cache at some level and run efficiently with respect to that cache. Further recursion may let it fit in another level in the cache hierarchy and run even faster.

Parallelizing a serial cache-oblivious algorithm is often straightforward because the algorithm already subdivides the problem into subproblems. All that remains is to solve the independent subproblems in parallel instead of serially. The recursive matrix multiply `MulAddR` on page 324 is a good example. The serial version would look like the parallel version, with plain calls instead of spawns. There are eight subproblems, which can be treated as two groups of four independent subproblems. The Cilk Plus code solves the subproblems in a group in parallel.

The common formulation of the Fast Fourier Transform (FFT) has poor cache behavior for very large data sets. One way to improve the behavior is to do an in-place transposition of the data partway through the transform [22]. The obvious nonrecursive way to transpose a $n \times n$ matrix has a doubly nested loop. For example, let a be a linear array representing an $n \times n$ matrix A, linearized in the usual way so that $A_{i,j} = a[i*n+j]$. The transposition code is:

```
for (int i=0; i<n; ++i)
    for( int j=0; j<i; ++j)
        std::swap(a[i*n+j], a[j*n+i]);
```

For large n, this code can perform abysmally because it uses the memory hierarchy poorly. The problem is that the subscript $j*n+i$ runs through memory with a large stride. It may touch each cache line once without reusing it, and worst yet, may touch each page only a few times before going to the next page. In the virtual memory system, there is a special cache called the translation lookaside buffer (TLB) for mapping virtual addresses to physical addresses. The TLB can hold information about a limited number of pages at any one time. If the inner loop touches more pages than the TLB can hold, performance drops dramatically because each inner iteration causes a TLB miss.

A recursive formulation of the above transposition avoids the problem. The formulation generalizes the problem of transposing a square matrix into a more general problem of both transposing and swapping two rectangular matrices, because the more general problem admits a recursive solution in terms of itself. Given an $m \times n$ matrix A and $m \times n$ matrix B, the routine exchanges A with B. Here is the serial code for the base case:

```
// Swap m × n array a with n × m array b, each with stride s between rows.
template<typename T>
void SerialTransposeSwap(size_t m, size_t n, T* a, T* b, size_t s) {
    if (a==b)
        for (size_t i=0; i<m; ++i)
            for (size_t j=0; j<i; ++j)
                std::swap(a[i*s+j], b[j*s+i]);
    else
        for (size_t i=0; i<m; ++i)
            for (size_t j=0; j<n; ++j)
                std::swap(a[i*s+j], b[j*s+i]);
}
```

The if-else distinguishes the special case of swap-transposing a matrix with itself, for which only transposition should be done.

The recursive parallel code performs the same operation recursively. It subdivides each matrix into quadrants, and swap-transposes the quadrants. Like the serial version, it has an if-else to deal with the special case of swap-transposing a matrix with itself.

```
// Cache oblivious version of SerialTransposeSwap.
template<typename T>
void ParallelTransposeSwap(size_t m, size_t n, T* a, T* b, size_t s) {
    const size_t TRANSPOSE_CUT = 32;
    if (m*n<=TRANSPOSE_CUT)
        SerialTransposeSwap(m, n, a, b, s);
    else {
        size_t m2 = m/2;
        size_t n2 = n/2;
        cilk_spawn ParallelTransposeSwap (  m2, n2, a,        b,    s);
        cilk_spawn ParallelTransposeSwap (m-m2, n2, a+m2*s, b+m2, s);
        if (a!=b)
            cilk_spawn ParallelTransposeSwap(m2, n-n2, a+n2, b+n2*s, s);
        ParallelTransposeSwap(m-m2, n-n2, a+m2*s+n2, b+n2*s+m2, s);
    }
}
```

Now `ParallelTransposeSwap(n,n,a,a,n)` can be called to accomplish the serial in-place transposition. Eventually the recursion gets down to a subproblem where the problem fits in cache (and fits in the TLB!) and runs at full speed. This algorithm is analyzed in [116].

A good cutoff for using the iterative algorithm can be found with a little experimentation. If in doubt, make it a little too small and perhaps lose a few cycles for recursive overhead, because if it is too large to use the TLB efficiently, the consequences can be dramatically slow code.

Transliterate OpenMP with Caution

Perhaps the biggest performance problems arise when programmers port OpenMP code to Cilk Plus. In particular, OpenMP does quite well with problems involving serial repetition of parallel sweeps over the same data set, when the data set is small enough to fit in cache, and the target system is dedicated, not multiprogrammed. In that case, OpenMP's `static` schedule mode for mapping iterations to threads is effective at maximizing reuse of data, because each thread repeatedly sees the same portion of the data set. Current implementations of `cilk_for` do not have this nice property for $P > 2$.[5]

Rethinking a problem to play to Cilk's strength at parallel recursion, however, can sometimes yield a Cilk Plus solution with significantly better performance than the iterative algorithm. In particular, the scenario of repetitive parallel sweeps is common in stencil computations. Cache-oblivious space-time blocking of stencils can sometimes do better at stencils, particularly when the data set does not fit in cache [118].

13.7 History

The best history of the entire Cilk family tree is in the *Encyclopedia of Parallel Computing* article on Cilk [177]. This section summarizes the pedigree path leading to Cilk Plus.

Cilk grew from the merger of three projects: theoretical work on scheduling multithreaded applications, a parallel chess program called StarTech [169], and a C-based package called PCM/Threaded-C [133] for scheduling continuation-passing-style threads on the Connection Machine Model CM5 Supercomputer.

The Cilk-1 system released in 1994 was a library, and because of lack of compiler support, required writing in explicit "continuation-passing style." Though this style has disappeared from Cilk, it reappeared in another library with similar aims: Intel Threading Building Blocks (Chapter 14). The earliest application of Cilk-1 was the ⋆Socrates chess program which, running on a 512-node CM5, won third place in the 1994 ACM International Chess Championship.

In 1995, Cilk-2 introduced spawn/sync syntax much like it looks today. It used a C-to-C preprocessor to lower the Cilk constructs to plain C and library calls [204].

Later that year, Cilk-3 was released, which supported a "dag-consistent" model for distributed shared memory [38].

In 1996, Cilk-4 introduced continuation-stealing semantics, which replaced "child-steal" semantics. It added support for speculative computation (`abort` and `inlet`). So far, these features have not appeared in commercial incarnations of Cilk.

---

5. Modifications to work stealing have been tried [2, 242], but so far these have required a level of user intervention that seems counter to the philosophy of Cilk Plus.

Cilk-5 was released in 1997, which featured a more portable runtime and could use OS threads instead of processes for workers. It also came with "Nondeterminator" tools that let programmers localize data-race bugs.

In 2006, as multicore processors became ubiquitous, MIT spun off a start-up, Cilk Arts, to commercialize Cilk technology. The product released in 2008, Cilk++ [176], was based on C++ instead of C, and introduced hyperobjects, the `cilk_for` keyword, full support for exceptions, and the ability to call C++ code from Cilk++ code. Furthermore, it commercialized automatic work/span analysis with Cilk View, and provably good race detection with Cilk Screen.

In 2009, Intel Corporation bought Cilk Arts and released Cilk Plus as part of its C/C++ compiler in 2010. A key improvement was that Cilk Plus code can be called from plain C++/C and vice-versa without any special markup or restrictions, thus greatly simplifying its integration into existing frameworks. Cilk Plus also added vectorization features. Pragma SIMD was inspired by OpenMP's parallel loop support, and array notation by Fortran 90 array expressions. Cilk Plus continues to evolve: in 2011 support for deterministic random-number generation was added to the Cilk Plus runtime [178].

In 2011, Intel announced the availability of an open-source experimental branch to GCC 4.7 that implements the Cilk and pragma SIMD portion of Cilk Plus. In early 2012, the array-notation portion was implemented in that branch. OpenMP 4.0 adopted a form of pragma SIMD. In 2015, `http://gcc.gnu.org/` announced that GCC 5.0 would have full support for Cilk Plus.

13.8   Summary

Cilk Plus allows simple expression of both thread and vector parallelism to speed up C/C++ programs, while retaining serial semantics. The linguistic model makes formal work-span analysis of algorithms straightforward, and the Cilk View tool automates that analysis for large pieces of software. Cilk Plus enforces a discipline of no dangling parallelism that allows hierarchical formal reasoning about races, and enables the Cilk Screen tool to efficiently analyze real programs for races. Most importantly, Cilk Plus offers a composable performance model. Software components written in Cilk Plus can be composed serially, in parallel, or in a nested manner, without concern for oversubscription. Thus, Cilk Plus gives parallel programmers a power that has been long appreciated by productive serial programmers: being able to write and reason about software hierarchically.

14 Intel Threading Building Blocks

Alexey Kukanov, Intel

14.1 Introduction

Threading Building Blocks (TBB) is a C++ library for parallelism being developed and maintained at Intel [238, 81]. It is aimed to ease development of applications that exploit thread-level parallelism of modern shared-memory multicore computers. Within the variety of approaches to parallel programming, ranging from using platform-dependent threading primitives to exotic new languages, the advantage of TBB is that it allows working at a higher level than raw threads, yet does not require exotic languages or compilers: you can use it with any compiler supporting ISO C++.

14.1.1 Overview

TBB provides a range of building blocks at various levels of abstraction to help write efficient parallel programs. Its high-level constructs—generic parallel algorithms and the flow graph—let developers easily express logical parallelism in the program, while leveraging its task-based programming model and work-stealing scheduler [166] to provide an efficient and composable execution environment. TBB containers, synchronization constructs, and memory allocators can be used from within its tasks or from raw threads. With these building blocks, developers have choice to express parallelism in the ways that best suite a given problem.

Similarly to C++ Standard Template Library (STL), TBB uses generic programming to provide users with efficient implementations that impose fewest constraints. Most of TBB interfaces are defined as C++ template classes or functions that specify requirements on types, but not particular types. This allows TBB to work with different data representations and deliver good performance for a broad variety of problems.

TBB works best for problems with sufficient parallel slackness, i.e., the amount of potential parallelism significantly exceeding available hardware concurrency. In particular, TBB is good for data-parallel programming, enabling multiple processor cores and threads to work on different parts of a data collection by dividing the collection into smaller pieces. The TBB runtime library automatically maps the parallelism onto the hardware in a way that makes efficient use of available resources and scales well with increasing numbers of cores.

At the same time, TBB offers high degree of composability to facilitate enabling parallelism in complex component-based applications and seamless integration of independently parallelized code blocks and components. It efficiently supports nested parallelism to build larger parallel components from smaller ones, and provides mechanisms for work isolation, priority, and cancellation [184]. TBB coexists well with other threading packages and can effectively adapt to changes in resources.

14.1.2 General Information

To use TBB in a program, include one of the TBB public headers into the code. The header that contains all of TBB API is `<tbb/tbb.h>`. It is also possible to only enable TBB components that are needed for the code, by including specific headers for these components. Most examples in the chapter use this latter approach.

Unless otherwise specified, the public TBB API functions and classes are defined in `namespace tbb`. It is recommended to use fully qualified names or selectively inject necessary TBB names into an appropriate scope with a `using` declaration.

The code that uses TBB is often more concise and looks closer to its serial equivalent with lambda expressions, a language feature introduced in C++11.[1] Lambda expressions provide a mechanism to specify code for a function object ("functor") right at the point of use, with the tedious work of defining and creating the functor done by the compiler. For example, the following listing shows how to run two functions in parallel with TBB, with explicit function objects and with lambda expressions. Most examples in the chapter use lambda expressions where appropriate.

```cpp
#include <tbb/tbb.h>
void foo( int );
void bar( int );
/* Call foo() and bar() in parallel via function objects */
class call_foo {
    int m_i;
public:
    call_foo( int i ): m_i( i ) {}
    void operator()( ) const { foo( m_i ); }
};
class call_bar {
    int m_j;
public:
    call_bar( int j ): m_j( j ) {}
    void operator()( ) const { bar( m_j ); }
};
void ParallelFooBar( int i, int j ) {
    tbb::parallel_invoke( call_foo( i ), call_bar( j ) );
}
/* Make it shorter and simpler with lambda expressions */
void ParallelFooBarWIthLambdas( int i, int j ) {
    using tbb::parallel_invoke; /* Selective name injection */
```

---

1. C++11 is a common informal name for the Third Edition of ISO C++ Standard, ratified in 2011.

```
parallel_invoke(
    [=i]( ){ foo( i ); },
    [=j]( ){ bar( j ); }
);
}
```

When compiling TBB programs, be sure to link in the TBB shared runtime library, otherwise undefined references will occur. Refer to the TBB documentation [84] for details.

14.2   Generic Parallel Algorithms

The recommended way to express parallelism with TBB is to use its generic parallel algorithms—template functions for several algorithmic patterns useful in a wide range of application domains. Through these functions, TBB provides support for various general forms of structured parallelism—functional, loop-based, recursive, pipelining—as well as parallel implementations of specific algorithms such as sorting and computing scan (e.g., a prefix sum). Most TBB generic algorithms emphasize a data-parallel approach by applying user-defined operations across a set of data.

TBB parallel algorithms have relaxed sequential semantics, i.e., they are expected to have a valid sequential execution. Parallel execution provides performance boost with extra hardware resources, but is not mandated for correctness. Relaxed sequential semantics enables efficient support for nested parallelism, helps dynamic load balancing, and may ease debugging. Since TBB does not guarantee execution by multiple threads, the TBB algorithms must not be used in scenarios where concurrency is mandated, such as the typical producer-consumer pattern,[2] or when computations are synchronized with a barrier.

14.2.1   Parallelizing Simple Loops

The simplest form of scalable parallelism is a loop of iterations that can run simultaneously without interfering with each other. For this, TBB provides generic functions that iterate over ranges and collections and apply a user-specified function object, a body of a TBB algorithm, to each element.

Suppose there is a function $F\colon \mathbb{R} \to \mathbb{R}$ and a set of values $x_i \in \mathbb{R}$ for $i \in \mathbb{N}, 0 \leq i < N$. Let us compute the values of $F(x_i)$ for all x_i. Typically, the original values and the results are stored in arrays, and the sequential code for the computation consists of a loop:

---

2. However, in some cases a producer-consumer pattern can be replaced with a parallel pipeline.

```
double F( double );
const int N = 1000;
double y[N], x[N];
...
for( int i=0; i!=N; ++i )
    y[i] = F( x[i] );
```

To execute such a loop in parallel, TBB provides the `tbb::parallel_for` template function:

```
#include <tbb/parallel_for.h>
...
tbb::parallel_for( 0, N,
    [&]( int i ) {
        y[i] = F( x[i] );
    }
);
```

In `tbb::parallel_for(first,last,step,body)`, the first three arguments must be of the same integral type, and the last argument be a function object for the loop body with a parameter of the same type. The iteration space of this loop goes from `first` to `last-1`,[3] with the given `step`. The step can be omitted (as in the above example), in which case it is implicitly `1`.

Processing a parallel algorithm, TBB creates tasks to be executed by its runtime library. Also, a separate copy (or copies) of the body functor might be created for each thread taking part in the execution. For `parallel_for`, tasks are created by recursive subdivision. TBB first divides the initial iteration space into two ranges, each roughly half of the space, and assigns each to a task. When a task executes, it decides whether to further subdivide its subrange into two tasks or to apply the loop's body serially to the subrange.

14.2.2 Processing Data in STL Containers

C++ programs often use STL containers instead of plain arrays for data storage. Let us consider the same example of calculating a function over a set of values, but additionally require that the data should be stored in lists. In this case, the serial code can iterate over two lists simultaneously, or can iterate over the list of x values and add computed values of $F(x)$ to another list:

---

3. TBB follows STL semantics of iteration ranges being half-open intervals [first, last).

```
std::list<double> y, x;
...
for( auto xiter=x.begin(); xiter!=x.end(); ++xiter )
    y.push_back( F( *xiter ) );
```

Typical loops that iterate over containers have loop carried dependencies that prohibit parallelization. In parallel programming, it is usually better to use dynamic arrays with random access, such as vector and deque; but sometimes it might be not an option and the data might need to be stored in a list or a map. For such cases TBB offers a special template function:

```
tbb::parallel_do( first, last, body );
```

The semantics of tbb::parallel_do follows std::for_each but adds parallel execution. An invocation of parallel_do applies body to the result of dereferencing every iterator in the range [first, last), possibly in parallel. Iterators first and last must refer to elements of the same sequence and satisfy the requirements of C++ input iterators. The sequence items must be safe to process in parallel.

The implementation of parallel_do recognizes different types of iterators and uses their properties to optimize behavior: for random access iterators the behavior is close to parallel_for, while for other iterator types the algorithm ensures that threads never act on the iterators concurrently.

To apply parallel_do to the function calculation example, the loop-carried dependency on the list of the output values still needs to be resolved. One possible solution is to combine input and output values in the same list, by using a structure that holds both x and $y = F(x)$:

```
double F( double );
struct XY
{
    double x;
    double y;
};
std::list<XY> data;
#include<tbb/parallel_do.h>
...
tbb::parallel_do( data.begin(), data.end(),
    []( XY& item ) {
        item.y = F( item.x );
    }
);
```

Since fetching of the work from an input stream without random access is inherently serial, the parallelism in parallel_do is not scalable in such a case. Moreover, the loop body should contain enough work, otherwise the internal overhead will swamp all parallelism gains. In the above example, computing $F(x)$ should take at least a few thousand instructions to get useful speedup over doing things sequentially.

Sometimes the loop body may add more iterations to process in the loop. In the function parallel_do, the body functor might take as its second argument a reference to tbb::parallel_do_feeder , and add new items to the iteration space by calling the feeder's add function. The invocation of parallel_do does not return until all items, both from the initial sequence and added through the feeder, have been processed.

As an example, for tree traversal with parallel_do, after processing a node you could add its descendant nodes into processing:

```
std::vector<TreeNode> forest; /* a set of root nodes */
...
tbb::parallel_do( forest.begin(), forest.end(),
    []( TreeNode& node, tbb::parallel_do_feeder<TreeNode>& feeder ) {
        Handle( node );
        TreeNode& child = node.get_first_descendant();
        while( child ) {
            feeder.add( child );
            child = node.get_next_descendant();
        }
    }
);
```

Adding work on the fly is also good to reduce the scalability limiting factor of serial data fetch. For good scaling, design your algorithm such that the body often adds more than one piece of work.

For compatibility with Microsoft's Parallel Patterns Library [58] and referring to the STL counterpart, TBB also provides tbb::parallel_for_each, which is a synonym to parallel_do but does not support the feeder functionality.

14.2.3   Complex Iteration Spaces

Processing linear iteration space and traversing through a container are basic building blocks of many programs. However, there are situations when these blocks are not enough. For example, algorithms running on multidimensional iteration spaces (dense matrix multiplication, stencil based computations, FFT, etc.) typically use two or more nested loops:

```
const int N = 1000;
double y[N][N], x[N][N];
...
for( int i=0; i<N; ++i )
    for( int j=0; j<N; ++j )
        y[i][j] = stencil_2d9pt( x, i, j );
```

While it is easy to make such code parallel by applying `tbb::parallel_for` to the outer or even to both loops, for big data sets it might result in suboptimal performance due to bad cache locality. Even serial code might get a performance boost from converting into either a blocked or cache-oblivious form.

```
const int blockSize = 10;
for( int ib=0; ib<N; ib+=blockSize )
    for( int jb=0; jb<N; jb+=blockSize )
        for( int ii=0; ii<blockSize; ++ii )
            for( int jj=0; jj<blockSize; ++jj ) {
                int i = ib*blockSize+ii;
                int j = jb*blockSize+jj;
                y[i][j] = stencil_2d9pt( x, i, j );
            }
```

The blocked form usually doubles the number of nested loops, as shown in the listing above. A cache-oblivious implementation typically uses recursive decomposition of the iteration space. While somewhat harder to implement and understand, cache-oblivious algorithms have some benefits over their blocking counterparts, as discussed in Chapter 13 of this book.

TBB provides a way to convert multidimensional nested loops into cache-oblivious form and, at the same time, process it in parallel. The template function `tbb::parallel_for` is overloaded to process generic iteration spaces, including multidimensional ones.

```
tbb::parallel_for( range, body, partitioner );
```

The first argument, `range`, describes an iteration space and defines how to divide it recursively into smaller ranges. The `body` argument is similar to other already discussed loop body functors; it takes an iteration range as the argument and defines how the range should be processed. The third argument, `partitioner`, specifies a policy for work partitioning and distribution [242]. It is optional and can be omitted.

TBB implementation of the example with nested loops may use `blocked_range2d`, a predefined range class for two-dimensional iteration space:

```
const int N = 1000;
double y[N][N], x[N][N];
#include<tbb/parallel_for.h>
...
tbb::parallel_for( tbb::blocked_range2d<int>( 0,N, 0,N ),
    []( const tbb::blocked_range2d<int>& block ){
        for( int i=block.rows().begin(); i!=block.rows().end(); ++i )
            for( int j=block.cols().begin(); j!=block.cols().end(); ++j )
                y[i][j] = stencil_2d9pt( x, i, j );
    }
);
```

The parallel_for recursively divides the blocked_range2d, dynamically selecting the dimension to split and making the whole iteration space "recursively blocked" in a way that improves cache locality. Once it decides that a subrange should not be further split, it invokes the lambda functor on the subrange.

TBB provides template classes for one-, two-, and three-dimensional iteration spaces: blocked_range, blocked_range2d, and blocked_range3d. A TBB blocked range object represents a half-open interval in the corresponding space. For each axis, it is possible to set (in a constructor) and get the range borders and a grain size—the value that specifies the splitting threshold along the dimension.

Historically, the range based form of parallel_for came first with TBB, and the simplified form for linear iteration was added later. While calling parallel_for with a blocked_range<int>(0,N) is almost equivalent to parallel_for(0,N,...), the range based form is more flexible due to possibility to select a grain size. Also explicit loop(s) in the body function sometimes make it easier for a vectorizing compiler to generate more efficient code.

An iteration space for tbb::parallel_for does not need to be blocked or even dimensional; the only requirement is that it should be recursively divisible. You may define your own iteration space as a class that specifies how it can be divided, by providing two methods and a "splitting constructor." If your class is called R, the methods and constructor should be as follows:

```
class R {
    // True if range is empty
    bool empty() const;
    // True if range can be split into nonempty subranges
    bool is_divisible() const;
    // Split r into subranges r and *this
    R( R& r, tbb::split );
    ...
};
```

The method `empty` should return true if the range is empty. The method `is_divisible` should return true if the range can be split into two, and such a split is worth the overhead. Obviously, `is_divisible` should be false for an empty range. The splitting constructor should take two arguments, the first be a reference to R and the second should be of type `tbb::split`. The second argument is not used; it serves only to distinguish the constructor from an ordinary copy constructor. The splitting constructor should attempt to split the range r roughly into two halves, update it to become the first half, and let the constructed object be the second half. The parallel algorithm templates call the splitting constructor on a range only if it is divisible, i.e., `r.is_divisible` returns true. If splitting can result in an empty range, the body functor must be able to handle it. `parallel_for` does not check if the range is empty before applying the body because in most cases it would just result in extra overhead.

14.2.4   Other Algorithms

There are more template functions representing generic parallel algorithms in TBB:

- `tbb::parallel_reduce` implements reduction—an operation of combining a set of values into a single one. Parallelism is achieved via reordering of pairwise combine operations on data elements; for correctness, the reduction operation must be associative. `parallel_reduce` operates over a recursively divisible interation space represented by a generic range as described in Section 14.2.3.

- `tbb::parallel_deterministic_reduce` is a special implementation of reduction that, unlike `parallel_reduce`, gives reproducible results for operations on floating point numbers.[4]

- `tbb::parallel_scan` computes a sequence of running totals—prefixes—for a given input sequence and a given operation. To break data dependencies and achieve parallelism, the algorithm uses two passes over the data and may apply the operation up to twice as many times as in the serial implementation, so it may need more than 2 hardware processing elements to achieve sufficient speedup.

- `tbb::parallel_invoke` calls specified functions in parallel, as shown in the example in Section 14.1.2. This pattern is useful for exploiting functional parallelism as well as expressing recursive divide-and-conquer algorithms.

- `tbb::parallel_pipeline` implements a pipeline pattern which applies a sequence of functions, each typically doing some data transformation, to a stream of

4. When applied multiple times to the same data set, the function will always produce the same result.

data items. Parallelism is achieved via processing multiple data items simultaneously, by different functions or even by the same function, if allowed by the user.

- `tbb::parallel_sort` is a parallel implementation of the quicksort algorithm.

14.3   Flow Graph

There are some applications that best express dependencies as messages passed between
nodes in a flow graph. These messages may contain data or simply act as signals that a
preceding computation has completed. At the same time, such an application might have
good opportunities for parallelism with parts of its flow graph working independently on
different data.

Until version 4.0, TBB provided only limited support for such parallelism. Possible options were to use the `tbb::parallel_pipeline` algorithm for linear data flow, the
`tbb::parallel_do` algorithm for control dependency graphs (with dependency management done by the application), or directly manipulate tasks and manage task dependencies. Adding support for "nonlinear pipelines" and "arbitrary DAG of tasks" were popular
users requests. In response to these requests, a high-level API for application flow graphs
was added to TBB.

14.3.1   Overview

The TBB flow graph API [287] is a family of classes to express parallelism through static
and dynamic control dependency graphs, as well as graphs that transfer and process data
messages. All these classes and auxiliary functions to build and use a flow graph reside in
`namespace tbb::flow`.

A TBB flow graph consists of a graph object, nodes, and edges.

A graph object is an instance of the `tbb::flow::graph` class. This object serves as
the handle to a particular flow graph in the program, and provides methods to modify and
query the state of the graph, to run user code that interacts with the graph, and to wait for
an execution of the graph to complete.

Flow graph nodes are instances of either predefined or user-defined classes that generate,
transform, pass, or buffer messages in accord with the topology of a graph and with the
node communication protocol described in Section 14.3.2. A variety of predefined node
types are provided by TBB, including functional nodes that execute user code, buffering
nodes with different policies, flow control nodes that split, join, and broadcast messages,
etc. Nodes are tied to a particular graph instance at creation, and exist until explicitly
destroyed.

A TBB flow graph is necessarily a directed graph. The structure of control or data flow in a graph is specified with edges that connect message senders to appropriate receivers. Edges are created by calls to the `tbb::flow::make_edge` function, and can be removed with the `tbb::flow::remove_edge` function. These functions can be called even if some messages are passing through the graph. Therefore, edges in a TBB flow graph are very dynamic and the graph topology can be modified on the fly.

A TBB flow graph is persistent and can be run multiple times after creation.

The TBB flow graph API resembles actor-based programming systems. However, unlike a typical actor system, the flow graph does not assign a separate thread to each node. Consequently, nodes do not contain a typical dispatch loop where a thread waits for messages to arrive. Instead, TBB tasks are created on demand (e.g., at message arrival) to execute node bodies and pass more messages to the successor nodes, as defined by the graph topology and user code. This is important to seamlessly integrate flow graph based codes with other TBB algorithms in a single application.

14.3.2   Node Communication Protocol

There can be situations when a message cannot be immediately processed by a receiving node. For example, the node might have a concurrency limit that does not allow it to process more than a certain number of messages (often, more than one) simultaneously. In such a case, we say that a message is rejected by its receiver. With a nonpreemptive TBB task scheduler, blocking send and receive methods would stop threads from doing useful work. At the same time, rejection also would not be handled efficiently by attempts to resend a message, as it would likely result in either excessive idle spinning or extra overhead.

To deal with message rejection, TBB applies a special node communication protocol where edges dynamically switch between push and pull state for passing messages.

For protocol description, let us consider a TBB flow graph as a triad $G = (V, E_1, E_2)$, where V is the set of nodes, E_1 is the set of edges that are currently in push state, and E_2 is the set of edges that are currently in pull state. For each edge (V_s, V_r), V_s is the sender node and V_r is the receiver node.

Messages over an edge from the push set E_1 are initiated by the sender, which tries to put to the receiver. When an edge is in the pull set E_2, messages are initiated by the receiver, which tries to get from the sender. If an attempt to send a message across an edge fails, the edge is moved to the other set. For example, if a put across the edge (V_s, V_r) fails, the edge is removed from the push set E_1 and placed in the pull set E_2. Thus, the responsibility to resume message flow across the edge is put onto the node that rejected the last message. Figure 14.1 summarizes this dynamic push/pull protocol.

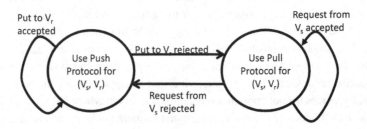

Figure 14.1: The state diagram for the TBB flow graph node communication protocol

The protocol is key to the performance of TBB flow graphs, as it allows graphs to work in the absence of blocking receives while avoiding inefficiencies of repeated sends. If a sender V_s generates data at higher rate than its successor V_r can process, the edge (V_s, V_r) will transition into pull mode, eliminating many rejections that V_s would see if it were to continue to send. On the other hand, if V_r works faster than V_s, the edge will stay in push mode, allowing V_s to send data at the generation rate.

One subtle point of the communication protocol is that rejected messages might get silently dropped. To avoid this, place a buffering node in front of a node that may reject. The predefined TBB buffering node types, `buffer_node`, `sequencer_node`, `queue_node`, and `priority_queue_node`, are unbounded and never reject messages.

14.3.3 Control Dependency Graphs

For an example of a control dependency graph, let us consider a simple 2D wavefront computation, where each node in a two-dimensional rectangular grid must be processed only after the nodes above and to the left of it. Correspondingly, after a node is processed, messages are sent to its neighbors below and to the right. While these messages can contain data, they typically just deliver a signal that a control dependency between nodes is satisfied.

With TBB, a graph of `tbb::flow::continue_node` objects would best represent a wavefront. This node type is designed specifically for implementing dependency graphs. `continue_node` does not receive data, but instead counts the number of input signals of type `tbb::flow::continue_msg`. Once signals from all predecessors are received, the node executes its user-specified body function, which must accept a `continue_msg` object[5] and should return an output message of the type specified as the template parameter to `continue_node`. Often, the output type is also a `continue_msg`; in this case the body does not have to return a value, as `continue_node` will pass the right message to its successors automatically.

In the next listing, a flow graph is used to update a two-dimensional matrix where dependencies between the elements form the diagonal wavefront pattern.

```cpp
// M and N are the number of rows and columns in the matrix
double value[M][N];

#include <tbb/flow_graph.h>
using tbb::flow::continue_msg;

tbb::flow::continue_node<continue_msg> * node[M][N];
tbb::flow::graph g;

double run_graph( ) {
    for( int i=0; i<M; ++i ) {
        for( int j=0; j<N; ++j ) {
            node[i][j] = new tbb::flow::continue_node<continue_msg>(
                g,
                [=]( const continue_msg& /*unused*/ ) {
                    update( i, j );
                }
            );
            if ( i > 0 )
                make_edge( *node[i-1][j], *node[i][j] ); // from above
            if ( j > 0 )
                make_edge( *node[i][j-1], *node[i][j] ); // from the left
        }
    }

    value[M-1][N-1] = 0;
    node[0][0]->try_put( continue_msg() );
    g.wait_for_all();
```

---

5. This requirement existed in TBB at the moment of writing this chapter. It might be removed in later TBB releases.

```
    for( int i=0; i<M; ++i )
        for( int j=0; j<N; ++j )
            delete node[i][j];
    return value[M-1][N-1];
}
```

The `for` loop in the function `run_graph` creates a set of `continue_node` objects, and adds edges according to the dependency pattern. Each node takes a reference to the graph object `g` it belongs to, and a lambda expression for the body, which updates the corresponding element of the matrix, probably using the data from its neighbor elements above and to the left.

Once the flow graph is set up, a `continue_msg` is put to the node in the upper left corner, `node[0][0]`, to start the wavefront propagation through the graph. The call to `g.wait_for_all()` blocks until the computation completes.

The body of a `continue_node` should have enough computation—of the same order as was recommended for iterations of TBB generic algorithms earlier in the chapter— to justify the overhead introduced by TBB. In the above example, if processing a single matrix element does not provide enough work, it makes sense to process data by blocks. In such cases, the wavefront pattern would be applied serially within a rectangular block of elements, and a `continue_node` would be associated with each of the blocks.

For the sake of comparison with the flow graph, an alternative wavefront implementation is shown that uses `tbb::parallel_do` together with `tbb::atomic` variables. This approach, though comparable in code size, requires a programmer to take care of details of thread-safe dependency management, while TBB flow graph allows one to express the high-level computation structure and let TBB do the rest.

```
// M and N are the number of rows and columns  in  the  matrix
double value[M][N];

#include <tbb/atomic.h>
#include <tbb/parallel_do.h>
#include <list>

tbb::atomic<int> dependency[M][N];

double run_graph( ) {
    struct index2d {
        int i, j;
        index2d( int ii, int jj ) : i( ii ), j( jj ) {}
    };
    for( int i=0; i<M; ++i )
        for( int j=0; j<N; ++j )
            dependency[i][j] = (i>0? 1 : 0) + (j>0? 1 : 0);
```

```
    std::list<index2d> top_left;
    top_left.push_back( index2d(0,0) );

    value[M-1][N-1] = 0;
    tbb::parallel_do( top_left.begin(), top_left.end(),
        []( const index2d& idx, tbb::parallel_do_feeder<index2d>& feeder )
        {
            update( idx.i, idx.j );
            if( idx.i < M-1 )
                if( --dependency[i+1][j] == 0 )      // decrement, check new value
                    feeder.add( index2d(i+1,j) );    // if 0, process element below
            if( idx.j < N-1 )
                if( --dependency[i][j+1] == 0 )
                    feeder.add( index2d(i,j+1) );     // same for the element at right
        }
    );

    return value[M-1][N-1];
}
```

14.3.4 Data Flow Graphs

Consider an application that processes data or requests coming from an external source, e.g., over the network. The external input might happen at an irregular rate, with both high activity and long wait periods possible. Data processing in response to the input might take significant time, potentially benefitting from extra hardware processing elements. Sometimes, the number of simultaneously processed inputs could be limited by availability of critical resources.

Such applications are often implemented with the producer-consumer pattern, with one or more producer actors polling external data sources in a loop, reading the input, and passing it to one or more consumer actors for processing. Actors are often implemented as threads that exchange data through shared queues and synchronize by sending and receiving signals.

The TBB flow graph API can also be suitable for such applications, but the design is not a typical producer-consumer pattern. Figure 14.2 shows the scheme of a TBB flow graph that implements an application like the one described above. It uses graph nodes of a few different types, each having its own iconic picture.

In the scheme, data is supplied to the graph by a polling loop. Since it waits for external events and may block for long, this loop should be external to the graph[6] and run in an application thread, not a TBB task. The polling loop puts obtained data items into a tbb::flow::limiter_node. This node counts the messages that pass through, and

---

6. Special support for coordination with an external activity might be added to the flow graph API in the future.

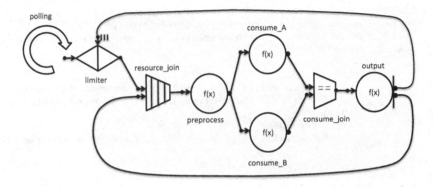

Figure 14.2: Scheme of a data flow graph

rejects its input when the count equals to a specified threshold. Put right at the beginning of the flow, it limits the number of data items simultaneously processed by the graph.

Next to the limiter is a `tbb::flow::join_node`, which accepts multiple inputs, combines those into a tuple and passes it down the graph. A `join_node` object has one of a few different input policies. The resource join node at the scheme uses the queuing policy, which means that input messages are buffered internally by the node, and passed down only when each of the input ports received a message. Thus, this node serves as the input data buffer between the producer and consumers, and also guarantees that for each data item the resources required for processing are available.

The tuple of the input data and a resource is then sent to the consumer part of the graph—a set of function nodes that process the input. Each `tbb::flow::function_node` executes a user-supplied body function that takes the node input as an argument, and returns a value to be passed to successors. Additionally, a `function_node` allows a limit to be set on the number of concurrent invocations. Two most useful values for the limit are `tbb::flow::unlimited`, which allows any number of invocations of the body to execute concurrently, and `tbb::flow::serial`, which allows only a single call of the body to run at any given time. However, any integer value can be used to limit node concurrency to the desired degree.

In the shown scheme, processing consists of four stages having "diamond" dependency.

preprocess precedes consume_A and consume_B; these stages can run independently, and supply their results to output. However, since a function_node can only have single input, the data from consume_A and consume_B should be combined before passing to output. For that, a key matching join_node is used. This node pairs together its inputs that have the same key, defined for each input by a user-specified function. With parallel consume stages, data items might come in an arbitrary order, therefore the key matching policy is important to combine proper parts together before sending it down.

The last node in the scheme, output, is a tbb::flow::multifunction_node. It also may have a concurrency limit; for example, if the output is sent to a channel that is not thread-safe, the node should operate in serial mode. multifunction_node differs from function_node in that its body is given a tuple of output ports, i.e., connections where it can send messages. After completing its work, the output node signals the limiter that one of the data tokens was fully processed, so that another one might start flowing through the graph. Also, this node returns the resource back to resource_join, thus allowing it to be reused in the processing of other inputs.

The next listing shows the source code that constructs and runs this graph. Since the example is schematic, the user-defined parts of the graph are not specified.

```cpp
#include <tbb/flow_graph.h>
class input;
class resource;
class consume_data;
int main() {
    using namespace tbb::flow; // for brevity
    const int token_limit = get_resource_limit();
    graph g;

    // Create graph nodes
    limiter_node< input >
        limiter ( g, token_limit );
    join_node< std::tuple<input, resource>, queueing >
        resource_join ( g );
    function_node< std::tuple<input, resource>, consume_data >
        preprocess( g, unlimited, preprocessor_body() );
    function_node< consume_data, consume_data >
        consume_A ( g, unlimited, consume_body_A() );
    function_node< consume_data, consume_data >
        consume_B ( g, unlimited, consume_body_B() );
    join_node< std::tuple<consume_data, consume_data>, tag_matching >
        consume_join ( g, tagger(), tagger() );

    // The multifunction node in more details
    typedef multifunction_node< std::tuple<consume_data, consume_data>,
                                std::tuple<resource, continue_msg> >
        output_node;
```

```
output_node output( g, tbb::flow::serial,
    []( std::tuple<consume_data, consume_data> data,
        output_node::output_ports_type & ports ) {
            auto combined = combine( data );
            send_result( combined );
            // Return the resource
            std::get<0>( ports ).try_put( combined.get_resource() );
            // Signal the limiter
            std::get<1>( ports ).try_put( continue_msg() );
    }
);
// Connect nodes with edges
make_edge( limiter, input_port<0>( resource_join ) );
make_edge( resource_join, preprocess );
make_edge( preprocess, consume_A );
make_edge( consume_A, input_port<0>( consume_join ) );
make_edge( preprocess, consume_B );
make_edge( consume_B, input_port<1>( consume_join ) );
make_edge( consume_join, output );
make_edge( output_port<0>( output ), input_port<1>( resource_join ) );
make_edge( output_port<1>( output ), limiter.decrement );

// Prepare the resources
for( int i=0; i<token_limit; ++i )
    input_port<1>( resource_join ).try_put( resource() );
// The polling loop
while( wait_for_input() ) {
    input new_item = get_new_input();
    // Feed the input into the graph through limiter
    while( limiter.try_put( new_item )==false ) {
        // perhaps token limit is reached; help processing
        g.wait_for_all();
    }
}
return 0;
}
```

An alternative TBB implementation might use parallel_pipeline, for this example. Some parts, e.g., limiting the number of simultaneously processed tokens, would be implicit; on the other hand, resource recycling would need to be implemented explicitly. But most important, there would be two major issues comparing to the flow graph. First, since parallel_pipeline is linear, the consumption stages would have to follow one another, resulting in reduced concurrency. And second, parallel_pipeline cannot be fed from outside, so combining it with the polling loop would likely require an intermediate buffer, resulting in more code and being less efficient.

Table 14.1: Comparison of various approaches to flow graph computations with TBB

	Task Graphs	parallel_do	parallel_pipeline	Flow Graph API
Expressiveness	Can express acyclic dependency graphs.	Can express acyclic dependency graphs.	Can express linear pipelines.	Can express acyclic dependency graphs as well as acyclic and cyclic messaging graphs.
Ease-of-use	Requires dependency book-keeping code and manipulations with tasks.	Requires dependency book-keeping code.	A concise, type safe interface.	More complex than `parallel_pipeline`, but avoids dependency book-keeping and task manipulations.
Persistence	Graphs are executed destructively and cannot be re-executed.	Can be executed multiple times.	Can be executed multiple times.	Can be executed multiple times.
Performance	Low overhead comparing to other approaches.	Overhead is higher than for task graphs, comparable to flow graphs.	Overhead is higher than for task graphs, comparable to flow graphs.	Overhead is comparable to `parallel_pipeline` and `parallel_do`.

14.3.5   Choosing Between a Flow Graph, Algorithms, or an Acyclic Graph of Tasks

The flow graph API adds significant functionality to TBB and makes it suitable to a wider variety of applications. At the same time, as discussed earlier, some applications suited to the flow graph can also be implemented using either the low-level support for acyclic graphs of tasks or the generic parallel algorithms. Table 14.1 compares these different approaches and provides characteristics that may help in selecting the most appropriate model to use.

14.4   Summary

The Intel TBB C++ template library provides a rich set of functionality for applications to exploit parallelism in modern multicore computers without focusing on low-level details of managing that parallelism. Besides generic parallel algorithms and the flow graph API described in this chapter, TBB offers a set of concurrency-friendly containers, a variety of synchronization classes, advanced classes to store and access thread-specific data, efficient and scalable memory allocators, and more. Most TBB components are independent of each other, and can be efficiently used together and mixed with other programming models for parallelism and concurrency.

While TBB is a mature product—with the first version released in 2006—it keeps evolving and expanding. The most recent documentation and other useful information about TBB can be found at `http://threadingbuildingblocks.org`.

15 Compute Unified Device Architecture

Wen-mei Hwu, University of Illinois, Urbana-Champaign
David Kirk, NVIDIA

Compute Unified Device Architecture (CUDA) C is an extension to the C programming language[1] with new keywords and application programming interface (API) for programmers to take advantage of the massively parallel graphics processing units (GPUs) in modern computers. For the rest of this chapter, we will refer to CUDA C simply as CUDA. To a CUDA programmer, the computing system consists of a host that is a traditional central processing unit (CPU), such an Intel Xeon microprocessor in personal computers today, and one or more devices that are massively parallel processors with a large number of arithmetic execution units and memory channels/banks. A CUDA device is typically a GPU. The CPUs and GPUs can be physically separated components connected by a system bus, such as PCI Express (PCIe), or integrated into the same chip package. In other cases, compiler-based tools also allow CPU cores, digital signal processing cores, or even field programmable gate arrays to be used as CUDA devices. As we will see in the rest of the chapter, CUDA gives programmers explicit, detailed control of the parallel execution, for predictable performance. Such control comes with programming details that are often abstracted away in higher-level programming interfaces.

15.1 A Brief History Leading to CUDA

Around the year 2000, the GPU industry began to move into general programmability. For example, in 2001, the NVIDIA GeForce 3 [179] took the first step toward true general shader programmability. It exposed the application developer to what had been the private internal instruction set of the floating-point vertex engine. This coincided with the release of Microsoft DirectX 8, and OpenGL vertex shader extensions. Later GPUs, at the time of DirectX 9, extended general programmability and floating-point capability to the pixel shader stage and made texture accessible from the vertex shader stage. The ATI Radeon 9700, introduced in 2002, featured a programmable 24-bit floating-point pixel shader processor programmed with DirectX 9 and OpenGL. The GeForce FX added 32-bit floating-point pixel processors. These programmable pixel shader processors were part of a general trend toward unifying the functionality of the different stages, as seen by the application programmer. By and large, however, the vertex and pixel stages were still based on different processor designs. For example, NVIDIA's GeForce 6800 series and 7800 series were built with separate processor designs dedicated to vertex and pixel processing.

The XBox 360 introduced an early unified-processor GPU in 2005, allowing vertex and pixel shaders to execute on the same processor. As the GPU hardware design evolved

---

1. CUDA C also supports a growing subset of C++ features. Interested readers should refer to the CUDA Programming Guide for more information about these features.

toward more unified processors, it increasingly resembled high-performance parallel computers. As DirectX 9 capable GPUs became available, some researchers took notice of the raw performance growth path of GPUs and started to explore their use for solving compute-intensive science and engineering problems. These exploratory efforts became known as the GPGPU (general-purpose GPU) movement. However, DirectX 9 GPUs had been designed only to match the features required by the graphics APIs. To access the computational resources, programmers had to cast their problem into graphics operations so that the computation could be launched through OpenGL or DirectX API calls. For example, in order to run many simultaneous instances of a compute function, the problem had to be written as a pixel shader. The collection of input data had to be stored in texture images and issued to the GPU by submitting triangles (with clipping to a rectangle shape, if that was what was desired). The output had to be cast as a set of pixels generated from the raster operations.

For the DirectX 10 generation graphics, NVIDIA had already begun work on a high-efficiency floating-point and integer processor that could run various simultaneous workloads to support the logical graphics pipeline. The designers of the Tesla architecture GPUs took another step. The shader processors became fully programmable processors with instruction memory, instruction cache, and instruction sequencing control logic. The cost of these additional hardware resources was amortized by having multiple shader processors share their instruction cache and instruction sequencing control logic. This design works well with graphics applications because the same shader program needs to be applied to a massive number of vertices or pixels. NVIDIA added memory load and store instructions with random byte addressing capability to support the requirements of compiled C programs.

Introduced in 2006, NVIDIA's GeForce 8800 GPU, which was based on the Tesla Architecture, mapped the separate programmable graphics stages to an array of unified processors; the logical graphics pipeline is physically a recirculating path that visits these processors three times, with much fixed-function graphics logic between visits. The unified processor array allows dynamic partitioning of the array to vertex shading, geometry processing, and pixel processing. Since different rendering algorithms present wildly different loads among the three programmable stages, this unification allows the same pool of execution resources to be dynamically allocated to different pipeline stages and achieve better load balance. Such unification of processors also makes GPUs, such as the GeForce 8800, more amenable to executing nongraphical applications.

For nongraphics application programmers, the Tesla architecture GPUs introduced a more generic parallel programming model with a hierarchy of parallel threads, barrier synchronization, and atomic operations to dispatch and manage highly parallel computing work. NVIDIA also developed the CUDA C/C++ compiler, libraries, and runtime software to enable programmers to readily access the new data-parallel computation model and develop applications. Programmers no longer need to use the graphics API to access the GPU parallel computing capabilities. The G80 chip was based on the Tesla architecture and was used in NVIDIA's GeForce 8800GTX. G80 was followed by G92, GT200, Fermi, and Kepler.

15.2   CUDA Program Structure

The structure of a CUDA program reflects the coexistence of a *host* and one or more *devices* in the computer. Each CUDA source file can have a mixture of both host and device code. By default, any traditional C program is also a CUDA program that contains only host code. One can add device functions and data declarations into any C source file. The functions or data declarations for the device are clearly marked with special CUDA keywords. Typically, these are functions that exhibit rich amount of data parallelism.

Once device functions and data declarations are added to a source file, it is no longer acceptable to a traditional C compiler. It must be compiled by a CUDA compiler, such as the NVIDIA C Compiler: NVCC. As shown at the top of Figure 15.1 , the NVCC compiler processes a CUDA program, using CUDA keywords to separate the program into host code and device code. The host code is straight ANSI C code, which is further compiled with the host's standard C/C++ compilers and is run as a traditional CPU process. The device code is marked with CUDA keywords for labeling data-parallel functions, called kernels, and their associated subroutines and data structures. The device code is typically further compiled by the NVCC and executed on a GPU device. One can also choose to execute the kernel on the CPU using tools such as MCUDA [144].

The execution of a CUDA program is illustrated in Figure 15.2. The execution starts with host (CPU) execution. When a kernel is called, or *launched*, it is executed by a device (GPU), where a large number of threads are used to take advantage of data parallelism. In CUDA, a kernel function specifies the code to be executed by all threads during a parallel phase. Since all these threads execute the same code, CUDA programming is an instance of the well-known single program, multiple data (SPMD) [19] programming style for massively parallel computing systems. It is also often referred to as SIMT (single instruction, multiple threads). All the threads that are generated by a kernel launch are collectively called a grid.

Figure 15.2 shows the execution of two grids of threads. When all threads of a kernel complete their execution, the corresponding grid terminates, and the execution continues on the host until another kernel is launched. Launching a kernel typically generates a large number of threads to exploit data parallelism. CUDA programmers can assume that these threads take few clock cycles to generate and schedule because of efficient hardware

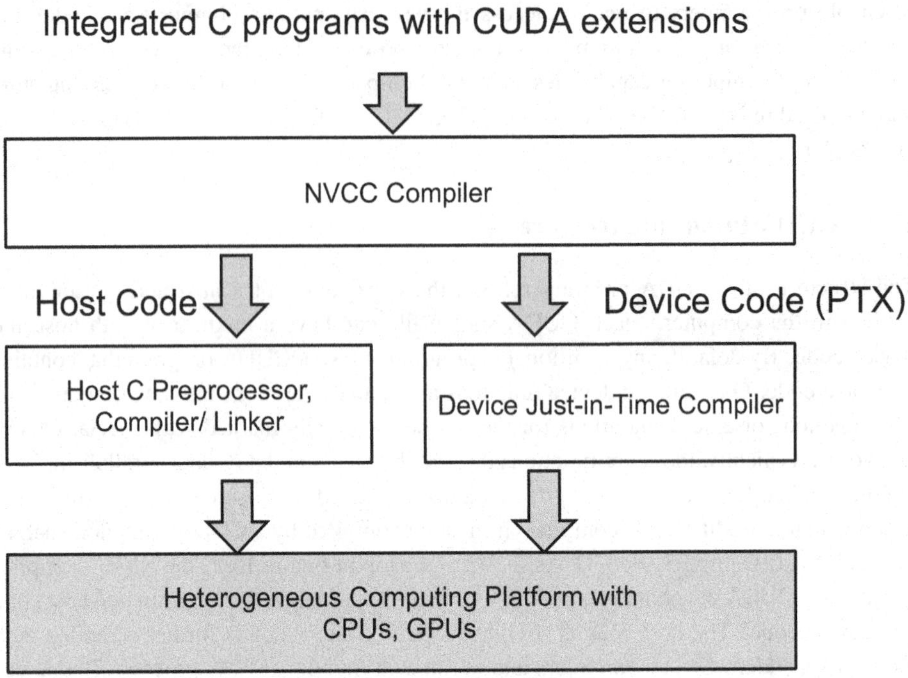

Integrated C programs with CUDA extensions

Figure 15.1: An Overview of the compilation process for a CUDA program.

support. This situation is in contrast with the CPU threads, which typically take thousands of clock cycles to generate and schedule.

15.3   A Vector Addition Example

Let us illustrate the basic concepts of CUDA with a vector addition example, where each element of the sum vector, C, is generated by adding an element of input vector A to an element of input vector B. For example, C[0] is generated by adding A[0] to B[0], and C[3] is generated by adding A[3] to B[3]. All additions can be performed in parallel. Therefore, the vector addition of two large vectors exhibits a rich amount of data parallelism.

Before we show the kernel code for vector addition, we first review how a conventional CPU-only vector addition function works. Figure 15.3 shows a simple traditional C program that consists of a main function and a vector addition function. Assume that the

CPU Serial Code

Device Parallel Kernel
KernelA<<< nBlk, nTid >>>(args);

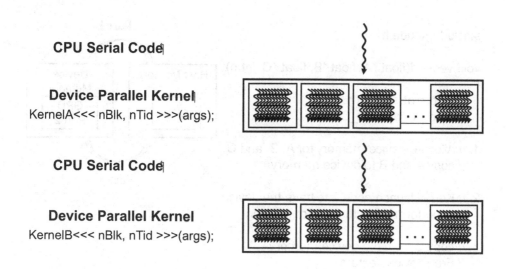

CPU Serial Code

Device Parallel Kernel
KernelB<<< nBlk, nTid >>>(args);

Figure 15.2: Execution of a CUDA program.

```
// Compute vector sum h_C = h_A+h_B
void vecAdd(float* h_A, float* h_B, float* h_C, int n)
{
  for (i = 0; i < n; i++) h_C[i] = h_A[i] + h_B[i];
}
int main()
{
    // Memory allocation for h_A, h_B, and h_C
    // I/O to read h_A and h_B, N elements each
      ...
    vecAdd(h_A, h_B, h_C, N);
}
```

Figure 15.3: C code example of a simple traditional vector addition.

vectors to be added are stored in arrays h_A, h_B, and h_C, that are allocated and initialized in the main program. For brevity, we do not show the details of how h_A and h_B are allocated or initialized. The pointers to these arrays are passed to the vecAdd() function, along with the variable N that contains the length of the vectors.

The vecAdd() function in Figure 15.3 uses a for loop to iterate through the vector elements. In the ith iteration, output element C[i] receives the sum of A[i] and B[i]. The vector length parameter n is used to control the loop so that the number of iterations matches the length of the vectors. The parameters A, B, and C are passed by reference so

```
#include <cuda.h>
...
void vecAdd(float *A, float *B, float *C, int n)
{
    int size = n* sizeof(float);
    float *d_A, *d_B, *d_C;
    ...
1. // Allocate device memory for A, B, and C
   // copy A and B to device memory

2. // Kernel launch code – to have the device
   // to perform the actual vector addition

3. // copy C from the device memory
   // Free device vectors
}
```

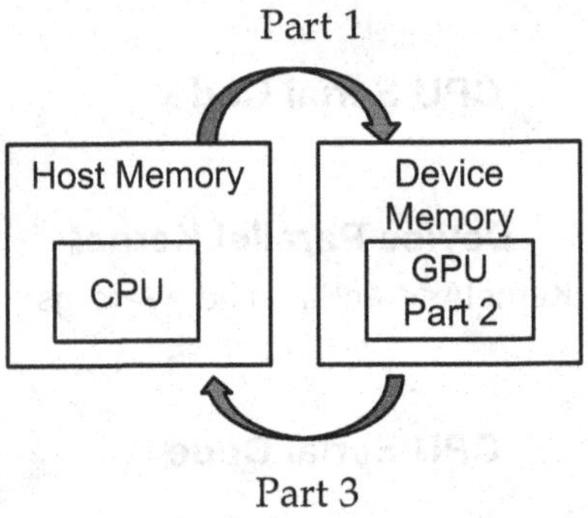

Part 1

Host Memory | Device Memory

CPU | GPU Part 2

Part 3

Figure 15.4: Vector addition host code.

the function reads the elements of h_A and h_B and writes the elements of h_C through the parameter pointers A, B, and C. When the vecAdd() function returns, the subsequent statements in the main function can access the new contents of h_C.

A straightforward way to execute vector addition in parallel is to modify the vecAdd() function and move its calculations to a CUDA device. The structure of such a modified vecAdd() function is shown in Figure 15.4. Part 1 of the function allocates device (GPU) memory to hold copies of the A, B, and C vectors and copies the vectors from the host memory to the device memory. Part 2 launches the parallel execution of the actual vector addition kernel on the device. Part 3 copies the sum vector C from the device memory back to the host memory.

Note that the revised vecAdd() function is essentially an outsourcing agent that ships input data to a device, activates the calculation on the device, and collects the results from the device. The agent does so in such a way that the main program does not need to even be aware that the vector addition is now actually done on a device. The details of the revised function, as well as the way to compose the kernel function, will be shown as illustrations as we introduce the basic features of the CUDA programming model.

15.4   Device Memories and Data Transfer

In CUDA, host and devices have separate memory spaces, as shown in Figure 15.4. This reflects the current reality that devices are often hardware units that come with their own dynamic random access memory. To execute a kernel on a device, the programmer needs to allocate memory on the device and transfer pertinent data from the host memory to the allocated device memory. This situation corresponds to Part 1 of Figure 15.4. Similarly, after device execution, the programmer needs to transfer result data from the device memory back to the host memory and free up the device memory that is no longer needed. This situation corresponds to Part 3 of Figure 15.4. The CUDA runtime system provides API functions to perform these activities on behalf of the programmer. From this point on, we will simply say that a piece of data is transferred from host to device, as shorthand for saying that the data is copied from the host memory to the device memory. The same holds for data movement in the opposite direction.

The CUDA runtime system provides API functions that help CUDA programmers manage data in the device memory. For example, Part 1 and Part 3 of the `vecAdd()` function in Figure 15.4 need to use these API functions to allocate device memory for A, B, and C; transfer A and B from host memory to device memory; transfer C from device memory to host memory; and free the device memory for A, B, and C. We will explain the memory allocation and deallocation functions first. The function `cudaMalloc()` can be called from the host code to allocate a piece of device global memory for an object. CUDA uses the standard C runtime library `malloc()` function to manage the host memory and adds `cudaMalloc()` as an extension to the C runtime library. By keeping the interface as close to the original C runtime libraries as possible, CUDA minimizes the time that a C programmer spends in relearning the use of these extensions.

The first parameter to the `cudaMalloc()` function is the address of a pointer variable that needs to point to the allocated object after allocation. The address of the pointer variable should be cast to (`void **`) because the function expects a generic pointer; the memory allocation function is a generic function that is not restricted to any particular type of objects. This parameter allows the `cudaMalloc()` function to write the address of the allocated memory into the pointer variable.[2] The host code passes this pointer value to the kernels that need to access the allocated memory object. The second parameter to the `cudaMalloc()` function gives the size of the object to be allocated, in terms of

---

2. Note that `cudaMalloc()` has a different format from that of the C `malloc()` function. The C `malloc()` function returns a pointer to the allocated object. It takes only one parameter, which specifies the size of the allocated object. The `cudaMalloc()` function writes to the pointer variable whose address is given as the first parameter. As a result, the `cudaMalloc()` function takes two parameters. The two-parameter format of `cudaMalloc()` allows it to use the return value to report any errors in the same way as other CUDA API functions.

bytes. The usage of this second parameter is consistent with the size parameter to the C `malloc()` function.

We now use a simple code example to illustrate the use of `cudaMalloc()`. This is a continuation of the example in Figure 15.4. For clarity, we will start a pointer variable with the letter "d_" to indicate that it points to an object in the device memory. The programmer passes the address of d_A (i.e., &d_A) as the first parameter after casting it to a void pointer. That is, d_A will point to the device memory region allocated for the A matrix. The size of the allocated region will be n times the size of a single-precision floating number, which is 4 on most computers today. After the computation, `cudaFree()` is called with d_A as input to free the storage space for the A matrix from the device global memory.

```
float *d_A
int size = n * sizeof(float);

cudaMalloc((void**)&d_A, size);
...
cudaFree(d_A);
```

The reader should complete Part 1 of the `vecAdd()` example in Figure 15.4 with similar declarations of d_B and d_C pointer variables and their corresponding `cudaMalloc()` calls. Furthermore, Part 3 can be completed with the `cudaFree()` calls for d_B and d_C.

Once the host code has allocated device memory for the data objects, it can request that data be transferred from host to device. This is accomplished by calling `cudaMemcpy()`, one of the CUDA API functions for data transfer between memories. The function takes four parameters. The first parameter is a pointer to the destination memory location for the data object to be copied. The second parameter points to the source location. The third parameter specifies the number of bytes to be copied. The fourth parameter indicates the types of memory involved in the copy: from host memory to host memory, from host memory to device memory, from device memory to host memory, and from device memory to device memory. For example, the memory copy function can be used to copy data from one location of the device memory to another location.

For the `vecAdd()` example, the host code calls the `cudaMemcpy()` function to copy A and B matrices from the host memory to the device memory, before adding them, and then to copy the C matrix from the device memory to the host memory, after the addition is done. Assume that A, B, d_A, d_B, and size have already been set as we discussed before; the required function calls are shown below. Note that the two symbolic constants, `cudaMemcopyHostToDevice` and `cudaMemcopyDeviceToHost`, are recognized, predefined constants of the CUDA programming environment. Also note that the same function can be used to transfer data in both directions by properly ordering the source and destination pointers and using the appropriate constant for the transfer type.

```
cudaMemcpy(d_A, A, size, cudaMemcpyHostToDevice);

cudaMemcpy(C, d_C, size, cudaMemcpyDeviceToHost);
```

A complete vecAdd() function is shown in Figure 15.5. It is responsible for allocating device memory, requesting data transfers, and launching the kernel that performs the actual matrix multiplication. We often refer to this type of host code as a stub function for launching a kernel. After the kernel finishes execution, vecAdd() also copies the result data from the device to host.

```
void vecAdd(float* A, float* B, float* C, int n)
{
    int size = n * sizeof(float);
    float *d_A, *d_B, *d_C;

    cudaMalloc((void **) &d_A, size);
    cudaMemcpy(d_A, A, size, cudaMemcpyHostToDevice);
    cudaMalloc((void **) &B_d, size);
    cudaMemcpy(d_B, B, size, cudaMemcpyHostToDevice);

    cudaMalloc((void **) &d_C, size);

    vecAddKernel<<<ceil(n/256.0), 256>>>(d_A, d_B, d_C, n);

    cudaMemcpy(C, d_C, size, cudaMemcpyDeviceToHost);

    // Free device memory for A, B, C
    cudaFree(d_Ad); cudaFree(d_B); cudaFree (d_C);
}
```

Figure 15.5: Detailed vecAdd() host code.

15.5   Kernel Functions and Threading

We are now ready to discuss more about the CUDA kernel functions and the effect of launching these kernel functions.

Figure 15.6 shows the kernel function for vector addition. The syntax is ANSI C with some notable extensions. First, there is a CUDA specific keyword, __global__, in front

```
// vector addition kernel − thread specification
__global__ void vecAddKernel(float *d_A, float *d_B, float *d_C, int n)
{
    // a global index based on Block index and Thread index
    int i = blockDim.x * blockIdx.x + threadIdx.x;

    // use global index to determine the element to work on
    if (i < n) C[i] = A[i] + B[i];
}
```

Figure 15.6: Kernel function vecAdd.

of the declaration of vecAddKernel(). This keyword indicates that the function is a kernel and that it can be called from a host function to generate a grid of threads on a device.

In general, CUDA extends the C language with three qualifier keywords in function declarations. The keyword, __global__, indicates that the function being declared is a CUDA kernel function. Note the two underscore characters on each side of the word global. A __global__ function is to be executed on the device and can be called only from the host code. The keyword, __device__, indicates that the function being declared is a CUDA device function. A device function executes on a CUDA device and can be called only from a kernel function or another device function.

The keyword, __host__, indicates that the function being declared is a CUDA host function. A host function is simply a traditional C function that executes on host and can be called only from another host function. By default, all functions in a CUDA program are host functions if they do not have any of the CUDA keywords in their declaration. This makes sense because many CUDA applications are ported from CPU-only execution environments. The programmer adds kernel functions and device functions during the porting process. The original functions remain as host functions. Having all functions default to host functions spares the programmer the tedious work of changing all the original function declarations.

Note that both __host__ and __device__ can be used in a function declaration. This combination tells the compilation system to generate two versions of the same function. One is executed on the host and can be called only from a host function. The other is executed on the device and can be called only from a device or kernel function. This design supports a common use case where the same function source code is recompiled with alternate flags to generate a device version. Many user library functions fall into this category.

The keywords threadIdx.x, blockIdx.x, and blockDim.x, are the second ex-

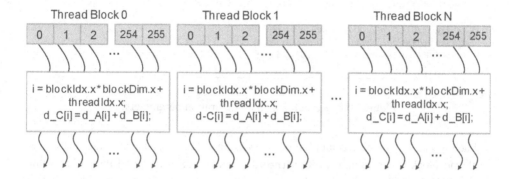

Figure 15.7: Mapping CUDA threads to data elements.

tension to ANSI C in Figure 15.6. Note that all threads execute the same kernel code. We need a way to distinguish them and direct each thread towards a particular part of the data structure. These keywords identify predefined variables that correspond to hardware registers that provide the identifying coordinates to threads. Different threads will see different values in their `threadIdx.x`, `blockIdx.x`, and `blockDim.x` variables. For the sake of simplicity in naming, we will refer to a thread as `threadblockIdx.x`, `threadIdx.x`. Note that the ".x" implies that there might be ".y" and ".z"—we will come back to this point soon.

A quick comparison between Figure 15.3 and Figure 15.6 reveals an important insight for CUDA kernels and CUDA kernel launch. The kernel function in Figure 15.6 has no loop that corresponds to the one in Figure 15.3. The loop is now replaced with the grid of threads. The entire grid forms the equivalent of the loop. Each thread in the grid corresponds to one iteration of the original loop. This concept is illustrated in Figure 15.7.

When a host code launches a kernel, the CUDA runtime system generates a grid of threads that are organized in a two-level hierarchy. Each grid is organized into an array of thread blocks. In CUDA 3.0 and beyond, each block can contain up to 1,024 threads.[3] Figure 15.7 shows an example where each block consists of 256 threads. The number of threads in each thread block is specified by the host code when a kernel is launched. The same kernel can be launched with different numbers of threads. For a given grid of threads, the number of threads in a block is available in the `blockDim` variable. In Figure 15.7, the value of the `blockDim.x` variable is 256. For hardware efficiency, the dimensions of thread blocks generally should be multiples of 32. We will revisit this point later.

---

3. Some earlier CUDA versions allow only up to 768 threads in a block.

```
int vectAdd(float* A, float* B, float* C, int n)
{
    // d_A, d_B, d_C allocations and copies omitted
    // Run ceil(n/256) blocks of 256 threads each
    vecAddKernel<<<ceil(n/256.0), 256>>>(d_A, d_B, d_C, n);
}
```

Figure 15.8: Kernel launch configuration parameters.

Each thread in a block has a unique `threadIdx` value. For example, the first thread in thread block 0 has value 0 in its `threadIdx` variable, the second thread has value 1, the third thread has value 2, and so forth. This deign allows each thread to combine its `threadIdx` and `blockIdx` values to create a unique global index for itself within the entire grid. In Figure 15.7, the global index is calculated as `i = blockIdx.x * blockDim.x + threadIdx.x`. Since `blockDim` is 256 in our example, the global index of threads in block 0 ranges from 0 to 255; the global index of threads in block 1 ranges from 256 to 511; the global index of threads in block 2 ranges from 512 to 767. That is, the `i` values of the threads in these three thread blocks form a continuous coverage of the values from 0 to 767. Since each thread uses `i` to access `d_A`, `d_B`, and `d_C`, these threads cover the first 768 iterations of the original loop. By launching the kernel with a larger number of blocks, one can process larger vectors. By launching a kernel with `n` threads, one can process vectors of length `n`.

Note the `if (i<n)` statement in `vecAddKernel()` in Figure 15.6. The reason is that not all vector lengths can be expressed as multiples of the block size. For example, if the vector length is 100 and the smallest efficient thread block dimension is 32, one would need to launch four thread blocks to process all the 100 vector elements. However, the four thread blocks would have 128 threads. We would, therefore, need to disable the last 28 threads in thread block 3 from doing work not expected by the original program. Since all threads are to execute the same code, all will test their `i` value against `n`, which is 100. With the `if (i<n)` statement, the first 100 threads will perform the addition whereas the last 28 will not. This design allows the kernel to process vectors of arbitrary lengths.

When the host code launches a kernel, it sets the grid and thread block dimensions via execution configuration parameters, as illustrated in Figure 15.8. The configuration parameters are given between the "<<<" and ">>>" before the traditional C function arguments. The first configuration parameter gives the number of thread blocks in the grid. The second specifies the number of threads in each thread block. In this example, each block has 256 threads. To ensure that we have enough threads to cover all the vector elements, we apply the C ceiling function to `n/256.0`. For example, if we have 1,000 threads, we will launch `ceil(1000/256.0) = 4` thread blocks. As a result, the statement will launch $4 \times 256 = 1024$ threads. With the `if (i < n)` statement in the kernel, the first 1,000 threads will perform addition on the 1,000 vector elements. The remaining 24 will not.

The code is hardwired to use thread blocks of 256 threads each. The number of thread blocks used, however, depends on the length of the vectors (n). If n is 750, then three thread blocks will be used; if n is 4,000, then 16 thread blocks will be used; if n is 2,000,000, then 7,813 blocks will be used. Note that all the thread blocks operate on different parts of the vectors. They can be executed in any arbitrary order. A small GPU with a small amount of execution resources may execute one or two of these thread blocks in parallel. A larger GPU may execute 64 or 128 blocks in parallel. This design gives CUDA kernels scalability with hardware. The same code runs at lower performance on small GPUs and higher performance on larger GPUs.

We point out that the vector addition example is used for its simplicity. In practice, the overhead of allocating device memory, input data transfer from host to device, and output data transfer from device to host and of deallocating device memory will likely make the resulting code slower than the original sequential code. The reason is that the amount of calculation done by the kernel is small relative to the amount of data processed. Only one addition is performed for two floating-point input operands and one floating-point output operand. Real applications typically have kernels where much more work is needed relative to the amount of data processed, thus making the additional overhead worthwhile. They also tend to keep the data in the device memory across multiple kernel invocations so that the overhead can be amortized.

15.6   More on CUDA Thread Organization

Recall that all CUDA threads in a grid execute the same kernel function and rely on coordinates to distinguish themselves from each other and to identify the appropriate portion of the data to process. These threads are organized into a two-level hierarchy: a grid consists of one or more blocks, and each block, in turn, consists of one or more threads. All threads in a block share the same block index, which can be accessed as the `blockIdx` variable in a kernel. Each thread also has a thread index, which can be accessed as the `threadIdx` variable in a kernel. To a CUDA programmer, `blockIdx` and `threadIdx` appear as built-in, preinitialized variables that can be accessed within kernel functions. When a thread executes a kernel function, references to the `blockIdx` and `threadIdx` variables return the coordinates of the thread. The execution configuration parameters in a kernel launch statement specify the dimensions of the grid and the dimensions of each block. These dimensions are available as predefined built-in variables `gridDim` and `blockDim` in kernel functions.

In general, a grid is a three-dimensional array of blocks, and each block is a three-dimensional array of threads. The programmer can choose to use fewer dimensions by setting the unused dimensions to 1. The exact organization of a grid is determined by the execution configuration parameters (within <<< >>>) of the kernel launch statement. The first execution configuration parameter specifies the dimensions of the grid in number of blocks. The second specifies the dimensions of each block in number of threads. Each such parameter is of dim3 type, which is a C struct with three unsigned integer fields: x, y, and z. These three fields correspond to the three dimensions.

For 1D or 2D grids and blocks, the unused dimension fields should be set to 1 for clarity. For example, the following host code can be used to launch the vecAddkernel() kernel function and generate a 1D grid that consists of 32 blocks, each of which consists of 128 threads. The total number of threads in the grid is $128 \times 32 = 4096$.

```
dim3 dimBlock(128, 1, 1);
dim3 dimGrid(32, 1, 1);
vecAddKernel<<<dimGrid, dimBlock>>>(...);
```

The grid and block dimensions can also be calculated from other variables. For example, the kernel launch in Figure 15.5 can be rewritten as follows.

```
dim3 dimGrid(ceil(n/256.0), 1, 1);
dim3 dimBlock(256, 1, 1);
vecAddKernel<<<dimGrid, dimBlock>>>(...);
```

This allows the number of blocks to vary with the size of the vectors so that the grid will have enough threads to cover all vector elements. Once vecAddKernel() is launched, the grid and block dimensions will remain the same until the entire grid finishes execution.

For convenience, CUDA provides a special shortcut for launching a kernel with one-dimensional grids and blocks. Instead of using dim3 variables, one can use arithmetic expressions to specify the configuration of 1D grids and blocks. In this case, the CUDA compiler simply takes the arithmetic expression as the x-dimension and assumes that the y- and z-dimensions are 1:

```
vecAddKernel<<<ceil(n/256.0), 256>>>(...);
```

The x field of the predefined variables gridDim and blockDim are preinitialized according to the execution configuration parameters. For example, if n is equal to 4,000, gridDim.x and blockDim.x in the vectAddkernel kernel function will be 16 and

256, respectively. Note that unlike the `dim3` variables in the host code, the names of these variables within the kernel functions are part of the CUDA specification and cannot be changed. That is, the `gridDim` and `blockDim` variables in the kernel function always reflect the dimensions of the grid and the blocks.

In CUDA, the allowed values of `gridDim.x`, `gridDim.y` and `gridDim.z` range from 1 to 65,536. All threads in a block share the same `blockIdx.x`, `blockIdx.y`, and `blockIdx.z` values. Among all blocks, the `blockIdx.x` value lies between 0 and `gridDim.x-1`, the `blockIdx.y` value between 0 and `gridDim.y-1`, and the `blockIdx.z` value between 0 and `gridDim.z-1`. For the rest of this chapter, we will use the notation (x, y, z) for a 3D grid with x blocks in the x-dimension, y blocks in the y-dimension, and z blocks in the z-dimension.

We now turn our attention to the configuration of blocks. Blocks are organized into three-dimensional arrays of threads. Two-dimensional blocks can be created by setting the z-dimension to 1. One-dimensional blocks can be created by setting both the y- and z-dimensions to 1, as in the `vecAddkernel` example. All blocks in a grid have the same dimensions. The number of threads in each dimension of a block is specified by the second execution configuration parameter at the kernel launch. Within the kernel, this configuration parameter can be accessed as the x, y, and z fields of the predefined variable `blockDim`.

The total size of a block is limited to 1024 threads, with flexibility in distributing these elements in the three dimensions as long as the total number of threads does not exceed 1024. For example, (512, 1, 1), (8, 16, 4) and (32, 16, 2) are allowable `blockDim` values, but (32, 32, 2) is not allowable since the total number of threads would exceed 1024.

15.7 Mapping Threads to Multidimensional Data

The choice of 1D, 2D, or 3D thread organizations is usually based on the nature of the data. For example, pictures are 2D array of pixels. It is often convenient to use a 2D grid that consists of 2D blocks to process the pixels in a picture. Assume that the host code uses an integer variable n to track the number of pixels in the x-dimension and another integer variable m the number of pixels in the y-dimension. We further assume that the input picture data has been copied to the device memory and can be accessed through a pointer variable d_Pin. The output picture has been allocated in the device memory and can be accessed through a pointer variable d_Pout. The following host code can be used to launch a 2D kernel to process the picture.

```
dim3 dimBlock(ceil(n/16.0), ceil(m/16.0), 1);
dim3 dimGrid(16, 16, 1);
pictureKernel<<<dimGrid, dimBlock>>>(d_Pin, d_Pout, n, m);
```

In this example, we assume for simplicity that the dimensions of the blocks are fixed at 16×16. The dimensions of the grid, on the other hand, depend on the dimensions of the picture. To process a $2,000 \times 1,500$ (3M pixel) picture, we will generate 14,100 blocks, 150 in the x-dimension and 94 in the y-dimension. Within the kernel function, references to built-in variables `gridDim.x`, `gridDim.y`, `blockDim.x` and `blockDim.y` will result in 150, 94, 16, and 16, respectively.

Before we show the kernel code, we need to first understand how C statements access elements of dynamically allocated multidimensional arrays. Ideally, we would like to access `d_Pin` as a two-dimensional array where an element at the row `j` and column `i` can be accessed as `d_Pin[j][i]`. However, the ANSI C standard, on which CUDA was developed, requires that the number of columns in `d_Pin` be known at compile time. Unfortunately, this information is not known at compiler time for dynamically allocated arrays. In fact, part of the reason one uses dynamically allocated arrays is to allow the sizes and dimensions of these arrays to vary according to data size at run time. Thus, the information on the number of columns in a dynamically allocated two-dimensional array is not known at compile time by design. As a result, programmers need to explicitly linearize, or "flatten," a dynamically allocated two-dimensional array into an equivalent one-dimensional array in current CUDA. Note that the newer C99 standard allows multidimensional syntax for dynamically allocated arrays. It is likely that future CUDA versions may support multidimensional syntax for dynamically allocated arrays.

A CUDA programmer should follow the row-major rule for linearizing a 2D array: rows are placed one after another into the memory space. Therefore, the one-dimensional equivalent index for the element in row `j` and column `i` is `((j × 4) + i)`, if there are four elements per row. The `(j × 4)` term skips over all elements of the rows before row `j`. The `i` term then selects the right element within the section for row `j`.

We show the source code of `pictureKernel()` in Figure 15.9. The kernel scales every pixel value in the picture by a factor of 2.0. The kernel code is conceptually simple. There are a total of `blockDim.x × gridDim.x` threads in the horizontal direction. As we learned in the `vecAddKernel()` example, the we can generate every integer value ranging from 0 to `((blockDim.x × gridDim.x) − 1)` using the expression `Col = (blockIdx.x × blockDim.x) + threadIdx.x`. We know that `(gridDim.x × blockDim.x)` is greater than or equal to n. We have at least as many threads as the number of pixels in the horizontal dimension. Similarly, we have at least as many threads as the number of pixels in the vertical dimension. Therefore, as

```
__global__ void PictureKernell(float* d_Pin, float* d_Pout, int n, int m) {
   // Calculate the row # of the d_Pin and d_Pout element to process
   int Row = blockIdx.y*blockDim.y + threadIdx.y;

   // Calculate the column # of the d_Pin and d_Pout element to process
   int Col = blockIdx.x*blockDim.x + threadIdx.x;
   // each thread computes one element of d_Pout if in range
   if ((Row < m) && (Col < n)) {
      d_Pout[Row*n+Col] = 2*d_Pin[Row*n+Col];
   }
}
```

Figure 15.9: Source code of `pictureKernel` showing a 2D thread mapping to data pattern.

long as we test and make sure that computation is performed only by the threads with both Row and Col values within the range (`(Col < n) && (Row < m)`), we will be able to cover every pixel in the picture. Since a row has n pixels, we can generate the one-dimensional index for the pixel at row Row and column Col as Row × n + Col. This one-dimensional index is used to read from the d_Pin array and write to the d_Pout array.

We can easily extend our discussion of 2D arrays to 3D arrays by including another dimension when we linearize arrays. We do so by placing each plane of the array one after another. Assume that the programmer uses variables m and n to track the number of rows and columns in a 3D array. The programmer also needs to determine the values of blockDim.z and gridDim.z when launching a kernel. In the kernel, the array index will involve another global index:

```
int Plane = blockIdx.z*blockDim.z + threadIdx.z
```

The linearized access to an array P will be in the form of P[(Plane × m × n) + (Row × n) + Col]. One would, of course, need to test whether all three global indices, Plane, Row, and Col fall within the valid range of the array.

15.8 Synchronization and Transparent Scalability

So far, we have discussed how to launch a kernel for execution by a grid of threads. We have also explained how one can map threads to process parts of the data structure. However, we have not yet presented any means to coordinate the execution of multiple threads. We will now study a basic coordination mechanism. CUDA allows threads in the same block to coordinate using a barrier synchronization function, __syncthreads(). Note that "__" consists of two "_" characters. When __syncthreads() is called by a kernel function, all threads in a block will be held at the calling location until every thread in the block reaches the location. This approach ensures that all threads in a block have completed a phase of their execution of the kernel before any of them can move on to the next phase.

In CUDA, a __syncthreads() statement, if present, must be executed by all threads in a block. When a __syncthreads() statement is placed in an if-statement, either all threads in a block execute the path that includes the __syncthreads() or none of them does. Furthermore, for an if-then-else statement, if each path has a __syncthreads() statement, either all threads in a block execute the __syncthreads() on the then-path or all of them execute the __syncthreads() on the else-path. The two calls to __syncthreads() are different barrier synchronization points. If a thread in a block executed the then-path and another executed the else-path, they would be end up at different barrier synchronization points waiting for each other forever. The programmers are responsible for writing their code so that these requirements are satisfied.

The ability to synchronize also imposes execution constraints on threads within a block. These threads should execute in close time proximity with each other to avoid excessively long waiting times. In fact, one needs to make sure that all threads involved in the barrier synchronization have access to the necessary resources to eventually arrive at the barrier. Otherwise, a thread that never arrived at the barrier synchronization point can cause everyone else to wait forever. CUDA runtime systems satisfy this constraint by assigning execution resources to all threads in a block as a unit. A block can begin execution only when the runtime system has secured all the resources needed for all threads in the block to complete execution. When a thread of a block is assigned to an execution resource, all other threads in the same block are also assigned to the same resource. This design ensures the time proximity of all threads in a block and prevents excessive or indefinite waiting time during barrier synchronization.

The design of CUDA barrier synchronization involves a major tradeoff. By not allowing threads in different blocks to perform barrier synchronization with each other, the CUDA runtime system can execute blocks in any order relative to each other since none of them need to wait for the others. This flexibility enables scalable implementations. In a low-cost system with only a few execution resources, one can execute a small number of blocks at the same time. In a high-end implementation with more execution resources, one can execute a large number of blocks at the same time.

The ability to execute the same application code at a wide range of speeds allows the production of a wide range of implementations according to the cost, power, and performance requirements of particular market segments. For example, a mobile processor may execute an application slowly but at extremely low power consumption, and a desktop processor may execute the same application at a higher speed while consuming more power. Both execute exactly the same application program with no change to the code. The ability to execute the same application code on hardware with different number of execution resources is referred to as transparent scalability; it reduces the burden on application developers and improves the usability of applications.

15.9 Assigning Resources to Blocks

Once a kernel is launched, the CUDA runtime system generates the corresponding grid of threads. As discussed in the preceding section, these threads are assigned to execution resources on a block-by-block basis. In the current generation of hardware, the execution resources are organized into streaming multiprocessors (SMs). Each device has a limit on the number of blocks that can be assigned to each SM. For example, a CUDA device may allow up to 8 blocks to be assigned to each SM. In situations with an insufficient amount of one or more types of resources needed for the simultaneous execution of 8 blocks, the CUDA runtime automatically reduces the number of blocks assigned to each SM until their combined resource usage falls under the limit. With limited numbers of SMs and limited number of blocks that can be assigned to each SM, the number of blocks that can be actively executing in a CUDA device is limited. Most grids contain many more blocks than this number. The runtime system maintains a list of blocks that need to execute and assigns new blocks to SMs as they complete executing the blocks previously assigned to them.

One of the SM resource limitations is the number of threads that can be simultaneously tracked and scheduled. Hardware resources are needed for SMs to maintain the thread and block indices and track their execution status. In more recent CUDA device designs, up to 1,536 threads can be assigned to each SM. These could be in the form of 6 blocks of 256 threads each, 3 blocks of 512 threads each, and so on. If the device allows only up to 8 blocks in an SM, 12 blocks of 128 threads each obviously is not a viable option. If a CUDA device has 30 SMs and each SM can accommodate up to 1,536 threads, the device can have up to 46,080 threads simultaneously residing in the CUDA device for execution.

15.10 CUDA Streams and Task Parallelism

A CUDA program calls the runtime to perform tasks such as memory copy and kernel execution. In many situations, the overall speed of a CUDA program can be significantly improved by exploiting the parallelism among these tasks, which we will refer to as task parallelism. Figure 15.10 illustrates such an opportunity in the vector addition example.

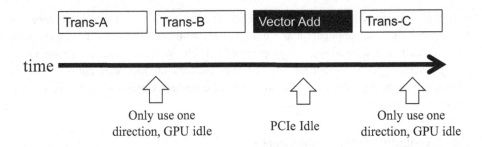

Figure 15.10: Sequential execution of CUDA tasks in the vector addition example.

Figure 15.10 shows the execution timing of the vector addition host code in Figure 15.5 and kernel code in Figure 15.6. The data copies are referred to as Trans-A (standing for "transfer A", copying vector A from host to device), Trans-B, Vector Add (execution of vecAddkernel()), and Trans-C (copying vector C from device to host). All tasks are done sequentially. Trans-B needs to wait for Trans-A to complete in order to have access to the system bus (PCIe). Vector Add needs to wait for both Trans-A and Trans-B for its input data. Trans-C needs to wait for Vector Add for its input data. Thus, the execution time of the program is the sum of execution time of four tasks.

Furthermore, the resources are poorly utilized. During Trans-A, the kernel execution resources are idle. During Vector Add, the PCIe system bus is idle. A more subtle form of resource underutilization also exists. The PCIe bus can transfer data in both directions. During Trans-A and Trans-B, only the direction from host to device is utilized. During Trans-C, only the direction from device to host is utilized. In both cases, only half the transfer bandwidth capacity of the PCIe bus is utilized.

Much better execution timing for vector addition can be achieved by converting some data parallelism into task parallelism. We observe that the computation of all elements in C can be done in parallel. Therefore, we can divide the input and output vectors into segments. An ideal case scenario for overlap is shown in Figure 15.11. We partition vector A into A.0, A.1, A.2, A.3, and so on. Vectors B and C are divided the same way. The data copying and vector addition can then be performed on a segment-by-segment basis.

During the first time period in Figure 15.11, we first perform Trans-A.0 and Trans-B.0. Since these are smaller sections of A and B, the data copy will take lesser time than that for the whole input vectors. As soon as we complete the data transfer for A.0 and B.0, we can perform kernel execution on A.0 and B.0 to generate C.0. This is shown as the second time period in Figure 15.11. Meanwhile, we can begin to transfer A.1 and B.1. This arrangement overlaps the data transfer for A.1 and B.1 with the kernel execution for

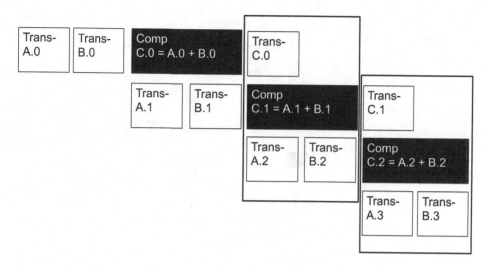

Figure 15.11: Ideal execution timing of vector addition.

A.0 and B.0 during the second time period.

During the third time period, we can begin to transfer A.2 and B.2 from the host to device, perform kernel execution on A.1 and B.1, and transfer C.0 from device to host. Notice that all three major types of resources—the PCIe link from host to device, the kernel execution resources, and the PCIe link from device to host—are utilized from the third time period on. For long vectors, the total execution time of the program will be close to the time of the longest of the three original activities: copying input vectors from host to device, kernel execution, and copying output vector from device to host. Of course, some extra time is needed to ramp up and ramp down the fully overlapped execution. The reader may recognize the similarity of the execution timing to software pipelining techniques commonly done for executing long loops in processors that support a high level of instruction-level parallelism.

The main mechanism for exploiting task parallelism in a CUDA application is CUDA streams. When a CUDA host code program needs to perform data transfer or kernel launch, it can specify a stream, as illustrated in Figure 15.12. All tasks in the same stream are executed in order: a task in a stream can start execution only if all previous tasks in the stream have finished execution. For any two tasks to execute in parallel, they must belong to different streams.

Figure 15.13 shows a vector addition host code that uses two CUDA streams to exploit task parallelism. Line 1 declares the two CUDA stream pointers, stream0 and stream1, with a predefined type, `cudaStream_t`. Line 2 and Line 3 call the CUDA function,

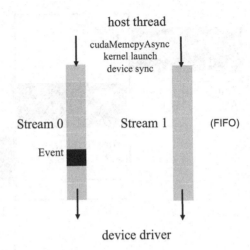

Figure 15.12: Exploiting task parallelism with CUDA streams.

```
1  cudaStream_t stream0, stream1;
2  cudaStreamCreate(&stream0);
3  cudaStreamCreate(&stream1);
4  float *h_A, *h_B, *h_C;
5  cudaHostAlloc((void **) &h_A, N* sizeof(float), cudaHostAllocDefault);
6  cudaHostAlloc((void **) &h_B, N* sizeof(float), cudaHostAllocDefault);
7  cudaHostAlloc((void **) &h_C, N* sizeof(float), cudaHostAllocDefault);
8  // I/O for reading A and B vectors are omitted for brevity
9  float *d_A0, *d_B0, *d_C0; // device memory for stream 0
10 float *d_A1, *d_B1, *d_C1; // device memory for stream 1
11 // cudaMalloc for d_A0, d_B0, d_C0, d_A1, d_B1, d_C1 go here
12 for (int i=0; i<n; i+=SegSize*2) {
13     cudaMemcpyAsync(d_A0, h_A+i, SegSize*sizeof(float),..,stream0);
14     cudaMemcpyAsync(d_B0, h_B+i, SegSize*sizeof(float),..,stream0);
15     cudaMemcpyAsync(d_A1, h_A+i+SegSize, SegSize*sizeof(float),..,stream1);
16     cudaMemcpyAsync(d_B1, h_B+i+SegSize, SegSize*sizeof(float),..,stream1);

18     vecAdd<<<SegSize/256, 256, 0, stream0>>>(d_A0, d_B0, ...);
19     vecAdd<<<SegSize/256, 256, 0, stream1>>>(d_A1, d_B1, ...);
20     cudaMemCpyAsync(d_C0, h_C+I; SegSize*sizeof(float),..,stream0);
21     cudaMemCpyAsync(d_C1, h_C+i+SegSize; SegSize*sizeof(float),..,stream1);
22 }
23 }
```

Figure 15.13: Vector addition host code that uses streams to exploit task parallelism.

`cudaStreamCreate()`, to create the two streams: `stream0` and `stream1`. We can then associate data transfer and kernel launch tasks to each stream.

Lines 5–7 allocate pinned (page locked) host memory for vectors A, B, and C. Note that pinned host memory must be used if we want to associate a data transfer task from host to device or from device to host, in CUDA streams. The allocation of pinned host memory can be done by using `cudaHostAlloc()` instead of the standard C `malloc()` function, when allocating a host memory object. After lines 5–7, `h_A`, `h_B`, and `h_C` can be used as source or destination in data transfers with streams.

Lines 9–10 declare two sets of pointers to device memory objects, where each will hold a segment of either an input or output vector elements. For brevity, we omitted the `cudaMalloc()` calls to allocate these device objects and assign their addresses to `d_-A0`, `d_B0`, `d_C0`, `d_A1`, `d_B1`, and `d_C1`. We need to have two sets of objects in order to sustain two-way task parallelism in the for loop that starts at line 12, which processes two segments in each iteration. This is why the loop variable `i` is incremented by twice the segment size after each iteration. Assume that `SegSize` is a variable that is initialized with the segment size somewhere else.

Lines 13–14 request that a segment of A (starting at location `h_A+i`) be copied to `d_A0` and a segment of B (starting at location `h_B+i`) to `d_B0`. Using `stream0` as their last parameter, these two tasks are inserted into the first stream. Lines 15–16 request that the next segment of A (starting at location `h_A+SegSize`) be copied to `d_A1` and the next segment of B be copied to `d_B1`. These two tasks are inserted into the second stream.

Line 18 launches `vecAddKernel()` on the segments of A and B copied in `stream0`. The additional parameter, `stream1`, in the kernel launch configuration inserts the kernel execution task into `stream1`. The kernel execution will wait for the completion of copies in lines 13–14, since they are in the same stream. It will, however, not wait for the copies in lines 15–16, since they belong to a different stream. Similarly, line 19 launches the `vecAddKernel()` on the segments of A and B copied in `stream1`. It will wait for the copies in lines 15–16 to complete.

Line 20 requests the output of `vecAddKernel()` (line 18) in `d_C0` be copied to a segment of C (starting at location `h_C+i`). This task will be in `stream0` and will wait for the kernel in line 18 to complete. Line 21 requests the output of `vecAddKernel()` (line 19) in `d_C1` be copied to the next segment of C (starting at location `h_C+i+SegSize`). This task will be in `stream1` and will wait for the kernel in line 19 to complete.

Figure 15.14 shows an approximate execution timing of the host code in Figure 15.13. During time period 0, the data copies on lines 13–14 will be executed. During this time period, the data copies on lines 15–16 will need to wait because the PCIe link is busy. During time period 1, data copies on lines 15–16 will be executed. The kernel call at line 18 will also be executed now that its predecessors in `stream0` are complete. During time

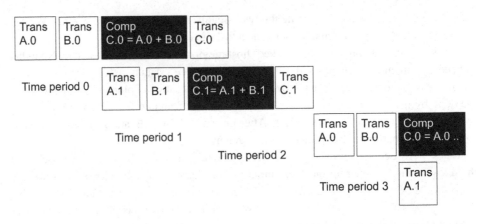

Figure 15.14: Approximate execution timing of a two-stream vector add host code.

period 2, the data copy on line 20 will be executed because its predecessors in stream0 are complete. Meanwhile, the kernel call at line 19 will also be executed now that its predecessors in stream1 are complete. This will be followed by the execution of the data copy on line 21.

The execution timing in Figure 15.14 is an improvement over that in Figure 15.10. During time period 1, the PCIe link from host to device and the kernel execution resources will both be utilized. During time period 2, the kernel execution resources and the PCIe link from device to host will both be utilized. One might expect that the Trans-A.0 and Trans-B.0 from the second iteration would start immediately after Trans-C.0 from the first iteration has completed, since the PCIe link from the the host to device is free at that point. But, in practice, that does not happen, as shown in Figure 15.14. One main reason for such behavior is that all data copy tasks are entered into a single copy engine queue in CUDA devices up to the Fermi generation. As a result, the copy of d_C1 blocks the copy of the segment of A at the next iteration. This design will, however, be improved by the Hyper-Q hardware in the Kepler generation.

Clearly, the timing is not quite as good as that shown in Figure 15.11. The timing of Figure 15.11 requires the exploration of three-way task parallelism. It can be achieved with three streams and three sets of device objects. The code that actually achieves such execution timing is much more complex. We leave it as an exercise to the interested reader.

15.11 Summary

This chapter provides a quick introduction to the CUDA programming model. CUDA extends the C language to support parallel computing. It provides a set of keywords and API functions to give programmers detailed control of the parallel execution. A CUDA program will likely have more predictable performance than its counterparts written in higher-level programming languages. It also requires the programmer to specify many of the details that are abstracted away by higher-level programming languages. The reader should refer to the CUDA Programming Guide for a comprehensive reference of all CUDA features.

Interested readers are referred to two more resources for further studies. In Kirk and Hwu's textbook of parallel programming [162], classic parallel programming code patterns are demonstrated with CUDA. Farber [105] provides a wealth of application design and development techniques for CUDA programmers.

16 OpenCL: the Open Computing Language

Tim Mattson, Intel

Successful programming models stand out by virtue of having large numbers of users as opposed to accumulating large numbers of research papers. Such models are born of necessity. A change in the computing landscape or a new application domain creates a need, and a programming model emerges to address that need. For OpenCL, that change was the emergence of heterogeneous platforms. The classic instance of a heterogeneous platform is a host CPU with an attached discrete GPU; but over time the market will support a much richer set of heterogeneous resources, including fixed-function processors, FPGAs, and multiple cores within a single many-core CPU.

Heterogeneous computing is relatively new, and consequently a great deal of confusion exists about what it is. The language we use to talk about heterogeneity and the programming associated with these systems are immature and shifting. With this chapter, I hope to diffuse that confusion by going beyond an exposition of the fundamental features of OpenCL to discuss the language we use when talking about heterogeneous computing.

16.1 The Language of Computing and OpenCL

Jargon permeates our lives. We need it. Without jargon, communication would be clogged with repetitive descriptions of recurring ideas. Jargon misused, however, breeds confusion. A statement is made and people nod their heads in agreement. All too often, however, only later do we realize that people hearing the statement may have applied different interpretations of key elements of jargon and have come away from the conversation with completely different meanings. With the children's game of "telephone" the result is comical. When decisions are made of serious import, the results can be dire.

For example, consider the word "thread." Here are a few meanings assigned to this single word:

- A lightweight, preemptable sequence of instructions with its own stack sharing the context of a process with other threads and scheduled for execution by an operating system (e.g., pthreads)

- A member of a set of nonpreemptable sequences of operations generated from a single sequence of instructions (e.g., SIMT threads)

- A generic term referring to any distinct sequence of instructions potentially executing concurrently with other threads (e.g., the informal concept of a thread)

Consequently, when the word "thread" is used, the actual meaning is left to the listener to deduce. With a tight-knit group of professionals all working within a shared context, this approach may be acceptable. For an outsider, however, the term "thread" has become almost useless. Likewise for "paradigm," "object," "commodity," "cloud" and many other terms destroyed by well-meaning computer scientists.

In this chapter, I will attempt to explain OpenCL. Taking my inspiration from the classic paper by Guy Steele, "Growing a Language" [257], I will carefully define each term before it is used. This leads to an unusual style of writing and will force us to cover material often taken as self evident. The result, however, will be a clear exposition of OpenCL. If I have done my job correctly, after a careful reading of this text no confusion will arise about what OpenCL is and how it works.

To launch this discussion properly, I also describe what we will not cover. This is not a tutorial on OpenCL. I will make no attempt to teach readers how to implement a significant application using OpenCL. Good books such as [206] accomplish that task, and to replicate the content here is of little value.

16.2   Base Definitions

I assume we share an understanding of the English language. Given the international nature of computer science, this is a tenuous assumption. But if we stick to common definitions from well-known dictionaries, we can make this work.

The *universe* holds all places, ideas, people and things. To make progress in any discussion, we must isolate a portion of the universe into a distinct unit we can work with in isolation. We call this isolated portion a *system*.

Systems can be complex. Hence we often simplify our work within a system by creating abstractions of the system. An *abstraction* is a mental construction that makes some features of the system explicit while hiding others. A specific instance of an abstraction is called a *model*.

People are model builders. Scientists who study how people think (*cognitive scientists*) describe the process whereby people understand systems and how they interact as one of building a set of models. We do this almost automatically and put great stock in the models we build.

Hence, it is not an overstatement to assert that to understand a system is to hold in your mind a set of models that provide a sufficiently useful abstraction of the system. This is what we will do for OpenCL.

16.3   Computers, Programming, and Heterogeneity

People have problems they want to solve. An *application* is a system that solves a problem of interest to one or more people we call "users." An important type of problem can be defined in terms of information input and later output from a system. When a well-defined output exists for any given input, we call the problem *computable*.

A *computer* is a machine designed to solve computable problems. For the vast majority of computers people are likely to use, the transformation from a particular set of input information to a set of output information is carried out according to a set of distinct instructions called a *program*. Except for the most trivial programs, a program must store intermediate representations of the problem as it converts input into output. This is stored as a collection of variables called the computer's *memory*. A distinct set of variables in memory at any given time, coupled with a special variable that keeps track of the next instruction to execute (the "instruction pointer"), defines an "agent" that manages how a program executes on a particular computer system. Hence an application is a program (the *software*) on a computer (the *hardware*) executed by an agent that solves a problem of interest to a user.

How we distinguish computers from each other is by their *instruction sets*, that is, the full set of instructions available for constructing programs. An instruction set is expressed in terms closely related to the physical implementation of the computer (the hardware). These instructions are not convenient for a human programmer to use. Hence, most programmers work with an abstraction of the computer's instructions called a *programming model*. An implementation of a programming model is called a *programming language*, and the human-readable text of a program is called the program's *source code*. The source code is transformed into the instructions from the computer's instruction set by a special program called a *compiler*.

A computer is a system that computes. In most cases, a computer is composed of smaller machines that compute. To avoid confusion, we often call these internal-computers *processors*. When these processors expose different instruction sets to the person creating a program (i.e., the programmer), we say that the computer is *heterogeneous*.

Heterogeneous computers are common. People interact with their computers through a visual representation of information presented on a display device. To generate these visual representations, computers include *graphics processing units* (GPUs). The basic transformation of input into output is carried out by a general-purpose processor called the *central processing unit* (CPU) while graphics output is handled by the GPU. The CPU and GPU use different instruction sets so the combination of the two is an example of a heterogeneous computer.

Programmers found these early heterogeneous computers reasonable to work with since the work of writing programs for the GPU was completely separate from writing programs for the CPU. The GPU programmer created a sequence of distinct program fragments called functions. A function has a set of input variables, a set of internal variables, and a set of output variables. The input and output variables together with the name of the function define an interface to the function. A collection of functions that are logically related and used to help a programmer solve a particular problem is called a library. The function names within the library plus their interfaces defines an application program interface (API). The GPU was exposed by an API specific to the jobs assigned to the GPU; hence, most programs just worried about programming the CPU and worked with the GPU only through its API (such as OpenGL for graphics).

The GPU is a specialized processor designed for the types of jobs found in graphics. Around the year 2000, programmers started experimenting with using the GPU to do more than graphics. They moved computing from the general-purpose processor (the CPU) to the more specialized GPU. In 2002, a term was coined for this type of programming. It was called GPGPU programming or general-purpose GPU programming. Early GPGPU programming was challenging, and frankly to many programmers GPGPU programming was considered an academic exercise or a stunt unworthy of serious consideration. Why? Because the GPGPU programmer had to work with programming languages designed for graphics. These languages were poorly suited to the needs of full applications, and hence GPGPU programming was largely ignored.

16.4   The Birth of OpenCL

This situation changed in 2006 when a company known for its work on GPUs released a new system for GPGPU programming called CUDA (see Chapter 15). With CUDA, a programmer could write a program for the GPU using a programming language similar to the languages used on a CPU. Thus, programmers interested in GPGPU programming did not need to learn specialized programming languages for graphics. With the release of CUDA, many programmers interested in applications that depended on high performance (high-performance computing) started to experiment with GPGPU programming. It was no longer viewed as a stunt.

CUDA made GPGPU programming a real possibility for many programmers. CUDA has one overarching problem, however. It is controlled by a single company (NVIDIA, a leading vendor of GPU technology). This can be an issue if users need to run their application on a different vendor's hardware. Or given that application software is used over a span of time much greater than the lifetime of a single computer, programmers needs to protect their software investments by writing software that can use both current and future hardware. In other words, to support a vibrant software industry, programmers need a system for creating application software that is portable between all important current and future hardware products. We call such a programming system an industry standard.

OpenCL is an industry standard for programming heterogeneous systems. OpenCL is more than a programming language. It includes an API to discover which processors make up the heterogeneous hardware, an API to select a subset of the hardware to be used for an application, an API to build programs to run on the various processors within the heterogeneous system, and an API to coordinate all the work within the heterogeneous computer as the application runs. We call a set of tools plus APIs for constructing software, a framework. OpenCL is an industry-standard framework for programming heterogeneous systems.

When designing frameworks for programming any type of computer system, the goals must be clearly understood if the resulting framework is to be well suited to its intended purpose. For OpenCL we made a deliberate decision to expose all the components that make up the heterogeneous system. The thinking was that in building an industry for heterogeneous systems, we ultimately need high-level frameworks to make the job faced by the typical application programmer easier, but we also need the low-level frameworks that give full control of every detail of the system. Where should one start? High level and abstract, or low level and detailed?

We chose to start with the low-level option. By creating a common low-level framework, we would enable a large number of framework developers to support higher-level abstractions for heterogeneous computing. The most effective high-level frameworks are tuned to the needs of a specific application domain; hence one high-level framework by design cannot meet the needs of every application domain. We, therefore, believed that to have the most impact in the minimum time, we needed a low-level framework for heterogeneous programming. It is still abstract, but the abstraction is focused on exposing the details of the hardware; in other words, the OpenCL framework presents programmers with a hardware abstraction layer.

OpenCL 1.0 was released in December 2008. Processors designed to effectively utilize large numbers of cores (so-called many-core processors) are evolving rapidly. Hence, we need to update OpenCL regularly to keep up. The goal is to release a new version of OpenCL approximately every 18 months. Currently, we have released OpenCL 1.0 (2008), OpenCL 1.1 (mid 2009), OpenCL 1.2 (late 2011), and OpenCL 2.0 (late 2013). OpenCL 2.0 was a major update of OpenCL, while 1.0 to 1.2 were based on the same core family of abstractions. We are currently working on OpenCL 2.1, which had a provisional release of its specification in March 2015.

16.5   OpenCL's Core Models

OpenCL is a framework for writing programs for heterogeneous systems. The framework defines resources and a set of interfaces that programmers use to construct an application. For example, as we will see shortly, an OpenCL programmer submits to a queue commands that are later executed on the OpenCL platform. The queue is an object or "an instance of a resource" within OpenCL. OpenCL also defines hardware resources. A common example of a hardware resource is a particular processor within a heterogeneous computer.

To help users understand the resources provided by the OpenCL framework and how they are used, the OpenCL specification defined a hierarchy of models.

- **Platform model:** defines the platform, that is, the heterogeneous system available for a computation and managed by the OpenCL framework.

- **Execution model:** defines how a computation is launched and makes progress (i.e., executes) on the platform

- **Memory model:** defines the disjoint set or regions into which the computer's memory, which is a collection of variables, is gathered. The model also defines how they interact with the execution model.

- **Programming model:** defines the fundamental abstractions used to map an algorithm onto source code.

To understand OpenCL, one needs to understand each of these models and how they interact with each other. For pedagogical reasons, we will present them sequentially in the order presented above. We advise, however, reading through these brief sections twice: once to understand the conceptual foundation of each model and a second time to appreciate how the models interact.

16.5.1 Platform Model

In general, a platform is a specific combination of hardware and software that defines a type of computer. Our goal with OpenCL requires that we be more specific with the concept of a platform. In particular, if a programmer wants to write a single program that runs on multiple OpenCL implementations, an abstraction of the platform is needed that can map onto any computer that supports OpenCL.

The OpenCL platform model is represented pictorially in Figure 16.1. An OpenCL platform consists of a single *host* resource. This is a general-purpose computer, by which we mean it can interact with a user, a file system, and the other functions we come to expect from a personal computer. Connected to the host are one or more OpenCL *devices*. An OpenCL device can be a CPU, a GPU, an FPGA, or a specialized processor. For OpenCL, the device is decomposed into one or more *compute units* each of which is composed of one or more *processing elements*. The reason for this division will become clear later when we describe the execution model.

At the highest level, the platform model defines memory that is resident on the host (*host memory*) and memory that is resident on the device (*device memory*). We will consider the structure of this memory in more detail later.

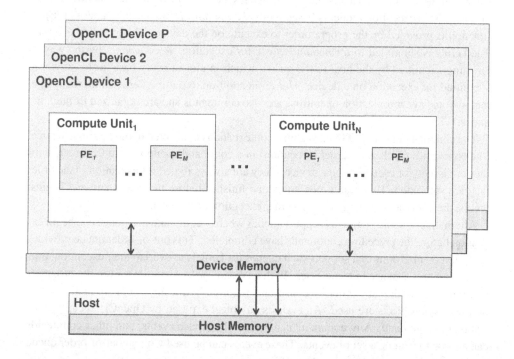

Figure 16.1: OpenCL platform model with a host and one or more devices. Each compute device has one or more compute units, which are composed of one or more processing elements.

16.5.2   Execution Model

A program starts much as any other program on the host. Inside the program, the platform is defined through calls to functions from the Platform API within OpenCL. This API provides functions to query the system concerning the number and types of devices as well as their features.

A program then defines a *context*. The context is a key concept in OpenCL. Everything that happens in an OpenCL program happens within a context. It is the platform, devices, memory space, and anything else required to define the environment within which the program executes.

The computation of most interest to the OpenCL programmer occurs on the device. The execution model for a device is the key to using OpenCL to exploit the concurrency in a problem. This execution model is based on the *kernel parallelism* design pattern [186]. A function is provided by the programmer to execute on the device. This is called a *kernel*. The kernel is submitted to a *command queue* for execution. A *command*, by the way, is anything submitted by the host to the queue, which in almost every case means anything submitted for execution on a device. Hence, in addition to putting kernels into the queue, memory and synchronization operations are also commands and are organized through the queue.

The command queue is defined within a context and is connected to only a single device. The commands (such as a kernel invocation) in a command queue wait in the queue until they are issued for execution on a device. They are always issued for execution in the order they are submitted. By default, one command finishes before the next command begins; that is, the command queue assures in-order execution of commands.

Alternatively, some platforms support queues where a command in a queue can begin execution before the preceding commands have completed. This out-of-order queue provides an option on platforms that support such queues for kernels to overlap their execution, thus improving performance in some cases. With an out-of-order queue, however, the programmer must ensure that any ordering constraints required by the algorithm are met. For this purpose event objects are used. An *event* is an object exposed by OpenCL to capture the status of a command. Any command can optionally expose events, and other commands can choose to wait on a set of events. These events can be used with an out-of-order queue to safely exploit concurrent execution of kernels.

Returning to our consideration of how an individual kernel executes within OpenCL, when a kernel is submitted to a queue (i.e., it is enqueued), an *NDRange* is specified. The kernel executes over an NDRange. The term "NDRange" at first may seem a bit strange, but if we take the term apart it will be clear. OpenCL, based on input from the programmer, creates an N-dimensional index space (*ND*) where in each dimension the indices range from 0 to some programmer input limit. OpenCL currently supports one-, two-, or three-dimensional index spaces. An instance of the kernel function executes on the processing elements of the device for each point in the index space. This instance is called a *work-item*. A work-item runs on a single processing element and runs to completion without interruption.

For example, consider the multiplication of two square matrices. The number of rows equals the number of columns, which defines the order of the matrices. In this case the order is equal to the value of the variable *Dim*. In Figure 16.2 we show a traditional

```
// Basic nested loop form to multiple two square (Dim x Dim) matrices
void mat_mul(int Dim, float *A, float *B, float *C)
{
    int i, j, k;
    for (i=0; i<Dim; i++){
        for (j=0; j<Dim; j++){
            for (k=0; k<Dim; k++) {
                C[i*Dim+j] += A[i*Dim+k] * B[k*Dim+j];
            }
        }
    }
}


// Simple Kernel form to multiple two square (Dim x Dim) matrices
// executing of a (Dim x Dim) 2 dimensional ND range.

__kernel void mat_mul(
                        const int Dim,
                        __global float *A,
                        __global float *B,
                        __global float *C)
{
    int i, j, k;
    i = get_global_id(0);
    j = get_global_id(1);
    for (k=0; k<Dim; k++){        // C(i,j) = sum(over k) A(i,k) * B(k,j)
        C[i*Dim+j] += A[i*Dim+k] * B[k*Dim+j];
    }
}
```

Figure 16.2: Matrix multiplication of order Dim matrices ... the triply nested loop version followed by the same function expressed as an OpenCL kernel.

representation of this problem in terms of nested loops. The outermost loops run over the dimensions of the output matrix, C, while the innermost loop computes the sum of the product of consecutive elements of a row of the A matrix with a column of the B matrix (a dot product). With kernel parallelism, we write a single kernel, an instance of which executes for each point in an index space defined by the outer two loops. The code for the kernel is also shown in Figure 16.2. As with any instance of kernel parallelism, the work-item begins by finding its place in the index space. It uses that information to define the computation it will perform, in this case the dot product to generate one element of the output matrix.

This defines the basic pattern of execution in kernel parallelism. The OpenCL execution model, however, goes further and defines how the work-items are organized for execution on a device. The number of work-items is generally much larger than the total number of processing elements provided by the OpenCL platform. This is done so that, while any given work-item may be unable to execute while waiting for variables to be provided from memory, other work-items are (one hopes) ready and able to execute. These excess work-items create excess capacity for doing useful work; thus, the overall limitation on how much computing can be done in a given interval of time is limited by the rate at which variables from memory can be streamed onto the device. A particular OpenCL device has a policy defined internal to the device to decide when work-items are actually executed on the system. This is called the schedule for executing the work-items. We refer to the "granularity" of a scheduling policy as the number of work-items that actually execute at the same time.

Work-items corresponding to a single kernel are organized into groups called *work-groups*. All the work-items in a work-group "logically" execute at the same time, where we use the term logically to refer to the fact that the system behaves "as if" the work-items execute at the same time even if "physically" the execution policy executes them in different sized blocks. The work-group has the same number of dimensions as the NDRange. The size of the work-group in each dimension must evenly divide the size of the NDRange. So an NDRange of 1,024 by 1,024 could be divided into a 32 by 32 grid of 32 x 32 work-groups or a 4 by 4 grid of 256 x 256 work-groups, and so forth. The common theme is that the work-groups are all of the same size, have dimension equal to the dimension of the NDRange, and in each dimension must evenly divide the corresponding size of the NDRange.

One can think of the execution of work-items mapping onto the platform in the following way: a kernel executes on a device, work-groups on a compute unit, and work-items on a processing element. The programmer through the host API can manage the sizes or NDRanges and work-groups. It is important to get the sizes right based on the needs of the target hardware. In particular, two factors must be considered.

First, the performance from most devices comes from high-throughput computing. This type of computing emphasizes completion of a large number of work-items in a period of time rather than completing an individual work-item in less time. The idea is to have so many work-items to execute that there is likely to be useful work to complete while carrying out other time-consuming activities (such as moving variables from memory onto and from a device). Hence, one wants the number of work groups in most cases to be much larger than the number of compute units.

Second, there exists s finer granularity of scheduling that is not directly exposed by OpenCL. Work-items are scheduled in small blocks that execute at the same time (i.e., we say they execute concurrently) corresponding to the natural SIMD width of the processing element. The term "SIMD width" is a bit confusing as it is not directly part of the OpenCL standard. It is an important part of every implementation of OpenCL, however, and is something a programmer must understand and take advantage of. Let us consider it in some detail.

The term SIMD comes from Flynn's taxonomy of parallel architectures [108]. It is an acronym that stands for single instruction, multiple data. It refers to a parallel architecture with multiple processing elements, driven by a single instruction unit, each operating together in "lock step" but operating on its own data. A classic example of a SIMD model is the vector units that have been included on CPUs since the late 1990s. One vector instruction causes an operation to occur on each element of the vectors associated with the vector unit. For example, with the SSE 4.2 vector instructions, each vector instruction is applied to four floating-point numbers; that is, the SIMD width of the vector unit is 4 over floats. On GPUs the analogous number is much larger; current 32 (the size of a "warp") on NVIDIA GPUs and 64 (the size of a wavefront) on AMD GPUs. This is the fundamental granularity limit in systems supporting OpenCL. If the work-items do not break down into blocks that match the SIMD width, the performance will suffer because the scheduler may need to execute incomplete blocks of work-items that are less than the full width, therefore leaving some of the processing elements idle. The result is that the number of work-items in a work-group must be evenly divisible by the SIMD width of the device.

Before leaving our discussion of the execution model, we emphasize that we are describing an abstraction of the actual hardware. Processing elements and compute units, even devices, may be virtual devices, by which we mean that the framework presents them as distinct resources but they do not map directly onto corresponding hardware elements. For example, on a multicore CPU implementation of OpenCL, the computer is designed to support multiple threads per core, with the threads swapping in and out of an active state based on their load. It may be natural to present more compute devices or "virtual cores" to the OpenCL programmer. Likewise on a CPU core with a vector unit, the number of processing elements depends on the data types used in the kernel. For example, with SSE 4.2 and kernels acting over doubles, a vector unit provides two virtual processing elements; but with float data the same hardware would provide four virtual processing elements. This is the essence of a good execution model. The model makes the key features of a system explicit and hides low-level details. And in doing so, these abstract representations allow a single abstraction to map onto many different systems.

16.5.3 Memory Model

A memory model is an abstraction that constrains the values of variables in memory that can be seen by multiple agents within a system. We need to understand three key groups of operations: reading a variable, writing a variable, and synchronization. To synchronize a set of agents is to bring them to a known state at distinct point in their execution. The most famous synchronization operation is a barrier. In a barrier, the agents involved in the barrier must all arrive at the barrier before any of them can continue executing instructions from the program that occur after the barrier. A closely related operation is a fence. This defines a point in a program where all reads and writes are committed to memory and made available to other agents before the agent invoking the fence continues. We have one more synchronization operation to consider. This is an operation where a variable is read, written, or changed completely and without interruption. This is called an atomic operation.

A memory model, therefore, specifies the rules that a programmer can depend on, to understand reads, writes, and synchronization operations of a set of variables when operated upon by one or more agents. This model must be complete, by which we mean it must apply to each distinct region of memory existing in the system.

OpenCL memory is organized into regions. A memory region defines a distinct range of addresses to reference a set of variables. These are logical entities; so while they may overlap in physical memory, OpenCL treats them as distinct. In OpenCL we define the following memory regions.

- **Host memory**: the memory available to and managed by the host. OpenCL uses the memory provided by the native host platform and hence does not define a detailed memory model for the host memory except where it pertains to OpenCL.

- **Global memory**: a memory region that is globally accessible to all work-items executing within a context. It is visible to the host through functions within the OpenCL API to read and write the memory or to map portions of global memory onto the host memory.

- **Constant memory**: a memory region that is globally accessible on the device that can be read only during the execution of a kernel. This is typically considered a part of the global memory. This memory is allocated and initialized by the host.

- **Local memory**: a memory region associated with a compute unit and visible to the work-items within a work-group

- **Private memory**: a memory region associated with a processing element and visible only within a work-item.

These memory regions, and how they relate to the platform model, are summarized in Figure 16.3.

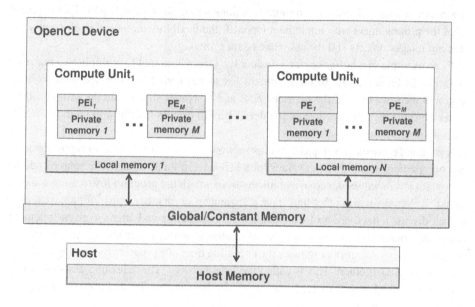

Figure 16.3: Memory regions defined by OpenCL and their relationship to the platform model.

The memory regions and the set of rules for safely working with variables within these memory regions are defined within a context. While a single OpenCL program can contain multiple OpenCL contexts, the rules of the OpenCL memory model are defined with respect to memory within a single context. We will start from the host and work inward toward the private memory within a processing element.

On the host and within a context, OpenCL defines memory objects that point to a block of one or more variables that resides in global memory. This is an example of a type of object used in computing called a handle. This means that the object contains information to access the contents pointed to through the handle rather than the contents themselves. This gives an implementation of OpenCL the flexibility to implement the system as needed to make it run efficiently on a particular computer system.

OpenCL defines two types of memory objects: a *buffer object* and an *image object*. The buffer object defines a collection of one or more variables that can be accessed inside a work-item through a pointer. An image object is used to support graphics applications. As with a buffer object, an image object defines a set of variables but those within an image object can be manipulated only through functions within the OpenCL API. This approach gives the programmers who implement OpenCL the flexibility they need to efficiently implement images objects and the associated data formats.

As an example of a buffer object, consider the OpenCL kernel to multiply two matrices, as shown in Figure 16.2. In the argument list to the kernel function are three pointers to global memory to hold the matrices A, B and C. Notice that inside the program these buffer objects are treated as normal pointers. We will discuss later how to interact with the memory objects on the host side.

A program consists of a sequence of instructions that act on variables to support generation of a particular set of output values for a given set of input values. The source code for a program is a serial sequence of statements from which the program instructions are generated. By serial we mean that they have a distinct order; in other words, for any statement we can discuss a fixed order of statements that occur before and after the given statement. Hence the source code defines an order of reads and writes to variables. We call this the "program order." A compiler reduces the execution time of a program by moving reads and writes around each other. This is called the "code order." The scheduler associated with a device may further reorder reads and writes leading to an order that appears in memory that could be different than the "code order." This called the "commit order." As long as the commit order is indistinguishable by an observer from the program order, the program is said to execute correctly on the system. Compilers are good at these sorts of reordering operations when a single agent is involved. When multiple agents are executing programs at the same time, however, and these programs are reading and writing variables into a single memory region, the reads and writes may collide, leading to a program whose output changes depending on the low-level details of how an agent is scheduled for execution. This is called a "race," and the specific operations causing the conflicting reads and writes are called a "race condition." The rules that a programmer must follow to prevent races are called the memory consistency model for a system.

With this basic vocabulary defined, we can now explore the rules for working with the memory regions from the host and multiple work-items.

- **private**: reads and writes to variables within a work-item's private memory are visible only to that work-item. Other work-items cannot access these variables. Hence, they appear to the work-item to occur in program order.

- **local**: reads and writes are accessible to the work-items within a single work-group but not to work-items from other work-groups. The reads and writes to a variable in local memory will appear in program order to a single work-item. Reads and writes to a single variable in local memory for multiple work-items in the same work-group occur in any order between synchronization events such as work-group barriers or work-group fences.

- **global**: reads and writes to memory objects in global memory are accessible to all work-items executing a given kernel. Direct synchronization between work-items running in different work-groups is not provided by OpenCL; therefore the order of updates to a single global variable is undefined during the execution of a kernel. Consistency for memory object in global memory is defined at kernel boundaries. OpenCL, however, does define optional atomic operations on global memory. A programmer can use these atomic operations to constrain orders of instructions across work-items in different work groups. Doing so can be complicated, however, and will not be discussed in more detail here.

The memory model in OpenCL is a weak memory model by which we mean it does not assure that every work-item sees updates to global or local memory variables in the same order and that order is not necessarily the program order. Consistency is enforced in local memory at barriers and fences. Consistency is enforced at the level of global memory at the boundaries between kernels.

16.5.4   Programming Models

An execution model defines an abstract representation of a computer system that a programmer can use to understand how a body of software will map onto a class of computer systems. A programming model is an abstract representation of an execution model tuned to the needs of a class of algorithms. In other words, it defines how a family of related algorithms map onto an execution model and from there onto a particular computer system.

OpenCL in principle supports two basic programming models.

- **Data parallelism**: a single sequence of instructions is applied concurrently to each element of a data structure.

- **Task parallelism**: A task is a sequence of instructions and the data required by those instructions. In task parallelism, multiple tasks are run concurrently.

Data parallelism is a natural fit to OpenCL. Consider the matrix multiplication example in Figure 16.2. The data fundamental to the problem (the three matrices) are aligned with the index space created when the kernels are enqueued. This is a straightforward data parallel algorithm with a dot product carried out for each point in the index space.

OpenCL goes well beyond data parallelism. A kernel can contain conditional logic to change the set of instructions that a work-item executes. So, while every work-item executes the same kernel in a data parallel style, the actual stream of instructions executed by each work-item can vary considerably. This is the well-known single program, multiple data design pattern.

Task parallelism in OpenCL is implemented by launching kernels that contain only a single work-item, thereby connecting the concept of a single task to a kernel. On an in-order queue, task parallelism is not parallel at all, since the kernels (i.e., the tasks) will execute in a serial order. If the tasks are enqueued to separate queues, or if they are enqueued to a queue with out-of-order execution enabled, then the task parallelism approach exposes concurrency that can be exploited in parallel. In both these cases, however, event objects must be used to enforce any ordering constraints between tasks. Events and their use go well beyond the scope of this quick introduction to OpenCL. Events are described in detail in [206].

16.6   OpenCL Host Programs: Vector Addition Example

The OpenCL programmer writes two programs: one that runs on the host (the host program) and one that runs on the device (the kernel). In this section, we explain the APIs in OpenCL used to write a host program using the elementwise addition of two vectors a and b to produce a new vector c, as our running example. The kernel for this example is simple. It is written by using the OpenCL C kernel programming language, which is based on a subset of the ISO/IEC 9899:1999 C language (commonly referred to as C99) with features that are difficult for a GPU to implement removed (such as recursion, bit fields, and function pointers).

Figure 16.4 shows the code for the vector addition kernel. The kernel is a void function marked with the `kernel` qualifier. The arguments are marked as belonging to one of several memory regions, as follows:

- `global`: This memory region is visible to all work-groups associated with a kernel's execution.

- `local`: This memory region is on the device and is shared between the work-items in a single work-group. We provide an example of the local address space later.

- `private`: This memory region is private to each work-item. Variables declared with standard C syntax inside a kernel are in this address space.

- `constant`: This is a part of the global memory region used to hold read-only variables.

```
//
// kernel: vadd
//
// input: a and b float vectors of length count
// output: c float vector of length count holding the sum a + b
//
const char *KernelSource = "\n" \
"__kernel void vadd(\n" \
"    __global float* a, \n" \
"    __global float* b, \n" \
"    __global float* c, \n" \
"    const unsigned int count) \n" \
"{    \n" \
"    int i = get_global_id(0);    \n" \
"    if(i < count)  \n" \
"        c[i] = a[i] + b[i];    \n" \
"}  \n" \
"\n";
```

Figure 16.4: Program for the vector addition kernel (include file vadd.cl).

For the kernel in Figure 16.4, we declare three global arrays and one simple value for the length of the arrays. We launch a work-item for each point in the index space. A kernel discovers its place within the computation by requesting its global ID:

```
int i = get_global_id(0);
```

The argument to this function identifies one of the dimensions of the index space; valid values range from 0 to the dimensionality of the underlying index space minus 1.

Note that the kernel is represented as a string. This is not the only option with kernels in OpenCL, but it is the easiest approach when getting started with OpenCL. For the duration of this chapter, we will omit the string assignment, quotes, and newline characters used when assigning a kernel to a string.

Although the kernel program for this case is simple, the host program is considerably more involved. The host program is where the programmer discovers the available resources of the heterogeneous platform, manages memory, prepares the kernels for execution, submits the kernel objects to the command-queue, and collects results. Programmers create the host program written in C (or C++) using the platform and runtime APIs defined in the OpenCL specification. These are large and complex APIs. In most cases, however, only a small subset of the full APIs are used, and these are used in similar ways from one program to the next. Therefore, one need not be alarmed by the complexity of the host program. In most cases the code is reused from one project to the next.

A host program for our vector addition kernel is shown in Figures 16.5 and 16.6. The program will launch a kernel to compute the sum of two vectors (a and b), each with LENGTH elements, to produce a third vector (c). This particular host program was developed for the OpenCL framework included in OS X version 10.6.2 (Snow Leopard). The host program begins with an include file that defines the APIs used with OpenCL.

```
#ifdef APPLE
#include <OpenCL/opencl.h>
#else
#include "CL/cl.h"
#endif
```

Notice that Apple placed the include file in a nonstandard location. A few lines later, we input the kernel as a string, using another include file.

```
// input kernel as a string assigned to "KernelSource"
#include "vadd.cl"
```

After defining the variables used on the host, including the two arrays for the input data (a_data and b_data) and the result array (c_res), the program declares the objects used to manage the OpenCL computation. We fill the arrays of data and then start the process of discovering the OpenCL platform.

```
// use whichever platform is the "first" one
    cl_uint numPlatforms;
    cl_platform_id firstPlatformId;

    err = clGetPlatformIDs(1, &firstPlatformId, &numPlatforms);

    // Connect to a GPU (use CL_DEVICE_TYPE_CPU for a CPU)
    err = clGetDeviceIDs(firstPlatformId,  CL_DEVICE_TYPE_GPU, 1,
                         &device_id, NULL);
```

These commands query the platform and request a device ID for a GPU within the platform. The variable device_id can now be used as a handle to reference the GPU within the platform. (Note: For simplicity, error handling has been omitted here and elsewhere in the examples.) With the GPU identified, we can create the context and the command-queue:

```
... <usual Unix includes >...
#ifdef APPLE
#include <OpenCL/opencl.h>
#else
#include "CL/cl.h"
#endif
#define TOL      (0.001)     // tolerance used in floating point comparisons
#define LENGTH (1024)        // length of vectors a, b, and c
// input kernel as a string assigned to "KernelSource"
#include "vadd.cl"

int main(int argc, char** argv)  {
    int             err;             // error code returned from OpenCL calls
    float           a_data[LENGTH];  // a vector
    float           b_data[LENGTH];  // b vector
    float           c_res [LENGTH];  // c vector (a+b) from the compute device
    unsigned int    correct;         // number of correct results
    size_t global;                   // global domain size
    size_t local;                    // local   domain (work-group) size
    cl_device_id      device_id;     // compute device id
    cl_context        context;       // compute context
    cl_command_queue  commands;      // compute command-queue
    cl_program        program;       // compute program
    cl_kernel         kernel;        // compute kernel
    cl_mem a_in;                     // device memory for the input  a vector
    cl_mem b_in;                     // device memory for the input b vector
    cl_mem c_out;                    // device memory for the output c vector
    int size;                        // buffer  size
    // Fill vectors a and b with random float values
    int i = 0;
    unsigned int count = LENGTH;
    for(i = 0; i < count; i++){
        a_data[i] = rand() / (float)RAND_MAX;
        b_data[i] = rand() / (float)RAND_MAX;
    }
    // use whichever platform is the "first" one
    cl_uint numPlatforms;
    cl_platform_id firstPlatformId;
    err = clGetPlatformIDs(1, &firstPlatformId, &numPlatforms);
    // Connect to a GPU (use CL_DEVICE_TYPE_CPU for a CPU)
    err = clGetDeviceIDs(firstPlatformId,  CL_DEVICE_TYPE_GPU, 1,
                        &device_id, NULL);
    // Create a compute context
    context = clCreateContext(firstPlatformId, 1, &device_id, NULL,
                        NULL, &err);
    // Create a command-queue
    commands = clCreateCommandQueue(context, device_id, 0, &err);
    // Create the compute program from the source buffer
    program = clCreateProgramWithSource(context, 1,
        (const char **) & KernelSource, NULL, &err);
```

Figure 16.5: Complete host program for the vector addition kernel (elementwise addition of two vectors ($c = a + b$), part 1 (continued in Figure 16.6).

```
// Build the program ... display error messages if unsuccessful
err = clBuildProgram(program, 0, NULL, NULL, NULL, NULL);
if (err != CL_SUCCESS)
{   size_t len;      char buffer[2048];
    printf("Error: Failed to build program executable!\n");
    clGetProgramBuildInfo(program, device_id, CL_PROGRAM_BUILD_LOG,
                  sizeof(buffer), buffer, &len);
    printf("%s\n", buffer);
    exit(1);
}
// Create the compute kernel from the program
kernel = clCreateKernel(program, "vadd", &err);
// Create the input (a, b) and output (c) arrays in device memory
size  = sizeof(float) * count;
a_in  = clCreateBuffer(context,  CL_MEM_READ_ONLY, NULL, NULL);
b_in  = clCreateBuffer(context,  CL_MEM_READ_ONLY, NULL, NULL);
c_out = clCreateBuffer(context,  CL_MEM_WRITE_ONLY, NULL, NULL);
// Write a and b vectors into compute device memory
err = clEnqueueWriteBuffer(commands, a_in, CL_TRUE, 0,
                  sizeof(float) * count, a_data, 0, NULL, NULL);
err = clEnqueueWriteBuffer(commands, b_in, CL_TRUE, 0,
                  sizeof(float) * count, b_data, 0, NULL, NULL);
// Set the arguments to our compute kernel
err = clSetKernelArg(kernel, 0, sizeof(cl_mem), &a_in);
err |= clSetKernelArg(kernel, 1, sizeof(cl_mem), &b_in);
err |= clSetKernelArg(kernel, 2, sizeof(cl_mem), &c_out);
err |= clSetKernelArg(kernel, 3, sizeof(unsigned int), &count);
// Set local to max work-group size for executing on this device
err = clGetKernelWorkGroupInfo(kernel, device_id,
          CL_KERNEL_WORK_GROUP_SIZE, sizeof(local), &local, NULL);
// Execute the kernel over the entire range of our 1d input data set
global = count;
err = clEnqueueNDRangeKernel(commands, kernel, 1, NULL,
                  &global, &local, 0, NULL, NULL);
// Wait for the commands to complete before reading back results
clFinish(commands);
// Read back the results (c_res) from the compute device
err = clEnqueueReadBuffer(commands, c_out, CL_TRUE, 0,
                  sizeof(float) * count, c_res, 0, NULL, NULL );
// Test the results
correct = 0;      float tmp;
for(i = 0; i < count; i++) {
    tmp = a_data[i] + b_data[i] - c_res[i];
    if(tmp*tmp < TOL*TOL)  correct++;
}
// cleanup and shutdown
clReleaseMemObject(a_in);          clReleaseMemObject(b_in);
clReleaseMemObject(c_out);         clReleaseProgram(program);
clReleaseKernel(kernel);           clReleaseCommandQueue(commands);
clReleaseContext(context);
return 0;
}
```

Figure 16.6: Complete host program for the vector addition kernel (elementwise addition of two vectors ($c = a + b$), part 2 (continued from Figure 16.5).

```
commands = clCreateCommandQueue(context, device_id, 0, &err);
```

The context is an important concept in OpenCL. It is the memory, programs, kernels, and anything else needed to execute commands on a compute device. This is provided as an explicit concept within OpenCL since it is possible for a platform to have multiple devices and hence the need for multiple contexts within a single host program.

The command-queue is used to schedule commands for execution on a device within a context. The command-queue is at the heart of OpenCL. All the real work of OpenCL happens through commands submitted to a queue, common commands being those to launch kernels or move memory objects between the host and compute devices. The queue is by default an in-order queue, which means that the commands are launched on the device in the order in which they are submitted to the queue, and one command finishes before the next one begins.

We turn the kernel source code defined in the string `KernelSource` into a program object that can later be used to construct the executable code for the kernel.

```
// Create the compute program from the source buffer
program = clCreateProgramWithSource(context, 1,
    (const char **) &KernelSource, NULL, &err);
```

We now move to the second part of the host program, shown in Figure 16.6, which begins with the following command to compile the program.

```
// Build the program ...  display error messages if unsuccessful
err = clBuildProgram(program, 0, NULL, NULL, NULL, NULL);
```

While we have omitted most error handling in order to save space, in this case we include the error handling and explain how it works. If any compilation errors exist, the call to `clBuildProgram()` will return something besides `CL_SUCCESS`. At least during program development we need to see these compilation errors. We do so by making a call to `clGetBuildProgramInfo()` to fill the `CL_PROGRAM_BUILD_LOG` in the `buffer`, which we subsequently print to see compilation errors. The OpenCL framework does not output compilation errors automatically, as one might expect, because that might not be acceptable on all platforms (e.g., cell phones and other consumer electronic devices).

The compiled program acts as a dynamic library. We select the desired function from this library and mark it as a kernel with the following lines:

```
// Create the compute kernel from the program
kernel = clCreateKernel(program, "vadd", &err);
```

The string "vadd" must match a kernel function within the program, as we will see in the next section. This function is now associated with the handle `kernel`.

Next, we create the memory objects in device memory for our three arrays. We do so with three calls to `clCreateBuffer()`, each of which returns a handle to the memory region. With the memory in place in the device's global memory (i.e., memory visible to work-items running on the device) we can copy data from host memory into device memory. We do this by enqueuing the write buffer operation onto the queue:

```
// Write a and b vectors into compute device memory
err = clEnqueueWriteBuffer(commands, a_in, CL_TRUE, 0,
                    sizeof(float) * count, a_data, 0, NULL, NULL);
err = clEnqueueWriteBuffer(commands, b_in, CL_TRUE, 0,
                    sizeof(float) * count, b_data, 0, NULL, NULL);
```

With the input data copied onto the device, we can now associate data in global memory with arguments in the kernel. The kernel (as shown earlier) has the following function prototype.

```
__kernel vadd(
    __global float* a,
    __global float* b,
    __global float* c,
    const unsigned int count)
```

The following operations connect OpenCL memory objects to arguments in the kernel.

```
// Set the arguments to our compute kernel
err =  clSetKernelArg(kernel, 0, sizeof(cl_mem), &a_in);
err |= clSetKernelArg(kernel, 1, sizeof(cl_mem), &b_in);
err |= clSetKernelArg(kernel, 2, sizeof(cl_mem), &c_out);
err |= clSetKernelArg(kernel, 3, sizeof(unsigned int), &count);
```

The programmer is responsible for making sure that there is one call to the function `clSetKernelArg` for each of the kernel's formal parameters and that everything (type, size, and initialization) matches up.

With the kernel and its arguments defined, we can now discuss how to execute a kernel. An instance of the kernel executes for each point in an index space. This defines a work-item. The work-items are organized into blocks called work-groups. The size of each dimension in a work-group must evenly divide the global index space; that is, all work-groups in a command are the same size. This size, however, must also be suitable for the compute device. The following function sets the variable `local` to the maximum allowed number of work-items in a work-group for our device and kernel.

```
// Set local to max work-group size for executing the kernel
// on the device
err = clGetKernelWorkGroupInfo(kernel, device_id,
            CL_KERNEL_WORK_GROUP_SIZE, sizeof(local), &local, NULL);
```

The name `local` was used because, from the point of view of a work-item, the size of a work-group is the size of the index space local to a work-group. For the example, we assume `local` evenly divides `count`. With code, index space, and arguments set, we can now submit the kernel object for execution with the following command.

```
// Execute the kernel over the entire range of our 1d input data set
global = count;
err = clEnqueueNDRangeKernel(commands, kernel, 1, NULL,
                          &global, &local, 0, NULL, NULL);
```

In our example, we have a one-dimensional NDRange index space with a global size of `count` broken into work-groups of size `local`. The function to enqueue a command returns immediately without waiting for the enqueued work to complete. If you want to insert a point in the command queue where you wait for all prior commands to finish (such as when timing kernel execution), you would use the command:

```
// Wait for the commands to complete before reading back results
clFinish(commands);
```

Once they have finished, we can read back the results from global memory to host memory.

```
// Read back the results (c_res) from the compute device
err = clEnqueueReadBuffer(commands, c_out, CL_TRUE, 0,
                       sizeof(float) * count, c_res, 0, NULL, NULL );
```

The rest of the host code checks the results and then cleanly shuts down the platform.

On first exposure, the host code may seem overly complex, but this complexity is what gives OpenCL its portability. The API available to the host exposes a wide range of details about the platform and any compute devices it contains. Since the kernel code is just a

```
#include <stdio.h>
#include <math.h>

int main () {
    int i;
    int num_steps = 1000000;
    double x, pi, step, sum = 0.0;

    step = 1.0/(double) num_steps;

    for (i=0;i< num_steps; i++)
    {
        x = (i+0.5)*step;
        sum = sum + 4.0/(1.0+x*x);
    }
    pi = step * sum;
    printf("pi %f\n",pi);
    return 0;
}
```

Figure 16.7: Sequential program to carry out a numerical integration to compute $\int_0^1 \frac{4}{1+x^2}\, dx$.

string, the kernel object can be dynamically generated based on features of the compute device. This extreme portability comes with a price, however, and that price is the complexity of the host code. Fortunately, the code in a host program can be reused from one case to the next. New host programs can be generated by starting with a working host program and modifying the definitions of memory objects and how they map onto the arguments of a kernel.

Example: Working with Local Memory

For a more complicated second example of OpenCL we consider the program in Figure 16.7. This program carries out a numerical integration with integrand and limits of integration chosen so the answer approximates π.

The program is simple; the crux of the calculation is a single loop that sums the value of the integrand for each point in the range of the integral. The loop iterations are naturally parallel, with the only complication being the reduction, that is, the accumulation of the summation into the variable sum. To parallelize this problem using OpenCL, we will need to explore the following.

- The OpenCL memory model with private, local, and global data.

- Synchronization between work-items in a work-group.

- The vector types in the OpenCL kernel programming language.

The biggest challenge is the reduction. Unlike many programing models (e.g., OpenMP or MPI), OpenCL does not provide a reduction primitive. Therefore, when a reduction is needed, a programmer must create one. We will use a relatively simple approach for the reduction. Work-items inside a single work-group can use synchronization constructs to orchestrate their execution. Coordination between work-groups, however, occurs only through the host. Hence, we will use local memory (shared between work-items in a work-group) to compute partial sums, and then we will finish the sum (across work-groups) on the host.

The host program is shown in Figure 16.8. We show only the parts of this program that are significantly different from the host program for the `vadd` kernel. OpenCL requires that the number of work-groups evenly divide the global number of work-items in each dimension. In a real application (as opposed to a simple example) we would adjust the number of integration steps, the size of each work-group, and the iterations per work-item to guarantee that these conditions are met for any input problem. To keep our example simple (and short), we avoid this problem by setting the total number of integration steps (`INSTEPS`) and the number of iterations per work-item (`ITERS`) to a power of 2. We also assume that the maximum work-group size on our platform is also a power of 2 (which is the case for a typical GPU). Once the final work-group size is defined, we can set the other integration parameters accordingly.

Each work-group will send a partial sum back to the host where the final reduction will take place. We need to define a global array long enough to hold these results from all work-groups.

```
// Create the output buffer to hold partial sums
partial_sums    = clCreateBuffer(context,  CL_MEM_WRITE_ONLY,
                    sizeof(float) * nwork_groups, NULL, NULL);
```

We then create the kernel program, compile it, and set up the kernel object, just as we did in the vector-addition example. Things get interesting when we consider the arguments to the kernel, however. Each work-item computes its own partial sum, but it must also cooperate with other work items in the same work-group to compute a partial sum for the work-group; this reduction operation requires an array shared among work-items. Since local memory is statically allocated within the host, we let the host allocate this space and pass it to the kernels as an argument.

```
// Set the arguments to our compute kernel.  Note argument 2 is a local
// array so all we do here is define  its  size (not assign a value).
err = clSetKernelArg(kernel, 0, sizeof(int),    &niters);
err |= clSetKernelArg(kernel, 1, sizeof(float), &step_size);
err |= clSetKernelArg(kernel, 2, sizeof(float)*work_group_size, NULL);
err |= clSetKernelArg(kernel, 3, sizeof(cl_mem), &partial_sums);
```

The function calls for arguments 0, 1, and 3 should look familiar because they are similar to those used in the vector addition host program. The function call for argument 2, however, is different. This is the argument that is declared by the kernel (the code for which we will show shortly) as a `local` memory object. In this case, we specify the size of the memory region (`sizeof(float) × work_group_size`), but we do not provide a value.

Once the arguments are defined, we issue the command to run the kernel.

```
// Execute the kernel
global = nwork_groups * work_group_size;
err = clEnqueueNDRangeKernel(commands, kernel, 1, NULL, &global,
                             &work_group_size, 0, NULL, NULL);
```

We then wait for the results and read back the `partial_sums` memory object, putting the results into the array `psum_data`, which we sum to produce the final answer.

The kernel program for our numerical integration problem is shown in Figure 16.9. Each work-item sums a different segment of the integral, where the segment in question is selected based on the number of work-items in a group, the ID of the work-group, and the ID of the work-item within the work-group (its local ID).

```
int num_wrk_items  = get_local_size(0);
int local_id       = get_local_id(0);
int group_id       = get_group_id(0);
```

The summation within a work-item is carried out and then each work-item places its result into an array shared between work-items in a group. This array, `local_sums`, is associated with an OpenCL memory object in the work-group's local address space, as indicated by the `local` qualifier in the argument list for the kernel.

```
__kernel void pi(
   const int        niters,
   const float      step_size,
   __local  float*  local_sums,
   __global float*  partial_sums)
```

```
#define INSTEPS  512*512*512   // numb integration steps
#define ITERS       65536      // iterations per work—item
float *psum_data;              // vector to hold partial sum
int in_nsteps = INSTEPS;       // number of integration steps
int niters = ITERS;            // iterations per work—item
int nsteps;                    // actual number integration steps
float step_size;               // step size for integration
size_t nwork_groups;           // number of work—groups
size_t global;                 // global domain size
float pi;                      // computed value of pi
size_t max_size, work_group_size = 32;
int i;
cl_mem partial_sums;           // device memory used for partial sums

// (code to define the platform, context, queue, program,
//   and kernel omitted)
// Find max work—group size for executing the kernel on the device
err = clGetKernelWorkGroupInfo(kernel, device_id,
      CL_KERNEL_WORK_GROUP_SIZE, sizeof(max_size), &max_size, NULL);
if(max_size > work_group_size) work_group_size = max_size;
// Now that we know the size of the work—groups, we can set the number
// of work—groups, the actual number of steps, and the step size
nwork_groups = in_nsteps/(work_group_size*niters);
nsteps = work_group_size * niters * nwork_groups;
step_size = 1.0/(float)nsteps;
psum_data = (float*)malloc(sizeof(float)*nwork_groups);
// Create the output buffer to hold partial sums
partial_sums    = clCreateBuffer(context, CL_MEM_WRITE_ONLY,
          sizeof(float) * nwork_groups, NULL, NULL);
// Set the arguments to our compute kernel. Note argument 2 is a local
// array so all we do here is define its size (not assign a value).
err = clSetKernelArg(kernel, 0, sizeof(int),    &niters);
err |= clSetKernelArg(kernel, 1, sizeof(float), &step_size);
err |= clSetKernelArg(kernel, 2, sizeof(float)*work_group_size, NULL);
err |= clSetKernelArg(kernel, 3, sizeof(cl_mem), &partial_sums);
// Execute the kernel
global = nwork_groups * work_group_size;
err = clEnqueueNDRangeKernel(commands, kernel, 1, NULL, &global,
          &work_group_size, 0, NULL, NULL);
// Wait for the commands to complete before reading back results
clFinish(commands);
// Read back the results from the compute device
err = clEnqueueReadBuffer( commands, partial_sums, CL_TRUE, 0,
          sizeof(float) * nwork_groups, psum_data, 0, NULL, NULL );
   // complete the sum and compute final integral value
for (i=0, pi=0.0;i<nwork_groups;i++)
    pi += psum_data[i];
pi = pi * step_size;
// (cleanup and shut down code omitted since it is the same as in
//   our earlier host program)
}
```

Figure 16.8: Host program for the numerical integration program, omitting those parts that are identical to the vector addition example shown earlier.

Once each work-item has finished its portion of the integration and has written its result into the local memory object, the results can be combined into a single partial sum for the whole work-group. But this process cannot be done until every work-item is complete. OpenCL provides a work-group barrier construct for just this kind of situation, which we can use as follows:

```
local_sums[local_id] = accum;
barrier(CLK_LOCAL_MEM_FENCE);
```

The barrier is a work-group function which means it applies to all the work-items within a single work group. It must be called by all the work-items in a work-group or by none of them. In other words, if there is conditional logic that causes different work-items to follow different paths through the code, it is essential that the paths converge before calling the barrier so all the work-items call the same barrier function.

Following the barrier, a single work-item (e.g., the one with local ID 0) combines the results and writes the final partial sum for this work-group into the global memory object we created earlier to hold partial sums from all work-groups.

To explore how this program scales with varying number of GPU compute units, we ran some experiments with an Apple PowerBook with OS X 10.6.2 and an NVIDIA GeForce 8600M GT GPU. We kept the number of steps fixed at $t = 512^3$ and the size of a work-group fixed at 512. By varying the number of loop iterations per work-item we were able to run the program with 1, 2, and 4 compute units. The problem showed nearly linear speedups, with runtimes of 0.248 sec, 0.126 sec, and 0.065 sec for 1, 2, and 4 compute units, respectively.

16.7   Closing Thoughts

In this chapter, we have provided an overview of OpenCL paying careful attention to the language we use in describing the sequence of models behind OpenCL. We have also discussed a small number of examples to explain how to construct a host program and some of the basic techniques in working with kernels.

On first exposure to OpenCL, people often complain about how complex the OpenCL framework is. This is a valid criticism. One must appreciate, however, that this complexity is fundamental to our goals for OpenCL. We set out to create a low-level hardware abstraction layer that exposes all the details of the heterogeneous platform. With all these details exposed, a programmer has the option of adapting to any particular platform and, in doing so, achieve a high degree of portability. Critics of OpenCL have often called this portability into question. They agree that by exposing everything, a programmer can write one

```
//
// The basic OpenCL "pi" kernel
//

   __kernel void pi(
      const int          niters,
      const float        step_size,
      __local  float*    local_sums,
      __global float*    partial_sums)
{
      int num_wrk_items  = get_local_size(0);
      int local_id       = get_local_id(0);
      int group_id       = get_group_id(0);
      float x, sum, accum = 0.0;
      int i,istart,iend;
      istart = (group_id * num_wrk_items + local_id) * niters;
      iend   = istart+niters;
      for(i= istart; i<iend; i++){
          x = (i+0.5)*step_size;
          accum += 4.0/(1.0+x*x);
      }
      local_sums[local_id] = accum;
      barrier(CLK_LOCAL_MEM_FENCE);
      if (local_id == 0){
        sum = 0.0;
         for(i=0; i<num_wrk_items;i++){
             sum += local_sums[i];
         }
         partial_sums[group_id] = sum;
      }
}
```

Figure 16.9: The `ocl_pi.h` include file holding the kernel function for the scalar-mode numerical integration program.

program that runs on a wide range of heterogeneous platforms. This one program, however, is unlikely to deliver a reasonably large fraction of the performance available from a heterogeneous platform. In other words, OpenCL programs are functionally portable, but they are not performance-portable.

On the one hand this is a legitimate point. OpenCL, as a low-level programming model, forces performance-oriented programmers to explicitly map their program onto the feature of any given platform. Is this situation fundamentally different, however, from programming with well-known standard programming languages? For example, a matrix multiplication program using the standard triply nested loop computing a distinct dot product for each element of the product matrix runs at 124 MFLOPS on an Intel Core 2 duo L9400 processor (dual core) running at 1.8 GHz using the C programming language. Rearranging the loops to produce a more efficient memory access pattern increased the performance to 1.2 GFLOPs! Reorganizing the program to access the matrices as panels mapped onto the specific sizes of different layers of the memory hierarchy, using both cores, and converting the innermost operations to fully utilize the SSE 4.2 instructions, the code runs at over 20 GFLOPS! The point is that programs, in general, are not performance-portable. OpenCL is no less performance-portable than any other general-purpose programming language. High-level languages tuned to the needs of a particular domain can achieve improved performance portability, but they do so by limiting the generality of the programming model.

With OpenCL, we set out to create a portable hardware abstraction layer for programming heterogeneous devices. Our goal was to enable development of higher-level tools by providing a common low-level target layer. We believe that OpenCL has achieved that goal admirably. However, OpenCL can be hard to use as a direct application programming model. To that end, creating simplified interfaces to OpenCL and eventually a high-level programming model based on a new C++ kernel programming language is an active area of work in the OpenCL community. We are also working on a standard intermediate language so that high-level languages can directly map onto the internals of an OpenCL framework. Moreover, we are exploring, for upcoming releases of the OpenCL API, expanded programming models to support more flexible task graphs and execution models that expand the range of algorithms that can be addressed within OpenCL.

OpenCL is a young and growing industry standard. The community's support is needed in working with the organizations behind OpenCL, so it evolves in ways that meet the needs of key user communities. People often fail to recognize the incredibly difficult social and business forces that make it so hard to create a widely adopted industry standard. The conditions to create such a standard emerge only at major inflection points (such as the emergence of heterogeneous computing) and even then only when the right set of visionaries come together to make something happen. Therefore, if you believe that having a common software framework that works across a wide range of heterogeneous platforms is important, you owe it to yourself to commit to OpenCL and help it evolve to meet your needs.

References

[1] *The OpenACC^{TM} Application Programming Interface (version 2.0)*, August 2013.

[2] U. A. Acar, G. E. Blelloch, and R. D. Blumofe. The data locality of work stealing. In *Proc. of the 12th ACM Annual Symp. on Parallel Algorithms and Architectures (SPAA 2000)*, pages 1–12, 2000.

[3] Bilge Acun, Abhishek Gupta, Nikhil Jain, Akhil Langer, Harshitha Menon, Eric Mikida, Xiang Ni, Michael Robson, Yanhua Sun, Ehsan Totoni, Lukasz Wesolowski, and Laxmikant Kale. Parallel programming with migratable objects: Charm++ in practice. In *Proceedings of the International Conference on High Performance Computing, Networking, Storage and Analysis*, SC '14, New York, NY, USA, 2014. ACM.

[4] M. F. Adams, H. H. Bayraktar, T. M. Keaveny, and P. Papadopoulos. Ultrascalable implicit finite element analyses in solid mechanics with over a half a billion degrees of freedom. In *ACM/IEEE Proceedings of SC2004: High Performance Networking and Computing*, 2004. Gordon Bell Award.

[5] ADLB web site. `https://www.cs.mtsu.edu/~rbutler/adlb/`.

[6] S. V. Adve and K. Gharachorloo. Shared memory consistency models: a tutorial. *Computer*, 29(12):66–76, December 1996.

[7] Foto N Afrati, Vinayak Borkar, Michael Carey, Neoklis Polyzotis, and Jeffrey D Ullman. Map-reduce extensions and recursive queries. In *Proceedings of the 14th International Conference on Extending Database Technology*, pages 1–8. ACM, 2011.

[8] Sudhir Ahuja, Nicholas Carriero, and David Gelernter. Linda and friends. *IEEE Computer*, 19(8):26–34, 1986.

[9] Volkan Akcelik, Jacobo Bielak, George Biros, Ioannis Epanomeritakis, Antonio Fernandez, Omar Ghattas, Eui Joong Kim, David O'Hallaron, and Tiankai Tu. High resolution forward and inverse earthquake modeling on terascale computers. In *Proceedings of SC2003*, 2003. A winner of the Gordon Bell Prize for special achievement at SC2003.

[10] Eric Allen, David Chase, Joe Hallett, Victor Luchangco, Jan-Willem Maessen, Sukyoung Ryu, Guy L. Steele Jr., and Sam Tobin-Hochstadt. *The Fortress language specification*. Sun Microsystems, Inc., 1.0β edition, March 2007.

[11] Robert Alverson, David Callahan, Daniel Cummings, Brian Koblenz, Allan Porterfield, and Burton Smith. The Tera computer system. In *Proceedings of the 4th International Conference on Supercomputing*, ICS '90, pages 1–6, New York, NY, USA, 1990. ACM.

[12] W. K. Anderson, W. D. Gropp, D. K. Kaushik, D. E. Keyes, and B. F. Smith. Achieving high sustained performance in an unstructured mesh CFD application. In *Proceedings of SC 99*, 1999. Winner of Gordon Bell Special Prize at SC1999.

[13] Edoardo Aprà, Alistair P. Rendell, Robert J. Harrison, Vinod Tipparaju, Wibe A. deJong, and Sotiris S. Xantheas. Liquid water: Obtaining the right answer for the right reasons. In *Proceedings of the Conference on High Performance Computing Networking, Storage and Analysis*, SC '09, pages 66:1–66:7, New York, NY, USA, 2009. ACM.

[14] T. G. Armstrong, Z. Zhang, D. S. Katz, M. Wilde, and I. T. Foster. Scheduling manytask workloads on supercomputers: Dealing with trailing tasks. In *Proc. MTAGS '10*, 2010.

[15] Timothy Armstrong. *Implicitly Parallel Scripting as a Practical and Massively Scalable Programming Model for High-Performance Computing*. PhD thesis, The University of Chicago, 2015.

[16] Timothy G. Armstrong, Justin M. Wozniak, Wilde Michael, and Ian T. Foster. Compiler techniques for massively scalable implicit task parallelism. In *Proc. CCGrid '14*, pages 299–310, November 2014.

[17] Timothy G. Armstrong, Justin M. Wozniak, and Michael Wilde. Exploring scientific discovery with large-scale parallel scripting. In *SCALE Challenge, CCGrid '13*, 2013.

[18] Timothy G. Armstrong, Justin M. Wozniak, Michael Wilde, and Ian T. Foster. Compiler techniques for massively scalable implicit task parallelism. In *Proceedings of Supercomputing 2014*, pages 299–310, 2014.

[19] Mikhail J. Atallah and Susan Fox, editors. *Algorithms and Theory of Computation Handbook*. CRC Press, Inc., Boca Raton, FL, USA, 1st edition, 1998.

[20] Cédric Augonnet, Samuel Thibault, Raymond Namyst, and Pierre-André Wacrenier. StarPU: a unified platform for task scheduling on heterogeneous multicore architectures. *Conc. Comput.: Pract. Exper.*, 23(2):187–198, 2011.

[21] D. H. Bailey. FFTs in external or hierarchical memory. In *Supercomputing, 1989. Supercomputing '89. Proceedings of the 1989 ACM/IEEE Conference on*, pages 234–242, November 1989.

[22] D. H. Bailey. FFTs in external or hierarchical memory. *Journal of Supercomputing*, 4(1):23–35, May 1990.

[23] Pavan Balaji, Darius Buntinas, David Goodell, William Gropp, Torsten Hoefler, Sameer Kumar, Ewing Lusk, Rajeev Thakur, and Jesper Larsson Träff. MPI on millions of cores. *Parallel Processing Letters*, 21(1):45–60, March 2011.

[24] S. Balay, S. Abhyankar, M. Adams, J. Brown, P. Brune, K. Buschelman, V. Eijkhout, W. Gropp, D. Kaushik, M. Knepley, L. Curfman McInnes, K. Rupp, B. Smith, , and H. Zhang. PETSc users manual. Technical Report ANL-95/11 - Revision 3.5, Argonne National Laboratory, 2015.

[25] Satish Balay, Kris Buschelman, Victor Eijkhout, William D. Gropp, Dinesh Kaushik, Matthew G. Knepley, Lois Curfman McInnes, Barry F. Smith, and Hong Zhang. PETSc users manual. Technical Report ANL-95/11 - Revision 3.0.0, Argonne National Laboratory, 2008.

[26] Satish Balay, William D. Gropp, Lois Curfman McInnes, and Barry F. Smith. Efficient management of parallelism in object oriented numerical software libraries. In E. Arge, A. M. Bruaset, and H. P. Langtangen, editors, *Modern Software Tools in Scientific Computing*, pages 163–202. Birkhäuser Press, 1997.

[27] Utpal Banerjee, Brian Bliss, Zhiqiang Ma, and Paul Petersen. A theory of data race detection. In *Proceedings of the 2006 workshop on Parallel and distributed systems: testing and debugging*, PADTAD '06, pages 69–78, New York, NY, USA, 2006. ACM.

[28] David M. Beazley. SWIG: an easy to use tool for integrating scripting languages with C and C++. In *Proc. USENIX Tcl/Tk Workshop*, Berkeley, CA, USA, 1996. USENIX Association.

[29] Aaron Becker. *Compiler Support for Productive Message-Driven Parallel Programming*. PhD thesis, Dept. of Computer Science, University of Illinois, 2012. http://charm.cs.uiuc.edu/media/12-44/.

[30] Michael A. Bender, Jeremy T. Fineman, Seth Gilbert, and Charles E. Leiserson. On-the-fly maintenance of series-parallel relationships in fork-join multithreaded programs. In *Proceedings of the Sixteenth Annual ACM Symposium on Parallel Algorithms and Architectures (SPAA 2004)*, pages 133–144, Barcelona, Spain, June 2004.

[31] P. Berenbrink, T. Friedetzky, and L. A. Goldberg. The natural work-stealing algorithm is stable. In *42nd IEEE Symposium on Foundations of Computer Science*, pages 178–187, 2001.

[32] Ian J. Bertolacci, Catherine Olschanowsky, Ben Harshbarger, Bradford L. Chamberlain, David G. Wonnacott, and Michelle Mills Strout. Parameterized diamond tiling for stencil computations with Chapel parallel iterators. In *29th International Conference on Supercomputing (ICS 2015)*, Newport Beach, CA, June 2015.

[33] James C. Beyer, Eric J. Stotzer, Alistair Hart, and Bronis R. de Supinski. OpenMP for accelerators. In *OpenMP in the Petascale Era*, pages 108–121. Springer, 2011.

[34] Abhinav Bhatele, Eric Bohm, and Laxmikant V. Kale. Optimizing communication for Charm++ applications by reducing network contention. *Concurrency and Computation: Practice and Experience*, 23(2):211–222, 2011.

[35] Abhinav Bhatelé, Laxmikant V. Kalé, and Sameer Kumar. Dynamic topology aware load balancing algorithms for molecular dynamics applications. In *23rd ACM International Conference on Supercomputing*, 2009.

[36] L. S. Blackford, J. Choi, A. Cleary, E. D'Azevedo, J. Demmel, I. Dhillon, J. Dongarra, S. Hammarling, G. Henry, A. Petitet, K. Stanley, D. Walker, and R. C. Whaley. *ScaLAPACK Users' Guide*. Society for Industrial and Applied Mathematics, Philadelphia, PA, 1997.

[37] L. S. Blackford, J. Choi, A. Cleary, E. D'Azevedo, J. Demmel, I. Dhillon, J. Dongarra, S. Hammarling, G. Henry, A. Petitet, K. Stanley, D. Walker, and R. C. Wha-

ley. *ScaLAPACK Users' Guide*. Society for Industrial and Applied Mathematics, Philadelphia, PA, 1997.

[38] Robert D. Blumofe, Matteo Frigo, Chrisopher F. Joerg, Charles E. Leiserson, and Keith H. Randall. An analysis of dag-consistent distributed shared-memory algorithms. In *Proceedings of the Eighth Annual ACM Symposium on Parallel Algorithms and Architectures*, pages 297–308, Padua, Italy, June 1996.

[39] Robert D. Blumofe and Charles Leiserson. Scheduling multithreaded computations by work stealing. In *Proc. of the 35th Symposium on Foundations of Computer Science (FOCS)*, pages 356–368, November 1994.

[40] Robert D. Blumofe and Charles E. Leiserson. Space-efficient scheduling of multi-threaded computations. In *Proceedings of the Twenty Fifth Annual ACM Symposium on Theory of Computing*, pages 362–371, San Diego, California, May 1993.

[41] Robert D. Blumofe and Charles E. Leiserson. Space-efficient scheduling of multi-tithreaded computations. *SIAM Journal on Computing*, 27(1):202–229, February 1998.

[42] Robert D. Blumofe and Charles E. Leiserson. Scheduling multithreaded computations by work stealing. *Journal of the ACM*, 46(5):720–748, September 1999.

[43] Jr. Robert L. Bocchino, Vikram S. Adve, Danny Dig, Sarita V. Adve, Stephen Heumann, Rakesh Komuravelli, Jeffrey Overbey, Patrick Simmons, Hyojin Sung, and Mohsen Vakilian. A type and effect system for Deterministic Parallel Java. In *Proceedings of OOPSLA'09, ACM SIGPLAN Conference on Object-Oriented Programming Systems, Languages and Applications*, pages 97–116, 2009.

[44] Robert L. Bocchino, Vikram S. Adve, and Bradford L. Chamberlain. Software transactional memory for large scale clusters. In *Proceedings of the ACM SIGPLAN Symposium on Principles and Practice of Parallel Programming*, 2008.

[45] Hans-J. Boehm and Sarita V. Adve. You don't know jack about shared variables or memory models. *Communications of the ACM*, 55(2):48–54, February 2012.

[46] Eric Bohm, Abhinav Bhatele, Laxmikant V. Kale, Mark E. Tuckerman, Sameer Kumar, John A. Gunnels, and Glenn J. Martyna. Fine grained parallelization of the Car-Parrinello ab initio MD method on Blue Gene/L. *IBM Journal of Research and Development: Applications of Massively Parallel Systems*, 52(1/2):159–174, 2008.

[47] D. Bonachea. Proposal for extending the UPC memory copy library functions and supporting extensions to GASNet, v1.0. Technical Report LBNL-56495, Lawrence Berkeley National Laboratory, 2004.

[48] Dan Bonachea. GASNet Specification, v1.1. Technical report, University of California at Berkeley, Berkeley, CA, USA, 2002.

[49] George Bosilca, Aurelien Bouteiller, Anthony Danalis, Thomas Herault, Pierre Lemarinier, and Jack Dongarra. DAGuE: A generic distributed DAG engine for high performance computing. Technical Report ICL-UT-10-01, U. Tennessee, 2010.

[50] Eric Boutin, Jaliya Ekanayake, Wei Lin, Bing Shi, Jingren Zhou, Zhengping Qian, Ming Wu, and Lidong Zhou. Apollo: Scalable and coordinated scheduling for cloud-scale computing. In *Proc. OSDI '14*, pages 285–300, Broomfield, CO, October 2014. USENIX Association.

[51] James Boyle, Ralph Butler, Terrence Disz, Barnett Glickfeld, Ewing Lusk, Ross Overbeek, James Patterson, and Rick Stevens. *Portable Programs for Parallel Processors*. Holt, Rinehart, and Winston, New York, NY, 1987.

[52] Richard P. Brent. The parallel evaluation of general arithmetic expressions. *Journal of the ACM*, 21(2):201–206, April 1974.

[53] Eugene D. Brooks III, Brent C. Gorda, and Karen H. Warren. The Parallel C Preprocessor. *Sci. Program.*, 1(1):79–89, January 1992.

[54] Derek Bruening. *Efficient, Transparent, and Comprehensive Runtime Code Manipulation*. PhD thesis, Department of Electrical Engineering and Computer Science, Massachusetts Institute of Technology, 2004.

[55] Z. Budimlic, A. Chandramowlishwaran, K. Knobe, G. Lowney, V. Sarkar, and L. Treggiari. Declarative aspects of memory management in the concurrent collections parallel programming model. In *Proceedings of DAMP 2009 Workshop (Declarative Aspects of Multicore Programming)*, 2009.

[56] Javier Bueno, Judit Planas, Alejandro Duran, Rosa M. Badia, Xavier Martorell, Eduard Ayguade, and Jesus Labarta. Productive programming of GPU clusters with OmpSs. In *Proc. IPDPS '12*, 2012.

[57] David Callahan, Bradford L. Chamberlain, and Hans P. Zima. The Cascade High Productivity Language. *9th International Workshop on High-Level Parallel Programming Models and Supportive Environments*, pages 52–60, April 2004.

[58] Colin Campbell and Ade Miller. *A Parallel Programming with Microsoft Visual C++: Design Patterns for Decomposition and Coordination on Multicore Architectures*. Microsoft Press, 1st edition, 2011.

[59] W. W. Carlson, J. M. Draper, D. E. Culler, K. Yelick, E. Brooks, and K. Warren. Introduction to UPC and language specification. Technical Report CCS-TR-99-157., IDA/CCS, Bowie, Maryland, May 1999.

[60] William W. Carlson and Jesse M. Draper. Distributed data access in AC. In *Proceedings of the fifth ACM SIGPLAN symposium on Principles and practice of parallel programming*, PPOPP '95, pages 39–47, New York, NY, USA, 1995. ACM.

[61] Denis Caromel, Ludovic Henrio, and Bernard Paul Serpette. Asynchronous sequential processes. *Information and Computation*, 207(4):459–495, 2009.

[62] J. Carson, S. Gandolfi, F. Pederiva, S. C. Pieper, R Schiavilla, K. E. Schmidt, and R. B. Wiringa. Quantum Monte Carlo methods for nuclear physics. *ArXiv e-prints*, 1412.3081, 2015. Accepted for publication in *Reviews of Modern Physics*.

[63] Brad Chamberlain. Why Chapel? *Cray Inc. Blog.* http://www.cray.com/blog/, June–October 2014.

[64] Bradford Chamberlain. [Ten] myths about scalable parallel programming languages. *IEEE TCSC Blog.* https://www.ieeetcsc.org/activities/blog, April–November 2012.

[65] Bradford L. Chamberlain. *The Design and Implementation of a Region-Based Parallel Language*. PhD thesis, University of Washington, November 2001.

[66] Bradford L. Chamberlain, David Callahan, and Hans P. Zima. Parallel programmability and the Chapel language. *International Journal of High Performance Computing Applications*, 21(3):291–312, August 2007.

[67] Bradford L. Chamberlain, Sung-Eun Choi, Steven J. Deitz, David Iten, and Vassily Litvinov. Authoring user-defined domain maps in Chapel. In *Cray User Group (CUG) 2011*, Fairbanks, AK, May 2011.

[68] Bradford L. Chamberlain, Sung-Eun Choi, Steven J. Deitz, and Angeles Navarro. User-defined parallel zippered iterators in Chapel. In *PGAS 2011: Fifth Conference on Partitioned Global Address Space Programming Models*, October 2011.

[69] Bradford L. Chamberlain, Sung-Eun Choi, Martha Dumler, Thomas Hildebrandt, David Iten, Vassily Litvinov, and Greg Titus. The state of the Chapel union. In *Cray User Group (CUG) 2013*, Napa Valley, CA, May 2013.

[70] Bradford L. Chamberlain, Sung-Eun Choi, E Christopher Lewis, Calvin Lin, Lawrence Snyder, and W. Derrick Weathersby. ZPL: A machine independent programming language for parallel computers. *IEEE Transactions on Software Engineering*, 26(3):197–211, March 2000.

[71] Bradford L. Chamberlain, Steven J. Deitz, David Iten, and Sung-Eun Choi. User-defined distributions and layouts in Chapel: Philosophy and framework. In *HotPAR '10: Proceedings of the 2nd USENIX Workshop on Hot Topics*, June 2010.

[72] Anthony Chan, William Gropp, and Ewing Lusk. An efficient format for nearly constant-time access to arbitrary time intervals in large trace files. *Scientific Programming*, 16(2-3):155–165, 2008.

[73] Ernie Chan, Marcel Heimlich, Avi Purkayastha, and Robert A. van de Geijn. Collective communication: Theory, practice, and experience. *Concurrency and Computation: Practice and Experience*, 19(13):1749–1783, 2007.

[74] Barbara Chapman, Tony Curtis, Charles Koelbel, Jeffery Kuehn, Stephen Poole, and Lauren Smith. Introducing OpenSHMEM: SHMEM for the PGAS community. In *Proceedings of the 2010 ACM Partitioned Global Address Space Conference*, PGAS'10, New York, NY, USA, 2010. ACM.

[75] Barbara Chapman, Gabriele Jost, and Ruud Van Der Pas. *Using OpenMP: portable shared memory parallel programming*. MIT press, 2008.

[76] Philippe Charles, Christian Grothoff, Vijay Saraswat, Christopher Donawa, Allan Kielstra, Kemal Ebcioglu, Christoph von Praun, and Vivek Sarkar. X10: an object-oriented approach to non-uniform cluster computing. In *Proceedings of the 20th annual ACM SIGPLAN conference on Object-oriented programming, systems, languages, and applications*, OOPSLA '05, pages 519–538, New York, NY, USA, 2005. ACM.

[77] Sanjay Chatterjee, Sağnak Taşırlar, Zoran Budimlic, Vincent Cave, Milind Chabbi, Max Grossman, Vivek Sarkar, and Yonghong Yan. Integrating asynchronous task parallelism with MPI. In *Proc. IPDPS '13*, 2013.

[78] Guang-Ien Cheng, Mingdong Feng, Charles E. Leiserson, Keith H. Randall, and Andrew F. Stark. Detecting data races in Cilk programs that use locks. In *Proceedings of the Tenth Annual ACM Symposium on Parallel Algorithms and Architectures (SPAA '98)*, pages 298–309, Puerto Vallarta, Mexico, June 28–July 2 1998.

[79] Pietro Cicotti. *Tarragon: a Programming Model for Latency-Hiding Scientific Computation*. PhD thesis, U. California, San Diego, 2011.

[80] Thomas H. Cormen, Charles E. Leiserson, Ronald L. Rivest, and Clifford Stein. *Introduction to Algorithms*. The MIT Press, third edition, 2009.

[81] Intel Corporation. Intel Threading Building Blocks open source web site.

[82] Intel Corporation. *Intrinsics for Low Overhead Tool Annotations*, 2011. Doc. No. 326357-001US.

[83] Intel Corporation. *Intel Cilk Plus Language Extension Specification Version 1.2*, 2013. Doc. No. 324396-003US.

[84] Intel Corporation. *Intel Threading Building Blocks documentation*, 2015.

[85] Cray Inc. Cray T3E^{TM} Fortran Optimization Guide - 004-2518-002.

[86] Cray Inc. Cray XT^{TM} System Overview. [Online] December 2009. [Cited: 26 August 2010.] http://docs.cray.com/books/S-2446-31/S-2446-31.pdf.

[87] Cray Inc. Man Page Collection (Unicos LC): Shared Memory Access SHMEM.

[88] Cray Inc. Man Page Collection (Unicos MP): Shared Memory Access SHMEM.

[89] Cray Inc., Seattle, WA. *Chapel Language Specification (version 0.97)*, April 2015. (Available from http://chapel.cray.com/language.html).

[90] Cray, The Super computing company, 2010. Cray Inc. The Gemini Network Rev 1.1 (White Paper). s.l.

[91] Jeff Daily and Robert R Lewis. Using the global arrays toolkit to reimplement numpy for distributed computation. *Proceedings of the 10th Python in Science Conference*, 2011.

[92] Jeff Daily, Abhinav Vishnu, Bruce Palmer, Hubertus van Dam, and Darren Kerbyson. On the suitability of MPI as a PGAS runtime. In *High Performance Computing (HiPC), 2014 21st International Conference on*, pages 1–10, December 2014.

[93] Jeffrey Dean and Sanjay Ghemawat. MapReduce: simplified data processing on large clusters. *Commun. ACM*, 51:107–113, January 2008.

[94] Steven J. Deitz. *High-Level Programming Language Abstractions for Advanced and Dynamic Parallel Computations*. PhD thesis, University of Washington, February 2005.

[95] Steven J. Deitz, David Callahan, Bradford L. Chamberlain, and Lawrence Snyder. Global-view abstractions for user-defined reductions and scans. In *PPoPP '06: Proceedings of the eleventh ACM SIGPLAN Symposium on Principles and Practice of Parallel Programming*, pages 40–47. ACM Press, 2006.

[96] Luiz DeRose. The Cray Compiling Environment: Bridging the user to high performance. `http://prace-portal.cscs.ch/uploads/tx_pracetmo/cpw09_craycce.pdf`, July 2009.

[97] James Dinan. *Scalable Task Parallel Programming in the Partitioned Global Address Space*. PhD thesis, The Ohio State University, 2010.

[98] James Dinan, Sriram Krishnamoorthy, D. Brian Larkins, Jarek Nieplocha, and P. Sadayappan. Scioto: A framework for global-view task parallelism. In *Proceedings of the 2008 37th International Conference on Parallel Processing*, ICPP '08, 2008.

[99] James Dinan, D. Brian Larkins, P. Sadayappan, Sriram Krishnamoorthy, and Jarek Nieplocha. Scalable work stealing. In *Proceedings of the Conference on High Performance Computing Networking, Storage and Analysis*, SC '09, 2009.

[100] Francisco Rodrigo Duro, Javier Garcia Blas, Florin Isaila, Jesus Carretero, Justin M. Wozniak, and Robert Ross. Exploiting data locality in Swift/T workflows using Hercules. In *Proc. Network for Sustainable Ultrascale Computing (NESUS) Workshop*, 2014.

[101] Derek L. Eager, John Zahorjan, and Edward D. Lazowska. Speedup versus efficiency in parallel systems. *IEEE Transactions on Computers*, 38(3):408–423, March 1989.

[102] Alexandre E Eichenberger, Christian Terboven, Michael Wong, and Dieter an Mey. The design of OpenMP thread affinity. In *OpenMP in a Heterogeneous World*, pages 15–28. Springer, 2012.

[103] Jaliya Ekanayake, Hui Li, Bingjing Zhang, Thilina Gunarathne, Seung-Hee Bae, Judy Qiu, and Geoffrey Fox. Twister: A runtime for iterative MapReduce. In *Proc.*

of 19th ACM Int'l Symp. on High Performance Distributed Computing, HPDC '10, pages 810–818, New York, 2010. ACM.

[104] Skevos Evripidou, Guang Gao, Jean-Luc Gaudiot, and Vivek Sarkar, editors. *1st Workshop on Data-Flow Execution Models for Extreme Scale Computing: DFM'11.* IEEE Computer Society, October 2011.

[105] Rob Farber. *CUDA Application Design and Development.* Morgan Kaufmann Publishers Inc., San Francisco, CA, USA, 1st edition, 2011.

[106] Mingdong Feng and Charles E. Leiserson. Efficient detection of determinacy races in Cilk programs. In *Proceedings of the Ninth Annual ACM Symposium on Parallel Algorithms and Architectures (SPAA)*, pages 1–11, Newport, Rhode Island, June22–25 1997.

[107] Mingdong Feng and Charles E. Leiserson. Efficient detection of determinacy races in Cilk programs. *Theory of Computing Systems*, 32(3):301–326, 1999. A preliminary version appeared as [106].

[108] M. J. Flynn. Some computer organizations and their effectiveness. *IEEE Transactions on Computers*, C-21(9), 1972.

[109] National Center for Supercomputing Applications. Blue Waters user portal, 2015. https://bluewaters.ncsa.illinois.edu/hardware-summary.

[110] I. Foster and S. Taylor. Strand: A practical parallel programming language. In *Proceedings of the North American Conference on Logic Programming*, pages 497–512, 1989.

[111] Ian Foster, Robert Olson, and Steven Tuecke. Productive parallel programming: The PCN approach. *Sci. Program.*, 1:51–66, January 1992.

[112] Ian Foster, Jens Voeckler, Mike Wilde, and Yong Zhao. The virtual data grid: A new model and architecture for data-intensive collaboration. In *Conference on Innovative Data Systems Research*, 2003.

[113] N. Francez and M. Rodeh. Achieving distributed termination without freezing. *IEEE Trans. on Software Engineering*, SE-8(3):287–292, May 1982.

[114] Matteo Frigo, Pablo Halpern, Charles E. Leiserson, and Stephen Lewin-Berlin. Reducers and other Cilk++ hyperobjects. In *Proceedings of the Twenty-First Annual ACM Symposium on Parallel Algorithms and Architectures (SPAA '09)*, Calgary, Canada, August 2009. To appear.

[115] Matteo Frigo and Steven G. Johnson. The design and implementation of FFTW3. *Proceedings of the IEEE*, 93(2):216–231, 2005. Special issue on "Program Generation, Optimization, and Platform Adaptation".

[116] Matteo Frigo, Charles E. Leiserson, Harald Prokop, and Sridhar Ramachandran. Cache-oblivious algorithms. In *40th Annual Symposium on Foundations of Computer Science*, pages 285–297, New York, New York, October 17–19 1999.

[117] Matteo Frigo, Charles E. Leiserson, and Keith H. Randall. The implementation of the Cilk-5 multithreaded language. In *Proceedings of the ACM SIGPLAN '98 Conference on Programming Language Design and Implementation*, pages 212–223, Montreal, Quebec, Canada, June 1998. Proceedings published ACM SIGPLAN Notices, Vol. 33, No. 5, May, 1998.

[118] Matteo Frigo and Volker Strumpen. Cache oblivious stencil computations. In *Proceedings of the 19th annual international conference on Supercomputing*, ICS '05, pages 361–366, New York, NY, USA, 2005. ACM.

[119] D. Frye, R. Bryant, H. Ho, R. Lawrence, and M. Snir. An external user interface for scalable parallel systems. Technical report, IBM, May 1992.

[120] E. Garbriel, G. E. Fagg, G. Bosilica, T. Angskun, J. J. Dongarra J. M. Squyres, V. Sahay, P. Kambadur, B. Barrett, A. Lumsdaine, R. H. Castain, D. J. Daniel, R. L. Graham, and T. S. Woodall. Open MPI: goals, concept, and design of a next generation MPI implementation. In *Proceedings, 11th European PVM/MPI Users' Group Meeting*, 2004.

[121] Al Geist, Adam Beguelin, Jack Dongarra, Weicheng Jiang, Bob Manchek, and Vaidy Sunderam. *PVM: Parallel Virtual Machine—A User's Guide and Tutorial for Network Parallel Computing*. MIT Press, Cambridge, Mass., 1994.

[122] David Gelernter. Generative communication in Linda. *ACM Trans. Program. Lang. Syst.*, 7(1):80–112, 1985.

[123] M. I. Gordon et al. A stream compiler for communication-exposed architectures. In *ASPLOS-X: Proceedings of the 10th international conference on Architectural support for programming languages and operating systems*, pages 291–303, New York, NY, USA, 2002. ACM.

[124] M. I. Gordon et al. Exploiting coarse-grained task, data, and pipeline parallelism in stream programs. In *ASPLOS-XII: Proceedings of the 12th international conference*

on Architectural support for programming languages and operating systems, pages 151–162, New York, NY, USA, 2006. ACM.

[125] R. L. Graham. Bounds for certain multiprocessing anomalies. *The Bell System Technical Journal*, 45:1563–1581, November 1966.

[126] W. Gropp, E. Lusk, and A. Skjellum. *Using MPI: Portable Parallel Programming with the Message-Passing Interface*. The MIT Press, Cambridge, MA, 1999.

[127] William Gropp, Torsten Hoefler, Rajeev Thakur, and Ewing Lusk. *Using Advanced MPI: Modern Features of the Message-Passing Interface*. MIT Press, Cambridge, MA, 2014.

[128] William Gropp, Ewing Lusk, and Anthony Skjellum. *Using MPI: Portable Parallel Programming with the Message Passing Interface,* 3rd edition. MIT Press, Cambridge, MA, 2014.

[129] William D. Gropp. Learning from the success of MPI. In Burkhard Monien, Viktor K. Prasanna, and Sriram Vajapeyam, editors, *8th International Conference on High Performance Computing – HiPC 2001*, number 2228 in Lecture Notes in Computer Science, pages 81–92. Springer, December 2001.

[130] William D. Gropp and Barry Smith. Chameleon parallel programming tools users manual. Technical Report ANL-93/23, Argonne National Laboratory, Argonne, IL, March 1993.

[131] Abhishek Gupta, Bilge Acun, Osman Sarood, and Laxmikant V. Kale. Towards realizing the potential of malleable parallel jobs. In *Proceedings of the IEEE International Conference on High Performance Computing*, HiPC '14, Goa, India, December 2014.

[132] Abhishek Gupta, Laxmikant Kale, Dejan Milojicic, Paolo Faraboschi, and Susanne Balle. HPC-aware VM placement in infrastructure clouds. In *Cloud Engineering (IC2E), 2013 IEEE International Conference on*, pages 11–20, 2013.

[133] Michael Halbherr, Yuli Zhou, and Chris F. Joerg. MIMD-style parallel programming with continuation-passing threads. In *Proceedings of the 2nd International Workshop on Massive Parallelism: Hardware, Software, and Applications*, Capri, Italy, September 1994.

[134] Robert Harper, David MacQueen, and Robin Milner. Standard ML. Technical Report ECS-LFCS-86-2, University of Edinburgh, Edinburgh EH9 3JZ, March 1986.

[135] Mihael Hategan, Justin Wozniak, and Ketan Maheshwari. Coasters: uniform resource provisioning and access for scientific computing on clouds and grids. In
Proc. Utility and Cloud Computing, 2011.

[136] Yuxiong He, Charles E. Leiserson, and William M. Leiserson. The Cilkview scalability analyzer. In *Proceedings of the 22nd ACM symposium on Parallelism in algorithms and architectures*, SPAA '10, pages 145–156, New York, NY, USA, 2010.
ACM.

[137] Michael A. Heroux, Roscoe A. Bartlett, Vicki E. Howle, Robert J. Hoekstra,
Jonathan J. Hu, Tamara G. Kolda, Richard B. Lehoucq, Kevin R. Long, Roger P.
Pawlowski, Eric T. Phipps, Andrew G. Salinger, Heidi K. Thornquist, Ray S. Tumi-
naro, James M. Willenbring, Alan Williams, and Kendall S. Stanley. An overview
of the Trilinos project. *ACM Trans. Math. Softw.*, 31(3):397–423, 2005.

[138] High Performance Computing Tools Group at the University of Houston and
Extreme Scale Systems Center, Oak Ridge National Laboratory. OpenSHMEM
Application Programming Interface. `http://www.openshmem.org/site/`
`sites/default/site_files/openshmem_specification_v1.`
`0-final.pdf`.

[139] Torsten Hoefler and Steven Gottlieb. Parallel zero-copy algorithms for fast Fourier
transform and conjugate gradient using MPI datatypes. In Rainer Keller, Edgar
Gabriel, Michael M. Resch, and Jack Dongarra, editors, *EuroMPI*, volume 6305 of
Lecture Notes in Computer Science, pages 132–141. Springer, 2010.

[140] Jay P. Hoeflinger and Bronis R. De Supinski. The OpenMP memory model. In
OpenMP Shared Memory Parallel Programming, pages 167–177. Springer, 2008.

[141] HPC challenge awards competetion. `http://www.hpcchallenge.org/`
`index.html`.

[142] Chao Huang. System support for checkpoint and restart of Charm++ and AMPI
applications. Master's thesis, Dept. of Computer Science, University of Illinois,
2004.

[143] Chao Huang, Gengbin Zheng, Sameer Kumar, and Laxmikant V. Kalé. Performance evaluation of Adaptive MPI. In *Proceedings of ACM SIGPLAN Symposium
on Principles and Practice of Parallel Programming 2006*, March 2006.

[144] Stratton, John A. and Sam S. Stone and Wen-Mei W. Hwu. MCUDA: An efficient
implementation of CUDA kernels for multi-core CPUs. In José Nelson Amaral,

editor, *Languages and Compilers for Parallel Computing*, pages 16–30. Springer-Verlag, Berlin, Heidelberg, 2008.

[145] Intel trace analyzer and collector 9.0. `http://software.intel.com/en-us/intel-trace-analyzer/`.

[146] Intrepid Technology, Inc. GNU Unified Parallel C (GNU UPC). `http://www.gccupc.org/`.

[147] Kenneth E. Iverson. *A Programming Language*. John Wiley & Sons, 1962.

[148] Pritish Jetley, Filippo Gioachin, Celso Mendes, Laxmikant V. Kale, and Thomas R. Quinn. Massively parallel cosmological simulations with ChaNGa. In *Proceedings of IEEE International Parallel and Distributed Processing Symposium 2008*, 2008.

[149] Pritish Jetley and Laxmikant V. Kalé. Static macro data flow: Compiling global control into local control. In *Proceedings of the IEEE International Parallel and Distributed Processing Symposium Workshops 2010*, 2010.

[150] Xiangmin Jiao, Gengbin Zheng, Phillip A. Alexander, Michael T. Campbell, Orion S. Lawlor, John Norris, Andreas Haselbacher, and Michael T. Heath. A system integration framework for coupled multiphysics simulations. *Engineering with Computers*, 22(3):293–309, 2006.

[151] JTC1/SC22/WG21. Working draft: Standard for programming language C++. Technical Report N3242=11-0012, ISO/IEC, February 2011. This is a not the actual standard, but a freely available late draft.

[152] Hartmut Kaiser, Maciej Brodowicz, and Thomas Sterling. ParalleX: An advanced parallel execution model for scaling-impaired applications. In *Int'l Conf. Parallel Processing Workshops (ICPPW) 2009*, pages 394–401, September 2009.

[153] L. V. Kale. The Chare Kernel parallel programming language and system. In *Proceedings of the International Conference on Parallel Processing*, volume II, pages 17–25, August 1990.

[154] L. V. Kalé and S. Krishnan. CHARM++: A portable concurrent object oriented system based on C++. In A. Paepcke, editor, *Proceedings of OOPSLA'93*, pages 91–108. ACM Press, September 1993.

[155] L. V. Kale and Sanjeev Krishnan. Charm++: Parallel programming with message-driven objects. In Gregory V. Wilson and Paul Lu, editors, *Parallel Programming using C++*, pages 175–213. MIT Press, 1996.

[156] L. V. Kale, Sameer Kumar, and Krishnan Vardarajan. A framework for collective personalized communication. In *Proceedings of IPDPS'03*, Nice, France, April 2003.

[157] L. V. Kale, B. H. Richards, and T. D. Allen. Efficient parallel graph coloring with prioritization. In *Lecture Notes in Computer Science*, volume 1068, pages 190–208. Springer-Verlag, August 1995.

[158] L. V. Kalé and V. Saletore. Parallel state-space search for a first solution with consistent linear speedups. *Internaltional Journal of Parallel Programming*, 19(4):251–293, 1990.

[159] Laxmikant V. Kalé. Application oriented and computer science centered HPCC research. In Uzi Vishkin, editor, *Developing a Computer Science Agenda for High-performance Computing*, pages 98–105. ACM, New York, NY, USA, 1994.

[160] Laxmikant V. Kale and Abhinav Bhatele, editors. *Parallel Science and Engineering Applications: The Charm++ Approach*. Taylor & Francis Group, CRC Press, November 2013.

[161] Ken Kennedy, Charles Koelbel, and Hans P. Zima. The rise and fall of High Performance Fortran. In *Proceedings of HOPL'07, Third ACM SIGPLAN History of Programming Languages Conference*, pages 1–22, 2007.

[162] David B. Kirk and Wen mei W. Hwu. *Programming Massively Parallel Processors: A Hands-on Approach*. Morgan Kaufmann Publishers Inc., San Francisco, CA, USA, 2nd edition, 2012.

[163] Kathleen Knobe and Carl D. Offner. TStreams: A model of parallel computation (preliminary report). Technical Report HPL-2004-78, HP Labs, 2004.

[164] Scott J. Krieder, Justin M. Wozniak, Timothy G. Armstrong, Michael Wilde, Daniel S. Katz, Benjamin Grimmer, Ian T. Foster, and Ioan Raicu. Design and evaluation of the GeMTC framework for GPU-enabled many task computing. In *Proc. HPDC '14*, New York, 2014.

[165] A. Krishnamurthy, D. E. Culler, A. Dusseau, S. C. Goldstein, S. Lumetta, T. von Eicken, and K. Yelick. Parallel programming in Split-C. In *Proceedings of the 1993 ACM/IEEE conference on Supercomputing*, Supercomputing '93, pages 262–273, New York, NY, USA, 1993. ACM.

[166] Alexey Kukanov and Michael J. Voss. The Foundations for Scalable Multi-core Software in Intel Threading Building Blocks. *Intel Technology Journal*, 11(4):309–322, 2007.

[167] Sameer Kumar, Yan Shi, Eric Bohm, and L. V. Kale. Scalable, fine grain, parallelization of the Car-Parrinello ab initio molecular dynamics method. Technical report, UIUC, Dept. of Computer Science, 2005.

[168] Sameer Kumar, Yanhua Sun, and L. V. Kale. Acceleration of an asynchronous message driven programming paradigm on IBM Blue Gene/Q. In *Proceedings of 26th IEEE International Parallel and Distributed Processing Symposium (IPDPS)*, Boston, USA, May 2013.

[169] Bradley Kuszmaul. The StarTech massively parallel chess program. Technical report, MIT Laboratory for Computer Science, January 1995.

[170] Lawrence Berkeley National Laboratory. MVICH: MPI for virtual interface architecture, August 2001.

[171] Leslie Lamport. How to make a multiprocessor computer that correctly executes multiprocess programs. *IEEE Transactions on Computers*, C-28(9):690–691, September 1979.

[172] Orion Sky Lawlor and L. V. Kalé. Supporting dynamic parallel object arrays. *Concurrency and Computation: Practice and Experience*, 15:371–393, 2003.

[173] Lawrence Berkeley National Laboratory and University of California, Berkeley. Berkeley UPC project homepage. http://upc.lbl.gov/.

[174] Lawrence Berkeley National Laboratory and University of California, Berkeley. GASNet project homepage. http://gasnet.cs.berkeley.edu/.

[175] I-Ting Angelina Lee, Silas Boyd-Wickizer, Zhiyi Huang, and Charles E. Leiserson. Using memory mapping to support cactus stacks in work-stealing runtime systems. In *Proceedings of the 19th international conference on Parallel architectures and compilation techniques*, PACT '10, pages 411–420, New York, NY, USA, 2010. ACM.

[176] Charles E. Leiserson. The Cilk++ concurrency platform. *Journal of Supercomputing*, 51(3):244–257, March 2010.

[177] Charles E. Leiserson. Cilk. In *Encyclopedia of Parallel Computing*, pages 273–288. Springer, 2011.

[178] Charles E. Leiserson, Tao B. Schardl, and Jim Sukha. Deterministic parallel random-number generation for dynamic-multithreading platforms. In *Proceedings of the 17th ACM SIGPLAN symposium on Principles and Practice of Parallel Programming*, PPoPP '12, pages 193–204, New York, NY, USA, 2012. ACM.

[179] Erik Lindholm, Mark J. Kilgard, and Henry Moreton. A user-programmable vertex engine. In *Proceedings of the 28th annual conference on Computer graphics and interactive techniques*, SIGGRAPH '01, pages 149–158, New York, NY, USA, 2001. ACM.

[180] Barbara Liskov, Alan Snyder, Russell Atkinson, and Craig Schaffert. Abstraction mechanisms in CLU. *Communications of the ACM*, 20(8):564–576, August 1977.

[181] Chi-Keung Luk, Robert Cohn, Robert Muth, Harish Patil, Artur Klauser, Geoff Lowney, Steven Wallace, Vijay Janapa Reddi, and Kim Hazelwood. Pin: building customized program analysis tools with dynamic instrumentation. In *PLDI '05: Proceedings of the 2005 ACM SIGPLAN Conference on Programming Language Design and Implementation*, pages 190–200, New York, NY, USA, 2005. ACM Press.

[182] E. Lusk, S. C. Pieper, and R. Butler. More scalability, less pain: A simple programming model and its implementation for extreme scale computing. *SciDAC Review*, 17:30–37, 2010.

[183] Alan M. Mainwaring and David E. Culler. Active message applications programming interface and communication subsystem organization. Technical Report UCB/CSD-96-918, EECS Department, University of California, Berkeley, October 1996.

[184] Andrey Marochko and Alexey Kukanov. Composable Parallelism Foundations in the Intel Threading Building Blocks Task Scheduler. In *Applications, Tools and Techniques on the Road to Exascale Computing, Proceedings of the conference ParCo 2011, 31 August - 3 September 2011, Ghent, Belgium*, pages 545–554, 2011.

[185] Friedemann Mattern. Algorithms for distributed termination detection. *Distributed Computing*, 2:161–175, 1987.

[186] Timothy G. Mattson and Beverly A. Sanders. *Patterns for Parallel Programming*. Addison Wesley, 2 edition, 2012.

[187] Chao Mei, Yanhua Sun, Gengbin Zheng, Eric J. Bohm, Laxmikant V. Kalé, James C. Phillips, and Chris Harrison. Enabling and scaling biomolecular simulations of

100 million atoms on petascale machines with a multicore-optimized message-driven runtime. In *Proceedings of the 2011 ACM/IEEE conference on Supercomputing*, Seattle, WA, November 2011.

[188] Mellanox. Mellanox releases scalableSHMEM 2.0, scalableUPC 2.0 for HPC. `http://www.hpcwire.com/hpcwire/2011-11-14/mellanox_releases_scalableshmem_2.0,_scalableupc_2.0_for_hpc.html`.

[189] John M. Mellor-Crummey and Michael L. Scott. Algorithms for scalable synchronization on shared-memory multiprocessors. *ACM Trans. Comput. Syst.*, 9(1):21–65, February 1991.

[190] Esteban Meneses, Greg Bronevetsky, and Laxmikant V. Kale. Evaluation of simple causal message logging for large-scale fault tolerant HPC systems. In *16th IEEE Workshop on Dependable Parallel, Distributed and Network-Centric Systems in 25th IEEE International Parallel and Distributed Processing Symposium (IPDPS 2011).*, May 2011.

[191] Esteban Meneses and Laxmikant V. Kale. CAMEL: Collective-aware message logging. *The Journal of Supercomputing*, 2015.

[192] Esteban Meneses, Celso L. Mendes, and Laxmikant V. Kale. Team-based message logging: Preliminary results. In *3rd Workshop on Resiliency in High Performance Computing (Resilience) in Clusters, Clouds, and Grids (CCGRID 2010).*, May 2010.

[193] Esteban Meneses, Xiang Ni, and Laxmikant V. Kale. Design and analysis of a message logging protocol for fault tolerant multicore systems. Technical Report 11-30, Parallel Programming Laboratory, Department of Computer Science, University of Illinois at Urbana-Champaign, July 2011.

[194] Esteban Meneses, Xiang Ni, Gengbin Zheng, Celso L. Mendes, and Laxmikant V. Kale. Using migratable objects to enhance fault tolerance schemes in supercomputers. In *IEEE Transactions on Parallel and Distributed Systems*, 2014.

[195] Esteban Meneses, Osman Sarood, and L. V. Kale. Assessing energy efficiency of fault tolerance protocols for HPC systems. In *Proceedings of the IEEE 24th International Symposium on Computer Architecture and High Performance Computing (SBAC-PAD)*, New York, USA, October 2012.

[196] H. Menon, L. Wesolowski, G. Zheng, P. Jetley, L. Kale, T. Quinn, and F. Governato. Adaptive techniques for clustered N-body cosmological simulations. *ArXiv e-prints*, September 2014.

[197] Harshitha Menon, Bilge Acun, Simon Garcia De Gonzalo, Osman Sarood, and Laxmikant Kalé. Thermal aware automated load balancing for HPC applications. In *Cluster Computing (CLUSTER), 2013 IEEE International Conference on*, pages 1–8. IEEE, 2013.

[198] Harshitha Menon, Nikhil Jain, Gengbin Zheng, and Laxmikant V. Kalé. Automated load balancing invocation based on application characteristics. In *IEEE Cluster 12*, Beijing, China, September 2012.

[199] Harshitha Menon and Laxmikant Kalé. A distributed dynamic load balancer for iterative applications. In *Proceedings of SC13: International Conference for High Performance Computing, Networking, Storage and Analysis*, SC '13, pages 15:1–15:11, New York, NY, USA, 2013. ACM.

[200] Message Passing Interface Forum. MPI: A Message-Passing Interface standard. *International Journal of Supercomputer Applications*, 8(3/4):165–414, 1994.

[201] Message Passing Interface Forum. MPI-2: A Message Passing Interface standard. *International Journal of High Performance Computing Applications*, 12(1–2):1–299, 1998.

[202] Message Passing Interface Forum. MPI: A message-passing interface standard, version 3.0. `http://www.mpi-forum.org/docs/mpi-3.0/mpi30-report.pdf`, September 2012.

[203] Phil Miller, Aaron Becker, and Laxmikant Kal. Using shared arrays in message-driven parallel programs. *Parallel Computing*, 38(12):66–74, 2012.

[204] Robert C. Miller. A type-checking preprocessor for Cilk 2, a multithreaded C language. Master's thesis, Massachusetts Institute of Technology Electrical Engineering and Computer Science, May 1995.

[205] Michael Mitzenmacher. Analyses of load stealing models based on differential equations. In *Proc. 10th Symposium on Parallel Algorithms and Architectures (SPAA '98)*, pages 212–221. ACM, 1998.

[206] Aaftab Munshi, Ben Gaster, Timothy G. Mattson, James Fung, and Dan Ginsburg. *OpenCL Programming Guide*. Addison Wesley, 2011.

[207] nCUBE Corporation. *nCUBE 2 Programmers Guide, r2.0*, December 1990.

[208] Robert H. B. Netzer and Barton P. Miller. What are race conditions? *ACM Letters on Programming Languages and Systems*, 1(1):74–88, March 1992.

[209] Xiang Ni, Laxmikant V. Kale, and Rasmus Tamstorf. Scalable asynchronous contact mechanics using Charm++. In *Proceedings of the IEEE International Parallel & Distributed Processing Symposium (to appear)*, IPDPS '15. IEEE Computer Society, May 2015. LLNL-CONF-663041.

[210] Xiang Ni, Esteban Meneses, Nikhil Jain, and Laxmikant V. Kale. ACR: Automatic checkpoint/restart for soft and hard error protection. In *ACM/IEEE International Conference for High Performance Computing, Networking, Storage and Analysis*, SC '13. IEEE Computer Society, November 2013.

[211] Xiang Ni, Esteban Meneses, and Laxmikant V. Kalé. Hiding checkpoint overhead in HPC applications with a semi-blocking algorithm. In *IEEE Cluster 12*, Beijing, China, September 2012.

[212] J. Nieplocha, R. Harrison, and R. Littlefield. Global arrays-A portable shared-memory programming model for distributed memory computers. In *Supercomputing '94, Proceedings*, page 340. IEEE, Comp. Soc.; Assoc. Comp. Machinery; Soc. Ind. Appl. Math., November 1994.

[213] J. Nieplocha, R. Harrison, and R. Littlefield. Global arrays: a nonuniform memory access programming model for high-performance supercomputers. *Journal of Supercomputing*, 10:169–189, 1996.

[214] J. Nieplocha, B. Palmer, V. Tipparaju, M. Krishnan, H. Trease, and E. Apra. Advances, applications and performance of the Global Arrays shared memory programming toolkit. *Int. J. High Perf. Comput. Applications*, 20(2):203–231, Summer 2006.

[215] Jarek Nieplocha, Robert J. Harrison, and Richard J. Littlefield. Global arrays: a portable "shared-memory" programming model for distributed memory computers. In *Proc. ACM/IEEE Conference Supercomputing (SC '94)*, pages 340–349, 1994.

[216] Rishiyur S. Nikhil. An overview of the parallel language Id. Technical report, DEC, Cambridge Research Lab., 1993.

[217] Rajesh Nishtala, Yili Zheng, Paul H. Hargrove, and Katherine A. Yelick. Tuning collective communication for partitioned global address space programming models. *Parallel Computing*, 37(9):576–591, 2011.

[218] Robert W. Numrich and John Reid. Co-array fortran for parallel programming. *SIGPLAN Fortran Forum*, 17(2):1–31, 1998.

[219] Martin Odersky, Philippe Altherr, Vincent Cremat, Burak Emir, Sebastian Maneth, Stéphane Micheloud, Nikolay Mihaylov, Michel Schinz, Erik Stenman, and Matthias Zenger. An overview of the Scala programming language. Technical Report IC/2004/64, École Polytechnique Fédérale de Lausanne, 1015 Lausanne, Switzerland, 2004.

[220] OpenMP: A proposed industry standard API for shared memory programming. OpenMP white paper, October 1997.

[221] OpenMP 4.0 Public Review Release Candidate Specifications. `http://www.openmp.org/mp-documents/OpenMP4.0.0.pdf`.

[222] The OpenMP 4.0 API examples document. `http://openmp.org/mp-documents/OpenMP4.0.0.Examples.pdf`.

[223] OpenSHMEM web site. `http://openshmem.org/`.

[224] J. K. Ousterhout. Scripting: Higher level programming for the 21st century. *Computer*, 31(3):23–30, March 1998.

[225] Kay Ousterhout, Aurojit Panda, Joshua Rosen, Shivaram Venkataraman, Reynold Xin, Sylvia Ratnasamy, Scott Shenker, and Ion Stoica. The case for tiny tasks in compute clusters. In *Proc. HotOS '13*, HotOS'13, pages 14–14, Berkeley, CA, USA, 2013. USENIX Association.

[226] B. Palmer, V. Gurumoorthi, A. Tartakovsky, and T. Sheibe. A component-based framework for smoothed particle hydrodynamics simulations of reactive fluid flow in porous media. *Int. J. High Performance Comp. Appl.*, 24(2):228–239, May 2010.

[227] Bruce Palmer, William Perkins, Yousu Chen, Shuangshuang Jin, David Callahan, Kevin Glass, Ruisheng Diao, Mark Rice, Stephen Elbert, Mallikarjuna Vallem, and Zhenyu (Henry) Huang. GridPACK^{TM}: A framework for developing power grid simulations on high performance computing platforms. In *Proceedings of the Fourth International Workshop on Domain-Specific Languages and High-Level Frameworks for High Performance Computing*, WOLFHPC '14, pages 68–77, Piscataway, NJ, USA, 2014. IEEE Press.

[228] Tim Peierls, Brian Goetz, Joshua Bloch, Joseph Bowbeer, Doug Lea, and David Holmes. *Java Concurrency in Practice*. Addison-Wesley Professional, 2005.

[229] PETSc Web page. http://www.mcs.anl.gov/petsc, 2015.

[230] James C. Phillips, John E. Stone, Kirby L. Vandivort, Timothy G. Armstrong, Justin M. Wozniak, Michael Wilde, and Klaus Schulten. Petascale Tcl with NAMD, VMD, and Swift/T. In *Proc. Workshop for High Performance Technical Computing in Dynamic Languages*, HPTCDL '14, pages 6–17, Piscataway, NJ, USA, 2014. IEEE Press.

[231] James C. Phillips, Gengbin Zheng, Sameer Kumar, and Laxmikant V. Kalé. NAMD: Biomolecular simulation on thousands of processors. In *Proceedings of the 2002 ACM/IEEE conference on Supercomputing*, pages 1–18, Baltimore, MD, September 2002.

[232] Paul Pierce. The NX/2 operating system. In *Proceedings of the Third Conference on Hypercube Concurrent Computers and Applications*, pages 384–390. ACM Press, 1988.

[233] John B. Plevyak. *Optimization of Object-Oriented and Concurrent Programs*. PhD thesis, University of Illinois Urbana-Champaign, 1996.

[234] Adrian Prantl, Thomas Epperly, Shams Imam, and Vivek Sarkar. Interfacing Chapel with traditional HPC programming languages. In *Proceedings of the Fifth Conference on Partitioned Global Address Space Programming Models*, Galveston Island, Texas, USA, October 2011.

[235] Quadrics Ltd. The Shmem Programming Manual.

[236] Ioan Raicu, Zhao Zhang, Mike Wilde, Ian Foster, Pete Beckman, Kamil Iskra, and Ben Clifford. Toward loosely coupled programming on petascale systems. In *Proc. SC '08*, 2008.

[237] V. Nageshwara Rao and Vipin Kumar. Parallel depth first search. part I. implementation. *International Journal of Parallel Programming*, 16(6):479–499, 1987.

[238] James Reinders. *Intel Threading Building Blocks*. O'Reilly & Associates, Inc., Sebastopol, CA, USA, first edition, 2007.

[239] Rice University. Coarray Fortran 2.0 at Rice University. http://caf.rice.edu/.

[240] Marshall C. Richmond, William A. Perkins, Timothy D. Scheibe, Adam Lambert, and Brian D. Wood. Flow and axial dispersion in a sinusoidal-walled tube: Effects

of inertial and unsteady flows. *Advances in Water Resources*, 62, Part B(0):215–226, 2013. A tribute to Stephen Whitaker.

[241] Mike Ringenburg and Sung-Eun Choi. Optimizing loop-level parallelism in Cray XMT™ applications. In *Cray User Group (CUG) 2009*, Atlanta, GA, May 2009.

[242] Arch Robison, Michael Voss, and Alexey Kukanov. Optimization via reflection on work stealing in TBB. In *IEEE Int. Symp. on Parallel and Distributed Processing*, pages 1–8. IEEE, April 2008.

[243] Eduardo R. Rodrigues, Philippe O. A. Navaux, Jairo Panetta, Alvaro Fazenda, Celso L. Mendes, and Laxmikant V. Kale. A comparative analysis of load balancing algorithms applied to a weather forecast model. In *Proceedings of 22nd International Symposium on Computer Architecture and High Performance Computing (SBAC-PAD)*, Itaipava, Brazil, 2010.

[244] Eduardo R. Rodrigues, Philippe O. A. Navaux, Jairo Panetta, Celso L. Mendes, and Laxmikant V. Kale. Optimizing an MPI weather forecasting model via processor virtualization. In *Proceedings of International Conference on High Performance Computing (HiPC)*, 2010.

[245] I. Sadooghi, S. Palur, A. Anthony, I. Kapur, K. Belagodu, P. Purandare, K. Ramamurty, Ke Wang, and I. Raicu. Achieving efficient distributed scheduling with message queues in the cloud for many-task computing and high-performance computing. In *Proc. CCGrid '14*, pages 404–413, May 2014.

[246] Vijay Saraswat, Bard Bloom, Igor Peshansky, Olivier Tardieu, and David Grove. *X10 Language Specification (version 2.5)*, June 2015.

[247] Osman Sarood, Akhil Langer, Abhishek Gupta, and Laxmikant V. Kale. Maximizing throughput of overprovisioned HPC data centers under a strict power budget. In *Proceedings of the International Conference on High Performance Computing, Networking, Storage and Analysis*, SC '14, New York, NY, USA, 2014. ACM.

[248] Osman Sarood, Akhil Langer, L. V. Kale, Barry Rountree, and Bronis de Supinski. Optimizing power allocation to CPU and memory subsystems in overprovisioned HPC systems. In *Proceedings of IEEE Cluster 2013*, Indianapolis, IN, USA, September 2013.

[249] Osman Sarood, Phil Miller, Ehsan Totoni, and L. V. Kale. 'cool' load balancing for high performance computing data centers. In *IEEE Transactions on Computer - SI (Energy Efficient Computing)*, September 2012.

[250] SGI. SGI Origin 350 Server System User's Guide, document number: 007-4566-001.

[251] SGI, Inc. SGI Shmem API Man Pages.

[252] Subodh Sharma, Sarvani Vakkalanka, Ganesh Gopalakrishnan, Robert M. Kirby, Rajeev M. Thakur, and William Gropp. A formal approach to detect functionally irrelevant barriers in MPI programs. In *EuroMPI*, pages 265–273, September 2008.

[253] Sameer S. Shende and Allen D. Malony. The Tau parallel performance system. *The International Journal of High Performance Computing Applications*, 20:287–331, 2006.

[254] Anthony Skjellum and Alvin P. Leung. *Zipcode:* A portable multicomputer communication library atop the Reactive Kernel. In *Proceedings of the Fifth Distributed Memory Computing Conference (DMCC5)*, pages 767–776. IEEE Press, April 1990.

[255] Lawrence Snyder. The design and development of ZPL. In *Proceedings of the third ACM SIGPLAN conference on History of programming languages*, HOPL III, pages 8-1–8-37, New York, NY, USA, 2007. ACM.

[256] Srinivas Sridharan, Jeffrey S. Vetter, Bradford L. Chamberlain, Peter M. Kogge, and Steven J. Deitz. A scalable implementation of language-based software transactional memory for distributed memory systems. Technical Report FTGTR-2011-02, Oak Ridge National Laboratory, Oak Ridge, Tennessee, USA, May 2011.

[257] Guy L. Steele,Jr. Growing a language. In *Addendum to the 1998 proceedings of the conference on Object-oriented programming, systems, languages, and applications (Addendum)*, OOPSLA '98 Addendum, pages 0.01–A1, New York, NY, USA, 1998. ACM.

[258] Yanhua Sun, Gengbin Zheng, Chao Mei Eric J. Bohm, Terry Jones, Laxmikant V. Kalé, and James C. Phillips. Optimizing fine-grained communication in a biomolecular simulation application on Cray XK6. In *Proceedings of the 2012 ACM/IEEE conference on Supercomputing*, Salt Lake City, Utah, November 2012.

[259] Yanhua Sun, Gengbin Zheng, L. V. Kale, Terry R. Jones, and Ryan Olson. A uGNI-based asynchronous message-driven runtime system for Cray supercomputers with

Gemini interconnect. In *Proceedings of 26th IEEE International Parallel and Distributed Processing Symposium (IPDPS)*, Shanghai, China, May 2012.

[260] Supercomputing Technologies Group, Massachusetts Institute of Technology Laboratory for Computer Science. *Cilk 5.4.2.3 Reference Manual*, April 2006.

[261] Michael Süß and Claudia Leopold. Common mistakes in OpenMP and how to avoid them. In *OpenMP Shared Memory Parallel Programming*, pages 312–323. Springer, 2008.

[262] Herb Sutter. Interrupt politely. *Dr. Dobb's*, April 2008.

[263] Swift team. Swift/T - high performance dataflow computing, 2015. `http://swift-lang.org/Swift-T/`.

[264] Sağnak Taşırlar and V. Sarkar. Data-driven tasks and their implementation. In *Proc. ICPP '11*, 2011.

[265] Olivier Tardieu, Benjamin Herta, David Cunningham, David Grove, Prabhanjan Kambadur, Vijay Saraswat, Avraham Shinnar, Mikio Takeuchi, and Mandana Vaziri. X10 and APGAS at petascale. In *Proc. PPoPP '14*, pages 53–66, 2014.

[266] Baba Arimilli, *et.al.* The PERCS high-performance interconnect. *2010 18th IEEE Symposium on High Performance Interconnects*, 2010.

[267] V. Aggarwal, *et.al.* Bridging parallel and reconfigurable computing with multilevel PGAS and SHMEM+.

[268] Rajeev Thakur and Alok Choudhary. An extended two-phase method for accessing sections of out-of-core arrays. *Scientific Programming*, 5(4):301–317, Winter 1996.

[269] Rajeev Thakur, William Gropp, and Ewing Lusk. Optimizing noncontiguous accesses in MPI-IO. *Parallel Computing*, 28(1):83–105, January 2002.

[270] Rajeev Thakur, Rolf Rabenseifner, and William Gropp. Optimization of collective communication operations in MPICH. *International Journal of High-Performance Computing Applications*, 19(1):49–66, 2005.

[271] The Parallel Computing Forum. PCF parallel fortran extensions. *SIGPLAN Fortran Forum*, 10(3):1–57, September 1991.

[272] Thinking Machines Corporation, Cambridge Massachusetts. *CMMD Reference Manual, Version 3.0*, May 1993. Document No. 700-009010.

[273] J. Nieplocha V. Tipparaju and M. Krishnan. High performance remote memory access computing: The ARMCI approach. *Int. J. High Perf. Comput. Applications*, 20(2):233–253, Summer 2006.

[274] Greg Titus, Sung-Eun Choi, and Brad Chamberlain. Chapel hierarchical locales: Adaptable portability for exascale node architectures. In *The International Conference for High Performance Computing, Networking, Storage and Analysis (SC14)*, November 2014. (an emerging technologies poster and presentation).

[275] Stephen Toub. Parallel programming and the .NET Framework 4.0. http://blogs.msdn.com/pfxteam/archive/2008/10/10/8994927.aspx, 2008.

[276] Jeffrey Travis and Jim Kring. *LabVIEW for Everyone: Graphical Programming Made Easy and Fun*. Prentice Hall, 2006. 3rd Edition.

[277] University of California, Berkeley. Titanium project home page. `http://titanium.cs.berkeley.edu/`.

[278] University of Houston. OpenUH: Open source UH compiler. `http://www2.cs.uh.edu/~openuh/`.

[279] UPC Consortium. UPC language specifications, v1.2. Technical Report LBNL-59208, Lawrence Berkeley National Laboratory, 2005.

[280] UPC Consortium. UPC language specifications, v1.2. Technical Report LBNL-59208, Lawrence Berkeley National Lab, 2005.

[281] UPC manual 1.2. `http://upc.gwu.edu/downloads/Manual-1.2.pdf`.

[282] M. Valiev, E. J. Bylaska, N. Govind, K. Kowalski, T. P. Straatsma, H. J. J. Van Dam, D. Wang, J. Nieplocha, E. Apra, T. L. Windus, and W. A. de Jong. NWChem: A comprehensive and scalable open-source solution for large scale molecular simulations. *Computer Physics Communications*, 181(9):1477–1489, 2010.

[283] Hubertus J. J. van Dam, Abhinav Vishnu, and Wibe A. de Jong. Designing a scalable fault tolerance model for high performance computational chemistry: A case study with coupled cluster perturbative triples. *Journal of Chemical Theory and Computation*, 7(1):66–75, 2011.

[284] Robert A. van de Geijn and Jesper Larsson Träff. Collective communication. In *Encyclopedia of Parallel Computing*, pages 318–327. Springer, 2011.

[285] Jeffrey S. Vetter and Michael O. McCracken. Statistical scalability analysis of communication operations in distributed applications. In Michael T. Heath and Andrew Lumsdaine, editors, *8th ACM SIGPLAN symposium on Principles and Practices of Parallel Programming (PPOPP)*, pages 123–132. ACM, 2001.

[286] A. Vishnu, J. Daily, and B. Palmer. Designing scalable PGAS communication subsystems on Cray Gemini interconnect. In *2012 19th International Conference on High Performance Computing (HiPC)*, HiPC 2012, 2012.

[287] Michael J. Voss. The Intel Threading Building Blocks Flow Graph. *Dr. Dobb's*, October 2011.

[288] Mattias De Wael, Stefan Marr, Bruno De Fraine, Tom Van Cutsem, and Wolfgang De Meuter. Partitioned global address space languages. *ACM Computing Surveys*, 47(4):62:1–62:27, May 2015.

[289] Ke Wang, Xiaobing Zhou, Tonglin Li, Dongfang Zhao, M. Lang, and I. Raicu. Optimizing load balancing and data-locality with data-aware scheduling. In *Proc. Int'l Conf. Big Data*, pages 119–128, October 2014.

[290] M. White and M. Oostrom. STOMP subsurface transport over multiple phases: Theory guide PNNL-12030 (UC-2010). Technical report, Pacific Northwest National Laboratory, Richland, WA, 2000.

[291] M. White and M. Oostrom. STOMP subsurface transport over multiple phases, version 4.0: User's guide PNNL-15782 (UC-2010). Technical report, Pacific Northwest National Laboratory, Richland, WA, 2006.

[292] Michael Wilde, Mihael Hategan, Justin M. Wozniak, Ben Clifford, Daniel S. Katz, and Ian Foster. Swift: A language for distributed parallel scripting. *Par. Comp.*, 37:633–652, 2011.

[293] R. B. Wiringa, Steven C. Pieper, J. Carlson, and V. R. Pandharipande. Quantum Monte Carlo calculations of A=8 nuclei. *Phys. Rev. C*, 62:014001, 2000.

[294] J. M Wozniak, T. G. Armstrong, M. Wilde, D. S. Katz, E. Lusk, and I. T. Foster. Swift/T: Large-scale applications via distributed-memory dataflow processing. In *Proc. CCGrid*, pages 95–102, 2013.

[295] Justin M. Wozniak, Timothy G. Armstrong, Ewing L. Lusk, Daniel S. Katz, Michael Wilde, and Ian T. Foster. Turbine: A distributed memory data flow engine for many-task applications. In *Proc. SWEET '12*, 2012.

[296] Justin M. Wozniak, Timothy G. Armstrong, Ketan Maheshwari, Ewing L. Lusk, Daniel S. Katz, Michael Wilde, and Ian T. Foster. Turbine: A distributed-memory dataflow engine for high performance many-task applications. *Fundamenta Informaticae*, 28(3), 2013.

[297] Justin M. Wozniak, Timothy G. Armstrong, Ketan C. Maheshwari, Daniel S. Katz, Michael Wilde, and Ian T. Foster. Interlanguage parallel scripting for distributed-memory scientific computing. In *IEEE Cluster*, 2015.

[298] Justin M. Wozniak, Tom Peterka, Timothy G. Armstrong, James Dinan, Ewing Lusk, Michael Wilde, and Ian Foster. Dataflow coordination of data-parallel tasks via MPI 3.0. In *Proc. EuroMPI '13*, 2013.

[299] Justin M. Wozniak, Hemant Sharma, Timothy G. Armstrong, Michael Wilde, Jonathan D. Almer, and Ian Foster. Big data staging with MPI-IO for interactive X-ray science. In *Proc. Big Data Conf.*, 2014.

[300] C. Eric Wu, Anthony Bolmarcich, Marc Snir, David Wootton, Farid Parpia, Anthony Chan, Ewing Lusk, and William Gropp. From trace generation to visualization: A performance framework for distributed parallel systems. In *Proc. of SC2000: High Performance Networking and Computing*, November 2000.

[301] William Wulf and Mary Shaw. Global variable considered harmful. *SIGPLAN Notices*, 8(2):28–34, 1973.

[302] Y. Yan, J. Zhao, Y. Guo, and V. Sarkar. Hierarchical place trees: A portable abstraction for task parallelism and date movement. In *Proceedings of the 22nd Workshop on Languages and Compilers for Parallel Computing*, 2009.

[303] Takeshi Yanai, George I. Fann, Zhengting Gan, Robert J. Harrison, and Gregory Beylkin. Multiresolution quantum chemistry in multiwavelet bases: Analytic derivatives for Hartree–Fock and density functional theory. *J. Chemical Physics*, 121(7):2866–2876, 2004.

[304] Jae-Seung Yeom, Abhinav Bhatele, Keith R. Bisset, Eric Bohm, Abhishek Gupta, Laxmikant V. Kale, Madhav Marathe, Dimitrios S. Nikolopoulos, Martin Schulz, and Lukasz Wesolowski. Overcoming the scalability challenges of epidemic simulations on Blue Waters. In *Proceedings of the IEEE International Parallel & Distributed Processing Symposium*, IPDPS '14. IEEE Computer Society, May 2014.

[305] Gengbin Zheng. *Achieving high performance on extremely large parallel machines: performance prediction and load balancing.* PhD thesis, Department of Computer Science, University of Illinois at Urbana-Champaign, 2005.

[306] Gengbin Zheng, Abhinav Bhatele, Esteban Meneses, and Laxmikant V. Kale. Periodic hierarchical load balancing for large supercomputers. *International Journal of High Performance Computing Applications (IJHPCA)*, March 2011.

[307] Gengbin Zheng, Esteban Meneses, Abhinav Bhatele, and Laxmikant V. Kale. Hierarchical load balancing for Charm++ applications on large supercomputers. In *Proceedings of the Third International Workshop on Parallel Programming Models and Systems Software for High-End Computing (P2S2)*, San Diego, California, USA, September 2010.

[308] Gengbin Zheng, Xiang Ni, and L. V. Kale. A scalable double in-memory checkpoint and restart scheme towards exascale. In *Proceedings of the 2nd Workshop on Fault-Tolerance for HPC at Extreme Scale (FTXS)*, Boston, USA, June 2012.

[309] Gengbin Zheng, Xiang Ni, Esteban Meneses, and Laxmikant Kale. A scalable double in-memory checkpoint and restart scheme towards exascale. Technical Report 12-04, Parallel Programming Laboratory, Feburary 2012.

[310] Gengbin Zheng, Lixia Shi, and Laxmikant V. Kalé. FTC-Charm++: An in-memory checkpoint-based fault tolerant runtime for Charm++ and MPI. In *2004 IEEE Cluster*, pages 93–103, San Diego, CA, September 2004.

[311] Yili Zheng, Amir Kamil, Michael B. Driscoll, Hongzhang Shan, and Katherine Yelick. UPC++: a PGAS extension for C++. In *28th IEEE International Parallel and Distributed Processing Symposium (IPDPS)*, 2014.

Scientific and Engineering Computation

William Gropp and Ewing Lusk, editors; Janusz Kowalik, founding editor

Data-Parallel Programming on MIMD Computers, Philip J. Hatcher and Michael J. Quinn, 1991

Enterprise Integration Modeling: Proceedings of the First International Conference, edited by Charles J. Petrie, Jr., 1992

The High Performance Fortran Handbook, Charles H. Koelbel, David B. Loveman, Robert S. Schreiber, Guy L. Steele Jr. and Mary E. Zosel, 1994

PVM: Parallel Virtual Machine–A Users' Guide and Tutorial for Network Parallel Computing, Al Geist, Adam Beguelin, Jack Dongarra, Weicheng Jiang, Bob Manchek, and Vaidy Sunderam, 1994

Enabling Technologies for Petaflops Computing, Thomas Sterling, Paul Messina, and Paul H. Smith, 1995

An Introduction to High-Performance Scientific Computing, Lloyd D. Fosdick, Elizabeth R. Jessup, Carolyn J. C. Schauble, and Gitta Domik, 1995

Parallel Programming Using C++, edited by Gregory V. Wilson and Paul Lu, 1996

Using PLAPACK: Parallel Linear Algebra Package, Robert A. van de Geijn, 1997

Fortran 95 Handbook, Jeanne C. Adams, Walter S. Brainerd, Jeanne T. Martin, Brian T. Smith, and Jerrold L. Wagener, 1997

MPI—The Complete Reference: Volume 1, The MPI Core, Marc Snir, Steve Otto, Steven Huss-Lederman, David Walker, and Jack Dongarra, 1998

MPI—The Complete Reference: Volume 2, The MPI-2 Extensions, William Gropp, Steven Huss-Lederman, Andrew Lumsdaine, Ewing Lusk, Bill Nitzberg, William Saphir, and Marc Snir, 1998

A Programmer's Guide to ZPL, Lawrence Snyder, 1999

How to Build a Beowulf, Thomas L. Sterling, John Salmon, Donald J. Becker, and Daniel F. Savarese, 1999

Using MPI-2: Advanced Features of the Message-Passing Interface, William Gropp, Ewing Lusk, and Rajeev Thakur, 1999

Beowulf Cluster Computing with Windows, edited by Thomas Sterling, William Gropp, and Ewing Lusk, 2001

Beowulf Cluster Computing with Linux, second edition, edited by Thomas Sterling, William Gropp, and Ewing Lusk, 2003

Scalable Input/Output: Achieving System Balance, edited by Daniel A. Reed, 2003

Using OpenMP: Portable Shared Memory Parallel Programming, Barbara Chapman, Gabriele Jost, and Ruud van der Pas, 2008

Quantum Computing without Magic: Devices, Zdzislaw Meglicki, 2008

Quantum Computing: A Gentle Introduction, Eleanor G. Rieffel and Wolfgang H. Polack, 2011

Using MPI: Portable Parallel Programming with the Message-Passing Interface, third edition, William Gropp, Ewing Lusk, and Anthony Skjellum, 2014

Using Advanced MPI: Modern Features of the Message-Passing Interface, William Gropp, Torsten Hoefler, Rajeev Thakur, and Ewing Lusk, 2014

Programming Models for Parallel Computing, edited by Pavan Balaji, 2015

Printed in the United States
by Baker & Taylor Publisher Services